1999 Guide to Board Compensation

Gail McGowan, Editor/Research Director

EXECUTIVE COMPENSATION ADVISORY SERVICES

This publication is designed to provide accurate and authoritative information in regard to the subject matter covered. It is sold with the understanding that the publisher is not engaged in rendering legal, accounting, or other professional services. If legal advice or other professional assistance is required, the services of a competent professional person should be sought.

Portions of this work were published in previous editions.

Printed in the United States of America

ISBN: 0-15-606305-0

98 99 00 IBT 4 3 2 1

Preface

In light of the revision of executive compensation disclosure rules by the Securities & Exchange Commission in 1992, implementation of the Section 162(m) "million dollar" deduction cap on non-performance-based pay in 1994, and steady criticism of perceived excesses in executive pay by the media and investors, the nonemployee corporate directors held responsible for those compensation decisions are being held increasingly accountable. This, in turn, has heightened competition among corporations to attract and retain experienced, informed directors.

The National Association of Corporate Directors' Blue Ribbon Commission recommended five principles for corporations to follow in achieving what the commission considered to be the two purposes of director compensation (linking board members' interests with shareholders and providing value to directors for the value received from their service):

- Align directors' compensation with shareholders' long-term interests
- Adequately compensate directors for their time and effort
- Approach directors' pay on an overall basis rather than as separate elements
- Use compensation to motivate director behavior
- Disclose board compensation fully to shareholders

Carefully crafted board compensation programs can both enhance a corporation's ability to acquire the best directors and help to focus their attention on enhancing returns to the company's owners—the shareholders who elect them. To help you design such programs, *1999 Guide to Board Compensation* updates our continuing analysis of trends in directors' pay practices at U.S. corporations, on the basis of the most recent company disclosures.

Note: To better reflect the year in which professionals will apply the information in this book, we titled it *1999 Guide to Board Compensation.* Last year's edition was titled *Board Compensation: 1997.*

For this edition, we expanded the study group to 225 companies in order to augment those in the under-$1 billion revenue range. The study group continues to represent a broad spectrum of public companies while providing significant data related to specific industry and revenue groups. Lists of the companies by revenue ranges are included in appendices.

All company information is based on disclosures filed at the Securities & Exchange Commission through July 1, 1998. As much as possible, ECAS reviewed plan documents in addition to corporate proxy statements, to collect data for this study (when no full text is available, we rely on proxy descriptions). Copies of actual plan documents may be ordered from ECAS.

Again this year your *Board Compensation* package includes a disk containing Excel and Lotus spreadsheets of selected data items for each study company, which we expanded to 24 fields for this edition (to include the number of meetings held). This premium enables you to re-sort meaningful board compensation information in order to customize a peer comparison group that may not match those used for analysis purposes in the printed study. It also provides an at-a-glance summary of the basic elements of each company's total program. Please refer to "About the Disk," page x, and to the "Read Me" file on your bonus disk.

1999 Guide to Board Compensation demonstrates both prevalent and innovative board compensation strategies utilized by leading corporations today, as well as the typical levels of specific pay elements—and total pay—being provided by companies in diverse industries and revenue classifications. In addition, the study examines significant governance-related developments, such as directors' ages and affiliations. This guidance is designed to enable you to establish compensation programs that are competitive, reasonable, and effective in motivating and rewarding valued directors.

Chapter 1—Overview of Directors' Compensation—includes a guide to directors' compensation elements that enumerates and explains the various types of fees, grants, benefits, and perks that may be included in the total pay packages designed for outside board members.

Chapter 2—Trends—highlights newly emerging pay techniques (such as director "bonuses") and pinpoints changes in board compensation programs in recent years.

Chapter 3—Direct Compensation—explains and analyzes the various types of retainers and fees that are delivered to directors on an annual basis. The 225 study companies are "ranked" according to the level of direct compensation they provide annually to a typical board member.

Chapter 4—Stock Compensation—explores the prevalence and characteristics of long-term equity-based grants, board stock programs and arrangements, and directors' stock ownership guidelines.

Chapter 5—Total Compensation—analyzes the mix of annual and long-term compensation in a typical director's package. The 225 study companies are again "ranked," this time according to the level of total compensation they provide to a typical or "average" director.

Chapter 6—Deferred Compensation—analyzes the deferred compensation arrangements, including account formats and earnings crediting, in use at the study companies.

Chapter 7—Retirement Benefits—examines both cash- and stock-based programs designed to furnish post-service benefits to outside directors. Cash-based pension plans maintained by the study companies are dissected. Also, cash-based pension plans that were terminated since last year's edition are indicated, with an explanation of how their accrued benefit obligations were settled.

Chapter 8—Other Benefits & Perquisites—pinpoints various perks, such as memorial gift programs, and insurance-related and other benefits offered to directors by the study companies.

Chapter 9—Governance & Compensation Committees—discusses shareholder proposals, board structure, and the composition of boards and Compensation Committees at the study companies.

Chapter 10—Company Summaries—outlines all aspects of each study company's most recently disclosed board compensation program.

Appendix 1 and Appendix 2 list the study companies according to their revenue and industry categories, respectively.

Appendix 3 lists the study companies in alphabetical order and includes the amount of "direct" and "total" compensation each company provides to a typical director annually.

Appendix 4 lists the members of each study company's Compensation Committee, by company.

Appendix 5 lists the Compensation Committee members by name, showing all the study company Compensation Committees on which they serve.

Contents

About the Disk

The data disk provided with *1999 Guide to Board Compensation* contains a spreadsheet of salient data elements for each of the 225 study companies.This electronic premium gives you two benefits:

1. It provides an at-a-glance summary of the basic components of each study company's board compensation program, and
2. It enables you to sort the study companies according to your own criteria, in order to analyze the data for a customized peer group. For example, you may wish to view the data for a revenue range that differs from the ranges used in the printed study. You also may add similar data for your own or additional companies, using the spreadsheet format, to further enhance a customized analysis and compare it to the trends pinpointed in *1999 Guide to Board Compensation.*

The spreadsheet contains the following data elements:

- Company—the name of the study company
- Industry code—a one-letter code designating the company's industry group, for analysis purposes in the study:
  - ⇨ F = Financial
  - ⇨ H = Health Care
  - ⇨ I = Industrial
  - ⇨ M = Manufacturing
  - ⇨ O = Other (e.g., conglomerates)
  - ⇨ S = Service
  - ⇨ T = High-Tech
  - ⇨ U = Utilities
- FY97 Revenue—the company's fiscal 1997 revenue, in millions
- Cash Retainer—the annual cash retainer amount paid to outside directors
- Stock Ret-$—the value of a share award paid as part of annual compensation (i.e., unrestricted shares)
- Stock Ret-#—a number of (unrestricted) shares paid as part of annual compensation
- Bd Mtg Fee—the value of the board meeting attendance fee
- Bd Meetings—the number of board meetings held in the last reported fiscal year
- Audit Committee Retainer—any annual retainer paid to Audit Committee members
- Audit Mtg Fee—the fee paid for attendance at each Audit Meeting (may not include

"same day" meetings)

- Audit Meetings—the number of Audit Committee meetings held in the last reported fiscal year
- Comp Committee Retainer—any annual retainer paid to Compensation Committee members
- Comp Mtg Fee—the fee paid for attendance at each Compensation Meeting (may not include "same day" meetings)
- Comp Meetings—the number of Compensation Committee meetings held in the last reported fiscal year
- Avg "Direct" Comp—the amount of direct annual compensation (cash + stock retainers, plus attendance fees) that would be received by a company director who was a member (not chairman) of the Audit and Compensation Committees and attended all indicated board and committee meetings
- Option Grant Value—the annualized value of any periodic stock options grant to outside directors
- Rest'd Award Value—the annualized value of any periodic award of restricted shares to outside directors
- Def'd Award Value—the annualized value of any periodic award of deferred shares or units to outside directors
- Share Award Value—the annualized value of any periodic award of shares (except time-based restricted) to outside directors; note: unless these are performance-based, they are also reflected under the applicable stock retainer column
- Average "Total" Compensation—the sum of a director's Average "Direct" Compensation and the annualized value of any periodic stock-based grants (excluding share awards that are not performance-based, since they are already reflected in "Direct" compensation); Average "Total" Compensation reflects the combined value of all cash and stock-based compensation that a typical outside director at the company received in the last fiscal year
- Stock Plan?—does the company maintain a stock plan for outside directors ("Yes" or "No")
- Deferral Plan?—does the company maintain an elective deferred comp plan for outside directors ("Yes" or "No")
- Retirement Plan?—does the company maintain a plan designed to provide post-service benefits for outside directors ("Yes" or "No")
- Retire Benefit Type—is the benefit cash-based ("C") or stock-based ("S")
- Insurance?—does the company provide insurance benefits for outside directors ("Yes" or "No")
- Perks?—do outside directors receive perks ("Yes" or "No")
- Charitable/Matching Gift?—does the company maintain a program for memorial gifts or matching gifts?

Chapter 1. Overview of Directors' Compensation

Compensation to nonemployee directors of public corporations typically involves one or a combination of the following:

- Cash, including retainers and meeting attendance fees
- Stock, which may be transferred as part of a retainer or fee, or may take the form of a long-term equity-based grant
- Benefits such as retirement, insurance, and deferred compensation programs
- Perks such as product discounts, spousal travel, and charitable giving plans.

There is no single ideal board compensation program—each corporation must determine the mix of cash, stock, and benefits most appropriate to meet its goals of attracting, motivating, and providing meaningful compensation to the individuals responsible for corporate governance and management oversight.

The following reference section defines and describes the various elements of board of director compensation and provides guidance on related tax and accounting issues. This will assist you in using the analyses and information provided in the study, to determine the structure and value of your director's pay program.

Directors' Fees

Directors' fees are delivered as part of the annual remuneration intended to compensate directors for the time and effort they expend to fulfill board service. Fees may consist of any or all of the following:

Board Retainer: An annual amount paid for board service (often paid on a monthly or quarterly basis)

Board Meeting Attendance Fee: Amount paid for attendance at each meeting of the board

Chairman of the Board Fee: Amount paid to a separate chairman of the board (COB) (i.e., one who is not also the CEO). May be paid in lieu of or in addition to regular board fees

Committee Meeting Attendance Fee: Amount paid for attendance at a board committee meeting

Committee Retainers: Annual fee paid to each member of a standing committee

Committee Chairman Fees: Additional amounts, paid either on an annual or per-meeting basis, to directors who chair board committees

Same Day Meeting Fee: Amounts paid for attendance at meetings held on the same day as a board or, in some cases, other committee meetings

Special Fees: Amounts paid for ad hoc services rendered in addition to regular board duties (e.g., visiting a company plant or representing the company at outside functions)

Telephone Fees: Amounts paid for meetings held via teleconferencing, which may differ from regular meeting attendance fees

Generally, only nonemployee or "outside" directors receive fees, but about 3% of current study companies pay at least nominal board compensation (typically, meeting attendance fees) to directors who are company employees.

Deferred Compensation

Many companies maintain programs or policies permitting board members to defer the receipt of fees (usually the annual retainer and meeting fees). Elections must be irrevocable. The director has no income tax liability (under plans that meet IRS requirements) until the fees are paid out (but FICA taxes may not be deferred).

Deferred amounts accrue earnings, with accounts denominated in cash (bearing interest) or stock (earning dividend equivalents). Some plans permit annual deferrals to be split between the two account types, and some permit periodic or one-time transfers. Companies also may offer directors a menu of investment choices (e.g., mutual funds). Under most arrangements, participants may elect to receive payouts in a number of installments (usually limited) beginning either on a date specified by the director or after termination of board service.

Some outside directors participate in the company's nonqualified employee deferred compensation programs, but most companies enact board-specific programs.

Change-of-control (COC) provisions in deferral plans typically provide for immediate payouts in the event of a COC. Many companies protect directors' deferrals via a rabbi trust.

A limited number of companies have instituted plans allowing outside directors to receive stock options in lieu of some or all cash compensation. Such options are often granted with exercise prices below the fair market value (FMV) of company common on their grant date. The number of option shares granted is calculated via a formula relating the amount of option-allocated cash fees to the exercise price.

Deferred Stock Awards

Deferred stock awards are grants of share "units" whose value is pegged to the company's common stock and which will be delivered in cash or shares at a future date, typically when the director leaves the board. Deferred share accounts are usually credited with dividend equivalents. Under some arrangements, the deferred stock vests (i.e., becomes nonforfeitable) over time, such as over 5 years or at the end of a director's 3-year term.

Deferred stock, sometimes termed "phantom shares" or "stock units," has become the common currency of the post-service benefits that have been replacing directors' cash-based pension programs.

Directors' Incentive Arrangements

A few companies link some portion of directors' compensation directly to the attainment of performance goals (generally involving the company's stock price). For example, the number of restricted shares to be granted or to vest might depend on the attainment of a particular stock price or stock price increase over a specified time period. A limited number of companies have begun experimenting with *cash bonuses* for outside directors.

Perks

Perks may include a variety of supplemental benefits, including charitable giving programs, health and life insurance coverage, product discounts or free use of products, spouse travel benefits, financial counseling, and use of company vehicles or planes.

> *Note: A much-touted board perk is insurance funded Charitable Award Programs, under which eligible board members may make substantial bequests (typically $1 million) to charities or educational institutions, at no cost to their estates. The legacies often are financed through second-to-die life insurance policies that the company purchases for directors (where two directors are insured, and the death benefit is paid only after the second dies; premiums are lower than for traditional life insurance policies). Other companies maintain traditional giving programs, under which the company matches a director's donations to charitable organizations.*

Rabbi Trusts

A rabbi trust (so named because the first one approved by the IRS was for a rabbi) is a nonqualified trust established to pay vested deferred compensation (to executives as well as directors). The trust is irrevocable and inaccessible to present or future management, so it provides security to protect funds in the event of a change of control or a change of heart by management. Rabbi trusts are available to creditors in the event of the company's bankruptcy, however, so the IRS has ruled that rabbi trust funds are not taxable until they are distributed (i.e., not at the time of contribution). Thus, rabbi trusts have become a favored vehicle for "funding" deferred compensation and cash-based board pension plans.

Retirement Programs

We define a board retirement program as one intended to furnish post-service benefits to nonemployee directors. This component of directors' pay has undergone dramatic change in the past couple of decades, beginning with the rapid spread of cash-based pension plans, which have now fallen out of favor but are just as rapidly being replaced with stock-based post-service compensation.

Traditional "defined benefit" cash-based plans generally cover only directors who satisfy certain conditions, such as age and service requirements. Most prohibit participation by directors who are or have been company employees. Eligibility requirements vary considerably but usually include a minimum retirement age (typically ranging from 65 to 72 years) and minimum service period (e.g., 5 or 10 years). Cash-based benefits tend to be expressed in terms of the annual retainer in effect upon the director's retirement (e.g., 100% of the retainer). Most plans also link benefits to the director's service in some manner—e.g., the annual benefit equals 10% of the retainer for each year of service completed by the director, *or* benefits are paid for a period equal to the director's years of service.

Some cash-based plans provide payments for the remainder of a retired director's life. Some specifically authorize death benefits, payable either to the director's spouse only or to any beneficiary. Many plans include noncompetition restrictions and/or a requirement that a director receiving benefits be available for advice and consultation.

Typical COC protections entail establishing a rabbi trust to keep benefits out of the hands of potentially hostile new managers. In addition, cash-based retirement plans may provide for automatic vesting and lump sum payment of benefits (without regard to age and service requirements) upon a COC or upon a director's termination of service in connection with a COC.

Board retirement programs spread rapidly during the 1980s, but the 1990s saw growing criticism of the practice of providing such benefits to outside directors (many of whom already receive pensions as retired employees). The National Association of Corporate Directors' blue ribbon commission on best practices for board compensation also recommended that such benefit plans be dropped from directors' pay packages.

As a result, companies began to jettison cash-based plans, but in many cases they concurrently adopted programs providing for stock-based compensation that vests or becomes payable after termination of a director's service. In contrast to cash-based "defined benefit" retirement plans, stock-based plans usually involve periodic defined contributions of restricted shares or deferred stock that will vest and/or be distributed (in shares or cash) when the director leaves the board. As with cash-based plans, payouts often may be in a lump sum or annual installments. Stock-based plans typically do not specify minimum service or retirement age requirements (beyond vesting terms), but some arrangements do condition payouts on the nature of the director's termination (e.g., retirement, death, disability, but not termination for cause). Many plans also limit benefit accruals to 10 years (i.e., the director receives a maximum of 10 annual grants of deferred stock).

Restricted Stock Awards

Restricted stock awards are awards of shares that may not be sold or transferred and may be forfeited if the director's service terminates before a specified time. The director has both dividend and voting rights during the restriction, or "vesting," period. Under some arrangements, the shares vest (i.e., become nonforfeitable) within a limited time frame but remain restricted from sale or transfer until the director leaves the board.

Vesting schedules vary, but they often match the length of a director's term of office (e.g., 3 years). Almost all plans provide for automatic vesting in the event of the director's death or disability retirement before the end of the vesting period. COC provisions generally also stipulate accelerated vesting.

Stock Awards/Stock Fees

"Stock awards/stock fees" refers to shares awarded either without transfer restrictions or for which such restrictions (and, typically, forfeiture conditions) lapse within one year. In this study, all such shares awarded are deemed to be a stock retainer and are reflected as part of annual "Direct Compensation" for analysis purposes (see Chapter 3).

Stock Options

Grants of stock options made to outside directors are always nonqualified (NSOs) for tax purposes; i.e., upon exercise, the director incurs ordinary income tax liability for the difference between the exercise price and fair market value (FMV) on the exercise date for the number of shares exercised; the company is entitled to a corresponding income tax deduction.

The exercise price of directors' stock options generally equals 100% of FMV on the grant date, but a few companies are experimenting with premium-priced options, where the exercise price is greater than market value at grant. Options that a director *elects* to receive in lieu of cash fees often have a lower-than-FMV exercise price, to reflect the inherent risk of deferring earned compensation in that form.

Stock Plans

"Stock plans" refers to a formal program establishing funding and grant terms for equity-based compensation (including share awards, restricted shares, and/or options) to nonemployee directors. COC provisions affecting directors' stock grants normally authorize immediate vesting and, in some cases, cash settlement of awards.

The SEC's adoption of new Rule 16b-3 in late 1996 made it easier for companies to exempt most stock-based compensation transactions between the company and its insiders from the reach of short-swing profit recovery. Among other things, the new rule eliminated the need to limit directors' stock-based compensation to formulaic awards (in order to qualify directors as "disinterested" for purposes of administering executive stock programs). As a result, companies have begun to provide directors' stock grants on a "discretionary" basis and dispense with formal stock plans for directors only. For example, board members may be included as potential participants in an "omnibus" stock plan, with their grants determined (and reported) annually, rather than "fixed" under the terms of a separate program.

Chapter 2. Trends

Directors' compensation continues to change in response to ongoing pressure to strengthen the link between their pay and performance, and to increase board members' accountability to shareholders. Companies are accomplishing this in several ways:

- Stock compensation (which aligns directors' interests with shareholders) is now being utilized by 96% of the study companies.
- Stock grants are increasingly replacing cash compensation and/or benefits (e.g., cash-based retirement plans). And a substantial 40% of the study companies now grant *more than one* type of stock (e.g., annual stock options and annual deferred stock grants).

  Note: SEC's liberalization of Rule 16b-3 helped to facilitate the substitution of stock for cash pay, since the revised rules enable companies to establish policies under which directors' equity grants are not formulaic and may vary from year to year in response to changing strategy and conditions.
- Companies are becoming more inclined to tie stock grants to company performance criteria (e.g., stock price appreciation or total shareholder return).
- For the first time since the *Board Compensation* study began, in 1992, two companies disclosed paying *cash* bonuses to directors, where the payout is directly contingent on company performance.
- An increasing number of companies are penalizing directors who fail to attend a requisite number of meetings.
- Also on the rise are companies insisting that directors acquire and maintain specified equity stakes, through the establishment of stock ownership guidelines.

Some of these trends, such as the substitution of stock for all or a portion of the cash retainer, are emerging slowly. But others, such as making directors eligible participants in umbrella stock plans without fixing their grant types or sizes, appear to be spreading rapidly.

Two elements of directors' pay programs that continue to *decline* are cash-based retirement benefits and insurance coverage. Charitable award programs, which appeared to be a rapidly expanding benefit just a few years ago, have leveled off. Several companies that adopted such programs now report they have been discontinued.

Clearly, most board compensation plan designers today are focusing on what type and how much stock should be provided, in order to:

1. Remain competitive in attracting experienced, skilled board members in a tight market,
2. Meet the short- and long-term needs of directors, and
3. Support the company's goals.

Figure 1 illustrates the evolving prevalence of several components of directors' remuneration since the initial *Board Compensation* analysis was published.

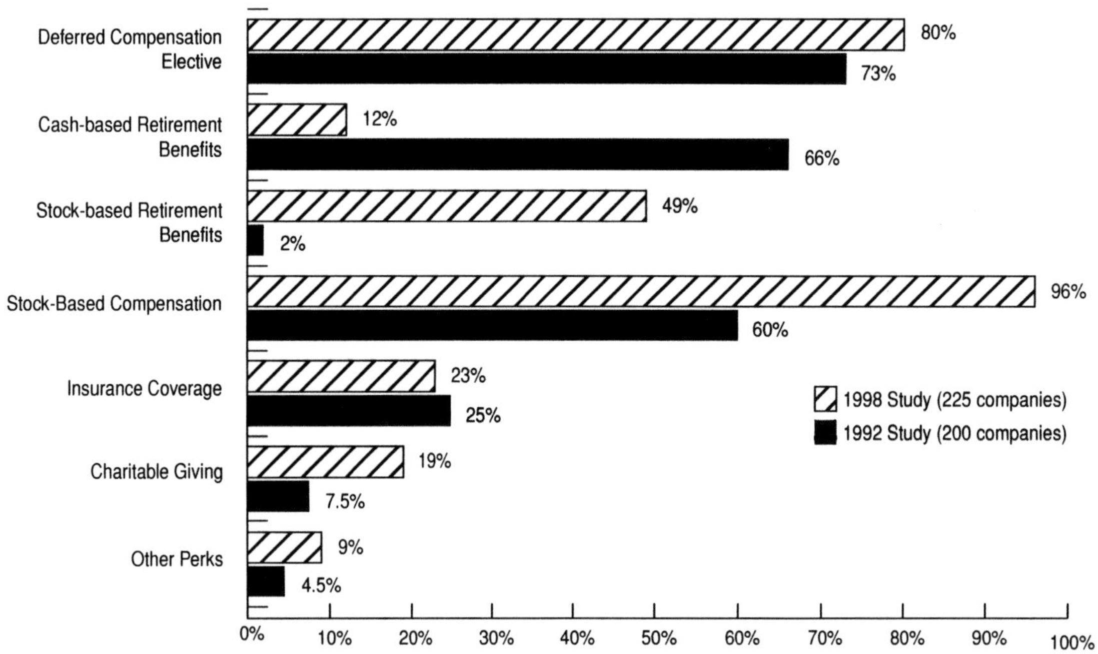

Figure 1. Board Compensation Trends at Study Companies

The most significant findings from this year's study are summarized below with respect to each element of directors' pay.

Retainers

- The value of *total* annual retainers for board service increased an average of 7.7% since last year. This was fueled by companies that eliminated board and/or committee meeting attendance fees and concurrently increased their board retainers.
- The number of companies that pay all or a portion of the annual retainer in unrestricted shares increased slightly, from 22% of the companies in last year's study to 24% this year.
- 12% of study companies now *require* directors to defer from 25% to 60% of their annual retainers in some form of stock until service terminates.

Meeting Fees

- Board meeting attendance fees remained fairly stable, with only 23 companies making a change to this component of directors' pay since last year's study.
- 21% of the study companies now pay *no* board meeting attendance fees, and 23% pay *no* committee meeting attendance fees.

Bonuses

- Incentive compensation, where the payout is based on company performance, is beginning to make its way into directors' pay packages. Two companies disclosed such cash payments in 1997.

Committee Chairman Fees

- The practice of delivering all or a part of chairmen's fees in stock has dramatically increased: nine study companies now do so, compared with only three last year.

Stock

- Providing stock to directors is now the norm—as of 1998, only 10 study companies *do not* include some form of stock in their board compensation programs.
- Companies are substituting stock for cash compensation or other benefits on an ever increasing basis. As a result, directors often receive more than one type of stock (e.g., stock options and deferred stock). In all, 40% of the study companies now grant more than one type of stock.
- Incentive grants continue to expand, with four study companies reporting that they link stock grants to performance criteria.
- An increasing number of companies are dropping a "fixed grant" approach for directors. This changed was spawned by the liberalization of Rule 16b-3, which eliminated the need for companies to ensure that the directors who administer employee stock plans are "disinterested." Twenty-one study companies (versus nine last year) now take a flexible approach to director stock grants.
- The tendency of companies that provide stock to outside directors to make grants on an annual basis continues: 85% of the study companies issue annual grants, compared with 81% in last year's study.
- An increasing proportion of study companies (15% this year vs. only 11% last year) are establishing personal stock ownership guidelines for nonemployee directors. The most prevalent guidelines are set at three- to five-times the retainer value.

Total Compensation

- The value of a typical director's total annual compensation (including fees and the value of periodic stock grants) at the 225 study companies rose 11.3%, on average, since last year's study, to $81,741.
- The proportion of stock-based compensation in directors' total pay packages increased again this year, and now represents almost 50% of total compensation. This compares to a 64%-to-36% ratio of cash to stock as recently as 1996.

Figure 2 highlights the of total compensation paid to an average director at the study companies, cut by revenue range.

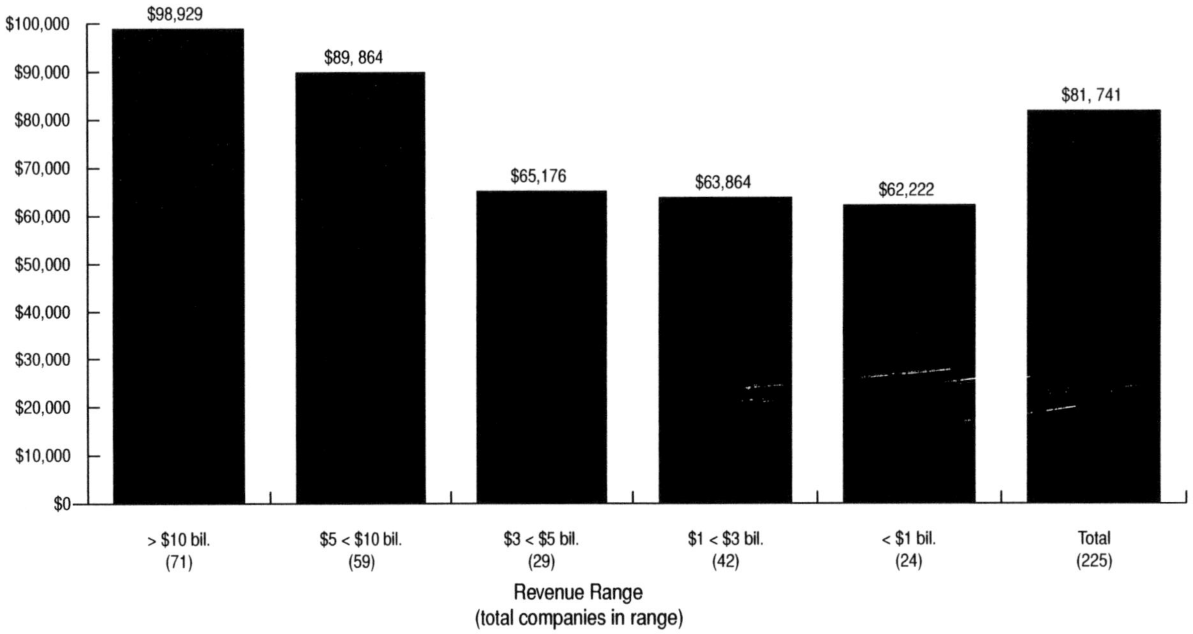

Figure 2. Average Total Compensation by Revenues

Deferred Compensation Programs

- The prevalence of elective deferred compensation arrangements for study company directors remained constant, at 80%, since last year.
- The decision to defer at least some compensation is being taken out of directors' hands to an increasing degree: 28 study companies (12%) now require a portion of the retainer (and sometimes other fees) to be deferred (in stock); the most prevalent retainer portions earmarked for deferral are 25% and 50%.
- A trend that emerged last year—for companies to provide directors with an array of investment choices for deferred compensation accounts—continues to advance: 9% of the study companies now take this approach to deferred earnings.
- At the same time, the proportion of study companies disclosing that a premium is or may be added to the specified earnings rate paid on deferred compensation—or that they pay above-market interest—rose from 10% last year to 13% this year.

Retirement Benefits

- Companies continue to abandon cash-based retirement plans, and only 12% of study companies now maintain them.
- On the other hand, 49% now make stock-based grants that will provide post-service compensation.
- The percentage of companies disclosing mandatory retirement requirements for outside

directors again increased significantly, from 34% last year to 39% in this year's study. The most prevalent mandatory retirement age is 70.

Other Benefits and Perquisites

- The prevalence of companies providing outside directors with additional benefits such as non-liability insurance and/or perks such as product discounts, which leveled off last year, has begun to decline: 37% of the study companies provide such supplementary remuneration, compared with 39% as of 1997.
- The proportion of companies that maintain charitable giving programs has stabilized at 19%, unchanged in the past two years.

Board/Compensation Committees

- Investor concern about directors' independent status remains intact, with nine shareholder proposals related to this issue in 1998 (vs. 10 the prior year).
- Corporations are responding slowly to shareholder pressures to declassify the board—the percentage of study companies that elect directors annually again rose only one percentage point (to 41%) from last year. But in a turnabout, four *companies* put forth proposals to change to annual director elections this year.

Chapter 3. Direct Compensation

The term *direct compensation*, as used in this study, refers to directors' fees that are received or that vest *in the year earned*. This includes:

- Cash retainers
- Stock awards (not restricted more than one year)
- Meeting attendance fees
- Committee member retainers
- Committee chairman fees
- Other special fees

Each of these elements is analyzed with respect to the study companies' most recent fee disclosures, through July 1, 1998. Elective deferrals of cash or stock compensation by directors are not factored into the study analyses. A list at the end of this chapter (see page 28) shows the study companies *ranked* by the level of direct compensation paid to a defined "average" or typical director, based on the disclosed fees.

Overall, the amount of direct compensation paid by study companies to their outside directors did not change significantly in the past year. About a fifth of the companies (21%) altered their cash retainer or board meeting attendance fees (the two most prevalent forms of cash compensation), but that represents a drop from almost 30% that made such changes as of the 1997 study. One trend continues to expand: Companies are requiring more compensation to be paid in stock rather than cash, and in some cases (12% of the study companies) the stock must be deferred until the director's service terminates (see Chapter 6, "Deferred Compensation" for a detailed discussion of this trend).

3.1 Annual Retainer

The most common component of directors' compensation is the annual retainer, which may take the form of cash, stock (with no restrictions beyond the current year), or both. The 225 study companies deliver the retainer portion of directors' pay as follows:

- 167 companies, or 74%, pay *only* a cash retainer.
- Five (2%) pay *only* a stock retainer (Campbell Soup, Chrysler, Colgate-Palmolive, Travelers, and Unicom).
- 49 companies (22%) pay a portion in cash and the remainder in stock.
- Four (2%) pay *no* annual retainer (Apple, Baxter, Manor Care, and Qualcomm).

3.1.1 Cash Retainers

A total of 216 companies (96%) pay a retainer in cash. The average cash retainer is $27,801. Only 17% of the study companies reported a change in their cash retainer level this year, compared with 27% last year. Of the 39 companies making changes, 31 increased the cash retainer, while eight reduced it. In other words, 14% of the companies paying a cash retainer increased the amount, and about 4% decreased it.

Five companies stated that the cash retainer was substantially increased because board (and/or) committee meeting attendance fees were eliminated (they are: AT&T, Ceridian, CISCO Systems, IKON Office Solutions, and Monsanto). One company, Enron, apparently dropped a prior requirement that 50% of the retainer be deferred in stock; thus its cash retainer effectively rose from $20,000 to $40,000. The remaining 25 companies raised their cash retainer level by an average of 22.7%.

The tendency to *decrease* cash stipends as a result of the substitution of stock for cash, which we have noted in the past few years, continued, although the pace has slowed. This year, eight companies reported such a change, compared with 12 in 1997 and 30 in 1996.

- **Apple**—replaced a $28,000 cash retainer and $1,000 board meeting fee with annual stock option grants
- **Ball**—now requires 50% of retainers to be paid in restricted stock
- **Baltimore Gas & Electric**—now requires 50% of retainer to be deferred in stock
- **Black & Decker**—changed from a $30,000 cash retainer to granting 500 shares of stock and paying the value of 500 shares in cash
- **Knight-Ridder**—now pays 50% of the retainer in shares of stock
- **Old Kent Financial**—now requires 50% of the retainer to be deferred in stock
- **Reebok**—now pays 40% of the retainer in shares of stock
- **Union Pacific**—increased from mandatory deferral of 10% of the retainer in shares to mandatory deferral of 50% of the retainer

As illustrated above, replacing cash with stock has been a significant trend, and the list of companies requiring that the stock be deferred until the director leaves the board also grew this year. As discussed in more detail in Chapter 6 ("Deferred Compensation"), 28 companies now require that portions ranging from 25% to 60% of the annual retainer be deferred until after the director's service terminates

3.1.2 Stock Retainers

A total of 54 companies (24% of the study group) now pay some or all of the board retainer in shares that are not restricted beyond the current year, up from 48 in 1997:

- Five companies pay 100% of the retainer value in stock (Campbell Soup, Chrysler, Colgate-Palmolive, Travelers, and Unicom).
- 49 pay a portion of the retainer value in stock.

To denominate the stock retainer, some companies specify a number of shares granted each year, and others determine a dollar value worth of shares that will be granted to directors each year. A few companies do both. The 54 companies that pay all or a portion of the annual retainer in stock split almost 50/50 between the two approaches, as shown below.

- 24 companies indicate a number of shares granted to directors each year (thus, the actual value of the retainer varies each year).

- 27 companies specify a dollar value of the shares granted to directors each year (thus, the value is constant).
- Three companies do both (Dexter, Marsh & McLennan, and Oryx Energy).

The average value of nonrestricted, nondeferred shares granted by the 54 companies that paid part (or all) of the retainer in stock is $28,602. This represents a 21% increase over the average value as of last year's report.

We further analyzed this group according to the denomination of the retainer (number of shares or dollar value). For the 24 companies that grant a specific number of shares each year, the number ranges from a low of 200 shares (granted by American Express) to a high of 2,400 shares (granted by Campbell Soup). The average number of shares granted is 717; the median is 500 shares.

Among the 27 companies that specify a dollar value, the levels range from a low of $5,000 (granted by Apache, Delta Air Lines, and Russell) to a high of $100,000 (granted by Travelers). The average value granted each year is $19,147; the median value is $15,000.

For the three companies that grant stock both as a number of shares and a dollar value, the average dollar value of the stock is $10,667, in addition to an average of 433 shares of stock.

3.1.3 Total Retainer Value

For the study analyses, all cash and any stock that is awarded annually to directors with no transfer restrictions or forfeiture risks beyond one year are included in the retainer value. To determine the value of stock portions expressed as a number of shares, we multiplied the number of shares granted by the company's 1997 year-end stock price.

The average retainer value (cash + unrestricted shares) among the 225 study companies is $33,554, representing a 7.7% increase since last year's analysis. Figure 3 depicts average retainer values (cash + stock) based on revenue ranges, demonstrating a general correlation between company size and the annual retainer value paid to outside directors. One notable exception is that the retainer value in the compensation of outside directors at companies with less than $1 billion in annual revenue is somewhat higher, on average, than at companies with revenue between $1 and $3 billion.

Figure 4 illustrates average retainers by industry groups. The variance between different industry averages is less pronounced this year than last, and there has been one significant change: Last year Utility companies paid on average only $22,657, which was substantially lower than the other industries; this year their average is $3,438 higher, and thus, much closer to the other industries. The shift is probably related to ongoing deregulation of the industry.

The highest paying group, Financials, far outpaced the other industries this year, and recorded a $7,288 increase in their average retainer value. This is most likely due to the fact that eight of the 25 companies in this group grant a fixed number of shares of stock as part of their retainer, and appreciation in their stock prices resulted in an increase in the total retainer value.

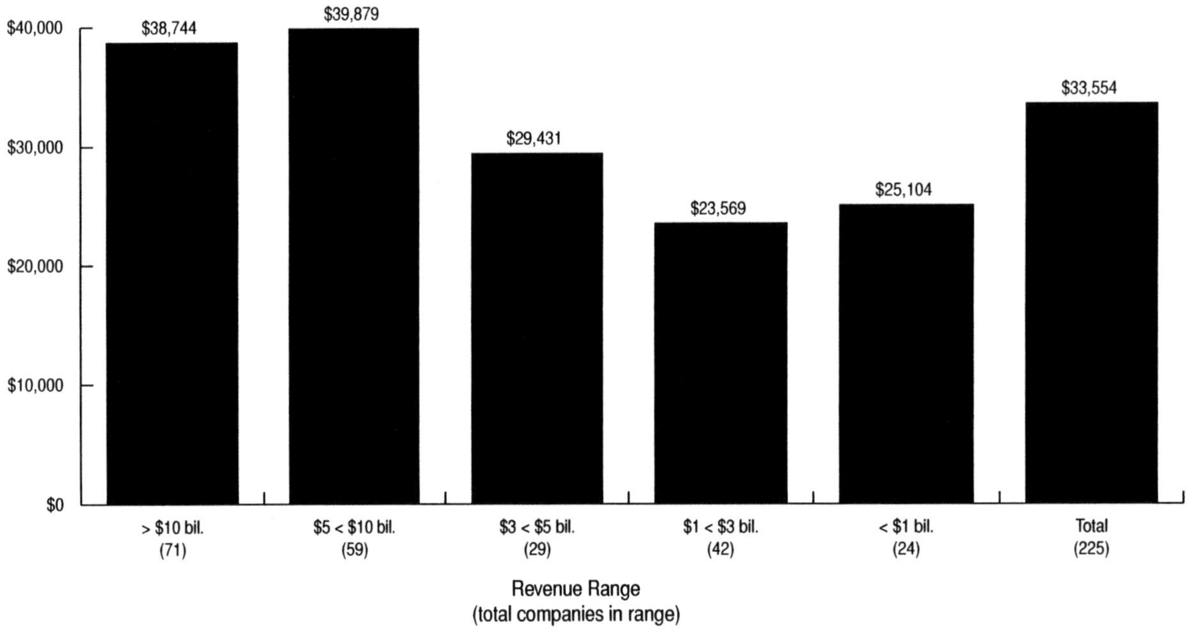

Figure 3. Average Retainer by Revenues

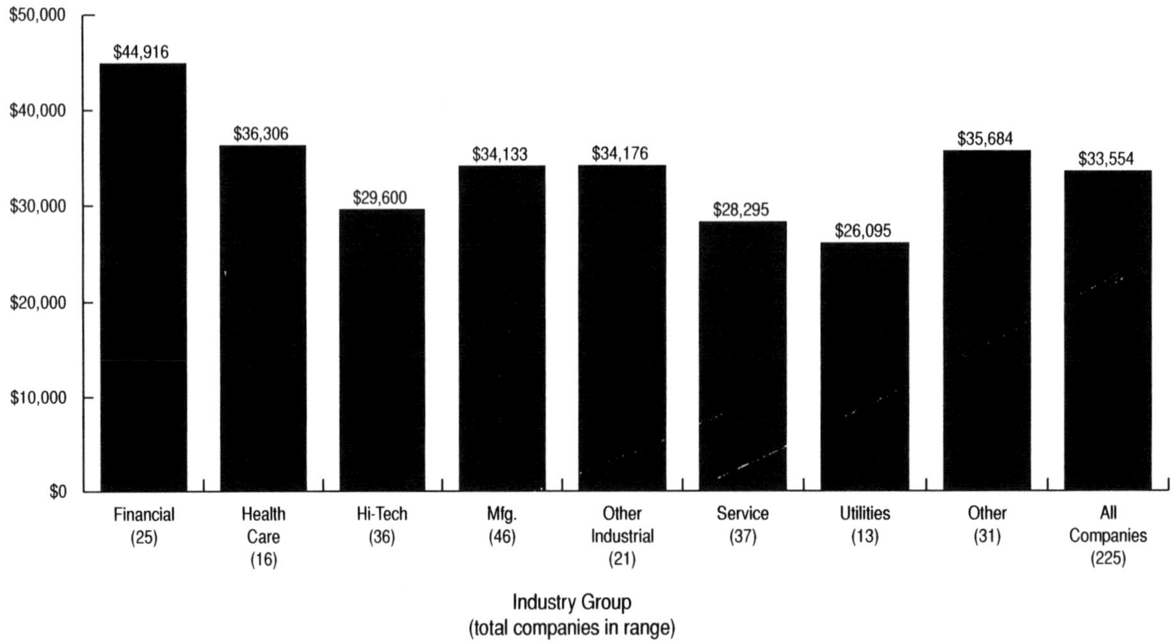

Figure 4. Average Retainer by Industry

3.2 Board Meeting Fee

The number and percentage of study companies that pay board meeting fees are broken out according to most prevalent fee levels in Table 1. As in past years, the most frequently paid amount continues to be $1,000 per board meeting. Interestingly, the number of companies paying *no* board meeting fee continues to rise. Last year 17% of the study companies paid no board meeting attendance fee, which increased to 21% as of 1998.

Table 1 Board Meeting Attendance Fees

Attendance Fee per Board Mtg	No. of Companies	% of Companies
$2,000–$3,500	22	10%
$1,050–$1,800	72	32%
$1,000	74	33%
$600–$950	9	4%
$0	48	21%
Total	225	100%

Only 23 study companies (10%) modified the board meeting attendance fee in the past year, as detailed below:

- 14 increased the fee (Baltimore Gas & Electric, BankAmerica, Bell Atlantic, Bestfoods, BMC Software, Cracker Barrel, Delta Air Lines, Idacorp, Knight-Ridder, McGraw-Hill, Neiman Marcus, Philip Morris, Pioneer Hi-Bred, and Unisys).
- One company decreased the amount (Qualcomm—resulting in identical board and committee meeting fee levels).
- Eight additional companies eliminated the board meeting fee altogether this year, up from four last year (the eight are: Apple, AT&T, Black & Decker, Brunswick, Ceridian, CISCO Systems, IKON Office, and Monsanto).

The average number of board meetings held in FY97 at the study companies was eight. Shoneys reported the most meetings, 18. BMC Software had the fewest, with only three. On the basis of the mean number of meetings (eight) multiplied by the median attendance fee ($1,000), the average amount paid to a typical director for attendance at all board meetings was $8,000.

Of interest: Dexter Corp. doubles the board meeting attendance fee, to $2,000, if the meeting is held outside of its headquarters.

3.2.1 Attendance Requirements

In a climate of concern about excessive compensation and accountability for executives and directors, a few companies penalize directors who fail to attend a requisite number of meetings. Seven study companies (up from five last year) hit directors in the pocketbook if they fail to attend meetings:

1. **AirTouch**—retainer is reduced by $3,000 for each meeting (after one) missed per year.
2. **American Express**—directors must attend 75% of the board *and* committee meetings or forfeit the fourth quarter retainer.
3. **Bob Evans**—directors who do not attend monthly meetings have $500 deducted from monthly retainer fee.
4. **CBS**—retainer may be reduced if 75% of all meetings are not attended (except because of illness).
5. **Gap**—retainer is reduced by $2,500 for each board and/or committee meeting day missed.
6. **Pioneer Hi-Bred**—if fees are elected to be paid in restricted stock and the director misses quarterly meeting, those shares are forfeited.
7. **Procter & Gamble**—the 4th quarter retainer payment is contingent upon a 75% attendance level at board meetings.

3.3 Committee Member Retainer and Meeting Fees

Remuneration for service on board committees is the third element of "direct" compensation. Only 15 study companies (6.7%) do *not* pay any fees for committee service: Apple, Burlington Resources, CISCO Systems, Fortune Brands, Gap, Media General, Mentor Graphics, PepsiCo, Procter & Gamble, Sonoco, SPX, St. Jude, Time Warner, Travelers, and Xerox. Fortune Brands states that the total annual retainer of $50,000 consists of a $35,000 board retainer and $15,000 for all committee service.

3.3.1 Committee Member Retainer

A total of 46 companies (20%) compensate committee members with an annual retainer. Frequently, the amount of the retainer varies by committee. For example, members of the Audit or Executive committee may receive a higher retainer than outside directors serving on other committees. At some companies (e.g., BankAmerica and Warner-Lambert) retainers are paid for service on only one or two committees, while the others receive none.

Average committee member retainers paid by study companies for the four most common board committees are enumerated in Table 2.

Table 2 Average Committee Retainers

Committee	No. of Companies	Avg. Committee Retainer
Audit	41	$5,017
Compensation	40	$4,761
Executive	16	$4,881
Finance-related	17	$4,735

The top committee retainer is $15,000, paid by Fortune Brands to members of the Executive Committee and by Merrill Lynch to both Audit and Compensation Committee members (their other committees receive no retainer). *Note: these two companies do not pay committee meeting attendance fees.*

Three companies (AFLAC, Boeing, and Pfizer) pay only one retainer (from $4,000 to $7,200) for multiple committee memberships.

3.3.2 Committee Meeting Attendance Fee

Unlike committee member retainers, committee meeting attendance fees *do not* tend to vary among committees. One hundred and seventy-four study companies (77%) pay committee meeting attendance fees. This is a small decline from last year when 81% reported such fees. The overall average committee meeting attendance fee is $1,065, which also reflects a slight *decrease* from last year's level of $1,088.

The highest committee meeting attendance fee is $2,500, paid by Electronic Data Systems. The most frequently paid amount is $1,000, which matches the most prevalent board meeting attendance fee. The distribution of various committee meeting fees is broken out in Table 3.

Compared with last year, more study companies are paying higher per meeting fees (e.g., 30 companies paid between $450 and $950 in 1997, but only 24 do so this year). However; the number of companies that pay *no* committee meeting fees also rose (41 last year vs. 51 this year). Thus, the overall average fee declined about 2%, from $1088 to $1,065.

Table 3 Committee Meeting Attendance Fees

Attendance Fee per Committee Meeting	No. of Companies	% of Companies
$1,600–$2,500	11	5%
$1,050–$1,500	45	20%
$1,000	94	42%
$500–$950	24	11%
$0	51	22%
Total	225	100%

The most prevalent practice is to pay the same attendance fee for both board meetings and committee meetings, as demonstrated below:

- 107 companies pay the same board meeting fee as committee meeting fee
- 57 companies pay a higher board meeting attendance fee than committee meeting fee
- 12 companies pay a board meeting fee, but not a committee meeting attendance fee (AFLAC, Chrysler, CSC, E.I. DuPont, Ford, Millipore, Pioneer Hi-Bred, Russell, Standard Register, St. Jude, United Healthcare, and U.S. Trust)
- Tenet Healthcare is the only company that pays a *lower* board meeting fee than its committee meeting fee
- Eight companies do *not* pay a board attendance fee, but *do* pay for committee meeting attendance (Bob Evans, Cooper, Cummins Engine, Johnson & Johnson, Manor Care, MGM Grand, Montana Power, and Waste Management)
- 39 companies pay neither board nor committee meeting attendance fees

Twenty-four of the study companies (11%) do not pay the customary committee meeting attendance fee if the committee meets on the same day as a board (or other committee) meeting. These "same day" policies are summarized below:

- 15 companies pay *no* fee if the committee meeting is on the same day as a board meeting (Allied-Signal, AMR, BMC Software, Boeing, Consolidated Natural Gas, Cummins Engine, Eli Lilly, Johnson & Johnson, Manor Care, Montana Power, Oshkosh B'Gosh, Owens-Corning, Policy Management, Qualcomm, and Unisys)
- Nine companies pay a reduced fee (Charles Schwab, Crestar Financial, Motorola, Omnicom, Rubbermaid, SunAmerica, Temple-Inland, Vanguard Cellular, and VF)

3.4 Committee Chair Fee

A total of 170 study companies (76%) pay special fees to directors who chair committees:

- 149 provide a specified retainer (e.g., $5,000 per year, or 500 stock options in the case of Sara Lee)
- 18 pay an additional amount for each committee meeting attended
- Ashland pays a $1,000 per year retainer *and* an additional $1,000 per meeting
- Philip Morris pays a $5,000 per year retainer ($10,000 for Audit and Compensation committees) *and* an additional $1,000 per meeting
- Cyprus Amax pays $250 per meeting for the Nominating Committee, $500 per meeting for the Employee Funds Investment Committee, and $5,000 per year or $500 per meeting (whichever is greater) for the Audit and Compensation committees

Like committee retainers, chair fees often vary depending on the committee. Table 4 details the average chair fees at the study companies that pay an annual retainer amount. *Note: for analysis purposes we included the $5,000 per year retainers for Cyprus Amax's Audit and Compensation committees.*

Table 4 Committee Chair Retainers

Committee	No. of Companies	Avg. Committee Chair Retainer
Audit	150	$4,443
Compensation	149	$4,370
Executive	71	$8,091
Finance-related	67	$4,113
Other	129	$4,076

At the 18 companies that pay chairmen an additional amount for each committee meeting attended (rather than an additional retainer), the extra fees range between $200 and $1,000, as shown in Table 5:

Table 5 Additional Meeting Fees Paid to Committee Chairmen

Additional Mtg Fee	No. of Companies	Companies
$1,000	7	Beverly, Federal Mogul, Harcourt General, Ingersoll-Rand, Schering-Plough, Silicon Graphics, Stone & Webster
$400–$750	5	Allergan, Beckman Coulter, Honeywell, Illinois Tool Works, Neiman Marcus
$200–$250	6	Bob Evans, Cracker Barrel, Louisiana-Pacific, Questar, Sherwin-Williams, VF

Note: Harcourt pays $1,000 per meeting to the Audit and Compensation committee chairmen; other chairmen receive an extra $500 per meeting.

The incidence of *stock* in chairmen's fees increased dramatically over the past year. A total of nine companies now deliver all or a part of the chairmen's fees in stock, compared with only three as of last year:

- **Baltimore Gas & Electric**—50% of chairmen's fee ($3,500) is mandatorily deferred in stock units; payout is at termination in cash.
- **Black & Decker**—pays chairmen 100 shares of stock (50% paid in cash and 50% paid in shares).
- **Brunswick**—50% of chairmen's fee is paid in stock.
- **CBS**—all of chairmen's fee ($5,000 per year) is paid in stock.
- **Chrysler**—chairmen's fee ($2,000 per year) is paid in stock (less cash to cover tax liability).
- **Monsanto**—50% of chairmen's fee ($10,000) is paid in stock options.
- **Questar**—pays $200 per meeting attended plus 800 additional stock options.
- **Rubbermaid**—50% of all cash fees are deferred in stock.
- **Sara Lee**—chairmen receive an additional 500 stock options each year.

Other unusual practices include:

- **Boeing** has only one chair fee ($4,000) which covers all committee service.
- **Citicorp** and **Corning** pay a chairman's fee in lieu of the committee meeting attendance fees.
- **Colgate-Palmolive** also pays a Deputy Chairman fee of $1,500 per year (versus $3,000 to chairmen).
- **IKON Office Solutions** pays $25,000 to the Chairman of the Independent Directors.

3.5 Chairman of the Board Fees

Five study companies pay special fees to a nonexecutive COB. The nonofficer COBs of Hannaford and Pharmacia & Upjohn received $76,000 and $100,000, respectively, *in lieu* of other board fees. At Allergan, Mentor Graphics, and TJX, COB fees of $250,000, $10,000, and $225,000, respectively, are paid *in addition* to other board fees.

3.6 Incentive Compensation

Two study companies (up from one, SPX, last year) reported that they pay outside directors a portion of *cash compensation* on the basis of company performance:

- **Ball Corp.**—pays an "incentive retainer" based on operating performance, with a target = 40% of the fixed retainer. Although no bonus value was disclosed for 1997, executive bonuses were paid based on "above target performance of the corporation" (therefore, we calculated a conservative bonus value = 100% of target for directors, or $8,800, in the study analyses).
- **SPX**—pays directors a bonus equal to $5,000 times the multiple of the target award earned by the CEO under the company's economic value added incentive plan. For 1997, directors received $18,097, with $8,731 allocated to "reserve accounts," as is typical under EVA programs. The plan is not clear on whether reserve balance is adjusted to reflect future performance (also typical in EVA plans), but it does state that with respect to directors, all "personal" performance goals will be deemed 100% satisfied, and reserve balances will be paid out immediately if the director's service terminates for any reason.

3.7 Employee Director Fees

The number of companies that pay *employee* directors for board service remains fairly stable. Only six study companies (compared with five last year) compensate employee directors:

1. **AFLAC**—$200 per month
2. **Bob Evans**—a $12,000 per year retainer
3. **Freeport McMoRan**—$1,000 per board meeting
4. **Hormel Foods**—$100 per meeting
5. **St. Joe**—$200 per board meeting
6. **Tootsie Roll**—fees are the same as outside directors, except the COB/CEO and Pres/COO do not receive any additional fees

3.8 Telephone Meeting Fees

Many boards engage in teleconferencing. Eighteen study companies (versus 16 in last year's study) disclose specific fees paid to directors who participate in board or committee meetings via telephone:

- Six companies set telephone fees equal to 50% of the regular fees (Consolidated Natural Gas, Harcourt General, Neiman Marcus, Qualcomm, Ryder, and Vanguard Cellular).
- Three companies (CSC, Snap-On, and Vulcan) pay the same as the regular fees, although

Vulcan Materials only pays for telephonic committee meetings, not board meetings.

- Five companies (Boise Cascade, Fleet Financial, Louisiana-Pacific, McDermott, and Wendy's) pay between 40% and 75% of the ordinary fees.
- Stanley Works pays just 20% of regular board meeting fee.
- Springs Industries has no regular board or committee meeting attendance fees, but pays $2,500 for special board meetings and $1,000 for special board meetings via telephone.

For the first time in the study, two companies (Oshkosh B'Gosh, and Policy Management) reported that telephone fees are based on the length of the meeting conducted:

- Oshkosh pays $1,000 for meetings of one hour or longer, and $600 for meetings up to one hour.
- Policy Management pays $500 for the first hour and $250 for each additional hour, up to a maximum of $1,000.

3.9 Former COB/CEO Fees

At 14 companies (6% of the overall study group), a former CEO who remains on the board received special fees. This may constitute compensation for serving as the current COB or be paid as part of a consulting arrangement. The companies are: Allergan, Black & Decker, Boeing, E.I. DuPont, Knight-Ridder, Lee Enterprises, Marsh & McLennan, PepsiCo, Reynolds Metals, Rouse, St. Joe, Talbots, VF, and Weyerhaeuser. The average fee paid to a former CEO at these companies was $227,774 in FY97.

At Ford Motor, the retired VCOB has an agreement for $100,000 per year plus an office, secretarial services, and security services.

3.10 Consulting Fees

Notwithstanding activists' demands that corporations ensure board members' "independence," a significant portion of companies continue to hire outside directors to provide special expertise when appropriate—but the practice remains limited. The proportion of study companies that reported paying consulting fees to outside directors or their firms remains at 14%, unchanged from 1997. The average amount paid for a director's consulting services dropped, however, from $163,123 last year to $132,640 this year (with a median value of $75,000).

The following study companies paid consulting fees to an outside director in FY97: AFLAC, American International, Becton Dickinson, Beverly, Boeing, CBS, Coca-Cola, Cracker Barrel, Cummins Engine, Dexter, Eaton, Freeport-McMoRan, General Dynamics, Hannaford, Illinois Tool Works, Lee Enterprises, MGM Grand, Millipore, Monsanto, Motorola, Nike, Owens-Corning, Pfizer, Pioneer Hi-Bred, Shoney's, Springs Industries, Tenet Healthcare, TRW, Unicom, Viacom, Wal-Mart, Walt Disney, and Wells Fargo.

The consulting fee paid by Freeport-McMoRan, $630,000, is in lieu of other director fees. Others appear to be in addition to board fees.

Table 6 shows the breakdown of director consulting fee levels for FY97. *Note: several companies paid consulting fees to more than one director.*

Table 6 Consulting Fees Paid to Directors

Consulting Fee Paid	No. of Companies
>$200,000	7
$101,000–$200,000	8
$51,000–$100,000	9
$26,000–$50,000	7
≤ $25,000	8

The St. Paul Companies maintains a policy prohibiting the hiring of a director (or his associated firm) except in exceptional circumstances and with the Governance Committee's consent.

3.11 Other Special Fees

Summarized below are various additional extraordinary fees or fee policies disclosed by companies in the study.

- 17 companies authorize payment of a fee for special services or assignments a director is asked to undertake (Allied-Signal, Ashland, Ball, Beckman Coulter, CBS, Ceridian, Chrysler, General Motors, Huffy, J.C. Penney, Northrop Grumman, Pittston, Rouse, Schering-Plough, Sun, Wal-Mart, and Warner-Lambert).
- 12 companies pay additional fees for any special meetings, functions, conferences, etc., that a director is asked to attend (Allied-Signal, American Electric, Cummins Engine, Eaton, Household, Huffy, Owens-Corning, Pioneer Hi-Bred, Policy Management, Public Service Enterprises, Sonoco, and Texas Instruments).
- 12 companies pay additional fees to directors who serve on a subsidiary board (American Express, American International, Baltimore Gas & Electric, Citicorp, Eaton, Harcourt General, J.C. Penney, Monsanto, Sprint, Stone & Webster, Venator, and Weyerhaeuser).
- Eaton paid one director a cash bonus of $300,000 for serving as the COB of a subsidiary during its divestiture process.
- Six companies pay a special fee when directors visit plant sites or make inspections (American Electric, Bestfoods, Huffy, Pfizer, Public Service Enterprises, and Texas Instruments).
- Two companies pay directors a fee for attending the annual shareholders' meeting (Bristol-Myers Squibb, and Marriott).
- Three companies pay a meeting attendance fee for written consents taken in lieu of an actual meeting (Boise Cascade, Quaker Oats, and Vulcan Materials).
- Air Products pays $15,000 per year to directors on the company's Japan Advisory Council, and $10,000 for the European Advisory Council.

- Dow Chemical compensates directors for attendance at the four quarterly Business Review meetings.
- Campbell Soup pays the "lead director" an additional $25,000 per year.
- IKON Office Solutions pays the Chairman of the Independent Directors (who coordinates the annual evaluation of the CEO and holds periodic meetings of the outside directors) $25,000 per year. It also pays trustees for the employee benefits plan $3,000 per year, $3,000 for chairmanship, and attendance fees of $1,000 per meeting.
- Citicorp pays directors who live abroad an additional $3,500 per board meeting. Exxon pays a director who travels more than 3,000 miles to attend meetings a travel allowance equal to the board meeting fee ($1,500) for each trip to North America.
- Dun & Bradstreet's meeting fees double if the meeting lasts more than half a day or if the committee meeting occurs on a different day than a board meeting.
- J.C. Penney pays directors who act as representatives under a trust agreement with Chase Manhattan Bank a fee of $5,000 per year and $600 per meeting attended.
- Monsanto granted a director who serves on a subsidiary board 15,000 shares of subsidiary stock in addition to the other subsidiary director fees.
- PG&E paid $100,000 to a director's nonprofit organization in 1997.
- Reebok has a sponsorship agreement with one outside director's sports team, involving a minimum royalty payment of $100,000 per year; Reebok also provides products to the team worth up to $140,000 per year.
- SBC Communications pays Advisory Directors the same fees as regular directors.
- Shoney's paid $10,000 to a director for assisting with a strategic review of the company operations in 1997.
- Tenet Healthcare pays a director $1,000 per month for serving as a Compensation Committee "advisor."

3.12 Tax Offset Payments

Six study companies make cash payments to directors to help them meet tax obligations arising from the receipt of stock:

1. **Colgate-Palmolive**—directors may elect to have 25% of their stock retainer (1,300 shares) paid in cash to meet tax obligations.
2. **Fluor**—a $2,000 tax allowance is paid each year.
3. **Nordstrom**—a $4,000 per year tax offset payment is paid in addition to the $10,000 stock portion of the retainer.
4. **Travelers**—$100,000 retainer is paid in stock, less the amount needed to cover tax liabilities.
5. **Chrysler**—the retainer ($25,000), committee member fees ($10,000), and chairman's fee ($2,000) are all paid in stock, less cash to cover tax liabilities.
6. **Interpublic**—the company may make tax offset payments for restricted stock awards (3,000 shares every 5 years, vesting after 5 years).

The additional tax allowances paid by Fluor and Nordstrom are included in the "Cash Retainer" value for analysis purposes. The other companies' tax provisions are not factored into our analyses.

3.13 Average Director's Direct Compensation

To enable comparisons of the direct compensation that each study company pays its board members, we defined a typical or "average" director and calculated the amount he or she would have been paid under the compensation program disclosed in the most recent proxy statement (through July 1, 1998). The analysis is based on the following assumptions:

- the director served on the Audit and Compensation committees (since they exist at all 225 companies)
- the director attended all board and Audit and Compensation Committee meetings
- the director was *not* a chairperson of either committee and did not receive any special fees
- all committee meetings were held on the same day as a board meeting (unless the company reported fewer board meetings than committee meetings)
- if stock-retainers are granted other than annually (e.g., every three or five years), the number of shares or dollar-value granted was divided by the grant frequency to determine an annual number of shares or value

To calculate the direct compensation amount paid to each company's "average director," the following were summed:

  Annual Retainer Value (cash + stock) — where necessary to determine the value of stock, the number of shares was multiplied by the 1997 year-end stock price
+ Number of Board Meetings x Board Meeting Attendance Fee
+ Committee Member Retainer Fee
+ Number of Audit and Compensation Committee Meetings x Committee Meeting Attendance Fee—if a different attendance fee applies for meetings held on the same day as a board meeting, this amount was used

---

= Average Director's Direct Compensation

The following were *not* factored into the calculation:

- actions taken by consent in lieu of a meeting, since meeting fees are not typically paid for them
- telephonic meetings where a different fee is paid
- fees paid under separate consulting arrangement
- any special fees paid in 1997 (e.g., additional cash or stock paid because of the extra services involved in the search for a new CEO)
- voluntary deferrals

- the value of *stock grants* (options and restricted shares/deferred shares that vest or become payable after more than one year)—see Chapters 4 ("Stock Compensation") and 5 ("Total Compensation")

On the basis of this analysis, the average level of direct compensation paid by the study companies to a typical director this year is $49,696. That is up just 3% over last year and was fueled primarily by stock price increases. The median direct compensation figure actually dropped by $400, to $46,000.

Campbell Soup continues to generate the largest direct compensation amount for an "average director," $167,000. Campbell Soup also ranked No. 1 in last year's study, and although no changes were made to the board compensation package, a stock split and stock price appreciation propelled an increase of $45,950 in its direct compensation since last year's analysis. The Bank of New York (No. 3 last year) is now the second-highest paying company, with $140,775 in average direct compensation.

New this year are two companies with *no* direct compensation paid to board members: Apple Computer and Manor Care. Apple eliminated its $28,000 annual retainer and $1,000 board meeting attendance fee and replaced them with annual grants of 10,000 stock options. Manor Care had abolished its cash fees last year (replaced by restricted shares) except for committee meeting attendance fees of $1,610, which it now pays only if the committee meets on a day other than when the board meets.

As illustrated in Table 7, there is a direct correlation between company revenues and the average level of direct compensation paid to directors: the bigger the company, the higher the compensation level. A comparison with last year's analysis shows that the smallest companies experienced the most significant increase in the direct compensation fees, however.

Table 7 Average "Direct Compensation" by Revenue Range

Revenue Range	No. of Companies	Avg. Direct Compensation	% Change Since 1997
$10-bil or more	71	$57,704	+ 2.1%
$5 < $10-bil	59	$56,895	+ 6.6%
$3 < $5-bil	29	$44,795	– 4.3%
$1 < $3-bil	42	$37,563	– 4.4%
Less than $1-bil	24	$35,463	+18.1%
Total	225	$49,696	+ 3.0%

Board members' direct compensation remained fairly stable across most industries, except Financials and Utilities, which each rose about 12% over last year. Table 8 shows the average direct compensation broken down by industry groupings.

Table 9 lists the 225 study companies, ranked in descending order according to their average director's "direct" compensation. The listing includes each company's FY97

Table 8 Average "Direct Compensation" by Industry Group

Industry Group	No. of Companies	Avg. Direct Compensation	% Change Since 1997
Financial	25	$67,399	+12.1%
Health Care	16	$52,250	– 0.4%
Hi-Tech	36	$42,529	– 5.2%
Manufacturing	46	$49,531	+ 3.9%
Other Industrials	21	$52,140	+ 1.9%
Service	37	$44,692	+ 2.2%
Utilities	13	$43,972	+ 11.9%
Other	31	$49,384	+ 1.8%
Total	225	$49,696	+ 3.0%

revenue (in millions) and Industry Group, using the following codes:

F = Financial
H = Health Care
I = Other Industrials
M = Manufacturing/Industrials
S = Service
T = High Tech
O = Other

Table 9 Average Director's Annual Direct Compensation Ranking

Avg. Direct Comp Rank	Company	FY97 Rev ($mil)	Ind	Avg. Direct Comp
1	Campbell Soup Co	$7,964	O	$167,000
2	Bank of New York Company, Inc	$5,697	F	$140,775
3	Schering-Plough Corp	$6,778	H	$125,338
4	Chase Manhattan Corp	$30,381	F	$123,432
5	American International Group	$30,520	F	$120,906
6	Philip Morris Companies Inc	$56,114	M	$116,673
7	Colgate-Palmolive Co	$9,057	M	$114,738
8	Marsh & McClennan Companies	$6,009	F	$113,738
9	Paine Webber Group, Inc	$6,657	F	$101,762
10	Travelers Group	$37,609	F	$100,000
11	General Mills, Inc	$5,609	O	$84,813
12	General Electric Co	$90,840	O	$83,600
13	American Express	$17,760	F	$81,850
14	Minnesota Mining & Mfg	$15,070	M	$80,400
15	American Financial Corp	$4,021	O	$78,000
16	Electronic Data Systems Corp	$15,236	T	$77,500
16	Exxon	$122,379	I	$77,500
18	Tenet Healthcare Corp	$8,691	H	$77,200
19	Coca-Cola Co	$18,868	M	$74,000
20	Aon	$5,751	F	$72,322
21	E.I. DuPont de Nemours	$41,304	I	$72,025

Avg. Direct Comp Rank	Company	FY97 Rev ($mil)	Ind	Avg. Direct Comp
22	FDX Corp	$11,520	S	$72,000
22	Pfizer Inc	$12,504	H	$72,000
24	Cooper Industries, Inc	$5,289	T	$70,600
25	Wells Fargo & Company	$9,608	F	$70,100
26	PepsiCo, Inc	$29,292	M	$70,000
27	Pharmacia & Upjohn, Inc	$6,710	H	$68,313
28	Fortune Brands, Inc	$7,001	M	$68,105
29	Quaker Oats	$5,016	O	$68,000
30	Bell Atlantic Corp	$30,194	T	$67,500
31	U.S. Trust Corp	$494	F	$67,050
32	Waste Management, Inc	$9,273	S	$67,000
33	Norfolk Southern Corp	$5,165	S	$66,200
34	Hewlett-Packard Co	$42,895	T	$65,100
35	Merrill Lynch & Co, Inc	$31,731	F	$65,000
36	Cigna Corp	$20,038	F	$64,250
37	Enron	$20,273	U	$63,000
38	Anheuser-Busch Companies, Inc	$11,066	M	$62,600
39	Sara Lee Corp	$19,734	O	$62,500
40	Bristol-Myers Squibb Co	$16,701	H	$62,250
41	BankAmerica Corp	$23,585	F	$62,000
42	SBC Communications	$24,856	T	$61,700
43	Dow Chemical Co	$20,018	I	$61,600
44	Morton International	$3,637	I	$60,938
45	American General	$8,927	F	$60,500
46	Honeywell	$8,028	T	$60,400
47	Chrysler	$61,147	M	$60,000
47	GTE Corp	$23,260	T	$60,000
47	Unocal Corp	$6,064	I	$60,000
50	McDermott International	$3,308	S	$59,950
51	Mobil Corp	$59,978	I	$59,750
52	Viacom Inc	$13,505	S	$59,500
53	Ryder System, Inc	$5,351	S	$59,300
54	Ford Motor Co	$153,627	M	$59,000
54	McDonald's	$11,409	S	$59,000
56	Houghton Mifflin	$797	S	$58,675
57	General Motors Corp	$178,174	M	$58,250
58	General Dynamics Corp	$4,062	T	$58,000
58	May Department Stores	$12,685	O	$58,000
58	Motorola	$29,794	T	$58,000
61	Allied-Signal Inc	$14,472	O	$57,800
62	Stone & Webster, Inc	$1,323	S	$57,750
63	Anadarko Petroleum	$673	I	$57,250
64	Merck & Co	$23,637	H	$57,200
65	Cummins Engine Co, Inc	$5,625	M	$57,000
66	Marriott International	$12,034	S	$56,250
67	PG&E	$15,400	U	$56,000

Avg. Direct Comp Rank	Company	FY97 Rev ($mil)	Ind	Avg. Direct Comp
68	Sun Company	$8,968	I	$55,900
69	Oryx Energy Co	$1,197	I	$55,750
70	Aetna Inc	$18,540	F	$55,000
70	AirTouch Communications	$3,594	T	$55,000
70	Burlington Resources Inc	$2,000	I	$55,000
70	CBS Corp	$9,632	T	$55,000
70	Eaton	$7,563	M	$55,000
70	Fruit of the Loom	$2,140	M	$55,000
70	Johnson & Johnson	$22,629	H	$55,000
70	Procter & Gamble Co	$35,764	M	$55,000
78	Northrop Grumman	$9,153	T	$54,000
79	Becton Dickinson & Co	$2,811	H	$53,000
79	FPL Group	$6,369	U	$53,000
79	Goodyear Tire & Rubber Co	$13,155	M	$53,000
79	Warner-Lambert Co	$8,180	H	$53,000
83	Sprint Corp	$14,874	T	$52,750
84	Emerson Electric Co	$12,299	T	$52,500
84	Texaco	$45,187	I	$52,500
86	Unicom Corp	$7,083	U	$52,200
87	Computer Sciences Corp	$5,616	T	$52,000
87	Fleet Financial Group	$8,095	F	$52,000
87	Walt Disney Co	$22,473	S	$52,000
90	Bestfoods Inc	$9,818	O	$51,250
91	Owens-Corning Fiberglas	$4,373	M	$51,063
92	Premark International	$2,407	M	$51,000
93	Brunswick Corp	$3,657	S	$50,000
93	St. Joe	$346	M	$50,000
93	Wal-Mart Stores, Inc	$119,299	O	$50,000
96	J. C. Penney	$30,546	O	$49,200
97	Ashland Inc	$13,567	I	$49,000
97	Citicorp	$34,697	F	$49,000
97	Temple-Inland, Inc	$3,625	M	$49,000
100	Public Service Enterprise Group	$6,370	U	$48,400
101	Ingersoll-Rand	$7,103	M	$48,000
101	Southern	$12,611	U	$48,000
101	Transamerica	$6,486	F	$48,000
104	Knight-Ridder, Inc	$3,139	S	$47,500
104	Sherwin-Williams Co	$4,881	M	$47,500
106	Lee Enterprises, Inc	$439	S	$47,381
107	Kimberly-Clark Corp	$12,547	M	$46,800
108	Pacific Enterprises	$2,777	U	$46,600
108	Textron	$10,544	O	$46,600
110	Vulcan Materials Co	$1,679	M	$46,500
111	Eli Lily & Co	$8,518	H	$46,200
112	Apache Corp	$1,176	I	$46,000
112	Boeing Co	$45,800	T	$46,000

Avg. Direct Comp Rank	Company	FY97 Rev ($mil)	Ind	Avg. Direct Comp
112	Reynolds Metals Co	$6,900	I	$46,000
115	Analog Devices, Inc	$1,243	T	$45,500
115	Rouse Co	$930	M	$45,500
117	AT&T	$53,261	T	$45,000
117	Dun & Bradstreet	$2,154	S	$45,000
117	Monsanto	$9,457	I	$45,000
117	Shoney's	$1,203	S	$45,000
117	Wendy's International, Inc	$2,037	S	$45,000
122	Cyprus Amax Minerals Co	$3,346	I	$44,688
123	Interpublic Group of Companies Inc	$3,126	S	$44,000
123	Sonoco Products Co	$2,848	M	$44,000
123	Stanley Works	$2,670	M	$44,000
126	Boise Cascade Corp	$5,493	M	$43,800
127	SPX Corp	$922	M	$43,597
128	Browning-Ferris Industries, Inc	$5,783	S	$43,500
129	Albertson's Inc	$14,690	O	$43,000
129	Delta Air Lines	$13,590	S	$43,000
131	Kelly Services	$3,853	S	$42,700
132	Dexter Corp	$1,159	I	$42,638
133	Weyerhaeuser Co	$11,210	M	$42,500
134	Snap-On Inc	$1,672	M	$42,250
135	Caterpillar	$18,925	M	$42,000
135	Fluor Corp	$14,299	S	$42,000
135	Nordstrom	$4,852	O	$42,000
135	Phelps Dodge Corp	$3,914	I	$42,000
135	Pioneer Hi-Bred International	$1,784	O	$42,000
135	PPG Industries, Inc	$7,379	M	$42,000
141	TJX Companies	$7,389	O	$41,750
142	American Electric Power	$6,161	U	$41,000
142	Hannaford Bros.	$3,226	O	$41,000
142	Reebok International Ltd	$3,637	M	$41,000
145	Charles Schwab Corp	$2,299	F	$40,600
146	Allergan, Inc	$1,138	H	$40,500
147	VF Corp	$5,222	M	$40,100
148	Beckman Coulter, Inc	$1,198	T	$40,000
148	Beverly Enterprises, Inc	$3,230	H	$40,000
148	Venator Group, Inc.	$6,624	O	$40,000
148	Xerox Corp	$18,166	T	$40,000
152	Black & Decker Corp	$4,941	M	$39,062
153	Kellogg	$6,830	O	$39,000
153	Omnicom Group	$3,125	S	$39,000
155	Dow Jones & Co	$2,573	S	$38,600
156	Hormel Foods	$3,257	O	$38,400
156	Pittston Co	$3,394	I	$38,400
158	Huffy Corp	$695	S	$38,250
159	AMR Corp	$18,570	S	$38,000

Avg. Direct Comp Rank	Company	FY97 Rev ($mil)	Ind	Avg. Direct Comp
159	Baltimore Gas & Electric	$3,308	U	$38,000
159	Consolidated Natural Gas Co	$5,710	U	$38,000
159	Household International	$5,503	O	$38,000
159	St. Jude Medical	$809	H	$38,000
164	Bowater Inc	$1,485	M	$37,600
165	Unisys Corp	$6,636	T	$37,500
166	Crestar Financial Corp	$1,997	F	$37,000
166	Dayton Hudson Corp	$27,757	O	$37,000
166	Freeport-McMoRan Copper & Gold	$2,001	I	$37,000
166	Standard Register Co	$966	T	$37,000
170	Harcourt General, Inc	$3,692	S	$36,750
171	Air Products & Chemicals	$4,662	I	$36,000
171	First Tennessee National Corp	$1,609	F	$36,000
171	Gap, Inc	$6,508	O	$36,000
171	Policy Management Systems	$583	T	$36,000
175	AFLAC	$7,251	F	$35,200
176	Illinois Tool Works Inc	$5,220	M	$35,000
176	MicroAge, Inc	$4,446	S	$35,000
176	Silicon Graphics	$3,663	T	$35,000
176	Texas Instruments	$10,562	T	$35,000
176	TRW	$10,831	O	$35,000
181	Mead Corp	$5,077	M	$34,900
182	Montana Power Co	$1,024	U	$34,840
183	McGraw-Hill, Inc	$3,534	S	$34,600
184	Corning Inc	$4,129	M	$34,500
185	MGM Grand, Inc	$828	S	$33,500
185	St. Paul Companies	$6,219	F	$33,500
187	Federal Mogul	$1,807	M	$33,000
187	Neiman Marcus Group, Inc	$2,210	O	$33,000
187	Nike, Inc	$9,187	M	$33,000
187	Universal Foods Corp	$826	O	$33,000
191	Louisiana-Pacific Corp	$2,403	M	$32,750
192	Southern New England Telecommunications	$2,022	T	$32,500
192	SunAmerica Inc	$2,084	F	$32,500
194	Genuine Parts Co	$6,005	S	$32,400
195	CISCO Systems, Inc	$6,440	T	$32,000
196	Idacorp, Inc	$749	U	$31,800
197	IKON Office Solutions, Inc	$5,128	O	$30,000
197	Sears, Roebuck & Co	$41,296	O	$30,000
197	Time Warner Inc	$13,294	S	$30,000
197	Union Pacific	$11,014	S	$30,000
201	Bob Evans Farms, Inc	$822	S	$29,900
202	Russell Corp	$1,228	M	$29,200
203	Cracker Barrel Old Country Store, Inc	$1,124	S	$29,000

Avg. Direct Comp Rank	Company	FY97 Rev ($mil)	Ind	Avg. Direct Comp
203	Tootsie Roll	$376	O	$29,000
205	Media General, Inc	$910	S	$27,500
206	Rubbermaid Inc	$2,400	M	$26,150
207	Ceridian Corp	$1,664	T	$26,000
207	United Healthcare Corp	$11,794	H	$26,000
209	Ball Corp	$2,389	M	$25,900
210	International Business Machines	$78,508	T	$24,000
210	Millipore Corp	$619	T	$24,000
210	United Technologies Corp	$24,713	T	$24,000
213	BMC Software, Inc	$731	T	$23,000
213	Oshkosh B'Gosh, Inc	$395	O	$23,000
213	Talbots, Inc	$1,054	O	$23,000
216	Old Kent Financial Corp	$1,306	F	$22,500
217	Baxter International Inc	$6,138	H	$22,000
218	Questar Corp	$933	U	$20,800
219	Mentor Graphics Corp	$455	T	$20,000
220	Vanguard Cellular Systems, Inc	$375	T	$18,500
221	Cintas Corp	$840	S	$18,400
222	Springs Industries, Inc	$2,226	M	$18,000
223	Qualcomm, Inc	$2,036	T	$10,000
224	Apple Computer, Inc	$7,081	T	$0
224	Manor Care, Inc	$1,617	H	$0

Chapter 4. Stock Compensation

The incorporation of stock-based compensation in directors' pay packages has nearly reached its saturation point among the study companies: an overwhelming 96% now utilize some form of stock, a rise of two percentage points from last year. Directors' stock compensation is delivered through:

- Fees paid in shares (this includes any shares that are not restricted more than one year)
- Nonqualified stock options (generally having exercise prices equal to 100% of FMV on the grant date)
- Restricted and deferred shares (including stock units or equivalents, which frequently are used as a vehicle to provide post-service "retirement" benefits)
- Plans allowing directors to receive all or a portion of their fees in stock.

Figure 5 depicts the prevalence of stock use by revenue. At this point, a significant proportion of virtually all revenue groups provide stock-based compensation to outside directors.

The burgeoning stock component of directors' packages has resulted in 40% of the study companies now granting more than one form of stock to board members. For example, part of the retainer may be paid in stock while the company also grants stock options, or directors may receive annual awards of restricted shares along with one-time grants of deferred stock. The breakdown of how the study companies use stock is shown below and further illustrated in Figure 6 and Table 10.

- 120 companies (54%) make only one type of grant (e.g., stock options).

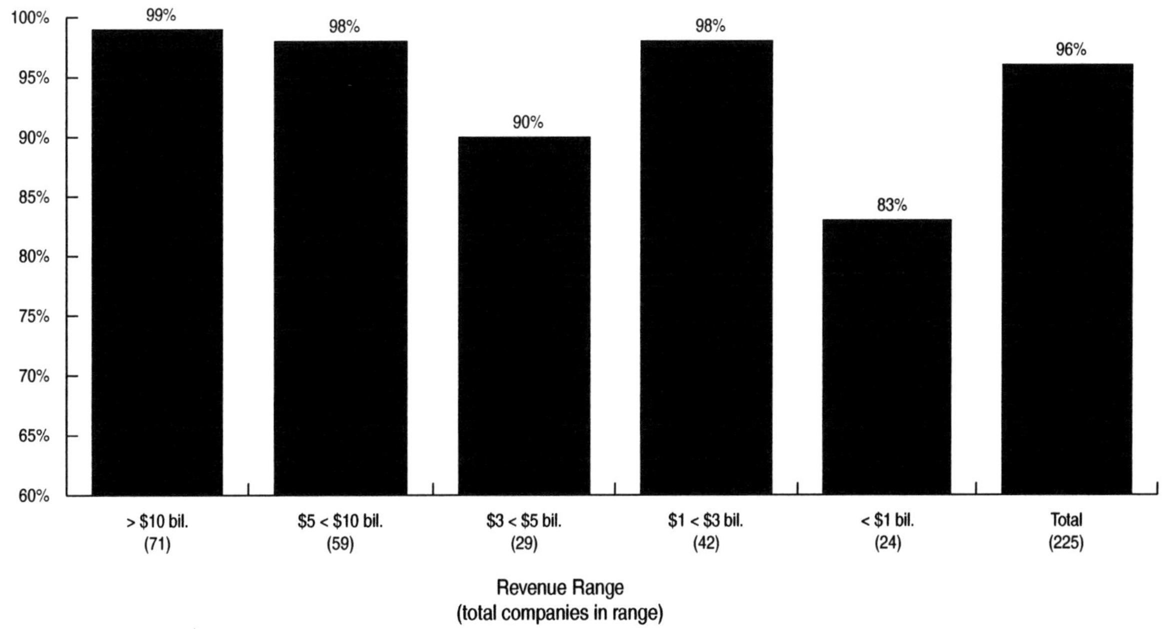

Figure 5. Prevalence of Stock Use by Revenues

- 78 companies (35%) utilize two types of stock grants (e.g., options and deferred stock).
- 12 companies (5%) utilize three types of stock grants (e.g., options, restricted and deferred stock); these include: Allied-Signal, Caterpillar, Ceridian, Cigna, Chrysler, Dun & Bradstreet, Federal-Mogul, Johnson & Johnson, Knight-Ridder, Northrop Grumman, PG&E, and United Technologies.
- Three companies (1%) provide only that directors will receive unspecified discretionary stock grants (Neiman Marcus, St. Joe, and Vanguard Cellular).
- Only 10 companies report *no* stock in their directors' pay package (Coca-Cola, General Dynamics, Genuine Parts, Harcourt General, Idacorp, Omnicom, Pacific Enterprises, Policy Management, Standard Register, and Tootsie Roll).
- Anheuser-Busch and Pioneer Hi-Bred only provide for elective stock.

Stock options continue to be the most popular type of equity grant. They are utilized by 120 of the study companies (53%), either alone or in combination with other grant types. Deferred stock is the second most prevalent grant type, reported by 77 study companies (34%). As further discussed in Chapters 6 (Deferred Compensation) and 7 (Retirement Benefits), the explosion in deferred stock has occurred in conjunction with:

1. Cancellation of cash-based retirement plans, which many companies replace with deferred stock, and

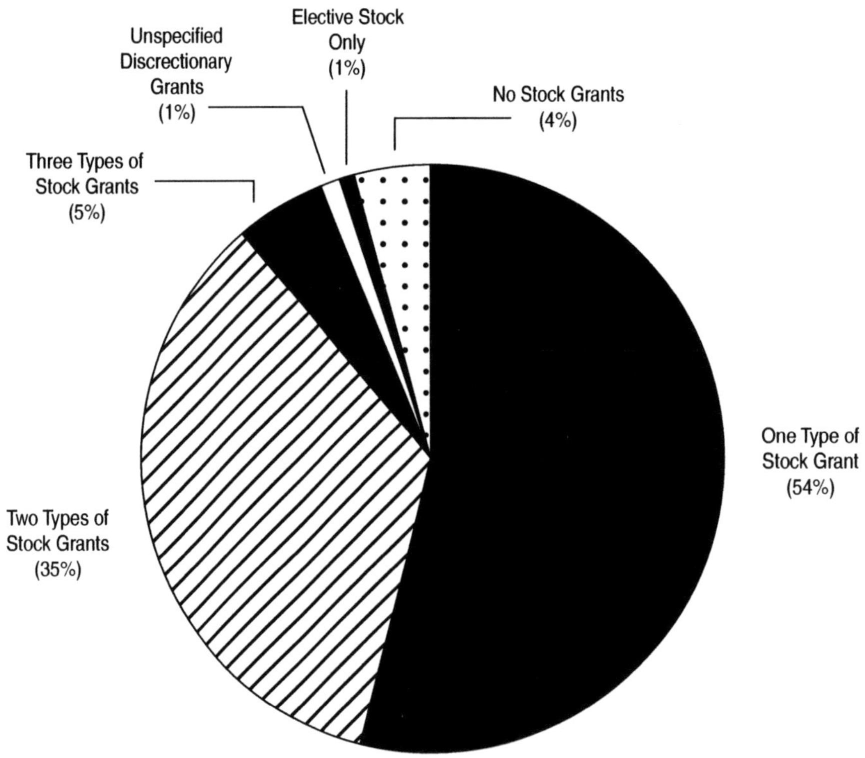

Figure 6. How Companies Use Stock in Directors' Pay

2. Mandatory deferral of portions of directors' cash compensation in a stock denominated form (12% of the study companies currently have such a requirement).

Table 10 details how the study companies utilize various types of stock and the percentage that each methodology represents among the 215 study companies that make stock grants.

Table 10 Prevalence of Stock Grant Types

Type of Grant(s)	No. of Companies	% of Companies
Stock options only	52	23%
Deferred stock only	30	13%
Stock award only	22	10%
Restricted stock only	16	7%
Options & stock award	21	10%
Options & deferred	18	8%
Options & restricted	18	8%
Restricted & deferred	11	5%
Stock award & deferred	7	3%
Stock award & restricted	3	1%
Options, restricted & deferred	6	3%
Options, deferred & stock award	4	2%
Options, restricted & stock award	1	0.5%
Restricted, deferred & stock award	1	0.5%
Unspecified discretionary grants only	3	1%
Elective stock only	2	1%
Do not use stock	10	4%

4.1 Incentive Stock

The pay-for-performance trend continues to reverberate in the boardroom, though not as loudly as in executive suites. Four study companies (up from three last year) now report that directors' stock grants are linked to performance criteria.

1. **Ashland**—stock option grants (1,000 shares per year) are contingent upon return on capital employed being 10% or more in the preceding fiscal year.
2. **Dun & Bradstreet**—target performance shares (1,000 for 1998) are earned if the company's total shareholder return (TSR) equals the 50th percentile of the S&P 500; up to 125% of target shares are delivered if TSR falls between the 50th and 60th percentiles, but only 75% of the number of target shares (i.e., 750 shares) are earned if D&B's TSR is below the 50th percentile.

3. **Hannaford Bros.**—deferred stock grants are based on projected future stock prices; payout depends on actual market performance + dividend equivalents (in 1997 each director received 1,400 performance shares).
4. **MicroAge**—vesting of stock options and restricted stock grants is 1/3 per year if stock price goals are met; stock price goals are 10% annual increases (e.g., grant price = $22.00, one year later price must be $24.20, etc.); if price targets are not met, options vest after 9 years.

Note: CBS, which previously set the exercise price of one-third of each annual option grant equal to 125% of FMV on the grant date, no longer grants premium-priced options.

4.2 Elective Stock

The proportion of companies that allow directors to *choose* to receive some or all of their fees in stock rather than cash continues to expand: 70 study companies (31%) permit elective stock, compared with 30% last year and only 14% in the 1994 study. All but two of the companies that have elective stock mechanisms also provide some other form of stock in their directors' pay packages (the exceptions are Anheuser-Busch, and Pioneer Hi-Bred).

The types of stock that directors may elect to receive are broken out in Table 11.

Table 11 Prevalence of Elective Stock Types

Type of Stock	No. of Companies	% of Group
Unrestricted common shares	42	60%
Stock options (may be discounted)	11	16%
Restricted stock	6	9%
May elect between two or more of above	10	14%
Deferred stock	1	1%

To encourage directors to increase their equity stakes, some companies offer enticements such as price discounts or award matching. Fourteen of the study companies that permit directors to elect *stock options* grant them with a discounted exercise price or other premium:

1. **Boise Cascade**—$2.50/share exercise price
2. **Enron**—50% of FMV exercise price
3. **First Tennessee**—85% of FMV exercise price
4. **Fruit of the Loom**—if director forgoes 50% of annual retainer ($20,500) for 4 years he or she receives 10,000 stock options
5. **Gap**—discount not disclosed
6. **Hannaford**—number of options = 3 times retainer) FMV
7. **Huffy**—number of options = amount forgone divided by (FMV less $1.00) times 1.5; the exercise price = $1.00
8. **IKON Office Solutions**—75% of FMV exercise price

9. **Premark International**—discount amount not disclosed
10. **Sara Lee**—number of options = 4 times amount forgone divided by FMV
11. **Sonoco**—grant value = 4 times amount deferred
12. **SunAmerica**—number of shares = 2.5 times amount forgone divided by FMV
13. **Temple-Inland**—exercise price = FMV minus (retainer) (2,000)
14. **Wells Fargo**—50% of FMV

Six of the companies that allow directors to substitute restricted or deferred stock for cash fees include a premium:

1. **Oryx Energy**—stock retainer may be deferred with the number of shares = 130% of those deferred
2. **Pioneer Hi-Bred**—if cash fees are deferred in restricted stock the value = 105% of foregone compensation for the next 3 years
3. **Ryder System**—in lieu of the $21,500 annual retainer, directors may take $15,000 worth of restricted shares plus $11,500 in cash (total value $26,500).
4. **St. Paul Companies**—shares awarded are valued at 110% of the forgone retainer amount and remain restricted for 5 years.
5. **Unocal**—shares are valued at 120% of forgone cash compensation, with restrictions lapsing after 5 years (or longer, if elected).
6. **Textron**—matches 25% of amounts the director elects to defer in excess of the $16,000 that the company requires to be deferred in stock units (that amount is also matched 25%).

4.3 Discretionary Stock Grants

The most significant development affecting director stock plans is the 1996 revision of Rule 16b-3, concerning exemption of compensatory stock-based transactions by insiders from the short-swing profit recovery provision of Section 16 of the Securities & Exchange Act of 1934. The new Rule eliminated the need for directors who administer executive stock plans to qualify as "disinterested" (a mandate that most companies had interpreted as requiring stock plans for such board members to be formulaic and nondiscretionary). In response, companies have begun to take a more flexible approach to directors' stock grants by forgoing shareholder approval, for example, or adopting plans that do not lock the company into fixed grants. Among other things, this has resulted in more directors being brought under the umbrella of the company's all-purpose executive stock plans, perhaps with an aggregate number of shares carved out for them.

As we expected, the proportion of companies authorizing non-formulaic stock grants ballooned from 4% in 1997 to 9% as of this year's study. Table 12 enumerates the companies that authorize discretionary grants, according to the type of plan that provides for them.

Table 12 "Discretionary" Stock Grants

Plan Type	No. of Companies	Companies
Separate director plan	4	Computer Sciences Corp., Marriott, MicroAge, and Sherwin-Williams
General stock incentive plan(includes executives and directors)	17	American General, Anadarko Petroleum, Ball, Bowater, CISCO Systems, Emerson Electric, Gap, Neiman Marcus, Shoney's, St. Joe, St. Jude Medical, Stone & Webster, Temple-Inland, TRW, Vanguard Cellular, VF, and Wal-Mart

4.4 Formulaic Stock Grants

A total of 213 study companies (95%) make one or more stock grants, such as stock options, restricted shares, unrestricted stock awards, and/or deferred shares (although three of these provide only for unspecified discretionary stock grants).

For calculation purposes, we "annualized" grants that are made at intervals of more than one year (e.g., every three or five years) by dividing the total number of shares by the frequency of the grant. We also distinguish between grants made periodically and those that are made on a one-time-only basis (since their numbers tend to differ dramatically, the latter are analyzed separately). Included in the "one-time grant" category are any awards made at the time a director is initially elected to the board, if such grants are larger than those reported to be made regularly.

Since some companies express equity grants as a number of shares and others as a dollar value, we converted them, as appropriate, using the following methodology:

- For restricted and deferred stock, the number of shares was multiplied by the year-end 1997 stock price to arrive at a dollar value; to convert dollars to shares, the number of shares was divided by the year-end 1997 stock price
- For stock options, the number of shares was multiplied by the year-end 1997 stock price and then divided by 3; or, vice-versa to convert a grant expressed in dollars to a number of options.

To put the study companies' stock grant practices into perspective, we considered them on the basis of two factors:

1. Whether grants are made annually or are "one-time," and
2. Whether only one or multiple types of stock are (e.g., an annual stock award plus stock options).

The analyses reveal a dramatic difference in the grant sizes, depending on whether the company uses only one type of stock or makes multiple grants (see Tables 13 and 14). For example, the average number of stock options granted by companies that grant *only* options is 3,991 shares, compared with an average of 1,994 shares among companies that grant a stock option *and* one or more other stock types. In other words, the companies that grant other stock-based awards in addition to options tend to grant only about half the number of option shares as those that use *only* stock options in the directors' compensation package. And the values of these grants diverge by about 45%, on average.

A similar though less pronounced pattern applies to restricted and deferred stock grants (Table 14). Stock awards are the only exception to this tendency—in their case, there is only about a 5% difference between the award sizes for companies that grant only stock awards and those that use additional stock.

Table 13 Average Annual/Periodic Stock Grants—Only One Type of Stock Granted

Grant Type	No. of Companies	Avg. No. of Shares Granted*	Avg. Award Value
Stock options	49	3,991	$50,712
Restricted stock	15	634	$28,314
Deferred stock	30	518	$29,262
Stock award	20	628	$30,596

**On an annualized basis*

Table 14 Average Annual/Periodic Stock Grants—Two or More Types of Stock Granted

Grant Type	No. of Companies	Avg. No. of Shares Granted*	Avg. Award Value
Stock options	65	1,994	$35,103
Restricted stock	27	386	$16,969
Deferred stock	43	403	$21,537
Stock award	33	600	$29,046

**On an annualized basis*

Predictably, stock grants that occur only one time tend to be much larger than those made periodically. Overall, one-time grants are three to seven times greater, on average, than periodic grants, but there is less distinction between companies that make only one-time stock grants and those that make them in combination with other stock-based grants. Tables 15 and 16 summarize average one-time grant sizes according to whether the company grants only one type of stock or multiple types.

Table 15 Average One-Time Grants—One Type of Stock Granted

Grant Type	No. of Companies	Avg. No. of Shares Granted	Avg. Award Value
Stock options	14	15,214	$196,662
Restricted stock	6	3,150	$163,940
Deferred stock	2	1,250	$75,422
Stock award	2	600	$20,419

Table 16 Average One-Time Grants—Two or More Types of Stock Granted

Grant Type	No. of Companies	Avg. No. of Shares Granted	Avg. Award Value
Stock Options	16	7,497	$108,581
Restricted Stock	14	1,720	$120,518
Deferred Stock	4	2,429	$107,703
Stock Award	4	1,744	$72,531

4.4.1 Stock Grant Frequency

A growing majority of study companies awards stock to directors *every* year, regardless of the grant type—options, restricted, or deferred shares. A total of 85% of the study companies grant some form of stock on an annual basis, compared with only 73% that followed that practice as of the 1996 study.

Table 17 highlights the frequency of stock grants to directors at the 225 study companies.

Table 17 Frequency of Stock Grants

Grant Frequency	No. of Companies	% of Companies
Annual	135	60%
2 or 3 years	4	2%
5 years	6	3%
One-time	6	3%
Both annual and another	57	25%
3/5 years & one-time	2	1%
No specific grants made*	15	6%
Total	225	100%

**Includes companies whose directors are only eligible for undisclosed non-formulaic grants*

4.4.2 Stock Grant Vesting Terms

Table 18 details the vesting periods applicable to stock grants made by the study companies.

With respect to deferred stock, if the award is not *paid out* until the director's service terminates (regardless of when it becomes vested) we considered it unvested until termination (and thus included in the "Term'n" column for purposes of the chart and related analyses). Most deferred stock awards are not released until the director's service terminates, regardless of any vesting timetables or other criteria.

By contrast, the predominant vesting period for directors' stock options runs from six months to one year, although about the same proportion of companies stretch the waiting period before options can be exercised over periods that range from 2 to 5 years. Restricted shares tend to vest over 2- to 5-year periods, but a substantial number of companies also hold restricted shares until the director leaves the board (see Chapter 7 for insight on how deferred stock is being used to provide post-service benefits).

Table 18 Stock Grant Vesting Terms

	Immed	6 mon –1yr	2–3 yrs	4–5 yrs	>5 yrs	Term'n	Other	Unknown	Total
				No. of Companies (% of Companies)					
Stock Options	8 (7%)	45 (37%)	26 (21%)	25 (21%)	1 (1%)	1 (1%)	1 (1%)	13 (11%)	120
Rest'd. Stock	0	0	12 (21%)	16 (28%)	4 (7%)	20 (36%)	2 (4%)	2 (4%)	56
Stock Awards	50 (85%)	8 (13%)	0	0	0	0	1 (2%)	0	59
Deferred Stock	0	0	0	4 (5%)	2 (3%)	66 (86%)	0	5 (6%)	77
Total	58 (19%)	53 (17%)	38 (12%)	45 (15%)	7 (2%)	87 (28%)	4 (1%)	20 (6%)	312

Note: For compensation analysis purposes, stock awards that vest within one year are considered part of the annual board retainer; we included all stock awards here in order to provide information about their vesting practices.

4.4.3 Unusual Stock Grants

While keeping their programs in line with prevalent practices, a number of companies tailor director's stock grants to meet specific cultural goals or to adopt innovative techniques. Here are some notable provisions among the study companies:

1. **Allergan**—made a 1-time grant of 5,000 restricted shares to the new outside COB.
2. **American International**—reimburses each nonemployee director for the purchase of 450 shares per year.
3. **AMR**—specifies annual grants of 450 deferred shares; the size of future grants may be increased on the basis of the average director's compensation paid by 20 other companies; if AMR falls below 85% of the median value, grants will be increased in 50-share increments.
4. **Bell Atlantic**—directors may elect to receive shares of stock in lieu of the 1,500 stock options granted annually.
5. **Boise Cascade**—provides that the committee may adjust the number of options granted annually (currently 1,500) up to once per year (at least 6 months prior to grant date).
6. **CBS**—Shares paid and/or received upon exercise of options must be held for (a) 3 years from exercise, or (b) 2 years from termination.
7. **Charles Schwab**—provides that if the exercise price (FMV at grant) of their annual 2,500 stock options equals less than $35.00 per share, the number of options granted increases to 3,750 shares.
8. **Chase Manhattan**—the value of annual 500-share awards may not be less than $37,500 or more than $50,000.

9. **Consolidated Natural Gas**—normally grants 200 shares of restricted stock annually, but directors may choose to receive 200 shares of deferred stock and 1,000 stock options instead.
10. **Dayton Hudson**—Vice Chair of the Executive Committee receives an additional $10,000 in restricted stock per year.
11. **Dun & Bradstreet**—grants target performance shares (1,000 for 1998) that are earned if the company's TSR = 50th percentile of S&P 500's TSR; up to 125% of target shares are paid if TSR ranks between the 50th and 60th percentiles; 75% of target if rank is below the 50th percentile.
12. **DuPont**—the COB receives 60,000 stock options in lieu of 400-share annual stock awards; the options vest after 1 year and have an exercise price = 100% of FMV, but the stock price must be at least 120% of FMV in order for the options to be exercised.
13. **Eli Lilly**—annual deferred stock awards = the *lesser* of (a) 800 shares, or (b) shares having a value equal to total annual compensation, assuming attendance at all board meetings.
14. **Enron**—annual restricted stock grants are based on 50% of average retainer from prior year divided by FMV, and the number of annual stock options = 4-times the number of restricted shares.
15. **Gap**—one director received a discretionary grant of 7,500 discounted stock options in 1998.
16. **General Motors**—directors may choose between $10,000 restricted stock units annually or 1,000 stock options which are exercisable after one year.
17. **Hannaford**—deferred stock grants are based on projected future stock price; payout depends on actual market performance plus dividend equivalents.
18. **Houghton Mifflin**—directors also participate in a Stock Purchase Program and may receive loans from the company to purchase shares.
19. **Louisiana-Pacific**—45,000 stock options, granted every 5 years, have an option exercise price = 85% of FMV.
20. **Mead**—annual stock option grants = 300 shares times [the average total compensation paid to directors at companies with sales > $4-bil, divided by $36,246 (the average total compensation for the same group in 1994)]; annual restricted stock grants = $5,000 times the same multiplier as above.
21. **Mentor Graphics**—the outside COB receives an additional 2,500 stock options per year.
22. **MicroAge**—stock option and restricted stock grants vest 1/3 per year if stock price goals are met (stock price goal = 110% increase per year); if goals are not met, the options vest after 9 years.
23. **PepsiCo**—up to $90,000 of their annual grants of $120,000 worth of stock options may be converted to capital stock at a ratio of 3 options per share.
24. **Philip Morris**—annual stock awards = the *lesser* of 1,200 shares or the value of the retainer (currently $40,000).

25. **Questar**—grants committee chairmen an additional 800 stock options per year.
26. **Reebok**—makes annual stock option grants = 3-times directors' average annual compensation in the prior year (initial grants = 6-times).
27. **Sara Lee**—grants an additional 500 stock options per year to committee chairmen.
28. **Sonoco**—annual grants of 2,000 stock options include "reload" options; also, the annual grants may be increased up to 10,000 per year without seeking shareholder approval.
29. **Texaco**—accrued deferred stock units (900 per year) are forfeited if a retired director engages in conduct detrimental to the company.
30. **Textron**—matches by 25% the $16,000 of the annual retainer that is mandatorily deferred in stock.
31. **United Technologies**—grants foreign nationals restricted stock units (2,000, one-time) instead of restricted shares.
32. **VF**—the number of annual stock options granted depends on the FMV of common on the grant date:

    < $5 = 1,200 shares
    $5–10 = 1,800 shares
    $10–15 = 2,400 shares
    $15–20 = 3,000 shares
    $20–25 = 3,600 shares
    $25–30 = 4,200 shares
    $30–35 = 4,800 shares
33. **Wendy's**—the company may cash out exercisable stock options without director's consent.

4.5 Stock Plans

Overall, 192 of the 215 companies that use stock (including two that provide only for elective stock in lieu of cash) do so under the auspices of a formal stock plan:

- 131 companies have a separate plan for directors' stock grants.
- 34 authorize directors' grants in the same plan as their executives.
- Seven have a separate plan for directors *and* provide for grants under the executive plan (Anadarko Petroleum, Ball, Mead, Marriott, Shoney's, Stone & Webster, and Wal-Mart).
- 11 provide for deferred stock grants, but they are administered under the directors' deferral plan.
- Six companies have a separate director plan and administer deferred stock under the deferral plan (Beverly, Boeing, Cigna, Delta Air Lines, General Motors, and United Technologies).
- Rouse and Rubbermaid have grants under their executive plans and their deferral plans.
- Federal Mogul makes stock-based grants under a separate director plan as well as the executive plan *and* the directors' deferral plan.

4.5.1 New Stock Plans

Because a substantial majority of study companies already included stock in directors' pay packages, the emergence of new equity plans at companies that previously did not report stock grants totaled only six this year, compared with 17 last year. The types of grants adopted by those companies are summarized in Table 19.

Table 19 Grant Types Utilized In New Director Stock Plans

Grant Type	No. of Companies	Companies
Stock awards	1	Russell
Restricted stock (elective)	1	Pioneer Hi-Bred
Stock options	1	Russell
Deferred stock	4	Baltimore Gas & Electric, Computer Sciences Corp., Old Kent Financial, and SBC Communications

4.5.2 Stock Plan Lives

Most director equity plans are designed to expire in no more than 10 years. Table 20 breaks out the most prevalent life spans among study company programs.

Table 20 Stock Plan Life-Spans

Plan Life	No. of Plans
5 year or less	9
6–10 years	61
>10 years	3
Indefinite	24

4.5.3 Stock Plan Kitties

Funding levels in directors' stock plans vary considerably but tend to range between 100,000 and 300,000 shares, as shown in Table 21. *Note: This analysis includes only shares authorized in separate stock programs for board members, excluding umbrella programs that cover executives as well as directors.*

Table 21 Director Stock Plan Funding

No. of Shares in Kitty	No. of Plans
1 million or more	6
500,000 > 1 million	10
300,000 > 500,000	17
100,000 > 300,000	48
50,000 > 100,000	18
Less than 50,000	5

Five companies utilize evergreen kitties (i.e., the plan is refueled each year) in their director stock plans:

1. **Boeing**—0.008% of common shares outstanding each year
2. **Cyprus Amax**—1/16th of 1% of common shares outstanding each year
3. **Kelly Services**—0.25% of common shares outstanding each year
4. **Sears, Roebuck**—0.1% of common shares outstanding each year
5. **Sonoco**—125,000 shares each year

4.5.4 Stock Plan Change of Control Provisions

Change of control (COC) provisions are included in 80 (55%) of the study company plans that provide solely for stock grants to directors. These typically stipulate accelerated vesting of outstanding awards upon a COC of the company.

4.6 Director Stock Ownership Guidelines

One consequence of the campaign to tie directors' interests more closely to shareholders' has been adoption of personal stock ownership goals for outside board members. This is becoming more prevalent, with 15% of the study companies now indicating they have ownership guidelines for nonemployee directors (vs. 12% last year). These guidelines are most often pegged to a dollar value, typically expressed as a multiple of the annual retainer amount. Shares that are "acquired" via grants made by the company (e.g., deferred stock)—and voluntary deferrals of cash fees into a stock-based account—are customarily considered for purposes of guideline attainment.

Stock ownership goals enacted among the study companies are depicted in Table 22. A majority express them as multiples of the annual retainer, with three to five times being most prevalent.

Most policies allow directors a period of time to comply with stock ownership guidelines, as summarized in Table 23. The breakdown indicates that companies instituting guidelines tend give directors a reasonable period (5 years) to meet the goal.

Table 22 Stock Ownership Guidelines for Outside Directors

Guideline	No. of companies	Companies
1x retainer	1	SPX
3x retainer	9	BankAmerica, Cooper, Cyprus Amax, Monsanto, Northrop Grumman, Oryx Energy, Union Pacific, Waste Management, and Sun (whose guideline includes 3X retainer + other fees)
4x retainer	1	Reebok
5x retainer	10	Ashland, Becton Dickinson, FDX, General Mills, Hannaford, McDonald's, Sears Roebuck, St. Paul Cos., Ford Motor (also includes committee fees) and AT&T (also includes stock retainer value in guideline)
6x retainer	1	Honeywell
10x retainer	1	Kellogg
Retainer x years of service	1	Allergan
$100,000	1	AirTouch (stock must be purchased within 30 days of initial election to the board; company loans are available)
1,000—3,000 shares	5	American Electric, Campbell Soup (the goal is 1,000 after one year of service, rising to 3,000 after three years), Phelps Dodge, Reynolds Metals, and Dow Chemical (directors' stock option grants are contingent on their acquiring "increasingly larger" amounts of stock, specified as 1,500 shares in 1994 up to 2,000 in 1999)
5,000 shares	1	Stanley Works
10,000 shares	2	American Express, Chrysler
Not disclosed	1	Bristol-Myers (indicates that guidelines have been established but they are not specified)

Table 23 Time-Frames for Stock Ownership Goal Compliance

Compliance Period	No. of Companies
30 days	1
1 year	1
3 years	4
5 years	18
Undisclosed	10

4.7 Changes to Stock Compensation

As corporations continuely to update their directors' pay packages, stock is frequently the focus. A substantial 28% of the study companies modified their approach to directors' equity grants in the past year. The changes are detailed in Table 24.

Table 24 Changes to Existing Directors' Stock Compensation

AFLAC	changed from granting 10,000 stock options one-time to every 5 years
Air Products	changed 200 deferred unit grants from one-time to annual grants
Allergan	increased restricted stock grants by 900 shares every 3 years
American Express	added annual stock awards of 200 shares to already existing 1,000 stock options annually
American General	disclosed one-time grants of 500 shares of restricted stock and 1,500 stock options—"future awards are subject to the discretion of the board"
Anadarko Petroleum	added one-time grant of $13,000 deferred units to already existing 5,000 stock options annually; a new 1998 stock plan provides for discretionary grants. *Note: cash retirement plan was eliminated.*
Analog Devices	amended stock plan to provide for annual stock option grants until a director terminates vs. only four annual grants previously
Apache	added annual $5,000 stock awards to already existing 1,000 share restricted stock awards every 5 years
Apple Computer	added annual 10,000 stock option grants; previously disclosed one-time grants of 10,000 warrants
AT&T	increased deferred unit grants from $4,500 per year to 45,000 shares per year. *Note: cash retirement plan was eliminated.*
Ball	now requires 50% of all retainers (fixed and "incentive") to be paid in restricted stock. *Note: cash retirement plan was eliminated.*

Beckman Coulter	added 100 share restricted stock grants to already existing annual grants of 2,000 stock options
Bestfoods	added 100 shares of deferred stock granted annually to already existing 50% of retainer being mandatorily deferred
Black & Decker	now pays 500 shares of stock as part of retainer; also increased annual stock option grants from 1,500 to 2,500 shares. *Note: cash retirement plan was frozen.*
Bristol-Myers	increased deferred unit grants from 300 to 500 shares
Brunswick	changed from $25,000 stock options annually to 3,000 stock options annually; changed from one-time deferred stock grants of $25,000 to one-time stock awards of $25,000
CBS	increased annual stock award and stock option grants from $15,000 to $25,000 each; eliminated premium-priced options
Ceridian	increased stock option grant from 1,500 to 2,000 shares annually; replaced one-time restricted stock grants = 4 times the retainer to = 2.5 times the retainer; changed from 50% of retainer paid in stock to now paid in deferred stock
Cigna	increased annual stock award from $12,000 to $20,000
Delta Air Lines	added $6,300 of deferred stock annually to already existing stock awards *Note: cash retirement plan was eliminated.*
Dexter	currently pays 200 shares of stock as part of retainer and now added $10,000 more of stock per year to the retainer value
Dow Chemical	added annual stock option grants = 45% of prior year's average retainer and fees to already existing one-time restricted stock grants of 1,500 shares and stock option grants every 5 years of 1,550 shares. *Note: cash retirement plan was eliminated.*
Emerson Electric	increased annual restricted stock awards from $25,000 to $35,000; also included directors as eligible participants in 1998 Stock Option Plan (although "not currently contemplated")
Enron	apparently no longer requires 50% of annual retainer to be deferred in stock
FDX	increased annual stock option grants from 1,000 to 2,000 shares. *Note: cash retirement plan was frozen.*
Federal Mogul	added annual stock option grants of 2,000 shares to already existing one-time grants of 1,000 restricted shares and $25,000 deferred shares granted every 5 years. *Note: cash retirement plan was eliminated.*

Fleet Financial	added annual grants of deferred units = 50% of retainer to already existing annual deferred unit grants = 25% of retainer. *Note: cash retirement plan was frozen.*
Fortune Brands	increased annual stock award from 300 to 482 shares
FPL	replaced one-time grants of deferred stock = retainer value with one-time stock awards of 200 shares
Gap	increased annual stock option grants from 2,000 to 3,750 shares
Goodyear	increased deferred unit grants from $8,000 to $10,000 per year
Household	increased stock option grants from 1,500 to 2,500 shares
Huffy	added annual 2,000 stock option grants to already existing stock option grants of 5,625 shares every 3 years
IKON Office Solutions	added annual restricted stock grants of 400 shares and one-time stock option grants of 25,000 shares to already existing annual stock option grants of 2,000 shares (increased from 800 shares). *Note: cash retirement plan was eliminated.*
J.C. Penney	dropped tandem grants of 200 restricted shares and 800 stock options annually, and replaced with 500 restricted shares annually
Johnson & Johnson	*reduced* the annual stock option grant from 1,100 to 900 shares
Knight-Ridder	now pays 50% of retainer in stock; added annual grants of 2,000 stock options to already existing annual grants of 600 deferred shares
Marriott	added annual stock awards with value = 50% of cash retainer to already existing annual grants of 250 shares of deferred stock
Marsh & McLennan	added 600 shares of stock granted annually to already existing stock grants of $10,000 per year. *Note: cash retirement plan was eliminated.*
May Dept. Stores	increased annual restricted stock grants from $40,000 to $45,000
McGraw-Hill	changed deferred stock grants from the greater of $30,000 or 50% of total prior year's compensation to 50% of total compensation ($17,000 for 1997)
Mead	changed from granting $37,500 worth of restricted stock every 5 years to $7,500 annually
MicroAge	increased annual stock option grants from 1,000 to 2,500 shares
Monsanto	replaced restricted stock grants of $50,000 every 5 years with annual stock option grants of $45,000 *Note: cash retirement plan was eliminated.*

Montana Power	no longer requires 25% of retainer to be paid in stock; added annual stock awards of 480 shares per year. *Note: cash retirement plan was frozen.*
Motorola	increased annual stock option grants from 1,000 to 2,500 shares
Oryx Energy	added stock option grants of 9,000 shares every 3 years to already existing annual stock awards of 50% of retainer plus 500 shares
Paine Webber	increased annual stock awards by 600 shares. *Note: cash retirement plan was eliminated.*
PG&E	added annual options and deferred stock grants with a combined value of $20,000 to already existing annual grants of $10,000 of restricted stock
Phelps Dodge	increased annual deferred units from 300 to 450 shares. *Note: cash retirement plan was eliminated.*
Qualcomm	replaced one-time 60,000 stock options grants with annual 10,000 share stock option grants
Reebok	now pays $10,000 of total annual retainer ($25,000) in stock; already grants stock options annually worth three times average annual compensation in prior year
Rubbermaid	increased annual deferred stock grants from $13,000 to $13,500
Schering-Plough	changed stock awards from the beginning of the 3-year term to annually
Southern	increased annual deferred stock from $10,000 to $19,000
Stanley Works	changed from granting 2,000 stock options every 2 years to 2,000 stock option annually
St. Paul Cos.	increased annual stock option grants from 1,000 to 1,500 shares
Tenet Healthcare	increased annual stock option grants from 5,000 to 7,500 shares
TJX	added annual grants of $10,000 deferred stock to already existing annual stock option grants of 1,000 shares (increase to 2,000) *Note: retirement plan was eliminated.*
Union Pacific	increased annual deferred stock awards from $6,000 to $30,000
Unisys	increased annual deferred stock awards from $12,000 to $22,500
Vulcan Materials	added annual restricted stock grants of 65 shares to already existing annual deferred unit grants = 40% of retainer value

Chapter 5. Total Compensation

Chapter 3 ("Direct Compensation") detailed trends in the pay that directors receive—and may spend—on an annual basis. Chapter 4 ("Stock Compensation") examined the long-term equity component of directors' pay, including grants of stock options, restricted stock, and deferred shares that involve a vesting period or grant life of more than one year. This section puts those two components together, to quantify the amount of total remuneration allocated to a typical director each year.

To calculate the total value of each study company's director package, we summed (1) the annualized value of periodic long-term stock grants made by each company and (2) the amount of "direct" compensation previously calculated for its "average" director (see Chapter 3, "Direct Compensation" for the methodology). When periodic stock grants occur other than annually (e.g., every three or five years), the number of shares or value granted was divided by the grant frequency to provide an annual value for this analysis. *One-time grants of stock are not included since they do not represent part of the regular annual package*.

When the company expresses the value of its stock grant or award in dollars, we use that figure in the Total Compensation calculation. When the grant is expressed in shares, it is valued using the company's 1997 year-end stock price and the following methodology:

- **Stock Options** =1/3 of the face value (i.e., number of shares times year-end stock price divided by three)
- **Restricted and Deferred Stock** = the face value (number of shares times year-end stock price)

5.1 Cash vs. Stock Compensation

To bring the directors' annual pay picture into better focus, we also looked at the mix between *all* forms of stock-based compensation (including current awards and long-term grants) and the amount that is delivered in cash. In other words, we subtracted from each company's average director's Total Compensation: (a) the value of annual/periodic stock grants and (b) the value of stock retainers. The remaining amount represents the pure cash portion of directors' total annual pay.

Figure 7 contrasts the average study company director's cash- versus stock-based compensation as of 1996 and 1998. The pie charts illustrate a significant overall increase—in just two years—in the proportion of a typical director's pay package being delivered in stock. The equity-based component—48%—nearly meets the guideline recommended by some investor activists. CalPERS, for example, advocates that at least 50% of a director's total compensation should be in the form of company stock.

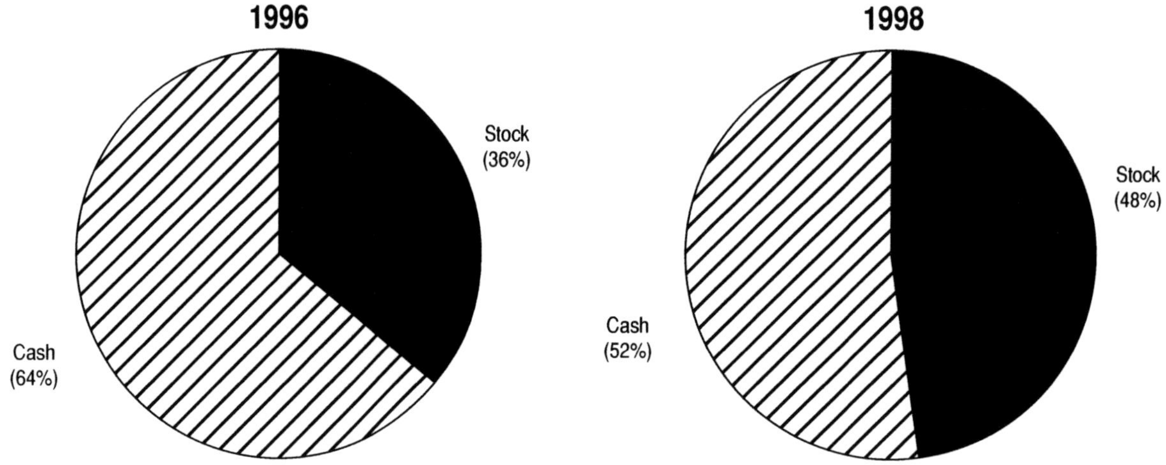

Figure 7 Total Compensation Paid in Cash vs. Stock

5.2 Average Total Compensation

Overall, the average value of one year's *Total Compensation* for a typical study company director is $81,741, up 11.3% since last year. The overall mean level of *Direct Compensation* is $49,696, and companies are annually granting their directors long-term equity awards with a value, on average, of $32,045.

An increased proportion of study companies (23% this year vs. 18% last year) deliver total compensation that exceeds $100,000 per year to a typical director. This compares with only 8% as of 1996.

Average Total Compensation for directors is broken out by revenue and industry groups in Tables 25 and 26.

Table 25 Average Total Compensation by Revenue Range

Revenue Range	No. of Companies	Avg. Total Compensation	% Change Since 1997
$10-bil or more	71	$98,929	+10.3%
$5 < $10-bil	59	$89,864	+20.1%
$3 < $5-bil	29	$65,176	-2.0%
$1 < $3-bil	42	$63,864	+2.2%
Less than $1-bil	24	$62,222	+22.8%
Total	225	$81,741	+11.3%

As also seen in Chapter 3, the average Direct Compensation and Total Compensation levels demonstrate a clear correlation between company size, measured by revenue, and the compensation paid to directors. This year, however, companies in the lowest revenue range (less than $1 billion) posted the largest percentage increase. Those in the $5- to $10-billion revenue range also showed a significant increase in total compensation, while companies in the $3- to $5-billion range exhibited a slight decrease.

With respect to industry groups (Table 26), all categories increased their Total Compensation levels compared with last year. As was the case with average Direct Compensation, board members of Financial companies saw the largest pay package gains for Total Compensation as well.

Table 26 Average Total Compensation by Industry

Industry Group	No. of Companies	Avg Total Compensation	% Change Since 1997
Financial	25	$94,312	+16.5%
Health Care	16	$104,021	+14.5%
Hi Tech	36	$92,280	+7.7%
Manufacturing	46	$73,915	+7.7%
Other Industrials	21	$81,253	+10.7%
Service	37	$67,624	+10.5%
Utilities	13	$58,551	+13.2%
Other	31	$86,380	+11.9%
Total	225	$81,741	+11.3%

5.3 Average Directors' Total Compensation

Table 27 ranks the 225 study companies, in descending order, according to the Total Compensation calculated for a hypothetical typical director (as defined in Chapter 3) at each company, based on their disclosures through July 1, 1998. For comparison purposes, the Total Compensation ranking is shown in the first column, and the same company's rank for average Direct Compensation (from Chapter 3) is shown in the second column of the chart.

An alphabetical list of the 225 study companies, with their rankings, is presented in Appendix V, page 376.

Average Directors' Total Compensation Chart: What the Headings Mean

Total Comp Rank: shows the company's Total Compensation ranking, within the 225 study companies

Avg Direct Comp Rank: shows the company's Direct Compensation ranking, for comparison purposes

Rev: shows the company's fiscal 1997 revenues, in millions of dollars

Ind: shows the company's industry group, using the following codes:

F - Financial
H - Health Care
I - Other Industrials
M - Manufacturing/Industrials
S - Service
T - Hi Tech
O - Other

Avg Direct Comp: shows the dollar figure calculated for an "average director" at the company (see page 26 in Chapter 3 for a detailed explanation of this technique). *Note: The value of any annual stock awards that are not restricted for more than one year is included in Avg. Direct Comp, as noted in the Comments column.*

+ **Grant Value**: reflects the annualized value of any annual or periodic stock grants received by directors (see methodology for calculating value on page 53).

= **Total Comp**: shows the sum of the company's Average Direct Compensation plus stock Grant Value

Comments: noted here are: (1) stock awards that are included in the retainer value, (2) one-time stock grants or "initial" awards that differ from regular periodic grants, and (3) the total number of shares/value in periodic grants that do not occur annually.

Table 27 Average Director's Total Compensation—by Rank

Total Comp Rank	Direct Comp Rank	Company	Rev ($mils)	Ind	Avg. Direct Comp	+ Grant Value	= Total Comp	Comments
1	5	Amer Int'l Group	30,520	F	120,906	181,250	302,156	675 shrs in retainer value
2	213	BMC Software	731	T	23,000	218,750	241,750	initial grant = 20,000 options
3	12	General Electric	90,840	O	83,600	146,750	230,350	
4	195	CISCO Systems	6,440	T	32,000	185,833	217,833	initial grant = 20,000 options
5	1	Campbell Soup	7,964	O	167,000	38,750	205,750	2,400 shrs in retainer value
6	22	Pfizer	12,504	H	72,000	115,475	187,475	
7	40	Bristol-Myers Sqb	16,701	H	62,250	119,146	181,396	
8	223	Qualcomm	2,036	T	10,000	168,333	178,333	initial grant = 20,000 options
9	7	Colgate-Palmolive	9,057	M	114,738	48,583	163,321	1,300 shrs in retainer value
10	18	Tenet Healthcare	8,691	H	77,200	82,813	160,013	
11	63	Anadarko Petroleum	673	I	57,250	101,146	158,396	initial grant = 10,000 options; also 1-time $13,000 def'd shrs
12	39	Sara Lee	19,734	O	62,500	93,854	156,354	
13	9	Paine Webber Group	6,657	F	101,762	51,844	153,606	1,162 shrs in retainer value; also 22,500 options every 5 yrs
14	3	Schering-Plough	6,778	H	125,338	25,000	150,338	1,100 shrs in retainer value
15	11	General Mills	5,609	O	84,813	59,688	144,501	500 shrs in retainer value
16	159	Household Inter'l	5,503	O	38,000	106,354	144,354	1-time 1,000 shrs stock award
17	30	Bell Atlantic	30,194	T	67,500	75,833	143,333	
18	135	Caterpillar	18,925	M	42,000	101,042	143,042	
19	115	Analog Devices	1,243	T	45,500	96,906	142,406	
20	2	Bank of New York	5,697	F	140,775	0	140,775	1,200 shrs in retainer value
21	217	Baxter International	6,138	H	22,000	117,688	139,688	4,000 res't shrs every 3 yrs
22	210	Int'l Bus Machines	78,508	T	24,000	104,750	128,750	
23	25	Wells Fargo & Co	9,608	F	70,100	56,573	126,673	
24	148	Xerox	18,166	T	40,000	86,563	126,563	

Total Comp Rank	Direct Comp Rank	Company	Rev ($mils)	Ind	Avg. Direct Comp	+ Grant Value	= Total Comp	Comments
25	78	Northrop Grumman	9,153	T	54,000	71,500	125,500	$8,400 shrs in retainer value
26	4	Chase Manhattan	30,381	F	123,432	0	123,432	500 shrs in retainer value
27	16	Electronic Data Syst	15,236	T	77,500	43,938	121,438	
28	87	Walt Disney	22,473	S	52,000	66,000	118,000	
29	6	Philip Morris	56,114	M	116,673	0	116,673	932 shrs in retainer value
30	101	Transamerica	6,486	F	48,000	68,250	116,250	
31	147	VF	5,222	M	40,100	74,400	114,500	
32	16	Exxon	122,379	I	77,500	36,713	114,213	initial grant = 4,000 res't shrs
33	8	Marsh & McClennan	6,009	F	113,738	0	113,738	$10,000 + 600 shrs in retainer value
34	104	Knight-Ridder	3,139	S	47,500	65,867	113,367	$15,000 shrs in retainer value
35	22	FDX	11,520	S	72,000	40,708	112,708	
36	43	Dow Chemical	20,018	I	61,600	51,088	112,688	1,550 options every 5 yrs; also 1-time 1,500 res't shrs
37	37	Enron	20,273	U	63,000	49,459	112,459	
38	47	GTE	23,260	T	60,000	52,250	112,250	
39	13	American Express	17,760	F	81,850	29,750	111,600	200 shrs in retainer value
40	29	Quaker Oats	5,016	O	68,000	42,200	110,200	
41	26	PepsiCo	29,292	M	70,000	40,000	110,000	
42	210	United Technologies	24,713	T	24,000	84,542	108,542	1-time 2,000 res't shrs
43	64	Merck & Co	23,637	H	57,200	50,333	107,533	
44	58	Motorola	29,794	T	58,000	47,656	105,656	
45	51	Mobil	59,978	I	59,750	43,313	103,063	
46	58	May Dept Stores	12,685	O	58,000	45,000	103,000	initial grant = 2,000 res't shrs
47	101	Ingersoll-Rand	7,103	M	48,000	54,675	102,675	
48	70	Fruit of the Loom	2,140	M	55,000	47,406	102,406	initial grant = 2,500 res't shrs
49	142	Hannaford Bros.	3,226	O	41,000	60,813	101,813	
50	70	Procter & Gamble	35,764	M	55,000	46,604	101,604	
51	84	Texaco	45,187	I	52,500	48,938	101,438	$15,000 shrs in retainer value
52	10	Travelers Group	37,609	F	100,000	0	100,000	$100,000 shrs in retainer value

Total Comp Rank	Direct Comp Rank	Company	Rev ($mils)	Ind	Avg. Direct Comp	+ Grant Value	= Total Comp	Comments
53	61	Allied-Signal	14,472	O	57,800	40,875	98,675	1-time 3,000 res't shrs
54	33	Norfolk Southern	5,165	S	66,200	30,500	96,700	1-time 3,000 res't shrs
55	176	TRW	10,831	O	35,000	61,688	96,688	
56	159	AMR	18,570	S	38,000	57,825	95,825	
57	47	Chrysler	61,147	M	60,000	35,188	95,188	$25,000 shrs in retainer value; also 1-time 6,000 def'd shrs
58	70	Johnson & Johnson	22,629	H	55,000	39,763	94,763	1-time $10,000 stock award
59	32	Waste Management	9,273	S	67,000	27,500	94,500	
60	28	Fortune Brands	7,001	M	68,105	25,042	93,147	482 shrs in retainer value
61	54	McDonald's	11,409	S	59,000	33,417	92,417	
62	70	Burlington Resources	2,000	I	55,000	37,344	92,344	initial grant = 3,000 options
63	20	Aon	5,751	F	72,322	20,000	92,322	675 shrs in retainer value
64	111	Eli Lily & Co	8,518	H	46,200	46,092	92,292	
65	207	United Healthcare	11,794	H	26,000	66,250	92,250	initial grant = 9,000 options
66	42	SBC Comm	24,856	T	61,700	30,500	92,200	
67	90	Bestfoods	9,818	O	51,250	40,800	92,050	
68	171	Air Products & Chem	4,662	I	36,000	55,867	91,867	
69	83	Sprint	14,874	T	52,750	39,083	91,833	1-time 2,500 def'd
70	15	Amer Financial Group	4,021	O	78,000	13,438	91,438	$20,000 shrs in retainer value; also initial grant = 5,000 options
71	197	Time Warner	13,294	S	30,000	61,000	91,000	
72	46	Honeywell	8,028	T	60,400	30,200	90,600	
73	117	AT&T	53,261	T	45,000	45,000	90,000	
74	191	Louisiana-Pacific	2,403	M	32,750	57,000	89,750	45,000 options every 5 yrs
75	166	Freeport-McMoRan	2,001	I	37,000	52,083	89,083	
76	153	Kellogg	6,830	O	39,000	49,625	88,625	
77	54	Ford Motor	153,627	M	59,000	29,425	88,425	2,000 res't shrs every 5 yrs
78	84	Emerson Electric	12,299	T	52,500	35,000	87,500	
79	24	Cooper Industries	5,289	T	70,600	16,333	86,933	400 shrs in retainer value

Total Comp Rank	Direct Comp Rank	Company	Rev ($mils)	Ind	Avg. Direct Comp	+ Grant Value	= Total Comp	Comments
80	134	Snap-On	1,672	M	42,250	43,625	85,875	$6,500 shrs in retainer value
81	166	Dayton Hudson	27,757	O	37,000	48,333	85,333	
82	35	Merrill Lynch	31,731	F	65,000	20,000	85,000	$100,000 def'd every 5 yrs
83	70	Eaton	7,563	M	55,000	29,750	84,750	initial grant = 5,000 options
84	128	Browning-Ferris Ind	5,783	S	43,500	40,833	84,333	initial grant = 5,000 options
85	56	Houghton Mifflin	797	S	58,675	25,583	84,258	1,000 shrs in retainer value
86	123	Interpublic	3,126	S	44,000	39,888	83,888	3,000 res't shrs every 5 yrs
87	207	Ceridian	1,664	T	26,000	56,542	82,542	1-time $65,000 res't shrs
88	57	General Motors	178,174	M	58,250	24,000	82,250	
89	41	BankAmerica	23,585	F	62,000	20,000	82,000	
89	87	Fleet Financial Group	8,095	F	52,000	30,000	82,000	
91	69	Oryx Energy	1,197	I	55,750	25,500	81,250	$12,000+500 shrs in retainer value; also 9,000 options every 3 yrs; initial stock award = 5,000 shrs
92	14	MMM	15,070	M	80,400	0	80,400	$35,000 shrs in retainer value
93	93	Brunswick	3,657	S	50,000	30,313	80,313	$25,000 shrs in retainer value; also 1-time $25,000 stock award
94	171	Gap	6,508	O	36,000	44,297	80,297	initial grant = 15,000 options
95	52	Viacom	13,505	S	59,500	20,719	80,219	1-time 10,000 options; also initial grant = 5,000 options
96	70	Aetna	18,540	F	55,000	24,697	79,697	initial grant = 1,500 def'd shrs
97	96	J. C. Penney	30,546	O	49,200	30,156	79,356	
98	67	PG&E	15,400	U	56,000	23,333	79,333	
99	187	Federal Mogul	1,807	M	33,000	45,708	78,708	$25,000 def'd every 5 yrs; also 1-time 1,000 res't shrs
100	127	SPX	922	M	43,597	34,500	78,097	
101	97	Ashland	13,567	I	49,000	28,634	77,634	1,000 res't shrs every 5 yrs
102	107	Kimberly-Clark	12,547	M	46,800	29,588	76,388	

Total Comp Rank	Direct Comp Rank	Company	Rev ($mils)	Ind	Avg. Direct Comp	+ Grant Value	= Total Comp	Comments
103	176	Silicon Graphics	3,663	T	35,000	41,042	76,042	initial grant = 30,000 options
104	117	Dun & Bradstreet	2,154	S	45,000	30,938	75,938	1-time $25,000 res't shrs
105	112	Boeing	45,800	T	46,000	29,575	75,575	initial grant = 1,500 options
106	123	Stanley Works	2,670	M	44,000	31,458	75,458	
107	36	Cigna	20,038	F	64,250	11,000	75,250	$20,000 shrs in retainer value; also 1-time 1,500 res't shrs
108	50	McDermott Int'l	3,308	S	59,950	15,260	75,210	
109	108	Textron	10,544	O	46,600	28,200	74,800	1-time 1,000 res't shrs
110	185	St. Paul Companies	6,219	F	33,500	41,031	74,531	
111	129	Albertson's	14,690	O	43,000	31,500	74,500	
112	19	Coca-Cola	18,868	M	74,000	0	74,000	
113	87	Computer Sciences	5,616	T	52,000	21,800	73,800	$109,000 res't shrs every 5 yrs
114	66	Marriott Int'l	12,034	S	56,250	17,313	73,563	$12,500 shrs in retainer value
115	62	Stone & Webster	1,323	S	57,750	15,625	73,375	400 shrs in retainer value; also initial grant = 2,000 options
116	79	Becton Dickinson	2,811	H	53,000	20,000	73,000	
116	79	Warner-Lambert	8,180	H	53,000	20,000	73,000	1-time 4,000 res't shrs
118	145	Charles Schwab	2,299	F	40,600	31,453	72,053	
119	31	U.S. Trust	494	F	67,050	5,000	72,050	400 shrs in retainer value
120	21	E.I. DuPont	41,304	I	72,025	0	72,025	400 shrs in retainer value
121	47	Unocal	6,064	I	60,000	12,000	72,000	
122	142	Reebok International	3,637	M	41,000	30,628	71,628	$10,000 shrs in retainer value; initial grant = 6X avg comp in prior year
123	152	Black & Decker	4,941	M	39,062	32,552	71,614	500 shrs in retainer value
124	112	Reynolds Metals	6,900	I	46,000	25,500	71,500	1,000 res't shrs every 5 yrs
125	146	Allergan	1,138	H	40,500	30,206	70,706	2,700 res't shrs every 3 yrs
126	148	Beckman Coulter	1,198	T	40,000	30,667	70,667	
127	53	Ryder System	5,351	S	59,300	10,917	70,217	
128	135	Phelps Dodge	3,914	I	42,000	28,013	70,013	

Total Comp Rank	Direct Comp Rank	Company	Rev ($mils)	Ind	Avg. Direct Comp	+ Grant Value	= Total Comp	Comments
129	197	Sears, Roebuck & Co	41,296	O	30,000	40,000	70,000	
130	175	AFLAC	7,251	F	35,200	34,083	69,283	initial grant = 10,000 options; 10,000 options every 5 yrs
131	70	AirTouch Comm	3,594	T	55,000	13,854	68,854	initial grant = 10,000 options
132	159	St. Jude Medical	809	H	38,000	30,500	68,500	
133	218	Questar	933	U	20,800	47,600	68,400	
134	27	Pharmacia & Upjohn	6,710	H	68,313	0	68,313	500 shrs in retainer value
135	123	Sonoco Products	2,848	M	44,000	23,125	67,125	
136	101	Southern	12,611	U	48,000	19,000	67,000	
136	135	PPG Industries	7,379	M	42,000	25,000	67,000	
138	104	Sherwin-Williams	4,881	M	47,500	18,500	66,000	
139	68	Sun Company	8,968	I	55,900	10,000	65,900	$19,880 shrs in retainer value
140	110	Vulcan Materials	1,679	M	46,500	18,638	65,138	
141	34	Hewlett-Packard	42,895	T	65,100	0	65,100	$22,500 shrs in retainer value
142	117	Wendy's Int'l	2,037	S	45,000	20,052	65,052	
143	148	Beverly Enterprises	3,230	H	40,000	23,400	63,400	
144	70	CBS	9,632	T	55,000	8,333	63,333	$25,000 shrs in retainer value
145	141	TJX Companies	7,389	O	41,750	21,459	63,209	initial grant = 1,000 options
146	79	Goodyear	13,155	M	53,000	10,000	63,000	
147	176	MicroAge	4,446	S	35,000	27,615	62,615	initial grant = 2,500 options and 1,000 res't shrs
148	38	Anheuser-Busch	11,066	M	62,600	0	62,600	
149	156	Pittston	3,394	I	38,400	22,978	61,378	initial grant = 17,000 options
150	44	Morton Int'l	3,637	I	60,938	0	60,938	500 shrs in retainer value
151	135	Fluor	14,299	S	42,000	18,688	60,688	1-time 1,570 res't shrs
152	45	American General	8,927	F	60,500	0	60,500	1-time 500 res't shrs; also 1-time 1,500 options
153	197	IKON Office Solut	5,128	O	30,000	30,000	60,000	1-time 25,000 stock options

Total Comp Rank	Direct Comp Rank	Company	Rev ($mils)	Ind	Avg. Direct Comp	+ Grant Value	= Total Comp	Comments
153	117	Monsanto	9,457	I	45,000	15,000	60,000	$50,000 res't shrs every 5 yrs
153	165	Unisys	6,636	T	37,500	22,500	60,000	
153	197	Union Pacific	11,014	S	30,000	30,000	60,000	1-time 1,785 res't shrs
157	115	Rouse	930	M	45,500	13,667	59,167	initial grant = 5,000 options
158	97	Citicorp	34,697	F	49,000	10,000	59,000	
159	126	Boise Cascade	5,493	M	43,800	15,125	58,925	
160	155	Dow Jones & Co	2,573	S	38,600	20,000	58,600	
161	58	General Dynamics	4,062	T	58,000	0	58,000	
162	100	Public Service Enterprs	6,370	U	48,400	9,544	57,944	$11,000 shrs in retainer value
163	65	Cummins Engine	5,625	M	57,000	0	57,000	$18,000 shrs in retainer value
164	142	Amer Electric Power	6,161	U	41,000	15,488	56,488	
165	213	Oshkosh B'Gosh	395	O	23,000	33,000	56,000	
166	158	Huffy	695	S	38,250	17,438	55,688	5,625 options every 3 yrs
167	205	Media General	910	S	27,500	27,500	55,000	
167	176	Texas Instruments	10,562	T	35,000	20,000	55,000	1-time 1,000 def'd
169	122	Cyprus Amax Min	3,346	I	44,688	10,250	54,938	500 shrs in retainer value
170	156	Hormel Foods	3,257	O	38,400	15,917	54,317	
171	192	SunAmerica	2,084	F	32,500	21,375	53,875	
172	181	Mead	5,077	M	34,900	18,372	53,272	
173	209	Ball	2,389	M	25,900	27,180	53,080	1,000 res't shrs every 3 yrs
174	176	Illinois Tool Works	5,220	M	35,000	18,038	53,038	900 res't shrs every 3 yrs; also 1-time 1,000 def'd
175	112	Apache	1,176	I	46,000	7,013	53,013	$5,000 shrs in retainer value; also 1,000 res't shrs every 5 yrs
176	79	FPL Group	6,369	U	53,000	0	53,000	1-time 200 shrs stock award
177	133	Weyerhaeuser	11,210	M	42,500	10,000	52,500	
178	164	Bowater	1,485	M	37,600	14,813	52,413	
179	219	Mentor Graphics	455	T	20,000	32,292	52,292	
180	86	Unicom	7,083	U	52,200	0	52,200	$36,200 shrs in retainer value

Total Comp Rank	Direct Comp Rank	Company	Rev ($mils)	Ind	Avg. Direct Comp	+ Grant Value	= Total Comp	Comments
181	183	McGraw-Hill	3,534	S	34,600	17,000	51,600	
182	91	Owens-Corning	4,373	M	51,063	0	51,063	500 shrs in retainer value; also 1-time 10,000 options
183	159	Baltimore Gas & Elec	3,308	U	38,000	13,000	51,000	
183	92	Premark International	2,407	M	51,000	0	51,000	1-time 1,000 shrs stock award
185	159	Consol Natural Gas	5,710	U	38,000	12,100	50,100	initial grant = 400 res't shrs
186	93	St. Joe	346	M	50,000	0	50,000	
186	93	Wal-Mart Stores	119,299	O	50,000	0	50,000	$25,000 shrs in retainer value
188	184	Corning	4,129	M	34,500	14,850	49,350	1,200 res't shrs every 3 yrs; also initial grant = 4,000 rest'd shrs
189	129	Delta Air Lines	13,590	S	43,000	6,300	49,300	$5,000 shrs in retainer value
190	97	Temple-Inland	3,625	M	49,000	0	49,000	1-time 10,000 options
191	192	So New England Tele	2,022	T	32,500	15,094	47,594	
192	106	Lee Enterprises	439	S	47,381	0	47,381	500 shrs in retainer value
193	213	Talbots	1,054	O	23,000	24,167	47,167	
194	210	Millipore	619	T	24,000	22,625	46,625	initial grant = 4,000 options
195	108	Pacific Enterprises	2,777	U	46,600	0	46,600	
196	117	Shoney's	1,203	S	45,000	1,083	46,083	5,000 options every 5 yrs
197	185	MGM Grand	828	S	33,500	12,042	45,542	initial grant = 5,000 options
198	166	Crestar Financial	1,997	F	37,000	8,000	45,000	$6,000 shrs in retainer value; also $40,000 res't shrs every 5 yrs
199	224	Apple Computer	7,081	T	0	43,750	43,750	initial grant = 30,000 options
200	131	Kelly Services	3,853	S	42,700	0	42,700	$10,500 shrs in retainer value
201	132	Dexter	1,159	I	42,638	0	42,638	$10,000 +200 shrs in retainer value
202	135	Nordstrom	4,852	O	42,000	0	42,000	$10,000 shrs in retainer value
202	135	Pioneer Hi-Bred	1,784	O	42,000	0	42,000	
204	224	Manor Care	1,617	H	0	41,667	41,667	initial grant = 5,000 options

Total Comp Rank	Direct Comp Rank	Company	Rev ($mils)	Ind	Avg. Direct Comp	+ Grant Value	= Total Comp	Comments
205	148	Venator Group	6,624	O	40,000	0	40,000	$20,000 shrs in retainer value
206	206	Rubbermaid	2,400	M	26,150	13,500	39,650	
207	153	Omnicom Group	3,125	S	39,000	0	39,000	
208	201	Bob Evans Farms	822	S	29,900	7,571	37,471	5,133 options every 5 yrs
209	166	Standard Register	966	T	37,000	0	37,000	
210	170	Harcourt General	3,692	S	36,750	0	36,750	
211	171	First Tennessee Nat'l	1,609	F	36,000	0	36,000	1-time 6,000 res't shrs
211	171	Policy Mgmt	583	T	36,000	0	36,000	
211	222	Springs Industries	2,226	M	18,000	18,000	36,000	
214	182	Montana Power	1,024	U	34,840	0	34,840	480 shrs in retainer value
215	187	Nike	9,187	M	33,000	0	33,000	1-time 30,000 options
215	187	Universal Foods	826	O	33,000	0	33,000	$5,500 shrs in retainer value
215	187	Neiman Marcus	2,210	O	33,000	0	33,000	
218	194	Genuine Parts	6,005	S	32,400	0	32,400	
219	196	Idacorp	749	U	31,800	0	31,800	
220	221	Cintas	840	S	18,400	13,000	31,400	
221	216	Old Kent Financial	1,306	F	22,500	8,500	31,000	
222	202	Russell	1,228	M	29,200	1,667	30,867	$5,000 shrs in retainer value
223	203	Cracker Barrel	1,124	S	29,000	0	29,000	regular grant of 25,312 opts not made because kitty was depleted
223	203	Tootsie Roll	376	O	29,000	0	29,000	
225	220	Vanguard Cellular Systems	375	T	18,500	0	18,500	

Chapter 6. Deferred Compensation

As the sun sets on directors' cash retirement plans, companies continue to implement alternative deferred compensation opportunities for outside board members. A trend emerging this year is the *mandatory* deferral of a portion of compensation in some form of stock.

The overall number of study companies disclosing deferred compensation arrangements for outside directors remained stable since last year, totaling 181 (80%), which also is just 7% higher than the proportion with deferral arrangements in the 1994 study. One hundred and eighty of these companies maintain elective deferral opportunities—only Media General, which requires that 50% of a director's annual compensation be deferred in stock, does not disclose any formal arrangement permitting *elective* deferral of the remaining portion of board compensation.

Figures 8 and 9 illustrate the prevalence of deferral programs in specific revenue and industry groups. The graphs show the total number of study companies in each category and the percentage of companies in the group that provide deferral arrangements for nonemployee directors. As with other aspects of directors' compensation, larger companies (measured by revenue) are most likely to offer deferral opportunities.

Knight-Ridder is the only company that appears to authorize deferrals under individual agreements rather than a formal deferral plan.

As mentioned above, corporations are beginning to take the decision to defer a portion of the annual retainer out of their directors' hands. Twenty-eight study companies (12%) now require a portion of the retainer (and sometimes other fees) to be deferred in some form of

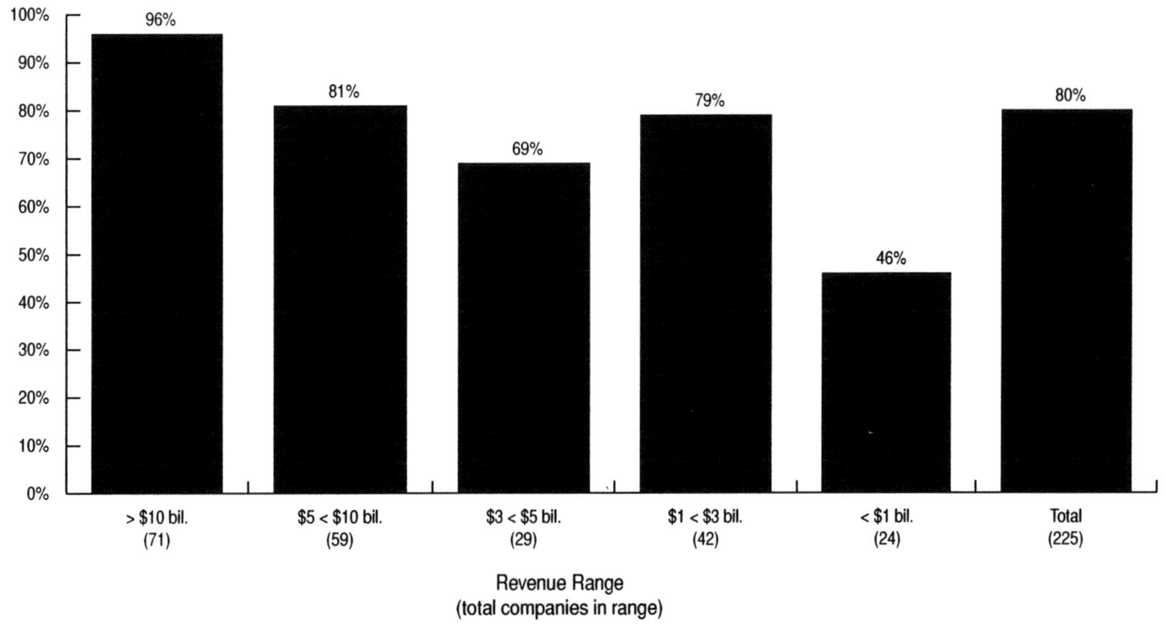

Figure 8 Deferred Compensation by Revenues

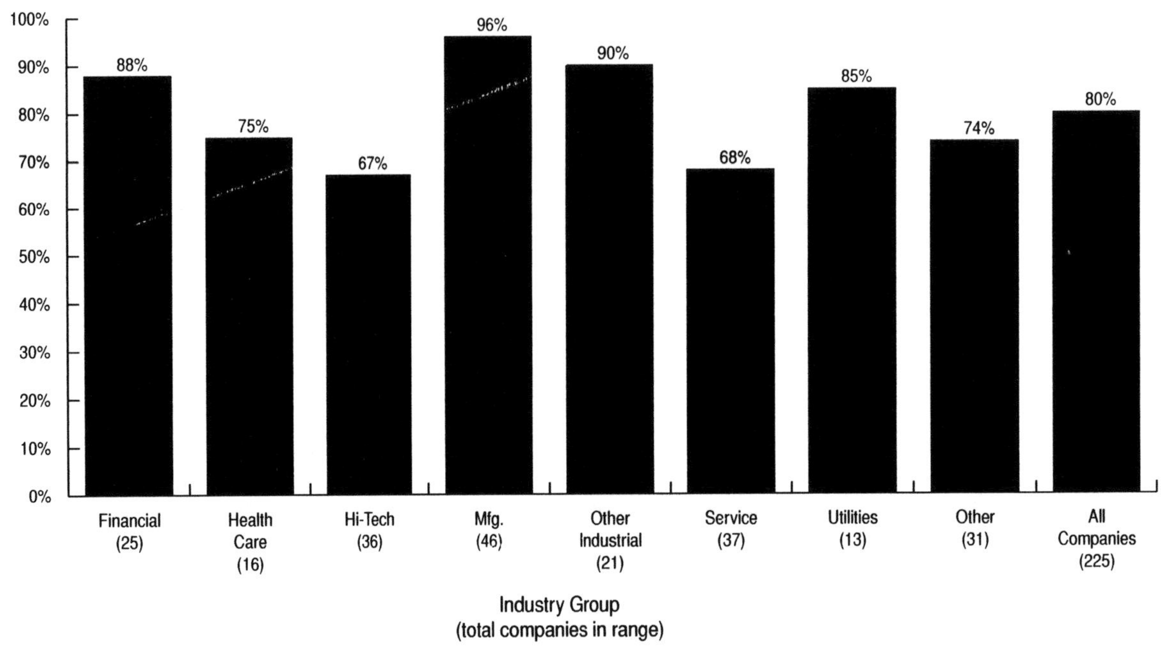

Figure 9 Deferred Compensation by Industry

stock. This technique enables companies to increase directors' equity stake and directly links board members' interests with shareholders'.

The companies that automatically defer a portion of directors' pay in a stock format, and the amount required to be deferred, are detailed below.

1. **Air Products**—12,000 of retainer ($48,000)
2. **Allied-Signal**—$15,000 of retainer ($50,000)
3. **Baltimore Gas & Electric**—50% of retainer ($26,000)
4. **BankAmerica**—50% of retainer ($40,000)
5. **Bestfoods**—50% of retainer ($60,000)
6. **Boeing**—$10,000 of retainer ($36,000)
7. **Bristol-Myers**—25% of retainer ($35,000) until undisclosed ownership guidelines are attained
8. **Browning-Ferris**—1/3 of retainer ($30,000)
9. **Citicorp**—$10,000 of retainer ($40,000)
10. **Fleet Financial**—25% of retainer ($40,000)
11. **Ford Motor**—25% of retainer ($40,000)
12. **General Motors**—35% of retainer ($40,000)
13. **Hewlett-Packard**—50% of retainer ($45,000)

14. **IBM**—60% of retainer ($60,000)
15. **Johnson & Johnson**—$20,000 of retainer ($65,000)
16. **Marsh & McLennan**—25% of retainer ($40,000)
17. **Media General**—50% of *annual compensation* ($55,000)
18. **Old Kent Financial**—50% of retainer ($17,000)
19. **PPG Industries**—1/3 of retainer ($30,000)
20. **Rubbermaid**—50% of *all fees* ($13,000 retainer, $1,100 meeting attendance fees, and $3,000 chairman fee)
21. **Southern**—$10,000 of retainer ($40,000)
22. **Stanley**—all fees must be deferred in stock until director owns 5,000 shares
23. **Texas Instruments**—50% of retainer ($40,000)
24. **Textron**—$16,000 of retainer ($41,000)
25. **TRW**—50% of retainer ($70,000)
26. **Union Pacific**—$6,000 of retainer ($60,000)
27. **United Technologies**—60% of retainer ($60,000)
28. **Weyerhaeuser**—$10,000 of retainer ($35,000)

Overall, compulsory stock deferrals tend to range from 25% to 50%, as shown in Table 28. And the predominant specified mandatory deferral amount is 50% of the retainer (followed by 25%).

Table 28 Mandatory Deferral of Board Retainers

% of Retainer Deferred	No. of Companies	% of Companies with Mandatory Deferral
25%–29%	8	30%
30%–39%	7	26%
50%	10	37%
More than 50%*	3	7%

* *Includes Stanley, where all fees may be required to be deferred*

6.1 Deferrable Compensation

As the system for delivering compensation to directors has evolved, so have deferral mechanisms.

- All of the 180 study companies that maintain elective deferral plans and pay a cash retainer permit the retainer to be deferred.
- Five companies (Baxter International, Campbell Soup, Colgate-Palmolive, Manor Care, and Unicom) have no cash retainer but allow deferral of their meeting and committee retainer fees.

- Among the 180 study companies with elective deferral programs, all but three (Caterpillar, Coca-Cola, and Monsanto) that pay meeting attendance fees and chairman fees allow these payments to be deferred.
- 45 of the companies with deferral plans (up from 37 last year) also pay a portion of the retainer in stock. Eighteen of these (40%) specifically provide that the stock portion of the retainer may be deferred at the director's option. This is a dramatic increase over last year when only 22% of the study companies provided for deferral of the stock retainer portion. The 18 companies are: Aon, Black & Decker, Brunswick, Chase Manhattan, Chrysler, CIGNA, Cooper, Crestar, E.I. DuPont, Fortune Brands, General Mills, Montana Power, Russell, Snap-On, Sun, Texaco, Travelers, and Wal-Mart.
- Chrysler provides for deferral of the proceeds from stock option exercises.
- Pepsico allows directors to defer their stock grants.
- Pfizer allows restricted stock dividends to be deferred.
- Warner-Lambert also provides that director's consulting fees may be deferred.

6.2 Account Types

The investment account types utilized by study company deferral programs are detailed in Table 29. The percentage of companies providing for deferrals only in cash accounts is decreasing (19% this year vs. 23% last year), while the proportion providing only for stock-denominated deferrals is rising (11% last year vs. 13% this year).

Table 29 Elective Deferral Account Types

Account Type	No. of Companies	% of Companies with Elective Deferral
Cash only	34	19%
Cash and stock	112	62%
Stock only	23	13%
Not disclosed	11	6%
Total	180	100%

Eighteen companies (compared with just 12 in 1994 and 18 last year) have plans or policies permitting outside directors to "defer" compensation by taking stock options in lieu of the annual retainer and, in some cases, meeting fees. "Deferral" options at a majority of these companies (78%) carry a discounted exercise price or other premium, as detailed below.

1. **Boise Cascade**—exercise price = $2.50/share
2. **Enron**—based on 50% of FMV
3. **First Tennessee**—exercise price = 85% of FMV
4. **Fruit of the Loom**—if director forgoes 50% of annual retainer ($20,500) for 4 years he or she receives 10,000 stock options

5. **Gap**—discount not disclosed
6. **Hannaford**—number of options = 3 times retainer divided by FMV
7. **Huffy**—number of options = amount forgone divided by (FMV less $1.00) times 1.5; the exercise price = $1.00
8. **IKON Office Solutions**—exercise price = 75% of FMV
9. **Premark International**—discount is not disclosed
10. **Sara Lee**—number of options = 4 times amount forgone divided by FMV
11. **Sonoco**—grant value = 4 times amount deferred
12. **SunAmerica**—number of shares = 2.5 times amount forgone divided by FMV
13. **Temple-Inland**—exercise price = FMV minus (retainer) 2,000)
14. **Wells Fargo**—exercise price = 50% of FMV

Fourteen companies utilize restricted stock as a deferral vehicle: Dayton Hudson, Dexter, EDS, Enron, Mead, Monsanto, Oryx Energy, Pioneer Hi-Bred, Ryder System, St. Jude, St. Paul Companies, Texaco, Unocal, and Xerox. Five of these companies include a premium:

1. **Oryx Energy**—the stock retainer may be deferred into a number of share units equal to 130% of those deferred
2. **Pioneer Hi-Bred**—if cash fees are deferred in restricted stock, then the value = 105% of foregone compensation for the next 3 years
3. **Ryder System**—in lieu of the $21,500 annual retainer, directors may take $15,000 worth of restricted shares plus $11,500 in cash (total value $26,500)
4. **St. Paul Companies**—shares awarded are valued at 110% of the forgone retainer amount and remain restricted for 5 years
5. **Unocal Corp**—shares are valued at 120% of forgone cash compensation, with restrictions lapsing after 5 years (or longer, if elected).

6.3 Earnings Crediting

One hundred and thirteen companies with deferral plans or policies disclose the measure used to credit earnings to participants' cash-based accounts. Table 30 summarizes the breakdown of the crediting rates associated with cash-based deferrals in the plans that disclose this information:

Table 30 Earnings Crediting in Elective Deferral Plans

Crediting Benchmark	No. of Plans	% of Plans with Cash Accounts
Government Securities (T-bills, T-notes)	25	22%
Prime rate	20	18%
Moody's index	11	10%
Company rate	19	17%
Other	38	33%

Springs Industries pays interest, at the prime rate, on the quarterly dividend equivalents that deferred stock accounts accumulate.

The trend we noted in the previous edition, of companies offering directors a variety of investment options for their deferred accounts, continues to grow. Last year 11 companies gave directors multiple investment options, compared with 16 companies (7% of the total) in this year's analysis, a 45% increase. The number of investment alternatives can be staggering—Ashland Oil's directors, for example, may choose among 25 different investment options! The companies providing various investment alternatives include: Ashland, Chase Manhattan, Chrysler, Dayton Hudson, Delta Airlines, Enron, General Mills, Merck, Old Kent Financial, Phelps Dodge, Philip Morris, Ryder System, Silicon Graphics, Snap-On, St. Paul Companies, and U.S. Trust.

6.4 Earnings Premiums

Thirteen percent of the companies indicate that they add or may add a premium to a specified earnings rate or that they pay above-market interest on deferred directors' fees. That compares with 10% in last year's study that reported some type of premium.

1. **AirTouch**—pays 8.53%
2. **Albertson's**—pays Moody's index + 3%
3. **Anadarko**—pays 20% per year (no deferrals have been made since 1990)
4. **AT&T**—10-yr T-note + 5%
5. **Ball**—Moody's index + 5%
6. **Beckman Coulter**—pays a premium of up to 30% depending on the percentage of annual compensation deferred above 40%
7. **Beverly Enterprises**—matches 25% of fees voluntarily deferred in stock
8. **Boise Cascade**—30% of Moody's index
9. **Bowater**—stock units are credited on the basis of 95% of FMV
10. **Cracker Barrel**—0-yr T-bill + 1.5%
11. **Dow Chemical**—125% of 10-yr average of 10-yr T-bills
12. **Eaton**—based on number of years until "normal" retirement, in most cases at higher than market rates
13. **EDS**—20% of the Federal Long-Term Rate
14. **Eli Lilly**—Prime rate + 2%
15. **Federal Mogul**—10-yr T-bill + 1%
16. **Fleet Financial**—12% for 1997
17. **Ford Motor**—T-bills + 0.75%
18. **Honeywell**—stock units = 110% of forgone fees

19. **Ingersoll-Rand**—matches 20% of fees voluntarily deferred
20. **Kimberly-Clark**—pays the 6-month T-bill rate *or* 6% if higher
21. **Louisiana-Pacific**—Moody's index + 2%
22. **McGraw-Hill**—Moody's index + 2% (maximum 150% of index)
23. **Mobil**—10-yr T-note + 1%
24. **Norfolk Southern**—rate is based on age at time of deferral: <age 45 = 7%; 45-54 = 10%; 55-60 = 11%; >age 60 = 12%
25. **Rubbermaid**—120% of the Federal Test Rate
26. **Stone & Webster**—Prime + 1%
27. **Textron**—stock unit deferrals are matched 25%
28. **Time Warner**—accounts are based on cash or stock, whichever yields the higher value at distribution
29. **Transamerica**—10-yr T-notes + up to 3% for 5-yr deferrals; Moody's index + 4% for longer deferrals

If we also consider the five companies that add a premium to fees "deferred" in restricted shares (see Section 6.2, page 71), the proportion of study companies using a premium to "incentivize" deferrals totals 15%, compared with 11% in last year's analysis.

6.5 COC Provisions

Eighteen percent (or 33) of the study company deferral plans specifically include change-of-control provisions, which is unchanged from last year. These mechanisms typically provide for rabbi trust funding and/or automatic payout of deferral accounts in the event of a COC. Seven companies specify informal funding vehicles:

- **Albertson's**—plan is life-insurance funded
- **Ball**—plan is backed by corporate-owned life insurance policies
- **Boise Cascade**—funds their plan with corporate-owned life insurance policies held in a rabbi trust
- **Enron**—plan is backed by life insurance
- **Norfolk Southern**—plan is funded by company-owned life insurance
- **PG&E**—protects deferred compensation via indemnity insurance policies
- **St. Paul Companies'**—benefits are backed by a grantor trust

6.6 Payment Provisions

Among the companies that disclose information about account distribution, plans stipulating that payouts will not occur until after the director's service terminates outnumber those that permit the participant to specify a payment date by almost 2-to-1. Here is the breakdown:

- Arrangements stipulating payout after service termination: 81 (up from 76 last year)
- Arrangements permitting the director to specify a payout date: 43 (same as last year)
- No payout parameters disclosed: 56

Three plans have unusual payment provisions:

1. **AT&T**—would distribute deferred compensation immediately if an ex-director competes or has a conflict of interest.
2. **Rubbermaid**—provides for payout at the earlier of age 70 or termination.
3. **Walt Disney**—provides for payout at a specified age or after termination.

Chapter 7. Retirement Benefits

Some of the most significant innovations in board of director compensation programs have involved post-service benefits. Cash pension plans for directors arose on a tidal wave in the 1980s, then ebbed just as quickly this decade after coming under attack by shareholders and the media as unjustified give-aways that provided little incentive to improve board or company performance. The study companies continue to abandon pure cash pension plans for directors, but—as demonstrated last year—for the most part those benefits are being replaced with additional stock-based compensation, particularly deferred stock. The trend is detailed in this section of the study.

A total of 137 of the 225 monograph companies (61%) provide some form of post-service benefit, either in cash and/or stock, for their nonemployee directors. As seen in Figure 10, only 12% of the study companies (26 companies) continue to maintain cash-based retirement plans. By contrast, stock grants that are stated or appear to be designed to provide post-service compensation are made by about half (49%) of the 225 study companies.

Figure 10 illustrates the prevalence of cash- vs. stock-based "retirement" programs by revenue range. There is a clear correlation between company size and the likelihood that a company will provide some type of post-retirement benefits. Larger companies tend to deliver the benefit in a stock format more often than smaller companies.

Figure 11 illustrates the prevalence of cash-based vs. stock-based retirement programs by industry groups. As was the case in last year's analysis, Health Care, Other Industrials, and Utilities companies are most likely to provide post-retirement compensation.

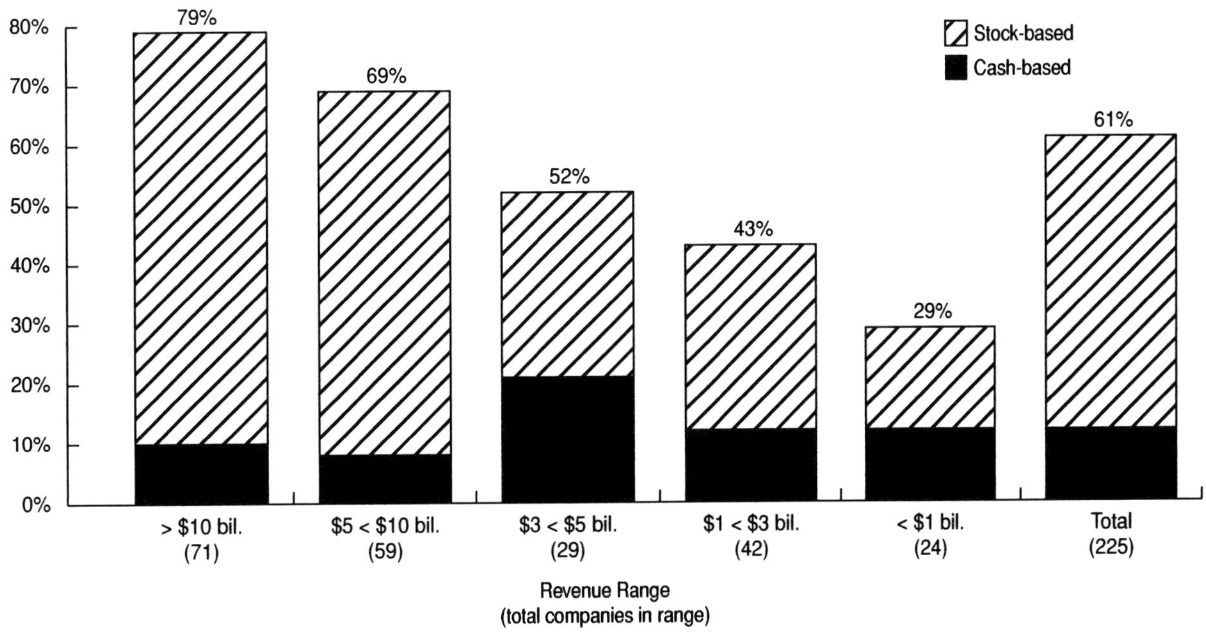

Figure 10 Post-Service Benefits by Revenues

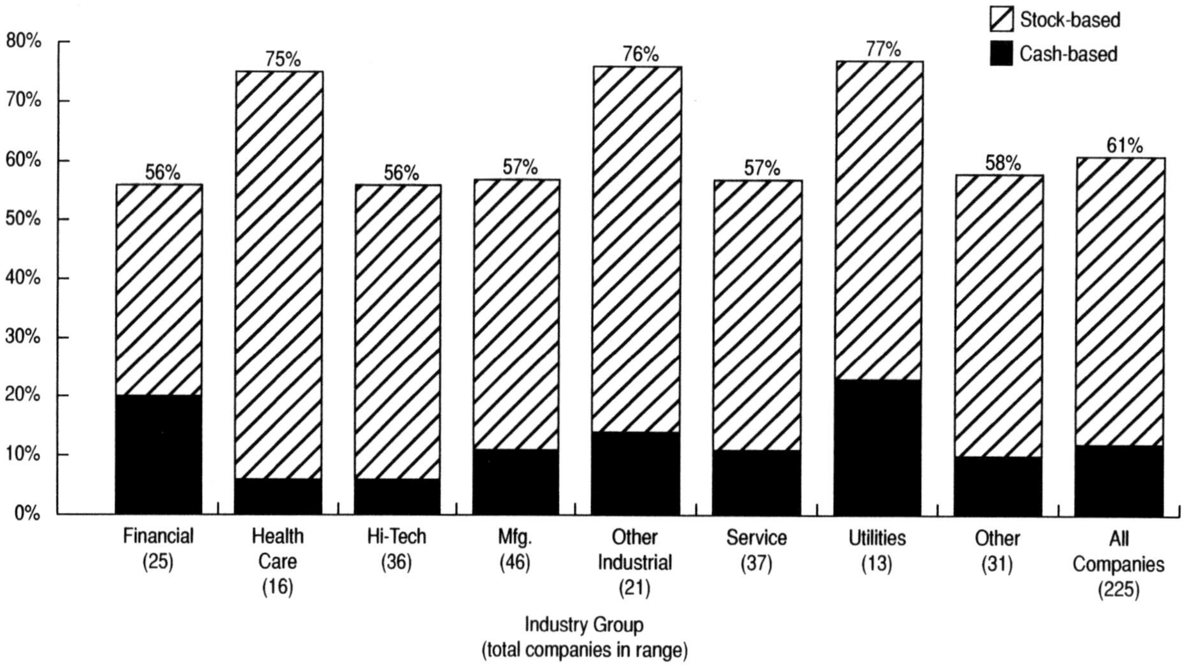

Figure 11 Post-Service Benefits by Industry

7.1 Terminated Cash-Based Plans

As indicated, a seismic shift has occurred in the way that companies accrue and deliver post-service benefits. Since last year's study, 20 additional companies eliminated cash-based board pension plans. That brings the total study population (since 1996) that has terminated or frozen such plans to 116, representing 52% of the 225 companies. This dramatic change in retirement benefits has been fueled by:

1. an increasing reliance on stock-based compensation to align directors' and shareholders' interests,
2. recommendations by investor and board governance advocacy groups (including the National Association of Corporate Directors' blue ribbon commission on outside director compensation principles and "best practices") to eliminate pensions for nonemployee directors, and
3. a general shift away from traditional "defined benefit" arrangements in favor of "defined contribution" programs (mirroring general trends in benefit techniques).

Last year, the study companies disposed of their cash retirement plans in various ways:

- Eight automatically converted accrued benefits to deferred stock/units, or restricted stock/units (Anadarko Petroleum, Ball, CSC, Dow Chemical, IKON Office Solutions, Phelps Dodge, Russell, and TJX).
- Three automatically froze accrued benefits (Black & Decker, FDX, and Montana Power).

- Two companies allowed directors to choose between receiving accrued benefits currently or deferring them (Monsanto and Paine Webber).
- Two companies gave directors a choice between continuing participation and converting accrued benefits to either (1) stock options (Federal Mogul) or (2) stock units (Fleet Financial).
- Two companies did not disclose specific information about accrued benefits from the terminated cash plan (Cyprus Amax, and Delta Air Lines).
- Three companies took other noteworthy actions:
    1. AT&T purchased deferred annuities to fund future retirement benefit obligations.
    2. Marsh & McLennan granted a one-time 4,000 shares of deferred stock to provide anticipated retirement benefits to current directors.
    3. SBC continued all current directors in the cash plan.

Nineteen of the 20 companies that terminated cash retirement plans since last year's analysis replaced them with some other benefit or compensation. A total of 18 (90% of the group) substituted some form of stock.

- Nine initiated grants of deferred or restricted stock (AT&T, CSC, Delta Air Lines, Fleet Financial, IKON Office Solutions, Marsh & McLennan, Phelps Dodge, SBC Communication, and TJX).
- Seven replaced pensions with either stock options (Black & Decker, Dow Chemical, FDX, and Federal Mogul) or a stock award (Montana Power, Paine Webber), and Russell now grants both options and a stock award.
- Anadarko Petroleum approved a new stock plan that provides for discretionary grants of stock options, restricted stock, stock awards, and other stock-based awards.
- Cyprus Amax is implementing new stock programs, although they will not become operative until 1999.
- Monsanto increased the cash retainer when retirement benefits were canceled.
- Ball is the only company that does not appear to have replaced its discontinued pension program.

The study companies that reported that they canceled or froze cash-based board pension plans since the 1997 study are listed below in alphabetical order. Details about the disposition of accrued benefits and adoption of any substitute (i.e., stock-based) plans can be found on the Individual Company Worksheets in Chapter 10.

Anadarko Petroleum	Fleet Financial
AT&T	IKON Office Solutions
Ball	Marsh & McLennan
Black & Decker	Monsanto
Computer Sciences Corp.	Montana Power
Cyprus Amax	Paine Webber

Delta Air Lines	Phelps Dodge
Dow Chemical	Russell
FDX	SBC Communications
Federal Mogul	TJX

Note: Stock and stock unit awards that are intended to provide post-service compensation are discussed in Chapter 4, along with other equity-based compensation. Unless otherwise noted, the analyses that follow in Sections 7.2 through 7.7 pertain to cash-based plans only.

7.2 Eligibility Requirements

As of this year, only 26 of the 225 study companies continue to maintain a cash-based retirement plan. A substantial 85% of these programs (and two plans that are stock-based, at Baxter International and Honeywell) have eligibility requirements that involve mandatory service and/or minimum retirement age levels. Cash benefit methodologies vary somewhat, but an eligible director typically receives payments based on the annual retainer in effect at retirement, either for life or for a period matching his or her service years.

Service Requirement—23 companies specify a service requirement, broken out in Table 31.

Table 31 Service Requirements for Post-Service Benefits

Service	No. of Plans	% of Plans with Requirement
Less than 5 years	5	22%
5 years	15	65%
10 years	3	13%
Total	23	100%

Minimum Retirement Age—12 companies require that a director remain on the board until a specified age in order to receive benefits (except, in some cases, in the event of earlier death, disability, or other approved terminations). Table 32 shows the breakdown.

Table 32 Age Requirements for Post-Service Benefits

Age Requirement	No. of Plans	% of Plans with Requirement
Age 55	4	34%
Age 60< 65	1	8%
Age 65	6	50%
Age 70	1	8%
Total	12	100%

7.3 Benefit Amount

Assuming that full eligibility requirements are met, more than half of the 26 *cash* plans set the value of the director's pension benefit at the annual retainer in effect when he or she retires (or the last retainer received).

Table 33 shows the proportion of the 26 plans that specify a "normal benefit" at that level, versus those providing for a lesser amount or a greater one. Included in the "Final Retainer" category are companies that pay 10% of the retainer value for each year of service, to a maximum of 100%.

Table 33 Benefit Levels in Cash-Based Pension Plans

Annual Benefit	No. of Plans	% of Cash-Based Plans
Final retainer	14	54%
Less than retainer	5	19%
More than retainer*	7	27%
Total	26	100%

**Typically includes meeting attendance fees and/or stock grant values or future retainer increases*

Other unusual benefit methodologies include:

1. **American Financial Group**—pays five times the retainer (but requires only 4 years of service)
2. **General Dynamics**—pays average annual income for the highest 3 years of service
3. **Idacorp**—pays $17,500 for 15 years (retainer = $19,800)
4. **McDermott**—pays the greater of: 50% of 3-year average compensation, or the annual retainer
5. **Merrill Lynch**—pays the retainer + $20,000 as an annual benefit
6. **Pacific Enterprises**—pays the retainer + 10 times the board meeting fee

7.4 Benefit Payment Periods

The 26 cash-based retirement plans provide for periodic payments for a stipulated time, usually the former director's lifetime or a period matching his or her board service. Table 34 shows the prevalence of various payout periods utilized in director pension plans.

Table 34 Payment Periods in Cash-Based Pension Plans

Specified Payment Periods	No. of Plans	% of Cash-Based Plans
Life of director	8	30%
Matching service*	14	54%
10 years	2	8%
Other	2	8%
Total	26	100%

**Sometimes capped at a number of years (e.g., 10 or 15)*

The two companies that make up the "Other" category are:

- **American Financial**—directors may elect a lump sum or installment payout of a retirement "bonus."
- **Idacorp** —the benefit is paid for 15 years.

7.5 Death Benefits

Fourteen of the cash-based plans (54%) stipulate that some or all benefits would continue in the event of the director's death (AFLAC, American Financial, Apache, Coca-Cola, Emerson Electric, General Dynamics, General Electric, Idacorp, McDermott, Merrill Lynch, St. Paul Cos., Temple-Inland, Tenet Healthcare, and Viacom). Seven of those permit post-death payments to an estate or beneficiary(ies), while seven limit them to the director's surviving spouse.

7.6 COC Provisions

Five cash-based pension programs (19%) specify COC protections, typically by authorizing rabbi trust funding or providing that vesting requirements would be waived and/or that benefits would be paid in a lump sum in the event of a change-of-control (Bank of New York, Bowater, St. Paul Cos., Temple-Inland and Tenet Healthcare).

7.7 Plans of Special Interest

- **American Financial**—if the director dies while serving (and was not an employee for at least 2 prior years) then the benefit (five times retainer) is paid to beneficiary whether or not the director was then eligible under the plan.
- **Bank of New York**—the benefit = 50% of retainer for 5 years of service + 10% for each additional year up to 100%; if director retires after age 70, then the benefit is paid for life (otherwise, it is paid for a period matching the director's service).
- **Baxter**—deferred shares granted as a retirement benefit vest after only 6 months, but are not paid out until termination.
- **Emerson Electric**—if director dies while serving, the spouse receives benefits for 5 years.
- **Ford Motor**—director may receive $15,000 for life, if life insurance coverage (also provided) is reduced from $200,000 to $100,000.
- **General Dynamics**—retirement before age 75 requires board approval.
- **General Electric**—director may take a $450,000 life insurance policy instead of a retirement benefit.
- **Harcourt General**—retirement benefits cease if the director joins the board or becomes an employee of a competitor within 3 years after retirement.
- **Idacorp**—pays a fixed retirement benefit ($17,500) apparently not related to the retainer

($19,800).

- **McDermott**—pays a benefit equal to the greater of: (a) 50% of 3-year average compensation, or (b) annual retainer.
- **Merrill Lynch**—benefits are payable after 5 years of service or age 65 with one year of service.
- **Nike**—life and medical insurance are also provided for life to directors who retire with at least 10 years of service.
- **St. Paul Companies**—the benefit paid is equal to the retainer *plus* the value of annual 1,500 share stock option grants.
- **Tenet Healthcare**—the plan was amended in 1994, to allow former employees to participate (service years are measured from the date employment terminates).

7.8 Mandatory Retirement

An increasing proportion of study companies are requiring outside directors to leave the board at a specified time or age. A total of 39% have now disclosed a mandatory retirement policy, up from 34% in last year's study. The requirements specified by the 87 companies that disclosed them this year are summarized below:

- 82 companies indicate a specific age.
- St. Paul specifies 15 years of service.
- Reebok requires directors retire after four full terms (3 years per term).
- Three companies establish a retirement age *and* limit directors to 15 years of service (Dayton Hudson, General Mills, and Honeywell).

As shown in Table 35, the most prevalent age specified is 70.

Table 35 Breakdown of Mandatory Retirement Ages

Mandatory Retirement Age	No. of Companies	% of Companies with Requirement
Greater than age 72	4	5%
Age 71–72	30	35%
Age 70	49	58%
Less than age 70	2	2%
Total	85	100%

General Dynamics sets a retirement age of 72, but permits it to extend to 75 for "special" reasons.

Chapter 8. Other Benefits and Perquisites

The total number of study companies that provide some form of additional benefits to outside directors declined slightly, from 39% to 37%, since last year's analysis. These include: charitable giving programs, non-liability insurance coverage, and perks such as product discounts, company cars, financial counseling, and spouse travel costs. The trend signals that the popularity of such directors' perks probably peaked in 1996, when 40% of the study companies reported such items.

Tables 36 and 37 demonstrate the prevalence of charitable giving, insurance, and other benefits in specific revenue ranges and industry groupings.

Table 36 Other Benefits by Revenue Ranges

Revenue Range	Charitable Giving		Insurance (non-liability)		Other Benefits/Perks	
(co's in range)	No. of Co's	% of Range	No. of Co's	% of Range	No. of Co's	% of Range
$10-bil + (71)	17	24%	23	32%	10	14%
$5 < $10-bil (59)	15	25%	21	36%	5	8%
$3 < $5-bil (29)	4	14%	4	14%	3	10%
$1 < $3-bil (42)	4	10%	3	7%	3	7%
< $1-bil (24)	2	8%	1	4%	0	0%
All Companies	42	19%	52	23%	21	9%

Table 37 Other Benefits by Industry Groups

Industry	Charitable Giving		Insurance		Other Benefits/Perks	
(co's in range)	No. of Co's	% of Range	No. of Co's	% of Range	No. of Co's	% of Range
Financial (25)	5	20%	7	28%	4	16%
Health Care (16)	1	6%	4	25%	0	0%
Hi-Tech (36)	5	14%	9	25%	5	14%

(Table continues)

(Table 37 continued)

Industry (co's in range)	Charitable Giving		Insurance		Other Benefits/Perks	
	No. of Co's	% of Range	No. of Co's	% of Range	No. of Co's	% of Range
Manufacturing (46)	12	26%	11	24%	1	2%
Other Indust (21)	6	29%	6	29%	1	5%
Service (37)	7	19%	5	14%	6	16%
Utilities (13)	0	0%	3	23%	1	8%
Other (31)	6	19%	7	23%	3	10%
All Companies (225)	42	19%	52	23%	21	9%

8.1 Charitable Giving Programs

Forty-two study companies have disclosed donation plans or policies for directors, as follows:

- 29 maintain only "memorial gift" programs, under which large donations are made to organizations designated by the director (often subject to company approval), usually following his or her death.
- 10 companies have only "matching gift" programs, under which the company matches a director's personal donation to charities, educational institutions, or other approved organizations.
- Fortune Brands and Bestfoods have both memorial gift and matching gift programs.

Memorial gift programs are typically funded by life insurance coverage on the directors, frequently utilizing "second-to-die" policies whereby donations are deferred until the death of the second director. Twenty-eight of the study company memorial gift programs (90% of the total) specify that they are funded by life insurance policies.

Six of the 31 companies (19%) stipulate that a portion of the payments must go to the company foundation (American Express, Bristol-Myers Squibb, Caterpillar, Norfolk Southern, Textron, and Union Pacific). Nine companies (29%) require a minimum service level before either any or full donations are made (Burlington Resources, Corning, Cummins Engine, E.I. DuPont, Rubbermaid, St. Paul Cos., Texas Instruments, Union Pacific, and Waste Management).

Two companies in the study—Ashland, and Monsanto—reported that they discontinued previously implemented charitable giving programs (four companies discontinued their programs last year).

The total donation levels and payment terms disclosed with respect to memorial gift programs that study companies continue to maintain are summarized in Table 38. Only Houghton Mifflin pays its memorial gifts after the director's retirement (rather than death), in 20 installments.

Table 38 Memorial Gift Programs

Company	Donation	Donee(s)
American Express	$1,000,000	50/50 to AmExp foundation and director designated charities
Aon	$1,000,000	tax qualified institutions; payout over 10 years
Brist-Myers Squibb	$1,000,000	50/50 to BMS foundation and up to 5 director-named charities
Burlington Resources	$1,000,000	one or more educational institutions/private foundations (vesting = 2 yrs' service)
Caterpillar	$1,000,000	50/50 to Caterpillar foundation and director-named charities
Corning	$1,250,000	one or more director-designated qualifying charities (vesting = 5 yrs' service)
Bestfoods	$1,000,000	up to 4 educational institutions
Cummins Engine	$1,000,000	one or more director-named institutions (undisclosed vesting requirement)
E.I. DuPont	$1,000,000	director-named institutions (vesting = 5 yrs' service)
Fortune Brands	$500,000	director selected charities, educational institutions or other qualified organizations
General Electric	$1,000,000	up to five charities
General Mills	$1,000,000	one or more qualifying institutions
Goodyear	$1,000,000	one or more qualifying charities recommend by director
GTE	$1,000,000	up to four charities
Houghton Mifflin	$500,000	one or more charitable organizations
J.C. Penney	$500,000	charities or educational institutions
Norfolk Southern	$1,000,000	50/50 to NS foundation and 1 or more tax exempt organizations
Owens-Corning	$1,000,000	up to 2 director selected charities
Pittston	$1,100,000	$1-mil to director-selected charity; $100,000 to company-selected one
PPG	$1,000,000	one or more director-designated charities
Procter & Gamble	$1,000,000	up to 5 director-designated charities
Rubbermaid	$500,000	up to 2 educational institutions (vesting = 3 yrs' service)
Ryder Systems	$1,000,000	up to 2 charities

Company	Donation	Donee(s)
St. Paul Companies	$1,000,000	up to 4 charities (vests 20%/yr in years 3–7 or at death, disability, or retirement at age 70)
SunAmerica	$500,000	up to 5 charities
Texaco	$1,000,000	one or more charities
Texas Instruments	$500,000	up to 3 educational institutions or approved charities (requires 5 yrs' svc)
Textron	$1,000,000	50/50 to company foundation and up to 5 director-selected charities
Union Pacific	$1,000,000	50/50 to company foundation and 1 or more director-named organizations (vesting = 20% per year)
United Tech.	$1,000,000	up to 4 charities
Waste Mgmt	$1,000,000	vesting = $100,000 for each service year up to 10

A total of 13 companies make direct contributions or "match" a director's donations to charities: Bestfoods, Browning Ferris Industries, CBS, Colgate-Palmolive, Cigna, Ford Motor, Fortune Brands, Freeport McMoRan, Household International, IBM, Lee Enterprises, Phelps Dodge, and VF.

8.2 Insurance Coverage

Fifty-one companies, representing 23% of the study group, provide outside directors with *one or more* of the following types of non-liability insurance (or make it available to them):

1. Travel/Accidental Death: 21 companies
2. Life: 33 companies
3. Medical and/or Dental: 18 companies
4. Accidental Death/Disability: 15 companies

Table 39 details the type and, as disclosed, the amount of coverage being provided to nonemployee members of study company boards. Each column shows the amount of coverage provided for the indicated type of insurance, or "Yes" if no amount was disclosed (a blank denotes no coverage for that insurance type).

Table 39 Non-liability Insurance Benefits

Company	Travel/ Accident	Life	AD&D	Medical/Dental
Aetna		$150,000		Yes
Allied Signal	$350,000	$100,000		Yes
American Elec Power			$1,000,000	
American Express		$50,000	$300,000	
Anheuser-Busch		$50,000		
AT&T	Yes	Yes		
Baxter International		Yes		Yes
Bell Atlantic	Yes	Yes		
Black & Decker	$200,000	$100,000		
Bob Evans		$50,000		Yes
CBS			$500,000	
Chase Manhattan		Yes	Yes	Yes
Chrysler	$250,000			
Cigna	$204,000	Yes		Yes
Coca-Cola	$200,000	$30,000	$100,000	Yes
Colgate-Palmolive	$300,000	$50,000		
Cons Natural Gas		Yes		
Bestfoods	$175,000	$100,000		
E.I. DuPont			$300,000	
Ford Motor		$200,000	$500,000	
Fortune Brands	Yes	Yes		
FPL Group	Yes			
Gap Stores				Yes
General Dynamics	Yes			
General Electric		$150,000		
General Mills	Yes			
Household International		$250,000		

Company	Travel/ Accident	Life	AD&D	Medical/Dental
IBM	$300,000	$50,000		
Kellogg	Yes			
McDermott Internat'l				Yes
Merrill Lynch	Yes	Yes		Yes
Mobil	$500,000	$100,000		
Monsanto	Yes			
Motorola			$500,000	
Nike		$500,000		Yes
Paine Webber				Yes
Phelps Dodge		$50,000		
Procter & Gamble			$750,000	
Reynolds Metals			$50,000	
Rubbermaid			$250,000	
Ryder Systems		$100,000	$100,000	Yes
SBC Comm.	Yes	$100,000		
Snap-On		Yes	Yes	
Southern N.E. Telecomm		Yes	Yes	
St. Paul Companies	$200,000	$100,000		
Tenet Healthcare		$1,000,000		
Texas Instruments	Yes	Yes		Yes
Union Pacific		$100,000		Yes
United Healthcare				Yes
Warner-Lambert		Yes	Yes	Yes
Waste Mgmt.				Yes
Total Plans	21	33	15	18

Ten companies, of which nine are also included in Table 40, provide other forms of insurance:

1. **Aetna**—directors may purchase long-term care insurance.

2. **American Express**—directors may purchase up to $50,000 of *additional* group life insurance.
3. **Cigna**—provides property/casualty insurance.
4. **Consolidated Natural Gas**—provides supplemental death benefits.
5. **Household**—insures personal excess liability equal to $10-mil.
6. **Phelps Dodge**—$25,000 life insurance for retired directors.
7. **Reynolds Metals**—death/disability benefit continues after retirement if director serves until age 65.
8. **Ryder Systems**—has long-term disability insurance for directors.
9. **Texaco**—offers group personal liability and property damage.
10. **Union Pacific**—provides excess liability insurance of $10-mil.

8.3 Perquisites

Eighteen study companies (8% of the total) disclosed perks for nonemployee directors, as follows:

1. **AirTouch Communications:** cellular equipment & services (up to $4,000 per year).
2. **AMR:** free transportation for the director and spouse on American Air (plus tax offset).
3. **Baltimore G&E:** one director, a former CEO, has a company car.
4. **Brunswick:** company products may be purchased at dealer's net cost; boats may be used for 2 years at no cost; other products up to $1,500.
5. **Charles Schwab:** directors who use Schwab for brokerage transactions receive a 20% discount on commission rates.
6. **Chrysler:** directors receive "product evaluation and lease vehicles."
7. **Cigna:** financial counseling services.
8. **Dayton Hudson:** discounts on company merchandise.
9. **Delta Air Lines:** complimentary transportation to directors and their spouses.
10. **The Gap:** merchandise discounts.
11. **McDonald's:** two directors have use of a company car.
12. **Merrill Lynch:** outside directors have an opportunity to invest personal funds in ML&Co sponsored employee partnerships.
13. **Motorola:** reimbursement of travel and lodging expenses of spouses traveling with directors on company business.
14. **SBC Communications:** telecommunications services and equipment (plus tax gross-ups).
15. **Southern New England Telecommunications:** telephone service concessions.
16. **Sprint:** residential long-distance service.
17. **Venator:** financial counseling services.
18. **Wells Fargo:** financial counseling up to $7,500 per year.

Chapter 9. Board/Compensation Committees

This section examines some aspects of board and Compensation Committee structure as well as several governance issues, specifically:

- Shareholder proposals involving directors' pay
- The prevalence of separate COBs
- Board election cycles
- Board sizes
- The average age of directors, and
- The background of Compensation Committee members.

Some practices have remained constant over the past few years (e.g., the prevalence of separate COBs) while others shifted significantly in the past year (e.g., the ratio of inside vs. outside directors on the board).

9.1 Shareholder Proposals

The number of compensation- or board-related proposals submitted by investors at the study companies' annual meetings decreased again, from 46 in 1997 to 40 in 1998. The topics of 1998 proposals generally matched those of 1997, although the emphasis shifted somewhat (see Table 40).

Demands to declassify the board (i.e., have annual rather than staggered terms) continue to be the most prevalent shareholder proposal, with 15 such propositions being submitted among the 225 study companies in 1998 (7%), which is slightly higher than the prior year's 6%. As discussed on page 92, most companies remain unmoved by this pressure—the percentage of study companies with annual elections did not significantly change.

Concern about directors' independent status continues to be significant, with a total of 11 shareholder proposals related to director autonomy submitted. The proposals range from recommending an independent, separate COB to requiring that members of all "key" committees be directors that are independent (i.e., "outsiders").

A shareholder proposal submitted for the first time to AT&T requested that a summary of each director's record on important matters, such as executive compensation, bonuses, stock option grants, acquisitions and divestitures, etc, be provided to stockholders. The stated intention was to enable shareholders to be more informed, and thus vote more intelligently, on proxy proposals and director elections. Table 40 summarizes the nature and number of shareholder proposals submitted to the study companies.

Table 40 Shareholder Proposals

No. of Proposals	Issue
15	Declassify board (to elect directors annually)
2	Ensure directors are independent
9	Have an independent COB, VCOB, or members of key committees
3	Limit the term directors may serve
3	Pay director compensation more (or all) in stock
4	Other

The number of proposals offered by a relatively small group of activist shareholders has decreased substantially. The individuals listed below represented half of all the shareholder proposals submitted to study companies in FY97. By contrast, they collectively submitted only 14 proposals (35%) in 1998.

Name	**1998 (No. in 1997)**
Evelyn Y. Davis	7 proposals (9)
Rossi family	3 proposals (5)
John Chevedden	3 proposals (5)
John & Margaret Gilbert	1 proposals (4)

Eight investment/pension funds or unions (up from seven last year) presented the following proposals:

1. **AFL-CIO Staff Retirement Plan**—make the Compensation Committee completely independent (E.I. DuPont)
2. **Amalgamated Bank of New York Long View Collective Investment Fund**—declassify board (FDX)
3. **California Public Employees' Retirement Systems (CALPERS)**—require an outside COB (Electronic Data Systems)
4. **College Retirement Equities Fund**—require a majority of directors to be independent (Walt Disney)
5. **Communication Workers of America**—cancel the director pension plan (General Electric)
6. **New York City Employees' Retirement System**—establish a Nominating Committee consisting solely of independent directors (Cyprus Amax)
7. **International Brotherhood of Electrical Workers Pension Benefit Fund**—only pay pension benefits if approved by shareholders (Sprint)
8. **Southwest Ohio District Council Pension Fund**—require a majority of directors to be independent (Marriott)

This year, two additional organizations submitted proposals:

1. The **Independent Association of Publishers' Employees** sought a vote to declassify the board at Dow Jones.
2. The **Presbyterian Church USA** resubmitted its proposal at American International Group to create a Nominating Committee consisting of at least four independent board members.

9.2 Annual vs. Staggered Elections

Many companies adopted a classified board structure, involving staggered terms, during the takeover mania of the 1980s. A classified system makes it more difficult for a raider to sweep out all board members, and thus may deter hostile takeovers. In recent years, however, staggered boards have been criticized for helping to entrench management, and shareholder proposals continue to advocate declassification.

The percentage of study companies that elect all board members annually inched up to 41% (92 companies) from 40% previously, while 59% (133 companies) maintain staggered board terms. On the other hand, four *companies* (Apple, Ashland, Walt Disney, and Waste Management) put forth proposals for annual director elections in 1998 (presumably in response to shareholder pressure; see page 91). In addition, Union Pacific is transitioning from staggered elections to annual.

9.3 Number of Board Members

The study companies have an average of 12 board members each. The largest boards are Bell Atlantic and Fleet Financial, containing 22 members each. The smallest have only five directors: Kelly Services and Tootsie Roll.

There is a clear correlation between company size and board size, as shown in Table 41.

Table 41 Average Number of Board Members

Revenue Range	Avg Number of Directors
> $10-bil	14
$5 < $10-bil	12
$3 < $5-bil	11
$1 < $3-bil	11
<$1 bil	10

Last year six of the eight industry groups categorized in the study had an average of 12 board members, and only Hi-Tech companies had fewer board members (11), on average. This year the picture changed somewhat:

- Financial companies continue to average 15 board members.
- Industrials, Utilities, and "Other" companies continue to average 12 board members.
- Health Care, Hi-Tech, Manufacturing, and Service companies now average 11 board members each.

Typically, only the company's top two or three executives sit on the board, with remaining directors being "outsiders." The average study company had three "inside" directors (defined, for purposes of this analysis, as employees, former employees, or relatives of the CEO) and nine "outside" directors. This remains unchanged since last year's study. Interestingly, 48 study companies (21%) have only *one* insider, presumably the COB/CEO.

The study company with the most inside directors is Dow Chemical, with 11 insiders and only seven outside directors. In all, only seven study companies have more insiders than outsiders serving on the board (down from eight last year). Along with Dow, they are: American Financial, Marsh & McLennan, MGM Grand, Nike, Talbots, and Tootsie Roll. Wal-Mart, which had more insiders in 1997, now has a majority of outsiders.

9.4 Separate COB

Another issue that has attracted supporters in recent years is splitting the COB and CEO positions at public corporations. But among the analysis group, the prevalence of separate COBs decreased, with only 29 companies (13%) now reporting an independent chairman versus 36 as of 1997.

While the trend of separating the COB and CEO positions appears to be declining overall, the number of study companies with a bona fide *outsider* COB actually increased dramatically. As of 1997, only three study companies had an outside COB (i.e., one who was not the former CEO), while eight of the companies with a separate COB in 1998 indicate that the chairman is an independent outsider (Allergan, Delta Air Lines, Fluor, Hannaford, Mentor Graphics, Pittston, Texas Instruments, and TJX).

9.5 Average Director Age

One measure of a company's innovative spirit may be the typical age of its outside board members. Younger new directors may have more exposure to the latest technologies and bring fresh ideas to the company's management. We calculated the average age of all outside directors at each study company and categorized them to identify prevalence patterns (see Table 42). The average outside director's age at a majority of the companies (59%) falls between 60 and 64.9, relatively unchanged from last year. The median age is 60.7 (up from 60.4).

Table 42 Average Age of Outside Directors

Average Age	No. of Companies	% of Companies
> 70.0	2	1%
65.0–69.9	4	2%
60.0–64.9	132	59%
55.0–59.9	75	33%
50.0–54.9	12	5%

American Financial Group has the "oldest" board, averaging 71.3 years of age (there are only three outside directors, ages 69 to 74). The oldest director is age 83 and sits on the board of Tootsie Roll. *Note: 87 study companies (39%) disclosed a mandatory retirement age ranging from 68 to 76.* *See Chapter 7, page 81 for more information on mandatory retirement requirements.*

In contrast, the "youngest" board serves at CISCO Systems. CISCO's five outside directors range in age from 40 to 66. The youngest director serving on a study company board is 31-year-old Carlos Fernandez, at Anheuser-Busch. He is VCOB of Grupo Modelo, S.A. de C.V., a Mexican company engaged in brewing and related operations.

9.6 Compensation Committees

The Compensation Committees of the 225 study companies had an aggregate number of 1,000 members, compared with a total of 1,004 members on the Comp Committees of the

220 companies analyzed last year. Thus, the average number of members per company declined from five to four.

In the world of "professional directors," individuals often serve on multiple boards, and even within the relatively small sample of 225 companies, 109 directors (about 12% of the total number of individuals serving) belong to Compensation Committees at more than one study company:

- 93 sit on two Compensation Committees
- 14 sit on three
- 2 sit on four

To gain perspective on who is responsible for setting executive compensation, we reviewed Compensation Committee members' biographies and categorized them using the following affiliations:

- Current executive
- Retired executive
- Consultant (to the company)
- Insider
- Academic
- Religious

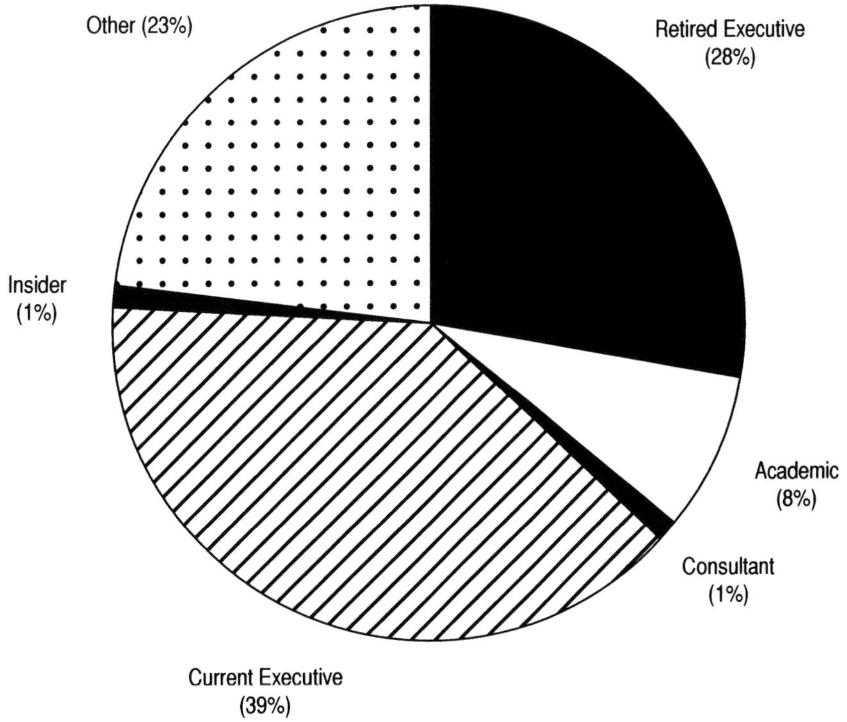

Figure 12 Compensation Committee Member Affiliations

- Other (e.g., attorney, investment fund manager, self-employed)

A breakdown of the affiliations of study company Compensation Committee members is illustrated in Figure 12. The mix is relatively unchanged since the previous study and indicates that the vast majority of Compensation Committee members are either current or retired corporate executives.

For your information, the study company Compensation Committee members are listed in Appendix III (page 341), showing all the members for each company, and in Appendix IV (page 357) showing all companies where each director serves.

Chapter 10. Company Summaries

The board compensation programs for each of the 225 study companies are enumerated in this chapter. Each company's entry is based on information disclosed through July 1, 1998.

This presentation gives you a detailed picture of the full directors' remuneration strategy being pursued by each study company. It also enables you to evaluate innovative techniques, such as performance-based stock grants, in relation to other elements of a company's director pay program. The company summaries break down as follows:

- "Direct" cash and stock compensation payment rates
- The terms of equity-based grants and awards
- The terms of deferred compensation, cash pension, and insurance and other benefit arrangements, and
- The changes that were made to the company's program since the prior year.

Each company summary includes the following categories:

Industry

The company's line of business is indicated.

FY97 Revenue

The company's revenues (in millions of dollars) for the last reported fiscal year (generally fiscal 1997) are cited here.

Board Structure/Fees

This section includes, as applicable:

- The number of board and committee meetings held in the last reported fiscal year
- The annual retainer (portions paid in cash and stock)
- Any committee membership fees
- The meeting attendance fee
- Any board or committee chairperson fees
  Note: unless otherwise indicated in the "Comments" section, chair fees represent an additional annual amount paid to the committee chairman.
- A typical or "average" director's annual direct compensation, based on the latest reported fees and the number of reported meetings (see page 26 in Chapter 3 for a detailed explanation of this calculation)

Stock-Based Compensation

This section summarizes the terms of directors' stock grants or awards, including options, discount options, restricted, deferred, or phantom shares, and stock awards (if made under a plan). Each entry indicates, as applicable and available:

- The grant type(s)—many companies provide more than one award (e.g., options and restricted shares)
- The number of shares covered by the grant or award
- The frequency of the grant or award
- The prescribed vesting term (generally accelerated in cases of death, disability, or approved retirement)
- The year-end price of the company's common stock
- The type of plan ("Separate" if it is solely for board members, or "Combined" if directors are participants in an omnibus plan that includes employees)
- The plan life (the number of years the plan is scheduled to be in effect)
- The number of shares authorized under the plan ("separate" board plans only)
- Whether the plan contains protections related to a change of control (typically, to accelerate vesting)

Compensation Deferral

This section highlights salient features of elective deferred compensation plans and arrangements for outside directors, including:

- The compensation eligible for deferral
- The account types used (cash, stock, or both)
- The interest rate or rates that may apply to cash-denominated deferrals (as last reported)
- The maximum number of annual installment payouts permitted
- Whether payout is at a date specified by the director or must be make after cessation of service
- Whether the program contains protections related to a change of control (typically, providing for rabbi trust funding and/or automatic payouts upon a change of control)

Cash Retirement Benefits

This segment summarizes the terms of programs or arrangements providing for cash-based post-service benefits to directors. It shows, as applicable and available:

- Any mandatory retirement age
- Any service requirements
- The minimum retirement age
- Whether a reduced benefit is available under some circumstances (e.g., if full eligibility requirements are not satisfied)
- The basic benefit amount or formula (*Retainer* generally refers to the last retainer received by the director before retirement)

- The payment term (*Life* = for the life of the director, *Matching Service* = a period matching the director's length of service on the board)
- Whether the arrangement includes a death benefit (i.e., allowing payments to continue or be settled in a lump sum) to the director's spouse or other beneficiary or estate
- Whether the program contains specific protections related to a change of control (typically, providing for rabbi trust funding and/or automatic vesting and/or settlement of benefits upon a change of control)

Insurance Benefits

This section lists any non-liability related insurance benefits and the associated coverage amount (as disclosed) that are provided or made available to outside directors, including life, travel/accident, and medical/dental.

Other Benefits

Cited here are any other perquisites that the company offers to outside directors, such as charitable giving programs, product discounts, car use, and spouse benefits.

Changes

This section highlights specific changes to the company's fees and programs since the prior year's study.

Aetna Inc.

Industry: Nonbank Financial FY97 Revenue (mils): $18,540

BOARD STRUCTURE/FEES

	No. of Mtgs	Retainer Cash	Retainer Stock	Member Fee	Meeting Fee	Chairman Fee
Board	10	$25,000	—	$ —	$1,000	$ —
Audit	4	—	—	4,000	1,000	3,000
Executive	2	—	—	4,000	1,000	—
Finance	3	—	—	4,000	1,000	3,000
Compensation & Organization	8	—	—	4,000	1,000	3,000
Nominating & Corp. Governance	3	—	—	4,000	1,000	3,000
Investment	4	—	—	4,000	1,000	—

Average director's annual compensation = $55,000
(assumes all meetings are attended and director sits on the Audit and Compensation committees)

STOCK-BASED COMPENSATION

Grant type(s):	**Deferred**
Number of shares:	350
Frequency:	Annual
Vesting:	12 months
Year-end stock price:	70.5625
Plan type:	Separate
Plan life	7 years
Plan kitty:	100,000
COC provision:	Yes

Comments: Director gets dividends (no voting rights); paid out at termination or upon a COC. Initial grant covers 1,500 shares, which vest over a 3-year period.

COMPENSATION DEFERRAL

Eligible comp: Retainer/meeting fees & dividend equivalents
Account types: Cash and/or stock
Interest rate: Company rate (6.6% for 1997)
Payment: After termination
Comments: Deferred stock dividends may be deferred

CASH RETIREMENT BENEFITS

Mandatory retirement age: 70
Cash plan terminated and accrued benefits put in deferred cash or stock accounts

INSURANCE BENEFITS

Group Life: $150,000
Medical/Dental and long-term care
Comments: Director may purchase medical/long-term care insurance similar to employees

OTHER BENEFITS None

CHANGES None

AFLAC Inc.

Industry: Nonbank Financial

FY97 Revenue (mils): $7,251

BOARD STRUCTURE/FEES

	No. of Mtgs	Retainer Cash	Retainer Stock	Member Fee	Meeting Fee	Chairman Fee
Board	5	$18,000	—	$ —	$2,000	$ —
Audit	3	—	—	7,200	—	12,000
Compensation	3	—	—	7,200	—	10,000
Nominating	1	—	—	7,200	—	—

Comments: Nonemployee directors receive $7,200 per year for service on one or more committees. Employee directors receive $200 per month for serving on committees. In 1997 consulting fees of $48,237 were paid to a director.

Average director's annual compensation = $35,200
(assumes all meetings are attended and director sits on the Audit and Compensation committees)

STOCK-BASED COMPENSATION

Grant type(s):	**Stock Option**
Number of shares:	10,000
Frequency:	5 years
Vesting:	20% per year, starting at grant
Year-end stock price:	51.125
Plan type:	Combined with exec.

Comments: Initial grant also covers 10,000 shares.

COMPENSATION DEFERRAL

None

CASH RETIREMENT BENEFITS

Mandatory service: 5 years
Min. retirement age: 55
Basic benefits: Retainer + board meeting fees
Payment term: Matching service
Death benefit: Yes (spouse only)

INSURANCE BENEFITS

None

OTHER BENEFITS

None

CHANGES

None

Air Products and Chemicals, Inc.

Industry: Chemicals

FY97 Revenue (mils): $4,662

BOARD STRUCTURE/FEES

	No. of Mtgs	Retainer Cash	Retainer Stock	Member Fee	Meeting Fee	Chairman Fee
Board	8*	$36,000	—	$ —	$ —	$ —
Audit	4	—	—	—	—	3,000
Executive	1	—	—	—	—	3,000
Finance	3	—	—	—	—	3,000
Mgmt Devel & Comp	5	—	—	—	—	3,000
Nominat & Corp. Governance	3	—	—	—	—	3,000
Env, Safety & Public Policy	2	—	—	—	—	3,000

* Includes one meeting of outside directors to review CEO's performance

Comments: $12,000 of total annual retainer ($48,000) is mandatorily deferred in stock units; directors on company's Japan Advisory Council receive $15,000 per year, and European Advisory Council receive $10,000.

Average director's annual compensation = $36,000

(assumes all meetings are attended and director sits on the Audit and Compensation committees)

STOCK-BASED COMPENSATION

Grant type(s):	**Stock Option**	**Deferred Units**	**Deferred Units**
Number of shares:	1,000	$12,000	200
Frequency:	Annual	Annual	Annual
Vesting:	6 months	After termination	Same
Year-end stock price:	82.25	Same	Same
Plan type:	Separate	(Deferral plan)	Same

COMPENSATION DEFERRAL

Eligible comp: Retainer/meeting
Account types: Cash/stock
Interest: Moody's LT A-rated industrial bond rate
Max. Installments: 10 years
Payment: After termination
COC provision: Yes
Comments: Deferred stock is paid out in shares; payouts are lump sum or installments

CASH RETIREMENT BENEFITS

Mandatory retirement age: 71

Cash plan terminated and directors with <6 years of service had value of accrued benefits converted to deferred stock units.

INSURANCE BENEFITS

None

OTHER BENEFITS

None

CHANGES

Changed 200 deferred unit grants from one-time to annual grants

Air Touch Communications, Inc.

Industry: Communications FY97 Revenue (mils): $3,594

BOARD STRUCTURE/FEES

	No. of Mtgs	Retainer Cash	Retainer Stock	Member Fee	Meeting Fee	Chairman Fee
Board	7	$55,000	—	$ —	$ —	$ —
Audit & Investment	4	—	—	—	—	5,000
Executive	4	—	—	—	—	5,000
Compensation & Personnel	5	—	—	—	—	5,000
Nominating & Director Affairs	4	—	—	—	—	5,000

Comments: Directors may elect to receive fees in either stock units or stock options; the number of options is calculated using a Black-Scholes pricing model; options are immediately vested and have a life of 7 years; stock units are based on FMV and are immediately vested and have a life of 10 years.

Attendance requirements: retainer is reduced by $3,000 for each meeting (after one) missed per year.

Average director's annual compensation = $55,000

(assumes all meetings are attended and director sits on the Audit and Compensation committees)

STOCK-BASED COMPENSATION

Grant type(s):	**Stock Option**
Number of shares:	1,000
Frequency:	Annual
Vesting:	1 year
Year-end stock price:	41.5625
Plan type:	Combined w/ exec
COC provision:	Yes

Comments: Initial grant covers 10,000 options.

Ownership guidelines: As a condition for receiving options, directors are required to purchase shares = $100,000 or more within 30 days of joining board; loans are available from the company.

COMPENSATION DEFERRAL

Eligible comp: Retainer/meeting
Account types: Cash
Interest: 8.53%

CASH RETIREMENT BENEFITS

None

INSURANCE BENEFITS

None

OTHER BENEFITS

Cellular service and equipment up to $4,000/yr.

CHANGES

- Increased retainer value by $10,000
- Changed attendance requirement, previously quarterly retainer payments were reduced by 20% if director missed one or more meetings

Albertson's Inc.

Industry: Food FY97 Revenue (mils): $14,690

BOARD STRUCTURE/FEES

	No. of Mtgs	Retainer Cash	Retainer Stock	Member Fee	Meeting Fee	Chairman Fee
Board	7	$30,000	—	$ —	$1,000	$ —
Executive	5	—	—	—	1,000	—
Audit	4	—	—	—	1,000	—
Compensation	2	—	—	—	1,000	—
Nominating	1	—	—	—	1,000	—
Non-Emp Director Defer'd Comp	0	—	—	—	1,000	—
Grantor Trust	1	—	—	—	1,000	—

Comments: $1,621,619 of office supplies/furniture were purchased from the firm of a director's son-in-law; $230,662 of food was purchased from a director's company.

Average director's annual compensation = $43,000

(assumes all meetings are attended and director sits on the Audit and Compensation committees)

STOCK-BASED COMPENSATION

Grant type(s):	**Stock Option**
Number of shares:	2,000
Frequency:	Annual
Vesting:	Immediate
Year-end stock price:	47.25
Plan type:	Separate
Plan life:	10 years
Plan kitty:	400,000

Comments: No more than 25,000 shares can be granted to an individual.

COMPENSATION DEFERRAL

Eligible comp: Retainer/meeting
Account types: Cash
Interest rate: Moody's
Max. installments: 15 years
COC provision: Yes

Comments: After retirement, death, disability, or a COC, interest rate jumps to Moody's + 3%; life insurance funded.

CASH RETIREMENT BENEFITS

None

INSURANCE BENEFITS

None

OTHER BENEFITS

None

CHANGES

None

Allergan, Inc.

Industry: Health Care FY97 Revenue (mils): $1,138

BOARD STRUCTURE/FEES

	No. of Mtgs	Retainer Cash	Retainer Stock	Member Fee	Meeting Fee	Chairman Fee
Board	5	$25,000	—	$ —	$1,300	$250,000
Audit	4	—	—	—	1,000	2,000
Organization & Comp	5	—	—	—	1,000	2,500
Finance	4	—	—	—	1,000	2,000
Corp. Governance	2	—	—	—	1,000	1,000
Science & Technology	2	—	—	—	1,000	1,000

Comments: Committee chairman fees reflect additional $500 per committee meeting attended; the COB fee is in addition to attendance fees; retired CEO is Chairman Emeritus, receiving $50,000 per year for consulting services, in addition to above fees; one director's (on the Comp. Committee) company provided marketing research data to Allergan for a total of $2.125-mil in 1997.

Average director's annual compensation = $40,500

(assumes all meetings are attended and director sits on the Audit and Compensation committees)

STOCK-BASED COMPENSATION

Grant type(s):	**Restricted**
Number of shares:	2,700
Frequency:	3 years
Vesting:	1/3 each year
Year-end stock price:	33.5625
Plan type:	Separate
Plan life:	10 years
Plan kitty:	50,000
COC provision:	Yes

Comments: Plan was amended in 1998 to increase from 600 to 900 shares per year; a one-time restricted stock grant of 5,000 shares was made to the new outside COB.

Ownership Guidelines: Shares equal in value to the retainer fee times the number of years served. Shares held in deferred accounts count toward guideline.

COMPENSATION DEFERRAL

Eligible comp: Retainer/meeting
Account types: Stock
Payment: After termination
Comments: Payouts are in cash.

CASH RETIREMENT BENEFITS

None

INSURANCE BENEFITS

None

OTHER BENEFITS

None

CHANGES

- Added COB fee
- Increased stock grants by 900 shares every 3 years

Allied Signal, Inc.

Industry: Conglomerate FY97 Revenue (mils): $14,472

BOARD STRUCTURE/FEES

	No. of Mtgs	Retainer Cash	Retainer Stock	Member Fee	Meeting Fee	Chairman Fee
Board	8	$35,000	—	$5,400	$1,500	$ —
Audit	5	—	—	5,400	1,000	4,000
Mgmt Devel & Compensation	6	—	—	5,400	1,000	4,000
Corporate Responsibility	3	—	—	5,400	1,000	2,000
Corp. Governance	2	—	—	5,400	1,000	2,000
Retirement Plans	3	—	—	5,400	1,000	2,000
Technology	2	—	—	5,400	1,000	2,000

Comments: $15,000 of the total cash retainer ($50,000) is mandatorily deferred in stock equivalents; $1,000 paid for special meetings; $1,000 per day for special assignments; $1,500 for alternate committee member attendance.

Same Day Meeting Fee: No committee meeting fee paid if on the same day as a board meeting.

Average director's annual compensation = $57,800

(assumes all meetings are attended and director sits on the Audit and Compensation committees)

STOCK-BASED COMPENSATION

Grant type(s):	**Restricted**	**Stock Option**	**Deferred Stock Units**
Number of shares:	3,000	2,000	$15,000
Frequency:	One-time	Annual	Annual
Vesting:	20% for each service yr	40% 1st yr, 30% in 2&3	After termination
Year-end stock price:	38.8125	Same	Same
Plan type:	Separate	Same	(Deferral plan)
Plan life:	Board discretion	Same	—
Plan kitty:	225,000	Same	—
COC provision:	Yes	Same	—

Comments: For restricted stock, shares remain restricted until service termination at age 65 or older.

COMPENSATION DEFERRAL

Eligible comp: Retainer/meeting
Account types: Cash and/or stock
Interest rate: Company rate (10% for 1998)
Max. installments: 10 years
COC provision: Yes
Payment: Date specified by director
Comments: Payouts are in cash following termination.

CASH RETIREMENT BENEFITS

Mandatory retirement age: 70

Cash plan terminated 1/97 with the present value of accrued benefits credited to their deferred accounts in either 100% stock or 50% stock and 50% cash, as elected by the director.

INSURANCE BENEFITS

Travel/accident: $350,000
Life: $100,000
Medical/Dental

OTHER BENEFITS: None

CHANGES: None

American Electric Power Company, Inc.

Industry: Utilities FY97 Revenue (mils): $6,161

BOARD STRUCTURE/FEES

	No. of Mtgs	Retainer Cash	Retainer Stock	Member Fee	Meeting Fee	Chairman Fee
Board	10	$23,000	—	$ —	$1,000	$ —
Audit	4	—	—	—	1,000	3,000
Human Resources	4	—	—	—	1,000	3,000
Corp Public Policy	2	—	—	—	1,000	3,000
Executive	0	—	—	—	1,000	3,000
Finance	4	—	—	—	1,000	3,000
Directors	2	—	—	—	1,000	3,000

Same Day Mtg Fees: only $1,000 fee for Board & Exec Committee meetings held on same day.

Comments: $1,000 inspection trip or conference fee; directors may elect to receive fees in stock.

Average director's annual compensation = $41,000

(assumes all meetings are attended and director sits on the Audit and Compensation committees)

STOCK-BASED COMPENSATION

Grant type(s):	**Deferred Units**
Number of shares:	300
Frequency:	Annual (up to 10)
Vesting:	After termination
Year-end stock price:	51.625
Plan type:	Separate
COC provision:	Yes

Comments: payout is proportionately reduced if director leaves with < 5 years service.

Ownership Guidelines: 2,000 shares within 5 years

COMPENSATION DEFERRAL

Eligible comp: Retainer/meeting
Account types: Cash and/or stock
Interest rate: Prime
Payment: After termination
Comments: Payout may be lump sum or installments

CASH RETIREMENT BENEFITS

Cash plan terminated 1/97 for future directors; current directors could elect to waive their rights under the plan and receive 300 shares of deferred units per year of service, up to 3,000 shares.

INSURANCE BENEFITS

Accidental death/disability: $1 million
Comments: Director gets annual tax offset payment of approximately $350 with respect to premium.

OTHER BENEFITS

None

CHANGES

None

American Express Company

Industry: Nonbank Financial

FY97 Revenue (mils): $17,760

BOARD STRUCTURE/FEES

	No. of Mtgs	Retainer Cash	Retainer Stock	Member Fee	Meeting Fee	Chairman Fee
Board	9	$64,000	200 shrs	$ —	$ —	$ —
Compensation & Benefits	4	—	—	—	—	10,000
Executive	0	—	—	—	—	10,000
Public Responsibility	2	—	—	—	—	10,000
Audit	5	—	—	—	—	10,000
Directors	2	—	—	—	—	10,000
Finance	3	—	—	—	—	10,000

Misc. Fees: subsidiary fees paid; $25,000 for service on subsidiary Board, + $1,000 for Board mtgs, $750 for committee mtgs; $5,000 to chairman of subsidiary Audit Committee

Attendance Require: must attend 75% of Board and committee meetings or forfeit 4th quarter retainer *and* lose 50 shares of the stock award

Average director's annual compensation = $81,850

(assumes all meetings are attended and director sits on the Audit and Compensation committees)

STOCK-BASED COMPENSATION

Grant type(s):	**Stock Option**	**Stock Award**
Number of shares:	1,000	200
Frequency:	Annual	Annual
Vesting:	1/3 per year	Immediate
Year-end stock price:	89.25	Same
Plan type:	Separate	Separate
Plan life:	5 years	—
Plan kitty:	200,000	—
COC provision:	Yes	—

Comments: If the director attends less than 75% of meetings, the stock award is reduced to 150 shares; the value of the stock award is reflected in "Stock Retainer" and "Average Director's Annual Compensation" above.

Ownership guidelines: Company has voluntary guideline of 10,000 shares or share equivalents, acquired over 5 years

COMPENSATION DEFERRAL

Eligible comp: Retainer/meeting
Account types: Cash and/or stock
Interest rate: Moody's Avg Corp Bond Yield
Max. installments: 10 years
Payment: Date specified by Director
Comments: Payouts are in cash; directors may switch between cash and stock accounts.

CASH RETIREMENT BENEFITS

Mandatory retirement age: 72

Cash plan frozen; directors who are elected for the first time after 3/31/96 are not eligible to participate

INSURANCE BENEFITS

Accidental Death/Dismemberment: $300,000

Group Term Life: $50,000

Comments: Directors may buy up to $50,000 of additional group term life insurance coverage.

OTHER BENEFITS

Charitable Award Program

Amount: $1,000,000; payout: Benefit payable 50/50 to AmEx Foundation & director's charity(ies); insurance funded.

CHANGES

- Added stock awards
- Added alternative for directors to make account transfers in the deferral plan

American Financial Corporation

Industry: Conglomerate FY97 Revenue (mils): $4,021

BOARD STRUCTURE/FEES

	No. of Mtgs	Retainer Cash	Retainer Stock	Member Fee	Meeting Fee	Chairman Fee
Board	7	$20,000	$20,000	$ —	$1,000	$ —
Executive	0	—	—	12,000	1,000	—
Audit	5	—	—	12,000	1,000	—
Compensation	2	—	—	12,000	1,000	—

Comments: committee member fees are also paid 50% in stock. Directors may elect to have all or a portion of cash fees paid in stock.

Average director's annual compensation = $78,000

(assumes all meetings are attended and director sits on the Audit and Compensation committees)

STOCK-BASED COMPENSATION

Grant type(s):	**Stock Option**	**Stock Award**
Number of shares:	1,000	$26,000
Frequency:	Annual	Annual
Vesting	Immediate	—
Year-end stock price	40.3125	Same
Plan type	Combined with exec.	Separate
Plan life	—	10 years
Plan kitty	—	100,000

Comments: initial stock option grant covered 5,000 shares; stock award includes 50% of annual retainer ($40,000) and 50% of the committee member fee ($12,000)

COMPENSATION DEFERRAL

None

INSURANCE BENEFITS

None

OTHER BENEFITS

None

CASH RETIREMENT BENEFITS

Mandatory service: 4 years
Min retirement age: 55
Basic benefits: 5 x retainer
Death benefit: Yes

Comments: Director may elect lump sum or installment payout of retirement bonus; must be available to consult for 5 years; if director dies while serving (and was not an employee for at least the 2 prior years), benefit is paid to beneficiary, whether or not eligible for retirement benefit.

CHANGES

None

American General Corporation

Industry: Nonbank Financial FY97 Revenue (mils): $8,927

BOARD STRUCTURE/FEES

	No. of Mtgs	Retainer Cash	Retainer Stock	Member Fee	Meeting Fee	Chairman Fee
Board	13	$32,000	—	$ —	$ 1,500	$ —
Audit	3	—	—	—	1,500	5,000
Executive	0	—	—	—	1,500	5,000
Personnel	3	—	—	—	1,500	5,000
Finance	(new)	—	—	—	1,500	5,000
Management Development	(new)	—	—	—	1,500	5,000

Average director's annual compensation = $60,500

(assumes all meetings are attended and director sits on the Audit and Compensation committees)

STOCK-BASED COMPENSATION

Grant type(s):	**Restricted**	**Stock Option**
Number of shares:	500	1,500
Frequency:	One-time	One-time
Vesting:	Undisclosed	Undisclosed
Year-end stock price:	54.0625	Same
Plan type:	Combined w/ exec.	Same

Comments: Shareholders approved a 1997 Stock and Incentive Plan, which provides for discretionary grants to outside directors; "future awards are subject to the discretion of the Board."

COMPENSATION DEFERRAL

None

CASH RETIREMENT BENEFITS

Mandatory retirement age: 70

Cash plan terminated 3/97, with current directors receiving stock units equal in value to the actuarial equivalent of the benefits due at age 70 with vesting requirements waived; in the future, directors are eligible for awards under the 1997 Stock and Incentive Plan.

INSURANCE BENEFITS

None

OTHER BENEFITS

None

CHANGES

Added two stock grants

American International Group, Inc.

Industry: Nonbank Financial | FY97 Revenue (mils): $30,520

BOARD STRUCTURE/FEES

	No. of Mtgs	Retainer Cash	Retainer Stock	Member Fee	Meeting Fee	Chairman Fee
Board	5	$15,000	675 shr	$ —	$ —	$ —
Audit	4	—	—	3,500	1,500	—
Stock Option & Comp	8	—	—	3,500	1,500	—
Executive	6	—	—	3,500	1,500	—
Finance	12	—	—	3,500	1,500	—

Misc. fees: subsidiary fees paid

Comments: one director has a consulting agreement for $600,000 in 1997.

Average director's annual compensation = $120,906

(assumes all meetings are attended and director sits on the Audit and Compensation committees)

STOCK-BASED COMPENSATION

Grant type(s):	**Stock Award**	**Stock Option**
Number of shares:	675	5,000
Frequency:	Annual	Not disclosed
Year-end stock price:	108.75	Same

Comments: Company reimburses each nonemployee director for purchase of 675 shares per year; stock award is reflected in "Stock Retainer" and "Average Annual Director's Comp" above. Initial grant of stock options covers 15,000 shares; the 1996 award was 5,000 options *Note: the company did not disclose any option grants in the 1998 proxy.*

COMPENSATION DEFERRAL

None

CASH RETIREMENT BENEFITS

None

INSURANCE BENEFITS

None

OTHER BENEFITS

None

CHANGES

None

AMR Corporation

Industry: Transportation

FY97 Revenue (mils): $18,570

BOARD STRUCTURE/FEES

	No. of Mtgs	Retainer Cash	Retainer Stock	Member Fee	Meeting Fee	Chairman Fee
Board	15	$20,000	—	$ —	$1,000	$ —
Audit	5	—	—	1,500	1,000	—
Compensation	7	—	—	1,500	1,000	—
Executive	4	—	—	1,500	1,000	—
Nominating/Governance	2	—	—	1,500	1,000	—

Same day fees: $1,000 paid per day regardless of number of meetings attended

Average director's annual compensation = $38,000

(assumes all meetings are attended and director sits on the Audit and Compensation committees)

STOCK-BASED COMPENSATION

Grant type(s):	**Deferred**
Number of shares:	450*
Frequency:	Annual
Vesting:	6 months
Year-end stock price:	128.50
Plan type:	Separate
Plan life:	10 years
Plan kitty:	100,000
COC provision:	Yes

Comments: Vested shares are delivered after director's service terminates.

* Future grants may be increased on the basis of the average director compensation paid by 20 other companies; if AMR falls below 85% of the median, grants will be increased in 50-share increments.

COMPENSATION DEFERRAL

Eligible comp: Retainer/meeting
Account types: Cash and/or stock
Interest rate: Prime
Payment: Date specified by director
Comments: Payouts are made in cash

CASH RETIREMENT BENEFITS

Cash plan discontinued for directors elected after 5/15/96 and replaced with 150 additional deferred shares for future directors; current directors continue in plan.

INSURANCE BENEFITS

None

OTHER BENEFITS

Free transportation for director, spouse, and dependents on American Air, plus related tax offset (the average value in 1997 was $44,800 per director)

CHANGES

None

Anadarko Petroleum Corporation

Industry: Fuel FY97 Revenue (mils): $673

BOARD STRUCTURE/FEES

		Retainer				
	No. of Mtgs	Cash	Stock	Member Fee	Meeting Fee	Chairman Fee
Board	4	$35,000	—	$ —	$1,250	$ —
Executive	0	—	—	—	1,250	3,000
Audit	3	—	—	3,000	1,250	3,000
Compensation & Benefits	6	—	—	3,000	1,250	3,000

Comments: Directors may elect to receive all or a portion of fees in stock; one director's companies were paid a total of $820,000 in 1997.

Average director's annual compensation = $57,250
(assumes all meetings are attended and director sits on the Audit and Compensation committees)

STOCK-BASED COMPENSATION

Grant type(s):	**Stock Option**	**Deferred Units**
Number of shares:	5,000	$13,000
Frequency:	Annual	One-time
Vesting:	1 year	Termination
Year-end stock price:	60.6875	Same
Plan type:	Separate	—
Plan life:	Indefinite	—
Plan kitty:	400,000	—
COC provision:	Yes	—

Comments: Initial option grant covers 10,000 options, vesting over a two-year period; a new 1998 Stock Plan provides for grants of options, restricted stock, stock awards, and other stock-based compensation as determined by the Board; additional deferred units may be granted in the future.

COMPENSATION DEFERRAL

Eligible comp: Retainer/meeting fees
Account types: Cash
Interest rate: 20% per annum
Max. installments: 10 years
Payment: Date specified by director
Comments: No deferrals have been made since 1990

CASH RETIREMENT BENEFITS

Cash plan terminated 1/98 and accrued benefits converted to deferred stock units

INSURANCE BENEFITS

None

OTHER BENEFITS

None

CHANGES

- Approved new stock plan providing for discretionary grants of options, restricted stock, stock awards or other stock-based compensation
- Eliminated cash retirement plan and converted accrued benefits to deferred stock units; granted $13,000 of deferred units for 1998

Analog Devices, Inc.

Industry: Electronics

FY97 Revenue (mils): $1,243

BOARD STRUCTURE/FEES

	No. of Mtgs	Retainer Cash	Retainer Stock	Member Fee	Meeting Fee	Chairman Fee
Board	7	$20,000	—	$ —	$2,500	$ —
Audit	5	—	—	—	1,000	—
Compensation	3	—	—	—	1,000	—
Nominating	2	—	—	—	1,000	—

Average director's annual compensation = $45,500

(assumes all meetings are attended and director sits on the Audit and Compensation committees)

STOCK-BASED COMPENSATION

Grant type(s):	**Stock Option**
Number of shares:	10,500
Frequency:	Annual
Vesting:	1/3 per year
Year-end stock price:	27.6875
Plan type:	Separate
Plan life:	7 years
Plan kitty:	550,000

Comments: Plan amended in 1998 to: (1) increase kitty by 150,000 shares, (2) extend plan life by 2 years, (3) authorize annual grants until directors' termination date (vs. only 4 annual grants previously), and (4) allow continued vesting of options after termination as a director if he/she becomes an employee of the company (vs. within 90 days after termination).

COMPENSATION DEFERRAL

None

CASH RETIREMENT BENEFITS

None

INSURANCE BENEFITS

None

OTHER BENEFITS

None

CHANGES

Amended stock option plan

Anheuser-Busch Companies, Inc.

Industry: Consumer Products FY97 Revenue (mils): $11,066

BOARD STRUCTURE/FEES

	No. of Mtgs	Retainer Cash	Retainer Stock	Member Fee	Meeting Fee	Chairman Fee
Board	11	$40,000	—	$ —	$ 1,400	$ —
Audit	4	—	—	—	1,200	10,000
Nominating	1	—	—	—	1,200	3,000
Executive Salaries	2	—	—	—	1,200	10,000
Finance	0	—	—	—	1,200	10,000
Pension	0	—	—	—	1,200	10,000
Conflict of Interest	0	—	—	—	1,200	10,000
Shareholder Meetings (Committee)	0	—	—	—	1,200	3,000

Misc. Fees: $1,200 paid for any Board meeting at which less than a quorum is present. Directors may elect to receive fees in stock or a combination of cash and stock. The COB/CEO sits on the Comp. Committee of an outside director's company; ABI turned over the rights to purchase a wholesalership to an outside director's son's company and it subsequently purchased $1.2-mil in products from ABI (over 11 days in 12/97).

Average director's annual compensation = $62,600

(assumes all meetings are attended and director sits on the Audit and Compensation committees)

STOCK-BASED COMPENSATION

None

COMPENSATION DEFERRAL

Eligible comp: Retainer/meeting
Account types: Cash and/or stock
Interest rate: Prime
Max. installments: 10 years
Payment: Date specified by Director

Comments: Interest is compounded quarterly; payouts are in cash, in lump sum or installments

CASH RETIREMENT BENEFITS

Cash plan terminated 12/95; present value of current directors' projected benefits were credited to deferred compensation accounts.

INSURANCE BENEFITS

Group Term Life: $50,000

OTHER BENEFITS

None

CHANGES

None

Aon Corporation

Industry: Nonbank Financial FY97 Revenue (mils): $5,751

BOARD STRUCTURE/FEES

	No. of Mtgs	Retainer Cash	Retainer Stock	Member Fee	Meeting Fee	Chairman Fee
Board	8	$20,000	675 shr	$ 750	$ —	$ —
Audit	3	—	—	750	1,000	2,500
Investment	5	—	—	750	1,000	2,500
Organization/Compensation	6	—	—	750	1,000	2,500
Nominating	0	—	—	750	1,000	2,500
Executive	1	—	—	750	1,000	—

Comments: The CFO serves on the board of a Compensation Committee member's firm.

Average director's annual compensation = $72,322

(assumes all meetings are attended and director sits on the Audit and Compensation committees)

STOCK-BASED COMPENSATION

Grant type(s):	**Stock Award**	**Deferred**
Number of shares:	675	$20,000
Frequency:	Annual	Annual
Vesting:	6 months	10% per year
Year-end stock price:	58.625	Same
Plan type:	Separate	Same
Plan kitty:	30,000	Same

Comments: Stock awards may be deferred to a stock unit account; award is reflected in "Average Annual Director's Comp" above; for service years before 1994 the amount contributed to deferred stock account is $10,000 per service year, up to $100,000; upon retirement, vested value is paid out in 10 installments of stock.

COMPENSATION DEFERRAL

Eligible comp: Retainer/meeting/stock award
Account types: Cash or stock
Interest rate: 1-year T-bills
Payment: Date specified by Director
Comments: (see STOCK also); payment date and schedule are elected by director.

CASH RETIREMENT BENEFITS

Mandatory retirement age: 72
(see STOCK)

INSURANCE BENEFITS

None

OTHER BENEFITS

Charitable award program
Amount: $1,000,000; payout: over 10 years to tax qualified institutions; life insurance funded

CHANGES

None

Apache Corporation

Industry: Oil & Gas

FY97 Revenue (mils): $1,176

BOARD STRUCTURE/FEES

	No. of Mtgs	Retainer Cash	Retainer Stock	Member Fee	Meeting Fee	Chairman Fee
Board	5	$20,000	$5,000	$ —	$ 1,000	$ —
Executive	0	—	—	2,000	1,000	4,000
Audit	6	—	—	2,000	1,000	4,000
Mgmt Development & Comp	6	—	—	2,000	1,000	4,000
Nominating	2	—	—	2,000	1,000	4,000
Stock Option Plan	7	—	—	2,000	1,000	4,000

Comments: A former subsidiary President/CEO and a retired company President serve on the Compensation Committee; 2 outside directors' companies operate wells in which Apache has interest (or visa versa)—one received $694,800 and paid Apache $482,000 in royalties in 1997, the second received $14.3-mil in royalties from Apache and paid $6.5-mil in drilling costs to Apache.

Average director's annual compensation = $46,000

(assumes all meetings are attended and director sits on the Audit and Compensation committees)

STOCK-BASED COMPENSATION

Grant type(s):	**Restricted**	**Stock Award**
Number of shares:	1,000	$5,000
Frequency:	5 years	Annual
Vesting:	1/5 per year	Immediate
Year-end stock price:	35.0625	Same
Plan type:	Separate	—
Plan life:	15 years	—
Plan kitty:	50,000	—

COMPENSATION DEFERRAL

Eligible comp: Retainer/meeting
Account types: Cash and/or stock
Interest rate: Company rate
Max. installments: 10 years
Payment: Date specified by director
Comments: Payouts may be in lump sum or installments.

CASH RETIREMENT BENEFITS

Basic benefits: 2/3 of retainer
Payment term: Matching service up to 10 years
Death benefit: Yes (spouse only)
Comments: Plan is unfunded.

INSURANCE BENEFITS

None

OTHER BENEFITS

None

CHANGES

- Added $5,000 stock retainer
- Added alternative to defer in stock accounts

Apple Computer, Inc.

Industry: Office Equipment & Services FY97 Revenue (mils): $7,081

BOARD STRUCTURE/FEES

	No. of Mtgs	Retainer Cash	Retainer Stock	Member Fee	Meeting Fee	Chairman Fee
Board	12	$ —	—	$ —	$ —	$ —
Audit & Finance	3	—	—	—	—	—
Director Affairs	3	—	—	—	—	—
Compensation	11	—	—	—	—	—

Average director's annual compensation = $0

(assumes all meetings are attended and director sits on the Audit and Compensation committees)

STOCK-BASED COMPENSATION

Grant type(s):	**Stock Option**
Number of shares:	10,000
Frequency:	Annual
Vesting:	Immediate
Year-end stock price:	13.125
Plan type:	Separate
Plan life:	10 years
Plan kitty:	400,000
COC Provisions:	Yes

Comments: Initial grants cover 30,000 options and then on the 4th anniversary of the initial grant annual 10,000 share grants begin.

COMPENSATION DEFERRAL

None

CASH RETIREMENT BENEFITS

None

INSURANCE BENEFITS

None

OTHER BENEFITS

None

CHANGES

- Eliminated annual retainer of $28,000 and $1,000 per Board meeting attended
- Added stock option grants

Ashland Inc.

Industry: Fuel

FY97 Revenue (mils): $13,567

BOARD STRUCTURE/FEES

	No. of Mtgs	Retainer Cash	Retainer Stock	Member Fee	Meeting Fee	Chairman Fee
Board	9	$30,000	—	$ —	$ 1,000	$ —
Audit	3	—	—	1,000	1,000	4,000
Directors	3	—	—	1,000	1,000	4,000
Personnel & Compensation	5	—	—	1,000	1,000	6,000
Finance	2	—	—	1,000	1,000	3,000
Public Policy/Environmental	1	—	—	1,000	1,000	2,000

Comments: Special assignment fee is $1,000 per day. Chairmen fee reflects additional $1,000 per committee meeting attended and additional $1,000 per year for committee service. Directors may elect to have fees paid in stock.

Average director's annual compensation = $49,000
(assumes all meetings are attended and director sits on the Audit and Compensation committees)

STOCK-BASED COMPENSATION

Grant type(s):	**Restricted**	**Stock Option/Incentive**
Number of shares:	1,000	1,000
Frequency:	5 years	Annual—if ROCE is 10% or more in preceding fiscal year
Vesting:	Retirement at age 70 or death/disability	6 months
Year-end stock price:	53.6875	Same
Plan type:	Separate	Same
Plan life:	10 years	Same
Plan kitty:	500,000	150,000 (out of 500,000)
COC provision:	Yes	Same

Comments: Directors must pay par value for restricted shares.

Stock Ownership Guidelines: 5x the annual retainer (must be achieved within 5 years)

COMPENSATION DEFERRAL

Eligible comp: Retainer/meeting
Account types: Cash and/or stock
Interest rate: 25 investment options
Max. installments: 20 years
Payment: After termination
COC provision: Yes

Comments: Compensation must be deferred in 25% increments; payouts may be lump sum or installments.

CASH RETIREMENT BENEFITS

Mandatory retirement age: 70

Cash plan terminated 1/97 except for current directors age 69 or greater who elected to continue in plan; the value of accrued benefits was converted to stock units for other current directors.

INSURANCE BENEFITS

None

OTHER BENEFITS

Terminated Charitable Award Program 1/97 for future directors

CHANGES

- Eliminated $1-mil charitable award program for future directors
- Changed deferral interest rate from prime to various investment options

AT&T Corporation

Industry: Telecommunications

FY97 Revenue (mils): $53,261

BOARD STRUCTURE/FEES

	No. of Mtgs	Retainer Cash	Retainer Stock	Member Fee	Meeting Fee	Chairman Fee
Board	17	$45,000	—	$ —	$ 0	$ —
Audit	5	—	—	—	0	7,500
Comp. & Empl. Benefits	9	—	—	—	0	7,500
Directors & Public Policy	4	—	—	—	0	5,000
Proxy	0	—	—	—	0	—
Executive	0	—	—	—	0	—
Finance	0	—	—	—	0	7,500

Comments: $1,500 fee paid for attendance at special Board or committee meetings

Average director's annual compensation = $45,000

(assumes all meetings are attended and director sits on the Audit and Compensation committees)

STOCK-BASED COMPENSATION

Grant type(s):	**Deferred Units**
Value of award:	$45,000
Frequency:	Annual
Year-end stock price:	61.3125
Plan type:	(deferral plan)

Ownership Guidelines: 5 times the annual cash retainer and deferred stock, within 5 years.

COMPENSATION DEFERRAL

Eligible comp: Retainer/meeting
Account types: Cash and/or stock
Interest rate: 10-year T-note +5%
Max. installments: 20 years

Comments: Immediate payout if ex-director competes or has conflict of interest; interest is compounded quarterly.

CASH RETIREMENT BENEFITS

Cash plan terminated 12/31/96; deferred annuities were purchased to pay equivalent benefit at retirement

INSURANCE BENEFITS

Travel/accident
Life

Comments: Company recaptures its expenses for life insurance at the earliest of (1) director's death, (2) age 70, or (3) 10 years after policy's inception; policy continues after retirement.

OTHER BENEFITS

None

CHANGES

- Increased cash retainer by $19,500
- Eliminated meeting attendance fees of $1,500
- Changed from mandatorily paying 15% of total annual retainer ($4,500) in deferred stock units to now granting $45,000 deferred stock units annually
- Eliminated cash retirement plan, purchasing annuities to pay benefit to current directors at retirement
- Added stock ownership guidelines

Ball Corporation

Industry: Containers & Packaging | FY97 Revenue (mils): $2,389

BOARD STRUCTURE/FEES

	No. of Mtgs	Retainer Cash	Retainer Stock	Member Fee	Meeting Fee	Chairman Fee
Board	6	$15,400	—	$ —	$ 1,000	$ —
Audit	3	—	—	—	750	3,000
Nominating	2	—	—	—	750	3,000
Human Resources	4	—	—	—	750	3,000
Executive	NA	—	—	—	1,000	—

Misc. fees: Special Assignments: $500 per day

Same day meeting fees: $750 paid for attending one or more committee meetings on same day

Comments: 50% of total fixed retainer value ($22,000) is paid in restricted stock; directors also receive an "incentive retainer" (or bonus) based on Ball's operating performance each year with a target = 40% of the "fixed" retainer; this is paid 50% in cash/50% in restricted stock. No bonus value was disclosed for 1997; however, executive bonuses were paid based on "above target performance of the corporation" and therefore the cash retainer above and the restricted stock grant below are calculated using a conservative bonus = 100% of target ($8,800) for directors.

Average director's annual compensation = $25,900

(assumes all meetings are attended and director sits on the Audit and Compensation committees)

STOCK-BASED COMPENSATION

Grant type(s):	**Restricted**	**Restricted**
Number of shares:	1,000	$15,400
Frequency:	3 years	Annual
Vesting:	Termination (except voluntary resignation)	Same
Year-end stock price:	35.375	Same
Plan type:	Separate	Combined with exec.
Plan kitty:	50,000	Same
COC provision:	Yes	Same

Comments: The 1997 Stock Incentive Plan provides for 50% of all retainers (fixed and "incentive") to be paid in restricted stock; no bonus value was disclosed for 1997 so for valuation purposes we used the 100% of target level or $8,800

COMPENSATION DEFERRAL

Eligible comp:	Retainer/meeting
Account types:	Cash
Interest rate:	Moody's Seasonal Corporate Bond + 5%
Max. installments:	15 years
Payment:	Date specified by Director

Comments: Backed by corporate owned life insurance policies; interest is credited annually.

CASH RETIREMENT BENEFITS

Mandatory retirement age: 70

Cash plan terminated 4/97 and accrued benefits converted to restricted stock

INSURANCE BENEFITS

None

OTHER BENEFITS

None

CHANGES

- Now require retainers to be paid 50% in cash/50% in restricted stock
- Eliminated cash retirement plan and converted accrued benefits to restricted stock

Baltimore Gas & Electric Company

Industry: Utilities FY97 Revenue (mils): $3,308

BOARD STRUCTURE/FEES

	No. of Mtgs	Retainer Cash	Retainer Stock	Member Fee	Meeting Fee	Chairman Fee
Board	10	$13,000	—	$ —	$1,250	$ —
Executive	0	—	—	—	1,250	3,500
Audit	3	—	—	—	1,250	3,500
Management (Comp. & Nomin)	7	—	—	—	1,250	3,500
Nuclear Power	3	—	—	—	1,250	3,500
Long Range Strategy	0	—	—	—	1,250	3,500
Workplace Diversity	2	—	—	—	1,250	3,500

Comments: Half of annual retainer value ($26,000) is mandatorily deferred in stock units; directors may elect to have additional amounts deferred; the COB/CEO serves on the Comp. Committee of a BG&E director's company.

Subsidiary fees: $20,000 annual retainer, $1,250 meeting attendance fees and $3,500 committee chairman's fee; 50% of retainers are mandatorily deferred

Average director's annual compensation = $38,000

(assumes all meetings are attended and director sits on the Audit and Compensation committees)

STOCK-BASED COMPENSATION

Grant type(s):	**Deferred Units**
Value of award	50% of retainer ($13,000)
Frequency:	Annual
Vesting	Termination
Year-end stock price	34.125

Comments: Half of annual retainer and committee chairman's fees are mandatorily deferred in stock units; payout at termination is in cash.

COMPENSATION DEFERRAL

Eligible comp: Retainer/meeting

Comments: 50% of annual retainer and committee chairman's fees are mandatorily deferred; directors may elect to defer additional amounts.

CASH RETIREMENT BENEFITS

Mandatory service: 5 years
Basic benefits: Retainer
Payment term: Life

Comments: Payment begins at the later of retirement or age 65.

INSURANCE BENEFITS

None

OTHER BENEFITS

Former COB/CEO who remains on the Board has company car for approximately $11,000/yr

CHANGES

- Increased total annual retainer value from $18,000 to $26,000, with half now deferred in stock units
- Increased meeting attendance fees by $250 each
- Increased Chairman's fee by $500
- Added requirement that half of annual retainer be deferred in stock units (also half of committee chairman fees)

The Bank of New York Company, Inc.

Industry: Banks

FY97 Revenue (mils): $5,697

BOARD STRUCTURE/FEES

	No. of Mtgs	Retainer Cash	Retainer Stock	Member Fee	Meeting Fee	Chairman Fee
Board	13	$30,000	1,200 shrs	$ —	$1,800	$ —
Executive	1	—	—	—	1,800	—
Nominating	2	—	—	—	1,800	3,000
Compensation & Organization	5	—	—	—	1,800	5,000
Audit	5	—	—	—	1,800	7,000
Pension	2	—	—	—	1,800	3,000

Comments: Fees are for service on corporate and bank boards.

Average director's annual compensation = $140,775

(assumes all meetings are attended and director sits on the Audit and Compensation committees)

STOCK-BASED COMPENSATION

Grant type(s):	**Stock Award**
Number of shares:	1,200
Frequency:	Annual
Year-end stock price:	57.8125

Comments: The value of the stock award is reflected in "Stock Retainer" and "Average Director's Annual Compensation" above.

COMPENSATION DEFERRAL

Eligible comp: Retainer/meeting
Account types: Cash and/or stock
Payment: After termination
COC provision: Yes
Comments: Payouts are in cash, except for stock fund accounts.

CASH RETIREMENT BENEFITS

Mandatory service: 5 years
Min. retirement age: 60
Basic benefits: 50–100% of retainer
Payment term: Matching service
Death benefit: No
COC provision Yes
Comments: 50% of retainer paid for 5 years' service and additional 10% for each additional year up to 100%. If director retires after age 70, benefit is paid for life.

INSURANCE BENEFITS

None

OTHER BENEFITS

None

CHANGES

- Increased cash retainer by $4,000

BankAmerica Corporation

Industry: Banks FY97 Revenue (mils): $23,585

BOARD STRUCTURE/FEES

	No. of Mtgs	Retainer Cash	Retainer Stock	Member Fee	Meeting Fee	Chairman Fee
Board	10	$20,000	—	$ —	$ 1,500	$ —
Audit & Examining	8	—	—	7,500	1,500	7,500
Executive	5	—	—	—	1,500	5,000
Exec. Personnel & Comp	5	—	—	—	1,500	8,000
Nominating	5	—	—	—	1,500	5,000
Public Policy	5	—	—	—	1,500	5,000

Comments: Retainer includes service on BAC and Bank boards. 50% of total retainer ($40,000) is paid in restricted units (see STOCK). One director's company has significant loans with the bank and he has a personal line of credit of $4-mil.

Average director's annual compensation = $62,000

(assumes all meetings are attended and director sits on the Audit and Compensation committees)

STOCK-BASED COMPENSATION

Grant type(s):	**Restricted Units**
Value of award:	$20,000
Frequency:	Annual
Vesting:	At termination
Year-end stock price:	73.00
Plan type:	(deferral plan)

Ownership Guidelines: 3 times annual retainer within 5 years

COMPENSATION DEFERRAL

Eligible comp: Retainer/meeting
Account types: Cash/stock
Payment: Upon termination
Comments: Mandatory 50% of retainer is deferred in share unit account; amounts are paid in cash in lump sum or installments.

CASH RETIREMENT BENEFITS

Mandatory retirement age: 70
Cash plan terminated 3/96; accrued benefits converted to restricted stock units under the deferred plan (directors with >10 years service could elect to continue participation in the cash plan, but none did).

INSURANCE BENEFITS

None

OTHER BENEFITS

None

CHANGES

- Increased chairman's fees by $2,000 (by $5,000 for Executive Personnel & Compensation)
- Increased meeting attendance fees by $300 each

Baxter International Inc.

Industry: Health Care | FY97 Revenue (mils): $6,138

BOARD STRUCTURE/FEES

	No. of Mtgs	Retainer Cash	Retainer Stock	Member Fee	Meeting Fee	Chairman Fee
Board	7	$ 0	—	$ —	$ 1,000	$ —
Executive	0	—	—	—	1,000	4,000
Audit	5	—	—	3,000	1,000	4,000
Compensation	4	—	—	3,000	1,000	4,000
Finance	6	—	—	3,000	1,000	4,000
Planning & Organization	5	—	—	3,000	1,000	4,000
Public Policy	3	—	—	3,000	1,000	4,000

Average director's annual compensation = $22,000

(assumes all meetings are attended and director sits on the Audit and Compensation committees)

STOCK-BASED COMPENSATION

Grant type(s):	**Restricted**	**Restricted**	**Deferred**
Number of shares:	3,000	1,000	1,000 per service year
Frequency:	3 years	3 years	At retirement
Vesting:	1/3 per year	1/3 per year	6 months after grant
Year-end stock price:	50.4375	Same	Same
Plan type:	Separate	Same	Same
COC provision:	Yes	Same	Same

Comments: 3,000-share grants made each 3 years are intended to replace a prior annual cash retainer of $25,000.

COMPENSATION DEFERRAL

Eligible comp: Meeting fees

Comments: no additional information disclosed

CASH RETIREMENT BENEFITS

Mandatory service: 5 years

Minimum retirement age: 65

Basic benefits: 1,000 shares deferred stock per year of service

Comments: Shares vest after 6 months

INSURANCE BENEFITS

Medical/dental

Life insurance

OTHER BENEFITS

None

CHANGES

None

Beckman Coulter, Inc. (formerly Beckman Instruments, Inc.)

Industry: Electronics FY97 Revenue (mils): $1,198

BOARD STRUCTURE/FEES

	No. of Mtgs	Retainer Cash	Retainer Stock	Member Fee	Meeting Fee	Chairman Fee
Board	7	$22,000	—	$ —	$1,000	$ —
Audit	6	—	—	—	1,000	3,000
Organization & Comp	5	—	—	—	1,000	2,500
Finance	6	—	—	—	1,000	3,000
Nominating	5	—	—	—	1,000	2,500

Comments: Additional meeting fee equal to Board meeting fee for each day or significant part of day spent on company business (not payable to a director who receives consulting fees). Chairman fees reflect additional $500 per meeting attended.

Average director's annual compensation = $40,000

(assumes all meetings are attended and director sits on the Audit and Compensation committees)

STOCK-BASED COMPENSATION

Grant type(s):	**Stock Option**	**Restricted**
Number of shares:	2,000	100
Frequency:	Annual	Annual
Vesting:	6 months	1/3 per year
Year-end stock price:	40.00	Same
Plan type:	Combined w/ exec	Same

COMPENSATION DEFERRAL

Eligible comp: Retainer/meeting
Account types: Stock
Payment: After termination

Comment: Accounts are paid out in cash. Beginning in 1998, deferred amounts receive a premium of up to 30% depending on the percentage of annual compensation deferred above 40% to 100%.

CASH RETIREMENT BENEFITS

Mandatory retirement age: 70

None

INSURANCE BENEFITS

None

OTHER BENEFITS

None

CHANGES

- Added deferral premium
- Stock plan amended 10/97 to increase grants from 1,000 to 2,000 options and add restricted stock grants
- New executive stock plan includes directors and replaces the previous director stock plan

Becton Dickinson and Company

Industry: Health Care

FY97 Revenue (mils): $2,811

BOARD STRUCTURE/FEES

	No. of Mtgs	Retainer Cash	Retainer Stock	Member Fee	Meeting Fee	Chairman Fee
Board	7	$45,000	—	$ —	$ —	$ —
Audit	3	—	—	—	1,000	2,000
Compensation & Benefits	5	—	—	—	1,000	2,000
Corporate Responsibility	3	—	—	—	1,000	2,000
Directors	2	—	—	—	1,000	2,000

Comments: $1,000 fee paid for "special" Board meetings; one director received $65,000 for consulting in 1997.

Average director's annual compensation = $53,000

(assumes all meetings are attended and director sits on the Audit and Compensation committees)

STOCK-BASED COMPENSATION

Grant type(s):	**Deferred Stock**
Number of shares:	400
Frequency:	Annual
Vesting:	After retirement
Year-end stock price:	50.00
Plan type:	(deferral plan)

Ownership guidelines: Within 5 years of inception, directors own stock equal to at least five times the annual retainer.

COMPENSATION DEFERRAL

Eligible comp: Retainer/meeting
Account types: Cash and/or stock
Payment: After termination
Max. installments: 10 years
Comments: No additional information disclosed

CASH RETIREMENT BENEFITS

Mandatory retirement age: 72

Cash plan terminated 12/1/96 and accrued benefits frozen; current directors could elect to (1) receive the present value of accrued benefits, or (2) enter in a consulting agreement and following retirement receive the then current retainer paid for the number of years matching service up to 12/96.

INSURANCE BENEFITS

None

OTHER BENEFITS

None

CHANGES

None

Bell Atlantic Corporation

Industry: Telecommunications FY97 Revenue (mils): $30,194

BOARD STRUCTURE/FEES

	No. of Mtgs	Retainer Cash	Retainer Stock	Member Fee	Meeting Fee	Chairman Fee
Board	9	$30,000	—	$ —	$1,500	$ —
Executive	1	—	—	—	1,500	5,000
Audit	5	—	—	—	1,500	5,000
Human Resources	11	—	—	—	1,500	5,000
Finance	5	—	—	—	1,500	5,000
Governance & Board Affairs	2	—	—	—	1,500	5,000
Public Responsibility	1	—	—	—	1,500	5,000

Average director's annual compensation = $67,500

(assumes all meetings are attended and director sits on the Audit and Compensation committees)

STOCK-BASED COMPENSATION

Grant type(s):	**Stock Option**	**Stock Option**
Number of shares:	1,000	1,500
Frequency:	Annual	Annual
Vesting:	12 months	Same
Year-end stock price:	91.00	Same
Plan type:	Separate	Same
Plan kitty:	100,000	Same

Comments: Directors may elect to receive shares, in lieu of the 1,500 stock options, with an equivalent value.

COMPENSATION DEFERRAL

Eligible comp: Retainer/meeting
Account types: Cash and/or stock
Interest rate: 10-year T-note
Max. installments: 10 years

Comments: Stock accounts are paid out in stock; installment period is capped at director's life expectancy.

CASH RETIREMENT BENEFITS

Mandatory retirement age: 70
Cash plan terminated 11/95 and replaced with additional stock options

INSURANCE BENEFITS

Travel/accident
Life

OTHER BENEFITS

Charitable Award Program was discontinued for directors elected after 1992.

CHANGES

- Increased annual retainer by $3,000
- Increased meeting attendance fees by $250 each

Bestfoods (formerly CPC International, Inc.)

Industry: Food

FY97 Revenue (mils): $9,818

BOARD STRUCTURE/FEES

	No. of	Retainer		Member	Meeting	Chairman
	Mtgs	Cash	Stock	Fee	Fee	Fee
Board	10	$30,000	—	$ —	$1,250	$ —
Audit	3	—	—	—	1,250	3,000
Compensation & Nominating	4	—	—	—	1,250	3,000
Corporate Affairs	3	—	—	—	1,250	3,000
Finance	3	—	—	—	1,250	3,000

Comments: $1,250 per day paid for visits to other company facilities. 50% of total retainer ($60,000) is mandatorily deferred in stock (see STOCK).

Average director's annual compensation = $51,250
(assumes all meetings are attended and director sits on the Audit and Compensation committees)

STOCK-BASED COMPENSATION

Grant type(s):	**Deferred**	**Deferred**
Value of award:	50% of Retainer ($30,000)	100 shares
Frequency:	Annual	Annual
Vesting:	6 months after Termination	Same
Year-end stock price:	108.00	Same
Plan type:	(deferral plan)	Same
COC provision:	Yes	Same

Comments: 50% of annual retainer is mandatorily deferred in stock.

COMPENSATION DEFERRAL

Eligible comp: Retainer/meeting
Account types: Cash and/or stock
Interest rate: Variable
Max. Installments: 10 years
Payment: After termination
COC provision Yes

Comments: no more than 10,000 shares may be credited to all directors' stock accounts per year; stock accounts may be paid in cash or shares.

CASH RETIREMENT BENEFITS

Mandatory retirement age: 70
Cash plan terminated 5/96 and the present value of accrued benefits converted to deferred stock units.

INSURANCE BENEFITS

Group Term Life: $100,000
Travel/Accident: $175,000

OTHER BENEFITS

Charitable Award Program
Amount: $1,000,000; payout: over 10 years to up to four educational institutions; life insurance funded
Matching Gift Program—up to $5,000 to charities will be double matched each year

CHANGES

- Increased meeting attendance fees by $250 each
- Added 100 shares of mandatorily deferred stock

Beverly Enterprises, Inc.

Industry: Health Care FY97 Revenue (mils): $3,230

BOARD STRUCTURE/FEES

	No. of Mtgs	Retainer Cash	Retainer Stock	Member Fee	Meeting Fee	Chairman Fee
Board	8	$25,000	—	$ —	$1,000	$ —
Audit	3	—	—	—	1,000	3,000
Quality Management	5	—	—	—	1,000	5,000
Compensation	4	—	—	—	1,000	4,000
Nominating	2	—	—	—	1,000	2,000
Executive	5	—	—	—	1,000	5,000

Comments: Chairman's fee reflects $1,000 per meeting attended.; one director was paid $50,000 for consulting in 1997.

Average director's annual compensation = $40,000

(assumes all meetings are attended and director sits on the Audit and Compensation committees)

STOCK-BASED COMPENSATION

Grant type(s):	**Stock Option**	**Deferred Units**
Number of shares:	3,375	675
Frequency:	Annual	Annual
Vesting:	1 year	After termination
Year-end stock price:	13.00	Same
Plan type:	Separate	(Deferral plan)
Plan life:	10 years	—
Plan kitty:	200,000	—
COC provision:	Yes	—

COMPENSATION DEFERRAL

Eligible comp: Retainer/meeting
Account types: Cash and/or stock
Interest rate: Prime
Max. installments: 10 years
Payment: After termination

Comments: the company matches 25% of fees that are voluntarily deferred in stock units; payouts may be lump sum or installments.

CASH RETIREMENT BENEFITS

Cash plan terminated 5/97 and replaced with deferred unit grants (see STOCK); no information disclosed about accrued benefits

INSURANCE BENEFITS

None

OTHER BENEFITS

None

CHANGES

None

The Black & Decker Corporation

Industry: Manufacturing

FY97 Revenue (mils): $4,941

BOARD STRUCTURE/FEES

	No. of Mtgs	Retainer: Cash	Retainer: Stock	Member Fee	Meeting Fee	Chairman Fee
Board	5	Value of 500 shrs	500 shrs	$ —	$ —	$ —
Executive	0	—	—	—	—	50 shrs + value of 50 shrs
Organization	5	—	—	—	—	"
Audit	3	—	—	—	—	"
Finance	5	—	—	—	—	"

Comments: Directors may elect to have cash fees paid in stock; stock may be deferred. The Organization Committee performs compensation and nominating functions. Former COB is part-time employee/consultant for $150,000 per year. *Note: for analysis purposes the cash retainer and chairman's fees were calculated using a stock price of $39.0625, or $19,531 for the cash retainer and $3,906 for the chairman's fees.*

Average director's annual compensation = $39,062

(assumes all meetings are attended and director sits on the Audit and Compensation committees)

STOCK-BASED COMPENSATION

Grant type(s):	**Stock Option**	**Stock Award**
Number of shares:	2,500	500
Frequency:	Annual	Annual
Vesting:	1 year	Immediate
Year-end stock price:	39.0625	Same
Plan type:	Separate	Separate
Plan life:	10 years	10 years
Plan kitty:	150,000	100,000
COC provision:	Yes	Yes

COMPENSATION DEFERRAL

Eligible comp: Retainer/stock

Account types: Stock

CASH RETIREMENT BENEFITS

Cash plan frozen in 1997

INSURANCE BENEFITS

Travel/Accident: $200,000

Term Life: $100,000

OTHER BENEFITS

None

CHANGES

- Eliminated meeting attendance fees of $1,500 per meeting
- Changed chairman's fee from $5,000 to 50 shares of stock + cash equal to the value of 50 shares
- Replaced $30,000 cash retainer with the cash value of 500 shares of stock
- Added stock retainer
- Increased stock option grants by 1,000 shares
- Changed deferral plan from cash-based to stock-based
- Froze cash retirement plan

BMC Software, Inc.

Industry: Office Equipment & Services — FY97 Revenue (mils): $731

BOARD STRUCTURE/FEES

	No. of Mtgs	Retainer Cash	Retainer Stock	Member Fee	Meeting Fee	Chairman Fee
Board	8	$20,000	—	$ —	$ 1,000	$ —
Audit	1	—	—	—	1,000	—
Compensation	5	—	—	—	1,000	—

Comments: Directors receive $1,000 for attendance at Board meetings in excess of 5 each year.

Same day fees: no fee paid for committee meetings held on the same day as a Board meeting

Average director's annual compensation = $23,000

(assumes all meetings are attended and director sits on the Audit and Compensation committees)

STOCK-BASED COMPENSATION

Grant type(s):	**Stock Option**
Number of shares:	10,000
Frequency:	Annual
Vesting	6.25% each quarter over 5 years
Year-end stock price	65.625
Plan type	Separate
Plan life	10 years
Plan kitty	400,000
COC provision	Yes

Comments: Upon initial election grants cover 20,000 options.

COMPENSATION DEFERRAL

None

CASH RETIREMENT BENEFITS

None

INSURANCE BENEFITS

None

OTHER BENEFITS

None

CHANGES

None

Bob Evans Farms, Inc.

Industry: Leisure

FY97 Revenue (mils): $822

BOARD STRUCTURE/FEES

	No. of Mtgs	Retainer Cash	Retainer Stock	Member Fee	Meeting Fee	Chairman Fee
Board	4	$26,400	—	$ —	$ —	$ —
Audit	3	—	—	—	500	600
Comp & Stock Option	4	—	—	—	500	800

Attendance requirement: Directors who do not attend monthly meetings have $500 deducted from monthly retainer fee.

Comments: Employee directors receive $12,000 per year for Board service; committee chairmen receive additional $200 per meeting attended.

Average director's annual compensation = $29,900

(assumes all meetings are attended and director sits on the Audit and Compensation committees)

STOCK-BASED COMPENSATION

Grant type(s):	**Stock Option**
Number of shares:	5,133
Frequency:	5 years
Vesting:	Undisclosed
Option life:	5 years
Year-end stock price:	22.125
Plan type:	Separate
Plan life:	Indefinite
Plan kitty:	73,333
COC provision:	Yes

COMPENSATION DEFERRAL

None

CASH RETIREMENT BENEFITS

None

INSURANCE BENEFITS

Life: $50,000
Group Hospitalization

OTHER BENEFITS

None

CHANGES

- Increased annual retainer fee by $2,400
- Increased meeting attendance fee by $50 each
- Added chairman's fees
- Added group hospitalization insurance

The Boeing Company

Industry: Aerospace — FY97 Revenue (mils): $45,800

BOARD STRUCTURE/FEES

	No. of Mtgs	Retainer Cash	Retainer Stock	Member Fee	Meeting Fee	Chairman Fee
Board	7	$26,000	—	$ —	$ 2,000	$ —
Audit	5	—	—	6,000	1,000	4,000
Compensation	7	—	—	6,000	1,000	4,000
Finance	5	—	—	6,000	1,000	4,000
Organization & Nominating	6	—	—	6,000	1,000	4,000

Same Day Meeting Fees: $1,000 paid for committee meetings held on days other than Board meetings

Comments: One committee member fee and chairman fee covers all committee service; $10,000 of total retainer value ($36,000) is mandatorily deferred in stock units; the former COB/CEO has a consulting agreement for $264,334; one retiring director has a consulting agreement for $27,000 per quarter.

Average director's annual compensation = $46,000

(assumes all meetings are attended and director sits on the Audit and Compensation committees)

STOCK-BASED COMPENSATION

Grant type(s):	**Stock Option**	**Deferred Units**
Number of shares:	1,200	$10,000
Frequency:	Annual	Annual
Vesting:	40% 1st yr, 30% 3rd & 5th yr	After termination
Year-end stock price:	48.9375	Same
Plan type:	Separate	(Deferral plan)
Plan life:	Indefinite	—
Plan kitty:	0.008% of shares outstanding each year	Same

Comments: Initial grant covers 1,500 shares; options vest one year after grant but become exercisable according to the schedule above.

COMPENSATION DEFERRAL

Eligible comp: Retainer/meeting
Account types: Cash and/or stock
Payment: After termination
Comments: Stock units are distributed in shares.

CASH RETIREMENT BENEFITS

Mandatory retirement age: 72
None

INSURANCE BENEFITS

None

OTHER BENEFITS

None

CHANGES

None

Boise Cascade Corporation

Industry: Paper/Forest

FY97 Revenue (mils): $5,493

BOARD STRUCTURE/FEES

	No. of Mtgs	Retainer Cash	Retainer Stock	Member Fee	Meeting Fee	Chairman Fee
Board	6	$30,000	—	$ —	$ 1,500	$ —
Executive	2	—	—	—	600	6,500
Outside Directors	2	—	—	—	600	6,500
Audit	3	—	—	—	600	6,500
Executive Compensation	5	—	—	—	600	6,500
Nominating	4	—	—	—	600	6,500

Misc. Fees: Telephone meetings: $600; actions by consent in lieu of meeting: $600

Comments: Directors may elect to have retainers and fees paid in discounted stock options (see STOCK).

Average director's annual compensation = $43,800

(assumes all meetings are attended and director sits on the Audit and Compensation committees)

STOCK-BASED COMPENSATION

Grant type(s):	**Discount Option**	**Stock Option**
Number of shares:	As elected by Director	1,500
Frequency:	Annual	Annual
Exercise price:	$2.50 per share	FMV
Vesting:	6 months	1 year
Option expiration:	3 years after termination	Same
Year-end stock price:	30.25	Same
Plan type:	Separate	Separate
Plan life:	10 years	10 years
Plan kitty:	100,000	100,000
COC provision:	Yes	Yes

Comments: Committee may adjust the number of options granted annually, up to once per year (at least 6 months prior to the grant date).

COMPENSATION DEFERRAL

Eligible comp: Retainer/meeting
Account types: Cash
Interest rate: 130% of Moody's
COC provision: Yes

Comments: 1983 plan rate = Moody's Corp Bond Avg +4%; since 1987, rate = 130% of Moody's; funded with corporate-owned life insurance policies held in a rabbi trust

CASH RETIREMENT BENEFITS

None

INSURANCE BENEFITS

None

OTHER BENEFITS

None

CHANGES

None

Bowater Inc.

Industry: Paper & Forest — FY97 Revenue (mils): $1,485

BOARD STRUCTURE/FEES

	No. of Mtgs	Retainer Cash	Retainer Stock	Member Fee	Meeting Fee	Chairman Fee
Board	8	$24,000	—	$ —	$1,000	$ —
Executive	1	—	—	—	800	—
Audit	3	—	—	—	800	—
Human Res & Compensation	4	—	—	—	800	—
Nominating & Governance	3	—	—	—	800	—
Finance	3	—	—	—	800	—

Average director's annual compensation = $37,600

(assumes all meetings are attended and director sits on the Audit and Compensation committees)

STOCK-BASED COMPENSATION

Grant type(s):	**Stock Option**
Number of shares:	1,000
Frequency:	Annual
Year-end stock price:	44.4375
Plan type:	Combined with exec.

Comments: Plan provides for discretionary grants to outside directors, who received 1,000 options in 1997.

COMPENSATION DEFERRAL

Eligible comp: Retainer/meeting
Account types: Cash and/or stock
Interest rate: Company
Payment: After termination
Max. installments: 10 years

Comments: Deferrals must be in 10% increments; shares are credited at FMV with a 5% discount; payout may be in lump sum or installments; may be paid in cash or stock; directors may transfer funds between cash/stock accounts.

CASH RETIREMENT BENEFITS

Mandatory service: 5 years
Minimum retirement age: 65
Basic benefits: 10% of retainer times years of service (up to 10 years)
Payment term: Life
Reduced benefit available: Yes
COC provision: Yes

Comments: a reduced payout is available for approved retirement after age 55 with 5 years of service.

INSURANCE BENEFITS

None

OTHER BENEFITS

None

CHANGES

None

Bristol-Myers Squibb Company

Industry: Health Care FY97 Revenue (mils): $16,701

BOARD STRUCTURE/FEES

	No. of Mtgs	Retainer Cash	Retainer Stock	Member Fee	Meeting Fee	Chairman Fee
Board	10	$26,250	—	$ —	$2,000	$ —
Audit	3	—	—	—	2,000	10,000
Compensation & Mgmt Devel	5	—	—	—	2,000	10,000
Directors & Corp. Goverrn	2	—	—	—	2,000	10,000
Executive	0	—	—	—	2,000	10,000

Comments: 25% of the annual retainer ($35,000) is mandatorily deferred in stock (see DEFERRAL), until stock ownership guidelines are attained (undisclosed); $2,000 for attendance at annual stockholders' meeting

Average director's annual compensation = $62,250

(assumes all meetings are attended and director sits on the Audit and Compensation committees)

STOCK-BASED COMPENSATION

Grant type(s):	**Stock Option**	**Deferred**	**Deferred Units**
Number of shares:	2,000	$8,750	500
Frequency:	Annual	Annual	Annual
Vesting:	25% per year	—	Undisclosed
Year-end stock price:	94.625	Same	Same
Plan type:	Separate	—	—
Plan life:	10 years	—	—
Plan kitty:	250,000	—	—

Ownership Guidelines: undisclosed (25% of annual retainer is mandatorily deferred in stock until guidelines are met)

COMPENSATION DEFERRAL

Eligible comp:	Retainer/meeting
Account types:	Cash and/or Stock
Interest rate:	6 month T-bill
Payment:	Date specified by Director
Max. installments:	10 years

Comments: 25% of annual retainer is mandatorily deferred in stock.

CASH RETIREMENT BENEFITS

Cash plan terminated 3/96 and all benefits vested. It appears the deferred stock units (above) replaced this benefit.

INSURANCE BENEFITS

None

OTHER BENEFITS

Charitable Award Program

Amount: $1,000,000; payout: 50% to BMS Foundation; 50% to up to five director-named charities; life insurance funded

CHANGES

- Increased deferred units by 200 shares per year

Browning-Ferris Industries, Inc.

Industry: Service Industries — FY97 Revenue (mils): $5,783

BOARD STRUCTURE/FEES

	No. of Mtgs	Retainer Cash	Retainer Stock	Member Fee	Meeting Fee	Chairman Fee
Board	6	$20,000	—	$ —	$1,000	$ —
Executive	2	—	—	10,000	—	—
Audit	2	—	—	8,000	500	4,000
Compensation	5	—		6,000	500	3,000
Corp. Responsibility	1	—	—	4,000	500	2,000
Director & Corp. Governance	4	—	—	4,000	500	2,000

Comments: 1/3 of annual retainer (currently $30,000) paid in restricted stock (see STOCK); Chairman of Executive and Finance committees (and all members of the Executive Committee) are employee directors.

Average director's annual compensation = $43,500

(assumes all meetings are attended and director sits on the Audit and Compensation committees)

STOCK-BASED COMPENSATION

Grant type(s):	**Restricted**	**Stock Option**
Award value:	$10,000	—
Number of shares:	—	2,500
Frequency:	Annual	Annual
Vesting:	3 years	25% per year
Year-end stock price	37.00	Same
Plan type	Separate	Same
Plan life:	10 years	Same
Plan kitty:	250,000	Same
COC provision:	Yes	Same

Comments: 1/3 of annual retainer fee paid in restricted stock; stock option repricing not allowed; initial stock option grants cover 5,000 shares.

COMPENSATION DEFERRAL

Eligible comp: Retainer/meeting
Account types: Cash/stock
Payment: Date specified by Director

CASH RETIREMENT BENEFITS

None

INSURANCE BENEFITS

None

OTHER BENEFITS

Company makes cash contributions directly to some organizations with which directors are affiliated (not a legacy donation program)

CHANGES

None

Brunswick Corporation

Industry: Leisure

FY97 Revenue (mils): $3,657

BOARD STRUCTURE/FEES

	No. of Mtgs	Retainer Cash	Retainer Stock	Member Fee	Meeting Fee	Chairman Fee
Board	9	$25,000	$25,000	$—	$—	—
Audit & Finance	5	—	—	—	—	$7,500
Human Res & Compensation	7	—	—	—	—	7,500
Executive	0	—	—	—	—	—
Corp. Governance	7	—	—	—	—	7,500

Comment: 50% of annual retainer and chairman fees are paid in stock; directors may elect to have all fees paid in stock; all stock may be deferred.

Average director's annual compensation = $50,000

(assumes all meetings are attended and director sits on the Audit and Compensation committees)

STOCK-BASED COMPENSATION

Grant type(s):	**Stock Option**	**Stock Award**	**Stock Award**
Number of shares:	3,000	$25,000	$25,000
Frequency:	Annual	Annual	One-time
Vesting:	50% per year	Immediate	Immediate
Year-end stock price:	30.3125	Same	Same
Plan type:	Separate	Separate	Same
Plan life:	10 years	Undisclosed	Same
Plan kitty:	200,000	250,000	Same
COC provision:	Yes	Yes	Same

Comments: Value of the annual stock award is reflected in "Stock Retainer" and "Average Director's Annual Compensation" above.

COMPENSATION DEFERRAL

Eligible comp: Retainer/Chairman fees/stock
Account types: Stock
Max. Installments: 15 years
Payment: After retirement
COC provision Yes

CASH RETIREMENT BENEFITS

Mandatory retirement age: 70

Cash plan was terminated in 1995 and one-time stock award (above) replaces retirement benefits

INSURANCE BENEFITS

None

OTHER BENEFITS

Company products may be purchased at dealers' net cost; boats may be used for 2 years at no cost; other products up to $1,500 may be received

CHANGES

- Eliminated meeting attendance fees of $1,500 and added $25,000 cash retainer
- Increased chairman's fee by $2,500
- Changed from $25,000 per year stock options to 3,000 shares
- Changed one-time grant of deferred stock to one-time grant of common stock

Burlington Resources Inc.

Industry: Fuel FY97 Revenue (mils): $2,000

BOARD STRUCTURE/FEES

	No. of Mtgs	Retainer Cash	Retainer Stock	Member Fee	Meeting Fee	Chairman Fee
Board	8	$55,000	—	$ —	$ —	$ —
Audit	2	—	—	—	—	—
Compensation & Nominating	5	—	—	—	—	—

Average director's annual compensation = $55,000

(assumes all meetings are attended and director sits on the Audit and Compensation committees)

STOCK-BASED COMPENSATION

Grant type(s):	**Stock Option**	**Deferred**
Number of shares:	1,000	500
Frequency:	Annual	Annual
Vesting:	Immediate	Termination
Year-end stock price:	44.8125	Same
Plan type:	Separate	Separate
Plan kitty:	100,000	—

Comments: initial stock option grant covers 3,000 shares; payouts of deferred stock accounts made in cash

COMPENSATION DEFERRAL

Eligible comp: Retainer/meeting

Comments: no additional information disclosed.

CASH RETIREMENT BENEFITS

Cash plan terminated in 1995 and replaced with deferred stock grants (above)

INSURANCE BENEFITS

None

OTHER BENEFITS

Charitable Award Program

Amount: $1,000,000; payout: donations may go to one or more educational institutions or private foundations; mandatory service: 2 years

CHANGES

None

Campbell Soup Company

Industry: Food

FY97 Revenue (mils): $7,964

BOARD STRUCTURE/FEES

	No. of Mtgs	Retainer Cash	Retainer Stock	Member Fee	Meeting Fee	Chairman Fee
Board	14	$0	2,400 shr	$ —	$1,250	$ —
Audit	3	—	—		1,000	4,000
Comp & Organization	7	—	—	—	1,000	4,000
Executive	0	—	—	—	1,000	—
Finance & Corp. Develop	7	—	—	—	1,000	4,000
Governance	5	—	—	—	1,000	4,000
Retirement	2	—	—	—	1,000	4,000

Comments: Director may elect to receive all compensation in stock; VCOB or lead director receives additional retainer of $25,000 in cash; one director received additional $25,000 as chairman of special Succession Committee

Average director's annual compensation = $167,000

(assumes all meetings are attended and director sits on the Audit and Compensation committees)

STOCK-BASED COMPENSATION

Grant type(s):	**Stock Award**	**Stock Options**
Number of shares:	2,400	2,000
Frequency:	Annual	Annual
Vesting:	—	Over 3 years
Year-end stock price:	58.125	Same
Plan type	Combined w/exec.	Same

Comments: stock award is reflected under "Stock Retainer" and "Average Director's Annual Compensation" above.

Ownership Guidelines: directors must own at least 2,000 shares within 1 yr after election and 6,000 shares within 3 years

COMPENSATION DEFERRAL

Eligible Comp: Meeting fees

Comments: No additional information disclosed.

CASH RETIREMENT BENEFITS

Mandatory retirement age: 70

Cash plan terminated 1/1/96 and accrued benefits liquidated.

INSURANCE BENEFITS

None

OTHER BENEFITS

None

CHANGES

None

Caterpillar, Inc.

Industry: Manufacturing FY97 Revenue (mils): $18,925

BOARD STRUCTURE/FEES

	No. of Mtgs	Retainer Cash	Retainer Stock	Member Fee	Meeting Fee	Chairman Fee
Board	6	$30,000	—	$ —	$1,000	$ —
Audit	3	—	—	—	1,000	5,000
Nominating	2	—	—	—	1,000	5,000
Compensation	3	—	—	—	1,000	5,000
Public Policy	3	—	—	—	1,000	5,000

Average director's annual compensation = $42,000

(assumes all meetings are attended and director sits on the Audit and Compensation committees)

STOCK-BASED COMPENSATION

Grant type(s):	Stock Option	Restricted	Deferred
Number of shares:	4,000	400	350
Frequency:	Annual	Annual	Annual
Vesting:	1/3 per year	3 years	Termination
Year-end stock price:	48.50	Same	Same
Plan type:	Combined w/ exec	Same	Same
COC provision:	Yes	Same	Same

Comments: continued service is not required for vesting.

COMPENSATION DEFERRAL

Eligible comp: 50% or more of Retainer
Account types: Cash and/or stock
Interest rate: Prime

CASH RETIREMENT BENEFITS

Mandatory retirement age: 72

Cash plan terminated 12/31/96 with the value of accrued benefits converted to restricted stock and held in escrow until termination of service; in the future awards of restricted stock are increased by 350 shares that will vest after service termination

INSURANCE BENEFITS

None

OTHER BENEFITS

Charitable Award Program

Amount: $1,000,000; payout: 10 installments (first five installments to director-selected charities and last five installments paid to Caterpillar Charitable Foundation); life insurance funded

CHANGES

None

CBS Corporation

Industry: Electronics FY97 Revenue (mils): $9,632

BOARD STRUCTURE/FEES

	No. of Mtgs	Retainer Cash	Retainer Stock	Member Fee	Meeting Fee	Chairman Fee
Board	15	$30,000	$25,000	$ —	$ —	$ —
Audit Review	3	—	—	—	—	5,000
Compensation	9	—	—	—	—	5,000
Environment & Health	1	—	—	—	—	5,000
Nominating & Governance	4	—	—	—	—	5,000

Comments: Chairman fees are paid in stock; $1,200 per day per diem is paid for special services performed outside normal board activities; one director received $6,000 for special services in 1997

Attendance requirements: retainers are forfeited on a pro-rata basis if a 75% attendance level is not met.

Average director's annual compensation = $55,000
(assumes all meetings are attended and director sits on the Audit and Compensation committees)

STOCK-BASED COMPENSATION

Grant type(s):	Stock Option	Stock Award
Value of award:	$25,000	$25,000
Frequency:	Annual	Annual
Vesting:	Jan 1st following grant if attendance requirements met	Same
Yr-end stock price	29.4375	Same
Plan type	Separate	Same
Plan kitty	600,000	Same
COC provision	Yes	Same

Comments: all shares paid and shares received upon exercise of options must be held for (a) 3 years from exercise or (b) 2 years from termination; the value of the stock award is reflected in "Stock Retainer" and "Average Director's Annual Compensation" above.

COMPENSATION DEFERRAL

Eligible comp: Retainer/meeting
Account types: Cash and/or stock
Interest rate: 1-year T-bill
Max. installments: 5 years
Payment: After termination
COC provision: Yes

Comments: deferrals are denoted in convertible debentures with a face value of $100, earning interest; payout = greater of (1) deferred amount + interest or (2) shares + interest.

CASH RETIREMENT BENEFITS

Cash plan terminated and present value of benefits deferred until directors' retirement

INSURANCE BENEFITS

Accidental Death/Disability: $500,000
Comments: covers directors when on company business.

OTHER BENEFITS

Charitable Award Program eliminated in 1996

Matching Gift Program: up to $2,000/year for educational institutions or $1,000 for charities

CHANGES

- Increased stock option grant by $10,000 and restricted stock by $10,000
- eliminated practices of setting a premium exercise price (125% of FMV) on 1/3rd of options granted
- Changed deferral interest from a link with convertible debentures (with interest at 10-year T-bond rate) to a simple 1-year T-bill rate

Ceridian Corporation

Industry: Office Equipment & Services | FY97 Revenue (mils): $1,664

BOARD STRUCTURE/FEES

	No. of Mtgs	Retainer Cash	Retainer Stock	Member Fee	Meeting Fee	Chairman Fee
Board	10	$26,000	$—	$—	$—	$—
Executive	0	—	—	—	—	—
Audit	3	—	—	—	—	5,000
Compensation & Human Res	7	—	—	—	—	5,000
Nominating & Board Govern	4	—	—	—	—	5,000
Strategy Review	3	—	—	—	—	5,000

Comments: $1,000 per day paid for time spent on other company business

Average director's annual compensation = $26,000
(assumes all meetings are attended and director sits on the Audit and Compensation committees)

STOCK-BASED COMPENSATION

Grant type(s):	Stock Option	Restricted	Deferred
Number of shares:	2,000	2.5 times Retainer	50% of Retainer ($26,000)
Frequency:	Annual	One-time	Annual
Vesting:	6 months	20% per year	Termination
Year-end stock price:	45.8125	Same	Same
Plan type:	Separate	Same	—
Plan life:	5 years	Same	—
Plan kitty:	125,000	Same	—
COC provision	Yes	Same	—

Comments: only new directors receive one-time grant of restricted stock rounded to the nearest 100 shares.

COMPENSATION DEFERRAL

None

CASH RETIREMENT BENEFITS

Mandatory retirement age: 70

Cash plan was previously terminated and replaced with larger stock option grant and restricted stock award (above); the present value of accrued benefits for directors with 4 years service was paid out in stock; directors with less than 4 years received transitional restricted stock grants.

INSURANCE BENEFITS

None

OTHER BENEFITS

None

CHANGES

- Increased total retainer from $30,000 to $52,000, with 50% paid in deferred stock
- Eliminated meeting attendance fees of $1,000
- Increased stock option grant by 500 shares
- Reduced one-time restricted stock grants from 4 times retainer to 2.5 times retainer

The Charles Schwab Corporation

Industry: Nonbank Financial FY97 Revenue (mils): $2,299

BOARD STRUCTURE/FEES

	No. of Mtgs	Retainer Cash	Retainer Stock	Member Fee	Meeting Fee	Chairman Fee
Board	8	$25,000	—	—	$1,500	—
Audit	3	—	—	—	1,000	3,000
Compensation	9	—	—	—	1,000	3,000
Customer Quality Assurance	2	—	—	—	1,000	3,000

Same day meeting fees: $300 paid for committee meetings on same day as board meetings

Average director's annual compensation= $40,600
(assumes all meetings are attended and director sits on the Audit and Compensation committees)

STOCK-BASED COMPENSATION

Grant type(s):	**Stock Option**
Number of shares:	2,250
Frequency:	Annual
Year-end stock price:	41.9375
Plan type:	Combined with exec.

Comments: if the exercise price (FMV at grant) equals less than $35.00, the number of options granted increases to 3,750 shares

COMPENSATION DEFERRAL

Eligible comp: Retainer/meeting
Account types: Stock
Payment: After termination

CASH RETIREMENT BENEFITS

None

INSURANCE BENEFITS

None

OTHER BENEFITS

Directors who do brokerage transactions at Schwab receive a 20% discount on commission rates

CHANGES

None

The Chase Manhattan Corporation

Industry: Banks

FY97 Revenue (mils): $30,381

BOARD STRUCTURE/FEES

	No. of Mtgs	Retainer Cash	Retainer Stock	Member Fee	Meeting Fee	Chairman Fee
Board	12	$25,000	500 shr	$ —	$1,250	$ —
Compensation & Benefits	6	—	—	8,000	1,250	8,000
Audit & Examining	8	—	—	8,000	1,250	8,000
Public Policy & Trust	3	—	—	5,000	1,250	5,000
Risk Policy	7	—	—	8,000	1,250	8,000
Governance	2	—	—	5,000	1,250	5,000

Comments: the COB/CEO served on the Compensation Committee of an outside director's firm.

Average director's annual compensation = $123,432
(assumes all meetings are attended and director sits on the Audit and Compensation committees)

STOCK-BASED COMPENSATION

Grant Type(s)	**Stock Award**
Number of shares	500
Frequency:	Annual
Year-end stock price	109.50

Comments: the value of the 500 shares will not be less than $37,500 or more than $50,000; the value of these shares is reflected in "Stock Retainer" and "Average Director's Annual Compensation" above. *Note: for analysis purposes we used 456 shares, which had a year-end 1997 value of $49,932.*

COMPENSATION DEFERRAL

Eligible comp: Retainer/meeting/Stock
Account types: Cash and/or Stock
Interest rate: Various investments
COC provision Yes
Comments: account transfers are permitted; cash accounts are paid out in cash; stock accounts are paid out in stock.

CASH RETIREMENT BENEFITS

Cash plan terminated 5/96 and benefits converted to deferred stock equivalents; payable at termination

INSURANCE BENEFITS

Group Term Life
Group Accident
Directors may participate in medical

OTHER BENEFITS

None

CHANGES

None

Chrysler Corporation

Industry: Automotive FY97 Revenue (mils): $61,147

BOARD STRUCTURE/FEES

	No. of Mtgs	Retainer Cash	Retainer Stock	Member Fee	Meeting Fee	Chairman Fee
Board	15	$ —	$25,000	$ —	$1,000	$ —
Audit	6	—	—	10,000	—	2,000
Corp Governance	7	—	—	10,000	—	2,000
Mgmt Resources & Compen	9	—	—	10,000	—	2,000
Pension Fund Review	2	—	—	10,000	—	2,000
Public & Legal Affairs	3	—	—	10,000	—	2,000

Comments: $2,000 per day for special services; annual retainer, committee member fee and chairman's fee are all paid in stock (less cash to cover tax liability).

Average director's annual compensation = $60,000

(assumes all meetings are attended and director sits on the Audit and Compensation committees)

STOCK-BASED COMPENSATION

Grant type(s):	Stock Option/SARs	Deferred	Stock Award
Number of shares:	3,000	6,000	$35,000
Frequency:	Annual	One-time	Annual
Vesting:	40% 1st yr, 30% 2nd & 3rd years	5 years	—
Year-end stock price:	35.1875	same	same
Plan type:	Combined with exec.	same	same
COC provision	Yes	same	same

Comments: Option grants include limited SARs; stock award includes annual retainer ($25,000) and committee member fee ($10,000); deferred units are intended to provide a retirement benefit, payable in cash or shares.

Ownership Guidelines: must own at least 10,000 shares within 3 years of election to the board

COMPENSATION DEFERRAL

Eligible comp: Retainer/meeting/Option proceeds
Account types: Cash and/or Stock
Interest rate: Various investments
Max. Installments: 10 years

Comments: proceeds from option exercises may also be deferred; payout may be lump sum or installments

CASH RETIREMENT BENEFITS

Mandatory retirement age: 72

Cash plan terminated in 1996 and accrued benefits converted to phantom stock units replaced with 1-time deferred stock grant (above)

INSURANCE BENEFITS

Travel/Accident: $250,000

OTHER BENEFITS

Directors receive product evaluation and lease vehicles.

CHANGES

None

Cigna Corporation

Industry: Nonbank Financial

FY97 Revenue (mils): $20,038

BOARD STRUCTURE/FEES

	No. of Mtgs	Retainer Cash	Retainer Stock	Member Fee	Meeting Fee	Chairman Fee
Board	6	$18,000	$20,000	$ —	$1,250	$ —
Executive	1	—	—	—	1,250	—
Audit	5	—	—	2,500	1,250	5,000
Corp. Governance	3	—	—	2,500	1,250	5,000
Finance	4	—	—	2,500	1,250	5,000
People Resources	6	—	—	2,500	1,250	5,000

Comments: Stock portion may be in shares or deferred stock. Directors may elect to receive all or a portion of fees in stock.

Average director's annual compensation = $64,250

(assumes all meetings are attended and director sits on the Audit and Compensation committees)

STOCK-BASED COMPENSATION

Grant type(s):	**Restricted**	**Deferred Stock Units**	**Stock Award**
Number of shares:	1,500	$11,000	$20,000
Frequency:	One-time	Annual	Annual
Vesting:	Death/disability/retirement/COC	Death/termination	—
Year-end stock price:	172.375	Same	Same
Plan type:	Separate	(Deferral plan)	—
Plan life:	Indefinite	—	—
COC provision:	Yes	—	—

Comments: restricted shares are forfeited upon termination for other reasons, unless a Board majority votes otherwise; the value of the stock award is reflected in Stock Retainer and Average Director's Annual Compensation above.

COMPENSATION DEFERRAL

Eligible comp: Retainer/meeting/stock retainer
Account types: Cash and/or Stock
Interest rate: Company Savings Plan rate
Max. Installments: 15 years
Comments: payouts from stock accounts may be in shares

CASH RETIREMENT BENEFITS

Mandatory retirement age: 70

Cash plan frozen as of 12/31/96; if elected by director, accrued benefits were transferred to a deferred stock account; two vested directors continue eligibility in the plan

INSURANCE BENEFITS

Travel/Accident: $204,000
Life: (same as employees)
Medical/Dental: (same as employees)
Property/Casualty personal lines insurance: (same as employees)

OTHER BENEFITS

Matching Gift Program (same as employees)
Financial Planning Services

CHANGES

- Increased stock retainer by $8,000
- Reduced chairman's fee by $2,500
- Increased travel/accident insurance by $104,000

Cintas Corporation

Industry: Service Industries — FY97 Revenue (mils): $840

BOARD STRUCTURE/FEES

	No. of Mtgs	Retainer Cash	Retainer Stock	Member Fee	Meeting Fee	Chairman Fee
Board	4	$9,200	—	$ —	$1,625	$ —
Executive	0	—	—	—	900	—
Audit	2	—	—	—	900	—
Compensation	1	—	—	—	900	—

* excludes actions taken by written consent

Average director's annual compensation = $18,400

(assumes all meetings are attended and director sits on the Audit and Compensation committees)

STOCK-BASED COMPENSATION

Grant type(s):	**Stock Option**
Number of shares:	1,000
Frequency:	Annual
Vesting:	25% per year
Year-end stock price:	39.00
Plan type:	Separate
Plan life:	10 years
Plan kitty:	30,000
COC provision	Yes

COMPENSATION DEFERRAL
None

CASH RETIREMENT BENEFITS
None

INSURANCE BENEFITS
None

OTHER BENEFITS
None

CHANGES
None

CISCO Systems, Inc.

Industry: Office Equipment & Services FY97 Revenue (mils): $6,440

BOARD STRUCTURE/FEES

	No. of Mtgs	Retainer Cash	Retainer Stock	Member Fee	Meeting Fee	Chairman Fee
Board	6	$32,000	$ —	$ —	$ —	$ —
Executive	0	—	—	—	—	—
Audit	3	—	—	—	—	—
Compensation/stock option	13	—	—	—	—	—
Nominating	0	—	—	—	—	—
Acquisition	3	—	—	—	—	—
Special stock option	0	—	—	—	—	—

Comments: An officer of CISCO is on the board of the Compensation Committee Chairman's company.

Average director's annual compensation = $32,000
(assumes all meetings are attended and director sits on the Audit and Compensation committees)

STOCK-BASED COMPENSATION

Grant type(s):	**Stock Option**
Number of shares:	10,000
Frequency:	Annual
Vesting:	50% per year
Option life:	9 years
Year-end stock price:	55.75
Plan type:	Combined w/ exec.
COC provision:	Yes

Comments: Outside directors who do not serve on the administering committee are also eligible for discretionary grants of options. Initial automatic grants cover 20,000 options.

COMPENSATION DEFERRAL

None

CASH RETIREMENT BENEFITS

None

INSURANCE BENEFITS

None

OTHER BENEFITS

None

CHANGES

- Increased annual retainer by $20,000
- Eliminated $1,000 Board meeting attendance fee

Citicorp

Industry: Banks — FY97 Revenue (mils): $34,697

BOARD STRUCTURE/FEES

	No. of Mtgs	Retainer Cash	Retainer Stock	Member Fee	Meeting Fee	Chairman Fee
Board	10	$30,000	$ —	$ —	$ 950	$ —
Audit	4	—	—	—	950	20,000
Directors	1	—	—	—	950	10,000
Executive	0	—	—	—	950	—
Personnel	6	—	—	—	950	20,000
Public Issues	0	—	—	—	950	10,000
Subsidiaries & Capital	0	—	—	—	950	—

Misc. Fees: Subsidiary fees paid; directors receive $10,000 to sit on Citibank board (or the consulting committee to that Board) + $950 for each Citibank board meeting; directors who reside abroad receive additional $3,500 per board meeting

Comments: committee chairmen receive a stipend in lieu of meeting fees; $10,000 of total retainer value ($40,000) is mandatorily deferred and payable in stock.

Average director's annual compensation = $49,000
(assumes all meetings are attended and director sits on the Audit and Compensation committees)

STOCK-BASED COMPENSATION

Grant type(s):	**Deferred**
Value of award:	$10,000
Frequency:	Annual
Vesting:	Retirement
Year-end stock price:	126.4375

COMPENSATION DEFERRAL

Eligible comp: Retainer/meeting
Account types: Cash and/or Stock
Interest rate: Company Savings Plan Rate
Comments: payouts from stock account are made in shares.

CASH RETIREMENT BENEFITS

None

INSURANCE BENEFITS

None

OTHER BENEFITS

None

CHANGES

None

The Coca-Cola Company

Industry: Consumer Products

FY97 Revenue (mils): $18,868

BOARD STRUCTURE/FEES

	No. of Mtgs	Retainer Cash	Retainer Stock	Member Fee	Meeting Fee	Chairman Fee
Board	8	$50,000	—	$ —	$1,500	$ —
Executive	0	—	—	—	1,500	5,000
Finance	5	—	—	—	1,500	5,000
Audit	3	—	—	—	1,500	5,000
Compensation	5	—	—	—	1,500	5,000
Directors	3	—	—	—	1,500	5,000
Public Issues Review	1	—	—	—	1,500	5,000

Comments: Company headed by a director provides consulting for $185,000/yr; one director's company leased office space to a Coca-Cola subsidiary for $271,000 in 1997; Compensation Committee chairman's company leased office space to Coca-Cola for $2.113-mil in 1997.

Average director's annual compensation = $74,000
(assumes all meetings are attended and director sits on the Audit and Compensation committees)

STOCK-BASED COMPENSATION

None

COMPENSATION DEFERRAL

Eligible comp: Retainer
Account types: Cash and/or stock
Interest rate: Prime
Payment: No earlier than the year after termination
Comments: Cash accounts are paid out in cash; stock accounts are paid out in stock.

CASH RETIREMENT BENEFITS

Mandatory service: 5 years
Min. retirement age: 55
Mandatory retirement age: 71
Basic Benefits: Retainer
Payment term: Matching Service
Death benefit: Yes (spouse only)
Comments: Payment may be in lump sum

INSURANCE BENEFITS

Travel/Accident: $200,000
Death/Disability: $100,000
Term Life: $30,000
Medical/Dental
Comments: aggregate 1997 cost = $39,269

OTHER BENEFITS

None

CHANGES

None

Colgate-Palmolive Company

Industry: Consumer Products FY97 Revenue (mils): $9,057

BOARD STRUCTURE/FEES

	No. of Mtgs	Retainer Cash	Retainer Stock	Member Fee	Meeting Fee	Chairman Fee
Board	9	$ —	1,300 shr	$ —	$1,000	$ —
Finance	6	—	—	—	1,000	3,000
Audit	3	—	—	—	1,000	3,000
Personnel & Organization	8	—	—	—	1,000	3,000
Directors (Nominating)	3	—	—	—	1,000	3,000

Comments: $1,500 annual retainer is paid to the Deputy Chair of each committee; directors may elect to have all or a portion of fees paid in stock; directors may elect to have 25% of stock paid in cash to meet tax obligations.

Average director's annual compensation = $114,738
(assumes all meetings are attended and director sits on the Audit and Compensation committees)

STOCK-BASED COMPENSATION

Grant type(s):	**Stock Award**	**Stock Option**
Number of shares:	1,300	2,000
Frequency:	Annual	Annual
Vesting:	Immediate	1/3 per year
Year-end stock price:	72.875	Same
Plan type:	Separate	Separate
Plan life:	Indefinite	10 years
Plan kitty:	—	150,000
COC provision	—	Yes

Comments: stock award reflected under "Stock Retainer" and "Average Director's Annual Compensation" above.

COMPENSATION DEFERRAL

Eligible comp: Meeting/chairman fees
Account types: Stock
Max. installments: 10 years
Payment: After Termination

Comments: must be deferred in 25% increments; distributions are made in shares, lump sum or installments.

CASH RETIREMENT BENEFITS

Mandatory retirement age: 72

Cash plan terminated 12/96 and replaced with additional 125 shares of stock; directors within 5 years of retirement who elect to continue with plan have 125 shares subtracted from their annual grant.

INSURANCE BENEFITS

Life: $50,000
Travel/Accident: $300,000

OTHER BENEFITS

Matching Gift Program for up to $8,000 to educational or medical institutions

CHANGES

None

Computer Sciences Corporation

Industry: Office Equipment & Services

FY97 Revenue (mils): $5,616

BOARD STRUCTURE/FEES

	No. of Mtgs	Retainer: Cash	Retainer: Stock	Member Fee	Meeting Fee	Chairman Fee
Board	8	$34,000	—	$ —	$1,000	$ —
Executive	32	—	—	—	—	—
Audit	3	—	—	5,000	—	—
Compensation	2	—	—	5,000	—	—

Comments: Meeting fee also applies to telephonic meetings; one director's company provided DP and consulting services to CSC for $22,788,000 in 1997.

Average director's annual compensation = $52,000
(assumes all meetings are attended and director sits on the Audit and Compensation committees)

STOCK-BASED COMPENSATION

Grant type(s):	**Restricted Units**
Value of award:	$109,000
Frequency:	5 years
Vesting:	Retirement
Year-end stock price:	$83.50
Plan type:	Separate
Plan life:	10 years
Plan kitty:	50,000

Comments: Award is based on projected value of retirement benefits over next 5 years; the next award may not be in restricted units—the plan provides for any type of stock-based grants; directors are eligible for discretionary grants, although not planned at this time.

COMPENSATION DEFERRAL

None

CASH RETIREMENT BENEFITS

Mandatory retirement age: 72

Cash plan terminated in 1997 for current and future directors; accrued benefits converted to restricted stock units; future benefits replaced with restricted stock units (above)

INSURANCE BENEFITS

None

OTHER BENEFITS

None

CHANGES

- Eliminated cash retirement plan and replaced with restricted stock units; accrued benefits were converted to restricted stock units
- New stock plan allows for discretionary stock-based grants

Consolidated Natural Gas Company

Industry: Utilities FY97 Revenue (mils): $5,710

BOARD STRUCTURE/FEES

	No. of Mtgs	Retainer Cash	Retainer Stock	Member Fee	Meeting Fee	Chairman Fee
Board	7	$24,000	—	$ —	$2,000	$ —
Audit	4	—	—	—	1,000	3,000
Human Resources	4	—	—	—	1,000	3,000
Compliance	4	—	—	—	1,000	3,000
Executive	0	—	—	—	1,000	3,000
Financial	6	—	—	—	1,000	3,000
Governance	4	—	—	—	1,000	3,000
International	6	—	—	—	1,000	3,000

Misc. Fees: Telephone Meetings: $1,000

Same Day Mtg Fees: $2,000 fee for Board attendance includes committee mtgs. on same day

Average director's annual compensation = $38,000

(assumes all meetings are attended and director sits on the Audit and Compensation committees)

STOCK-BASED COMPENSATION

Grant type(s):	**Restricted***
Number of shares:	200*
Frequency:	Annual
Vesting:	25% per yr/retirement at 70/death/disability
Year-end stock price:	60.50
Plan type:	Combined with exec.

* Directors may receive 200 shares of deferred stock and 1,000 stock options instead.

Comments: initial grants cover 400 shares (or 400 deferred shares and 2,000 options).

COMPENSATION DEFERRAL

Eligible comp:	Retainer/meeting
Account types:	Cash and/or stock
Interest rate:	Prime
Max. installments:	10 years
Payment:	After termination

Comments: interest compounded quarterly; payouts are in cash in lump sum or install; lump sum payment if director dies before distribution.

CASH RETIREMENT BENEFITS

Mandatory retirement age: 70

Cash plan terminated 1/97 for future directors; current directors may elect to have the present value of expected benefits converted to restricted stock or deferred stock

INSURANCE BENEFITS

Split Dollar Life

Supplemental Death Benefit

OTHER BENEFITS

None

CHANGES

None

Cooper Industries, Inc.

Industry: Electronics FY97 Revenue (mils): $5,289

BOARD STRUCTURE/FEES

	No. of Mtgs	Retainer Cash	Retainer Stock	Member Fee	Meeting Fee	Chairman Fee
Board	4	$45, 000	400 shr	$ —	$ —	$ —
Audit	3	—	—	—	1,000	6,000
Executive	0	—	—	—	1,000	6,000
Finance	2	—	—	—	1,000	6,000
Mgmt Devel & Compensation	3	—	—	—	1,000	6,000
Nominations & Corp Govern	4	—	—	—	1,000	6,000

Comments: $2,000 paid for each special Board or committee meeting attended; the maximum number of shares granted to an individual = 1,200; directors may elect to receive fees in stock, that may be further deferred

Average director's annual compensation = $70,600
(assumes all meetings are attended and director sits on the Audit and Compensation committees)

STOCK-BASED COMPENSATION

Grant type(s):	**Stock Option**	**Stock Award**	**Stock Award**
Number of shares:	1,000	400	As elected by director
Frequency:	Annual	Annual	Annual
Vesting:	3 years	—	Date specified by director
Year-end stock price:	49.00	Same	Same
Plan type:	Separate	Same	Separate
Plan life:	10 years	Same	10 years
Plan kitty:	200,000	Same	100,000
COC provision	Yes	—	Yes

Comments: The maximum number of shares granted under the elective stock plan = 1,200 shares.
Ownership Guidelines: Three times annual cash retainer within 5 years

COMPENSATION DEFERRAL

Eligible comp: Retainer/meeting/stock retainer
Account types: Cash
Payment: Date apecified by Director
Comments: no additional information disclosed.

CASH RETIREMENT BENEFITS

Cash plan was previously terminated and replaced with stock option grants (above); existing accrued benefits were grandfathered

INSURANCE BENEFITS

None

OTHER BENEFITS

None

CHANGES

- Added new stock plan where directors may elect to receive cash fees in stock, which may be deferred
- Added stock ownership guidelines

Corning Inc.

Industry: Manufacturing FY97 Revenue (mils): $4,129

BOARD STRUCTURE/FEES

	No. of Mtgs	Retainer Cash	Retainer Stock	Member Fee	Meeting Fee	Chairman Fee
Board	7	$22,500	—	$ —	$ 750	$ —
Audit	4	—	—	—	750	6,500
Compensation	5	—	—	—	750	3,000
Nominating	2	—	—	—	750	3,000

Comments: The now retired COB of Corning is on the Compensation Committee of a director who is on Corning's Compensation Committee. Committee chairmen receive retainer in lieu of meeting fees.

Average director's annual compensation = $34,500
(assumes all meetings are attended and director sits on the Audit and Compensation committees)

STOCK-BASED COMPENSATION

Grant type(s):	**Restricted**
Number of shares:	1,200
Frequency:	3 years
Vesting:	3 years
Year-end stock price:	37.125
Plan type:	Separate
Plan kitty:	100,000

Comments: Shares are awarded upon election for a 3-year term; initial grants cover 4,000 shares.

COMPENSATION DEFERRAL

Eligible comp: Retainer/meeting
Account types: Cash and/or stock
Interest rate: Prime
Payment: Date specified by Director

Comments: Stock accounts may be based on either the company's market value or book value; payouts are in cash.

CASH RETIREMENT BENEFITS

Mandatory retirement age: 70

INSURANCE BENEFITS

None

OTHER BENEFITS

Charitable Award Program

Amount: $1,250,000 payout: made to one or more qualified charities selected by director; life insurance funded; 5 years' service required for participation

CHANGES

None

Cracker Barrel Old Country Store, Inc.

Industry: Leisure FY97 Revenue (mils): $1,124

BOARD STRUCTURE/FEES

	No. of Mtgs	Retainer Cash	Retainer Stock	Member Fee	Meeting Fee	Chairman Fee
Board	5	$20,000	—	$ —	$1,000	$ —
Executive	6	—	—	—	1,000	—
Audit	3	—	—	—	1,000	600
Stock Option	1	—	—	—	1,000	200
Compensation	1	—	—	—	1,000	200

Comments: Executive Committee also serves as nominating committee; chairman fees reflect an additional $200 for each committee meeting attended; one director received $373,801 in lease payments, $75,000 for legal services, and $22,750 for rent of his personal jet; another director's firm received $24,000 for P.R. services.

Average director's annual compensation = $29,000
(assumes all meetings are attended and director sits on the Audit and Compensation committees)

STOCK-BASED COMPENSATION

Grant type(s):	**Stock Option**
Number of shares:	25,312
Frequency:	Annual
Vesting:	6 months
Year-end stock price:	33.375
Plan type:	Separate
Plan kitty:	1,518,750

Comments: options have no expiration date; due to the kitty being exhausted, there were no options granted for 1996 or 1997.

COMPENSATION DEFERRAL

Eligible comp: Retainer/meeting
Account types: Cash
Interest rate: 10-year T-bill + 1.5%

CASH RETIREMENT BENEFITS

None

INSURANCE BENEFITS

None

OTHER BENEFITS

None

CHANGES

- Increased annual retainer by $6,000
- Increased meeting attendance fees by $100 or $200 each
- Decreased chairmans' fees by $200 per meeting

Note: the two directors receiving payments for leasing and consulting were pulled off the Compensation Committee.

Crestar Financial Corporation

Industry: Banks FY97 Revenue (mils): $1,997

BOARD STRUCTURE/FEES

	No. of Mtgs	Retainer Cash	Retainer Stock	Member Fee	Meeting Fee	Chairman Fee
Board	13	$12,000	$6,000	$ —	$1,000	$ —
Audit	5	—	--	—	1,000	3,500
Nominating & Governance	5	—	--	—	1,000	3,500
Human Res & Compensation	7	—	--	—	1,000	3,500
Executive	10	—	—	—	1,000	—

Same day fees: $500 paid for second meeting in a day; stock may be deferred

Average director's annual compensation = $37,000
(assumes all meetings are attended and director sits on the Audit and Compensation committees)

STOCK-BASED COMPENSATION

Grant type(s):	Restricted	Stock Award
Value of award:	$40,000	$6,000
Frequency:	5 years	Annual
Vesting:	20% per year	—
Year-end stock price:	57.00	same
Plan type:	Separate	—
COC Provisions:	Yes	—

COMPENSATION DEFERRAL

Eligible comp:	Retainer/meeting/stock
Account types:	Cash and/or stock
Payment:	After termination
Max. installments:	20 years
COC provision:	Yes

Comments: payout may be lump sum or installments.

CASH RETIREMENT BENEFITS

None

INSURANCE BENEFITS

None

OTHER BENEFITS

None

CHANGES

None

Cummins Engine Company, Inc.

Industry: Automotive

FY97 Revenue (mils): $5,625

BOARD STRUCTURE/FEES

	No. of Mtgs	Retainer Cash	Retainer Stock	Member Fee	Meeting Fee	Chairman Fee
Board	5	$27,000	$18,000	$ —	$ —	$ —
Audit	4	—	—	6,000	1,000	3,000
Compensation	4	—	—	6,000	1,000	3,000
Nominating & Organization	5	—	—	6,000	1,000	3,000
Executive	1	—	—	6,000	—	—
Business Dev & Finance	0	—	—	6,000	1,000	3,000
Employee Dev & Corp. Resp.	0	—	—	6,000	1,000	3,000
Proxy	0	—	—	—	1,000	—
Technology	0	—	—	6,000	1,000	3,000

Same day fees: no fee paid for committee meetings held in conjunction with a Board meeting

Comments: $1,000 paid for "special" Board meetings; director Harold Brown received $50,000 in consulting fees in 1997 and chairs the Science & Technology Advisory Council for $17,000/yr plus $3,000 per meeting.

Average director's annual compensation = $57,000

(assumes all meetings are attended and director sits on the Audit and Compensation committees)

STOCK-BASED COMPENSATION

Grant type(s):	Stock Award
Award value:	$18,000
Frequency:	Annual
Vesting:	6 months
Year-end stock price:	59.0625
Plan type:	Separate
Plan life:	8 years

Comments: shares from Executive Stock Plan are used for director grants; value is reflected under "Stock Retainer" and "Avg Director's Annual Compensation" above.

COMPENSATION DEFERRAL

Eligible comp:	Retainer/meeting
Account types:	Cash
Max. installments:	10 years
Payment:	After termination
COC provision:	Yes

Comments: payouts may be lump sum or installment.

CASH RETIREMENT BENEFITS

Cash plan terminated in 1997 and replaced with additional $12,000 of stock each year; vested directors could elect to have accrued benefits converted to phantom stock units

INSURANCE BENEFITS

None

OTHER BENEFITS

Charitable Award Program

Amount: $1,000,000; payout: 10 install. to 1 or more institutions; subject to vesting based on director's years of service; life insurance funded

CHANGES

None

Cyprus Amax Minerals Company

Industry: Metal/Mining FY97 Revenue (mils): $3,346

BOARD STRUCTURE/FEES

	No. of Mtgs	Retainer Cash	Retainer Stock	Member Fee	Meeting Fee	Chairman Fee
Board	6	$25,000	500 shr	$ —	$1,000	$ —
Audit	3	—	—	—	1,000	5,000
Compensation	3	—	—	—	1,000	5,000
Nominating	1	—	—	—	1,000	250
Executive	2	—	—	—	1,000	—
Empl. Funds Investment	2	—	—	—	1,000	1,000

Comments: Chairmen fees reflect additional $250 per meeting for Nominating, $500 per meeting for Employee Funds Investment, and $5,000 per year or $500 per meeting, whichever is greater, for Audit and Compensation & Benefits committees

Average director's annual compensation = $44,688
(assumes all meetings are attended and director sits on the Audit and Compensation committees)

STOCK-BASED COMPENSATION

Grant type(s):	**Stock Award**	**Stock Option**
Number of shares:	500	2,000
Frequency:	Annual	Annual
Vesting:	—	50% per year
Year-end stock price:	15.375	Same
Plan type:	Separate	Same
Plan life:	Indefinite	Same
Plan kitty:	1/16 of 1% of outstanding common/year	Same
COC provision:	Yes	Same

Comments: stock award is reflected in "Stock Retainer" and "Average Director's Annual Compensation" above.
Ownership Guidelines: must own three times annual retainer within 5 years

COMPENSATION DEFERRAL

Eligible comp: Retainer/meeting
Account types: Cash or stock
Payment: After termination
COC provision: Yes
Comments: paid out in cash or shares on any January 1st after retirement

CASH RETIREMENT BENEFITS

Mandatory retirement age: 70
Cash plan terminated 4/98; the plan is amended so that no current Board member will receive a benefit >$25,000

INSURANCE BENEFITS

None

OTHER BENEFITS

None

CHANGES

- Substantial changes have been approved and will become effective 1/1/99
- Eliminated cash retirement plan

Dayton Hudson Corporation

Industry: Retailing FY97 Revenue (mils): $27,757

BOARD STRUCTURE/FEES

	No. of Mtgs	Retainer Cash	Retainer Stock	Member Fee	Meeting Fee	Chairman Fee
Board	6	$25,000	$ —	$ —	$1,000	$ —
Executive	3	—	—	—	1,000	(see stock below)
Audit	3	——	—	—	1,000	—
Compensation	3	—	—	—	1,000	—
Corp. Responsibility	2	—	—	—	1,000	—
Finance	2	—	—	—	1,000	—
Nominating	2	—	—	—	1,000	—

Comments: Executive Committee (headed by CEO) reviews all recommendations made by Compensation Committee. Directors may have the company forward fees to a broker to purchase common shares (company pays brokerage fees). Directors may take additional restricted stock in lieu of cash fees.

Average director's annual compensation = $37,000
(assumes all meetings are attended and director sits on the Audit and Compensation committees)

STOCK-BASED COMPENSATION

Grant type(s):	**Restricted**	**Stock Option**
Value of award:	$15,000	$100,000
Frequency:	Annual	Annual
Vesting:	After 15 years or approved termination	1 year
Year-end stock price:	67.50	Same
Plan type:	Separate	Separate
Plan life:	—	Indefinite
Plan kitty:	—	100,000
COC provision	Yes	Yes

Comments: Vice Chair of Executive Committee receives an additional $10,000 in restricted stock each year.

COMPENSATION DEFERRAL

Eligible comp: Retainer/meeting
Account types: Cash and/or stock
Interest rate: Various investment alternatives
Comments: Deferred fees may go to a broker to purchase stock; the company pays broker fees.

CASH RETIREMENT BENEFITS

Mandatory retirement age: 68 (or after 15 years of svc)
Cash plan terminated 12/96 and accrued benefits frozen; directors now receive $50,000 more stock options and $5,000 more restricted stock each year

INSURANCE BENEFITS

None

OTHER BENEFITS

Directors receive discounts on company merchandise (same as employee discounts)

CHANGES

- Added deferral alternative of stock-based accounts and various investment alternatives for directors to choose from for deferred amounts

Delta Air Lines, Inc.

Industry: Transportation — FY97 Revenue (mils): $13,590

BOARD STRUCTURE/FEES

	No. of Mtgs	Retainer Cash	Retainer Stock	Member Fee	Meeting Fee	Chairman Fee
Board	12	$20,000	$5,000	$ —	$1,000	$ —
Benefit Funds Investment	3	—	—	—	1,000	7,500
Audit	2	—	—	—	1,000	7,500
Corporate Governance	(new)	—	—	—	1,000	7,500
Executive	0	—	—	—	1,000	7,500
Finance	6	—	—	—	1,000	7,500
Personnel, Comp & Nom	4	—	—	—	1,000	7,500

Comments: Directors may elect to have fees paid in stock.

Average director's annual compensation = $43,000
(assumes all meetings are attended and director sits on the Audit and Compensation committees)

STOCK-BASED COMPENSATION

Grant type(s):	**Stock Award**	**Deferred**
Number of shares:	$5,000	$6,300
Frequency:	Annual	Annual
Year-end stock price:	119.00	Same
Plan type:	Separate	(deferral plan)
Plan life:	10 years	—
Plan kitty:	250,000	—

COMPENSATION DEFERRAL

Eligible comp: Retainer/meeting
Account types: Cash and/or stock
Interest rate: 17 investment choices
Max. Installments: 10 years
Payment: Date specified by director
COC provision: Yes
Comments: amounts deferred prior to 10/26/95 earn interest at Prime

CASH RETIREMENT BENEFITS

Mandatory retirement age: 70
Cash plan terminated 10/96 and replaced with annual deferred stock grants

INSURANCE BENEFITS

None

OTHER BENEFITS

Director & spouse are eligible for complimentary transportation

CHANGES

- Added $5,000 stock retainer
- Increased meeting attendance fees by $200 each, and chairman's fee by $1,500
- Eliminated cash retirement plan and replaced with deferred stock grants
- Added alternative for deferral in stock accounts

Dexter Corporation

Industry: Chemicals

FY97 Revenue (mils): $1,159

BOARD STRUCTURE/FEES

	No. of Mtgs	Retainer Cash	Retainer Stock	Member Fee	Meeting Fee	Chairman Fee
Board	6	$10,000	$10,000+ 200 shrs	$ —	$1,000	$ —
Compensation & Organization	5	—		—	1,000	4,000
Audit	3	—	—	—	1,000	4,000
Environmental & Safety	3	—	—	—	1,000	4,000

Comments: Directors may elect to have all or a portion of fees paid in stock which may be restricted at the director's election until death, disability, retirement, termination, or COC. Board meetings held outside headquarters pay $2,000.

Average director's annual compensation = $42,638
(assumes all meetings are attended and director sits on the Audit and Compensation committees)

STOCK-BASED COMPENSATION

Grant type(s):	**Stock Award**	**Stock Award**
Number of shares:		200
Value of shares:	50% of retainer ($10,000)	
Frequency:	Annual	Annual
Year-end stock price:	43.1875	Same
Plan type:	Separate (1996 plan)	Separate (1994 plan)
Plan life:	10 years	10 years
Plan kitty:	50,000	25,000

Comments: The value of both stock awards is reflected in the "Stock Retainer" and "Average Director's Annual Compensation" above.

COMPENSATION DEFERRAL

None

CASH RETIREMENT BENEFITS

The annual 200 share stock awards are intended to replace the prior plan, which was terminated in 1993.

INSURANCE BENEFITS

None

OTHER BENEFITS

None

CHANGES

- Increased chairman's fee by $2,000
- Increased total retainer value from $10,000 to $20,000, with 50% paid in common stock
- Eliminated $300 telephone meeting fee

The Dow Chemical Company

Industry: Chemicals | FY97 Revenue (mils): $20,018

BOARD STRUCTURE/FEES

	No. of Mtgs	Retainer Cash	Retainer Stock	Member Fee	Meeting Fee	Chairman Fee
Board	7	$32,000	$ —	$ —	$1,200	$ —
Executive	12	—	—	—	1,200	—
Audit	4	—	—	4,000	1,200	2,000
Directors	4	—	—	4,000	1,200	2,000
Compensation	7	—	—	4,000	1,200	2,000
Environ, Health & Safety	4	—	—	—	1,200	3,000
Finance	7	—	—	—	1,200	3,000
Investment Policy	4	—	—	—	1,200	3,000

Comments: $1,200 paid for special committee meetings and each of 4 quarterly Business Review meetings.

Average director's annual compensation = $61,600
(assumes all meetings are attended and director sits on the Audit and Compensation committees)

STOCK-BASED COMPENSATION

Grant type(s):	**Restricted**	**Stock Option**	**Stock Option**
Number of shares:	1,500	Formula*	Formula**
Frequency:	One-time	5 years	Annual
Vesting:	—	1/3 per year	5 years
Year-end stock price:	101.50	Same	Same
Plan type:	—	Separate	Separate
Plan life:	—	10 years	—

Comments: The option grants made every 5 years are contingent on director owning increasingly larger amounts of stock (1,500 shares as of 1994; will be 2,000 in 1999).

*Formula is based on annual retainer and price of stock (1,550 shares granted in 1994). *Note: for valuation purposes, this grant is annualized to 310 shares and added to the other option grant.*

** Formula = 45% of prior year's average retainer and fees ÷ Black Scholes valuation (currently 30%) and stock price (1,200 shares for 1998).

COMPENSATION DEFERRAL

Eligible comp:	Retainer/meeting
Account types:	Cash and/or stock
Interest rate:	125% of 10-yr avg of 10-year T-bills
Max. installments:	10 years
Payment:	After termination or age 70

CASH RETIREMENT BENEFITS

Cash plan terminated 12/97 and accrued benefits converted to deferred stock

INSURANCE BENEFITS

None

OTHER BENEFITS

None

CHANGES

- Eliminated cash retirement benefit with accrued benefits converted to deferred stock accounts
- Replaced cash retirement plan with annual stock option grants

Dow Jones and Company

Industry: Publishing/Broadcasting — FY97 Revenue (mils): $2,573

BOARD STRUCTURE/FEES

	No. of Mtgs	Retainer Cash	Retainer Stock	Member Fee	Meeting Fee	Chairman Fee
Board	8	$20,000	$ —	$ —	$1,200	$ —
Executive	3	—	—	—	1,000	3,000
Audit	4	—	—	—	1,000	3,000
Compensation	5	—	—	—	1,000	3,000
Nominating	2	—	—	—	1,000	3,000

Comments: Committee meeting fee paid to nonmembers invited to attend.

Average director's annual compensation = $38,600
(assumes all meetings are attended and director sits on the Audit and Compensation committees)

STOCK-BASED COMPENSATION

Grant type(s):	**Deferred**
Value of award:	$20,000
Frequency:	Annual
Vesting:	Not disclosed
Year-end stock price:	53.6875
Plan type:	(deferral plan)

COMPENSATION DEFERRAL

Eligible comp: Retainer/meeting
Account types: Cash and/or stock
Interest rate: Prime
Max. installments: 15 years

Comments: payable in lump sum or installments; deferred stock is paid out in cash or stock; cash accounts are paid in cash.

CASH RETIREMENT BENEFITS

Mandatory retirement age: 70
Cash plan terminated 11/96 and accrued benefits converted to deferred cash and/or stock accounts

INSURANCE BENEFITS

None

OTHER BENEFITS

None

CHANGES

None

Dun & Bradstreet Corporation

Industry: Publishing/Broadcasting — FY97 Revenue (mils): $2,154

BOARD STRUCTURE/FEES

	No. of Mtgs	Retainer Cash	Retainer Stock	Member Fee	Meeting Fee	Chairman Fee
Board	9	$25,000	--	$ --	$1,000	$ --
Audit	6	–	--	–	1,000	4,000
Exec Comp & Stock Option	5	–	--	–	1,000	4,000
Nominating	3	–	--	–	1,000	4,000
Finance	1	–	--	–	1,000	4,000
Employee Benefits	1	–	--	–	1,000	4,000
Policy & Planning	2	–	--	–	1,000	4,000
Executive	0	–	--	–	1,000	4,000

Same Day Mtg Fees: fee doubles if Board/Committee meeting exceeds a half day or occurs on different day

Average director's annual compensation = $45,000
(assumes all meetings are attended and director sits on the Audit and Compensation committees)

STOCK-BASED COMPENSATION

Grant type(s):	**Restricted**	**Performance Shares**	**Stock Option**
Number of shares:	Value = Retainer	1,000	3,000
Frequency:	One-time	Annual	Annual
Vesting:	5 years	If TSR 50% of S&P 500 TSR	1 year
Year-end stock price:	30.9375	Same	Same
Plan type:	Separate	Same	Same
Plan life:	Indefinite	Same	Same
Plan kitty:	50,000	Same	Same
COC provision	Yes	Same	Same

Comments: target performance shares (1,000 for 1998) are earned if the company's TSR = 50th percentile of S&P 500's TSR; up to 125% of target shares are paid if TSR = 50th - 60th percentile; 75% of target if < 50th percentile achieved; shares may be deferred if elected by director.

COMPENSATION DEFERRAL

Eligible comp: Retainer/meeting
Account types: Cash
Interest rate: Company rate
Max. installments: 10 years
Payment: After termination
COC provision: Yes
Comments: interest compounded annually; paid in lump sum, five or ten installments.

CASH RETIREMENT BENEFITS

Mandatory retirement age: 70
Cash plan terminated 12/96 and accrued benefits converted to phantom stock units; for directors with 3-5 years of service accrued benefits were accelerated and became vested

INSURANCE BENEFITS

None

OTHER BENEFITS

None

CHANGES

None

E. I. Dupont de Nemours and Company

Industry: Chemicals

FY97 Revenue (mils): $41,304

BOARD STRUCTURE/FEES

	No. of Mtgs	Retainer Cash	Retainer Stock	Member Fee	Meeting Fee	Chairman Fee
Board	7*	$35,000	400 shrs	$ —	$ —	$300,000
Strategic Direction	3	—	—	9,000	—	6,000
Audit	3	—	—	6,000	—	9,000
Compensation	4	—	—	6,000	—	9,000
Environmental Policy	3	—	—	6,000	—	9,000
Corp. Governance	4	—	—	6,000	—	9,000

* Includes one special meeting

Comments: $1,000 fee is paid only for special meetings of the Board and stockholder meetings held on day Board does not meet; former COB/CEO retired from company and remains COB, receiving fee in lieu of other retainer/fees/stock. Stock awards may be deferred.

Average director's annual compensation = $72,025
(assumes all meetings are attended and director sits on the Audit and Compensation committees)

STOCK-BASED COMPENSATION

Grant type(s):	**Stock Award**
Number of shares:	400
Frequency:	Annual
Year-end stock price:	60.0625
Plan type:	Separate
Plan life:	Indefinite

Comments: the COB received a stock option grant of 60,000 shares in lieu of stock award. The options vest after 1 year, have an exercise price of 100% of FMV, but the stock price must be at least 120% of FMV in order for options to be exercised.

COMPENSATION DEFERRAL

Eligible comp: Retainer/meeting/stock retainer
Account types: Cash and/or stock
Interest rate: Prime
Payment: Date specified by director
Comments: payable in installments or lump sum; stock account is payable in shares; stock retainer may be deferred.

CASH RETIREMENT BENEFITS

Mandatory service: 5 years
Mandatory retirement age: 70
Basic Benefits: 50% of Cash retainer
Payment term Lesser of life or 10 years
Death benefit: No

INSURANCE BENEFITS

Accidental Death & Disability: $300,000

OTHER BENEFITS

Charitable Award Program

Amount: $1,000,000; payout: Five installments to organizations designated by director; participation is vested after 5 years' service or upon director's death/disability; may be funded by life insurance policies

CHANGES

None

Eaton Corporation

Industry: Automotive

FY97 Revenue (mils): $7,563

BOARD STRUCTURE/FEES

	No. of Mtgs	Retainer Cash	Retainer Stock	Member Fee	Meeting Fee	Chairman Fee
Board	10	$30,000	—	$ —	$1,000	$ —
Audit	3	—	—	3,000	1,000	2,000
Compensation & Organization	6	—	—	3,000	1,000	2,000
Executive	0	—	—	—	1,000	—
Finance	2	—	—	3,000	1,000	2,000
Corp. Respons & Public Policy	2	—	—	3,000	1,000	2,000

Misc. Fees: Subsidiary fees paid

Comments: $1,000 paid for special presentation attended on non-board meeting days; one director received $22,750 and 10,000 phantom stock options and a one-time cash bonus of $300,000 in 1997.

Average director's annual compensation = $55,000

(assumes all meetings are attended and director sits on the Audit and Compensation committees)

STOCK-BASED COMPENSATION

Grant type(s):	**Stock Option**
Number of shares:	Formula*
Frequency:	Annual
Vesting:	6 months
Year-end stock price:	89.25
Plan type:	Combined w/ exec.

* Formula = 4 times the annual retainer ÷ stock price (for 1997 1,000 options were granted)

Comments: initial grant covers 5,000 shares.

COMPENSATION DEFERRAL

Eligible comp: Retainer/meeting
Account types: Cash and/or stock
Payment: Date specified by director
COC provision Yes

Comments: interest rate based on number of years until "normal" retirement, normally at higher than market rates; directors elected before 1996 may defer up to $30,000 at higher than prevailing market rate or at Prime; others receive 10-yr T-note +3% for retirement deferrals, or 13-week T-bill rate for short-term deferrals.

CASH RETIREMENT BENEFITS

Cash plan terminated 1/96 for future elected directors; accrued benefits were frozen.

INSURANCE BENEFITS

None

OTHER BENEFITS

None

CHANGES

- Changed stock option grants from 1,000 annually to a formula = 4 times the annual retainer ÷ stock price

Electronic Data Systems Corporation

Industry: Office Equipment & Services FY97 Revenue (mils): $15,236

BOARD STRUCTURE/FEES

	No. of Mtgs	Retainer Cash	Retainer Stock	Member Fee	Meeting Fee	Chairman Fee
Board	6	$35,000	$ —	$ —	$2,500	$ —
Audit	5	—	—	—	2,500	5,000
Compensation & Benefits	6	—	—	—	2,500	5,000
Governance	3	—	—	—	2,500	5,000

Comments: directors may elect to receive stock options or restricted stock in lieu of cash fees

Average director's annual compensation = $77,500
(assumes all meetings are attended and director sits on the Audit and Compensation committees)

STOCK-BASED COMPENSATION

Grant type(s):	**Stock Option**	**Restricted**
Number of shares:	1,500	500
Frequency:	Annual	Annual
Vesting:	1/3 per year	1/3 per year
Year-end stock price:	43.9375	Same
Plan type:	Combined with exec.	Same

COMPENSATION DEFERRAL

Eligible comp: Retainer/meeting
Account types: Cash and/or stock
Interest: 120% of Federal LT rate
Payment: After termination
Max installments: 5 years

Comments: interest is compounded monthly; payout is in lump sum or installments.

CASH RETIREMENT BENEFITS

None

INSURANCE BENEFITS

None

OTHER BENEFITS

None

CHANGES

None

Eli Lilly and Company

Industry: Health Care | FY97 Revenue (mils): $8,518

BOARD STRUCTURE/FEES

	No. of Meetings	Retainer Cash	Retainer Stock	Member Fee	Meeting Fee	Chairman Fee
Board	7	$35,000	—	$ —	$1,600	$ —
Audit	3	—	—	—	1,600	—
Compensation & Mgmt Dev	6	—	—	—	1,600	—
Directors & Corp Govern	2	—	—	—	1,600	—
Public Policy	3	—	—	—	1,600	—
Finance	2	—	—	—	1,600	—
Science & Technology	3	—	—	—	1,600	—

Same Day Mtg Fees: $1,600 meeting fee paid for meetings held on a day other than Board meetings
Comments: the COB/CEO is on the Compensation Committee of one of the outside director's company
Average director's annual compensation = $46,200
(assumes all meetings are attended and director sits on the Audit and Compensation committees)

STOCK-BASED COMPENSATION

Grant type(s):	**Deferred**
Number of shares:	Formula*
Frequency:	Annual
Vesting:	Termination of service
Year-end stock price:	69.625
Plan type:	(Deferral plan)

Comments: dividends earn interest at prime + 2%; directors who are former employees receive deferred cash instead of shares;

* The number of shares = lesser of (a) 800 shares, or (b) shares = in value to total annual cash compensation assuming attendance at all board meetings (in 1997 662 shares were granted)

COMPENSATION DEFERRAL

Eligible comp: Retainer/meeting
Account types: Cash and/or stock
Interest rate: Prime + 2%
Max. Installments: 10 years
Comments: deferred amounts must exceed $1,000; payment may be lump sum or installments.

CASH RETIREMENT BENEFITS

Cash plan terminated 2/96; accrued benefits transferred to deferred stock accounts.

INSURANCE BENEFITS

None

OTHER BENEFITS

None

CHANGES

None

Emerson Electric Company

Industry: Electronics

FY97 Revenue (mils): $12,299

BOARD STRUCTURE/FEES

	No. of Mtgs	Retainer Cash	Retainer Stock	Member Fee	Meeting Fee	Chairman Fee
Board	10	$30,000	—	$ —	$1,250	$ —
Executive	0	—	—	—	1,000	5,000
Audit	5	—	—	—	1,000	5,000
Comp & Human Resources	5	—	—	—	1,000	5,000
Finance	0	—	—	—	1,000	5,000
Pension	0	—	—	—	1,000	5,000
Public Policy	0	—	—	—	1,000	5,000

Comments: The SrVP/Chief Admin Officer is a director at an outside director's company.

Average director's annual compensation = $52,500
(assumes all meetings are attended and director sits on the Audit and Compensation committees)

STOCK-BASED COMPENSATION

Grant type:	**Restricted**
Value of award:	$35,000
Frequency:	Annual
Vesting:	retirement/death/resignation
Year-end stock price:	56.4375

Comments: Directors are eligible for discretionary awards under the new 1998 Stock Option Plan (although "not currently contemplated").

COMPENSATION DEFERRAL

Eligible comp: Retainer/meeting
Account types: Cash and/or stock
Interest rate: Prime
Comments: payments are made in cash only.

CASH RETIREMENT BENEFITS

Mandatory service: 5 years
Mandatory retire age: 74
Basic Benefits: 50–100% of retainer
Payment term Life
Death benefit: Yes (spouse only)
Comments: payment begins at later of age 72 or retirement; benefit = 50% of retainer + 10% for each service year over 5, up to 10; if director dies while serving spouse receives benefits for 5 years.

INSURANCE BENEFITS

None

OTHER BENEFITS

None

CHANGES

- Increased restricted stock grants by $10,000
- Directors are now eligible for discretionary awards under the new 1998 Stock Option Plan

Enron Corporation

Industry: Utilities FY97 Revenue (mils): $20,273

BOARD STRUCTURE/FEES

	No. of Mtgs	Retainer Cash	Retainer Stock	Member Fee	Meeting Fee	Chairman Fee
Board	8	$40,000	—	$ —	$1,250	$ —
Executive	11	—	—	—	1,000	5,000
Audit	5	—	—	—	1,000	5,000
Compensation	8	—	—	—	1,000	5,000
Finance	5	—	—	—	1,000	5,000
Nominating	2	—	—	—	1,000	5,000

Comments: Directors may elect to take restricted stock (as described in STOCK) or discounted stock options (exercise price =50% of FMV) in lieu of cash fees. One director on Compensation Committee is a former executive of a subsidiary and continues to maintain business arrangements with Enron.

Average director's annual compensation = $63,000
(assumes all meetings are attended and director sits on the Audit and Compensation committees)

STOCK-BASED COMPENSATION

Grant type(s):	**Restricted**	**Stock Option**
Number of shares:	Formula	Formula
Frequency:	Annual	Annual
Vesting:	20% per year	20% at 6 mon & 1st through 4th anniv
Year-end stock price:	41.5625	Same
Plan type:	Combined w/ exec.	Same

Comments: number of restricted shares = 50% of average retainer from prior year divided by FMV; number of options = 4x number of restricted shares; for 1997, each director received 510 shares of restricted stock (@ $41.375/sh) and 2,040 options (@ $41.375/sh).

COMPENSATION DEFERRAL

Eligible comp: Retainer/meeting
Account types: Cash and/or stock
Interest rate: 10 investment choices
Payment: Date Specified by director
Comments: life insurance backed.

CASH RETIREMENT BENEFITS

None

INSURANCE BENEFITS

None

OTHER BENEFITS

None

CHANGES

- No longer require 50% of annual retainer to be deferred in stock

Exxon Corporation

Industry: Fuel FY97 Revenue (mils): $122,379

BOARD STRUCTURE/FEES

	No. of Mtgs	Retainer Cash	Retainer Stock	Member Fee	Meeting Fee	Chairman Fee
Board	10	$40,000	—	$ —	$1,500	$ —
Audit	3	—	—	3,000	1,500	5,000
Advisory on Contributions	2	—	—	3,000	1,500	5,000
Compensation	8	—	—	3,000	1,500	5,000
Board Affairs	4	—	—	3,000	1,500	5,000
Public Issues	3			3,000	1,500	5,000
Executive	0	—	—	—	1,500	—
Finance	4	—	—	3,000	1,500	5,000

Comments: director who travels more than 3,000 miles to attend meetings receives a travel allowance equal to the board meeting fee for each trip to North America.

Average director's annual compensation = $77,500
(assumes all meetings are attended and director sits on the Audit and Compensation committees)

STOCK-BASED COMPENSATION

Grant type(s):	**Restricted**
Number of shares:	600
Frequency:	Annual
Vesting:	age 70/disability/death
Year-end stock price:	61.1875
Plan type:	Separate

Comments: initial awards cover 4,000 shares; board may allow early vesting.

COMPENSATION DEFERRAL

Eligible comp: Retainer/meeting
Comments: no additional information disclosed.

CASH RETIREMENT BENEFITS

Mandatory retirement age: 70
Comments: stock awards are intended to provide pension.

INSURANCE BENEFITS

None

OTHER BENEFITS

None

CHANGES

None

FDX Corporation (formerly Federal Express Corp.)

Industry: Transportation

FY97 Revenue (mils): $11,520

BOARD STRUCTURE/FEES

	No. of Mtgs	Retainer Cash	Retainer Stock	Member Fee	Meeting Fee	Chairman Fee
Board	7	$40,000	—	$ —	$ 2,000	$ —
Audit	8	—	—	—	1,200	8,000
Compensation	7	—	—	—	1,200	8,000

Average director's annual compensation = $72,000
(assumes all meetings are attended and director sits on the Audit and Compensation committees)

STOCK-BASED COMPENSATION

Grant type(s):	**Stock Option**
Number of shares:	2,000
Frequency:	Annual
Vesting:	1 year
Year-end stock price:	61.0625
Plan type:	Combined w/ exec.

Comments: beginning 9/99 the grants will increase to 4,000 options; FDX may make interest-free loans for option exercises.

Ownership Guidelines: Directors must own shares = 5 times the retainer by 3/2000; vested stock options do *not* count towards guideline

COMPENSATION DEFERRAL

None

CASH RETIREMENT BENEFITS

Mandatory retirement age: 72

Cash plan frozen 7/97; vesting was accelerated for all directors; benefits will be paid upon retirement

INSURANCE BENEFITS

None

OTHER BENEFITS

None

CHANGES

- Increased annual retainer by $8,000, committee attendance fees by $200 each, and chairman fees by $1,750
- Increased stock option grants by 1,000 shares
- Added stock ownership guidelines
- Froze cash retirement plan benefits, accelerating vesting for unvested directors

Federal Mogul Corporation

Industry: Automotive FY97 Revenue (mils): $1,807

BOARD STRUCTURE/FEES

	No. of Mtgs	Retainer Cash	Retainer Stock	Member Fee	Meeting Fee	Chairman Fee
Board	8	$16,000	—	$ —	$1,000	$ —
Audit	3	—	—	—	1,000	3,000
Compensation	6	—	—	—	1,000	6,000
Nominating	2	—	—	—	1,000	2,000
Pension	2	—	—	—	1,000	2,000

Comments: Chairman fees reflect additional $1,000 per committee meeting attended; directors may elect to have all or a portion of fees paid in restricted stock, with restrictions lapsing 6 months after grant

Average director's annual compensation = $33,000
(assumes all meetings are attended and director sits on the Audit and Compensation committees)

STOCK-BASED COMPENSATION

Grant type(s):	**Stock Option**	**Deferred**	**Restricted**
Number of shares:	2,000	$25,000	1,000
Frequency:	Annual	5 years	One-time
Vesting:	6 months	20% per year	20% per year
Year-end stock price:	61.0625	Same	Same
Plan type:	Combined w/ exec.	(deferral plan)	Separate
Plan kitty:	—	Same	50,000

Comments: deferred stock awards were made in 1996, representing a $5,000 increase in the annual retainer to become vested over 5 years.

COMPENSATION DEFERRAL

Eligible comp: Retainer/meeting
Account types: Cash and/or stock
Interest rate: 10-year T-note + 1%
Max. Installments: 10 years
Comments: see STOCK

CASH RETIREMENT BENEFITS

Cash plan terminated 2/98 and, if elected, accrued benefits converted to stock options

INSURANCE BENEFITS

None

OTHER BENEFITS

None

CHANGES

- Increased committee meeting attendance fee by $200 and committee chairman fee from $250 per meeting to $1,000 per meeting
- Eliminated cash retirement plan and converted accrued benefits to stock options
- Added annual stock option grants

First Tennessee National Corporation

Industry: Banks FY97 Revenue (mils): $1,609

BOARD STRUCTURE/FEES

	No. of Mtgs	Retainer Cash	Retainer Stock	Member Fee	Meeting Fee	Chairman Fee
Board	5	$22,000	—	$ —	$ 1,000	$ —
Audit	4	—	—	—	1,000	3,000
Human Resources	5	—	—	—	1,000	3,000

Comments: Human Resources Committee also functions as nominating and compensation committee. Director may take discount stock options (exercise price = 85% of FMV), which vest in 6 months, in lieu of cash fees; number of shares = cash divided by 15% of FMV.

Average director's annual compensation = $36,000
(assumes all meetings are attended and director sits on the Audit and Compensation committees)

STOCK-BASED COMPENSATION

Grant type(s):	**Restricted**
Number of shares:	6,000
Frequency:	One-time
Vesting:	10% per year
Year-end stock price:	66.125
Plan type:	Combined w/ exec.
COC provision	Yes

COMPENSATION DEFERRAL

Eligible comp:	Retainer/meeting
Account types:	Cash
Interest rate:	10-year T-note
Max. installments:	15 years

CASH RETIREMENT BENEFITS

None

INSURANCE BENEFITS

None

OTHER BENEFITS

None

CHANGES

- Increased annual retainer by $2,000
- Increased chairman's fee by $600

Fleet Financial Group, Inc.

Industry: Banks FY97 Revenue (mils): $8,095

BOARD STRUCTURE/FEES

	No. of Mtgs	Retainer Cash	Retainer Stock	Member Fee	Meeting Fee	Chairman Fee
Board	8	$30,000	—	$ —	$ 1,500	$ —
Audit	5	—	—	—	1,000	5,000
Human Resources & Planning	5	—	—	—	1,000	5,000
Risk Management	4	—	—	—	1,000	5,000
Executive	2	—	—	—	1,000	5,000
Empl. Develop & Public Policy	4	—	—	—	1,000	5,000

Telephone Mtg fee: $1,000 for board meetings and $750 for committee meetings

Comments: 25% of $40,000 annual retainer is mandatorily deferred in stock units; the COB sits on the Compensation Committee of two directors companies (one is on Fleet's Compensation Committee); Fleet's subsidiaries have several partnerships with companies of outside directors; they also lease New York Stock Exchange seats owned by an outside director and his family for $160,000 per year.

Average director's annual compensation = $52,000
(assumes all meetings are attended and director sits on the Audit and Compensation committees)

STOCK-BASED COMPENSATION

Grant type(s):	**Deferred Units**	**Deferred Units**
Value of award:	25% of annual retainer ($10,000)	Value = 50% of retainer ($20,000)
Frequency:	Annual	Same
Vesting:	After termination	Same
Year-end stock price:	75.125	Same

COMPENSATION DEFERRAL

Eligible comp: Retainer/meeting
Account types: Cash or stock
Interest rate: 12% for 1997
Payment: After termination
Comments: 25% of annual retainer is mandatorily deferred in stock account; payouts are in cash

CASH RETIREMENT BENEFITS

Mandatory retirement age: 68
Cash plan frozen 4/98; directors may convert accrued benefits to deferred stock units or leave in retirement plan; annual grants of $20,000 deferred units replace future accruals

INSURANCE BENEFITS

None

OTHER BENEFITS

None

CHANGES

- Eliminated cash retirement plan; accrued benefits may be converted to deferred stock units or left in plan; future accruals replaced with $20,000 annual awards of deferred stock units
- Changed mandatory deferrals from phantom stock to deferred stock units

Fluor Corporation

Industry: Service Industries FY97 Revenue (mils): $14,299

BOARD STRUCTURE/FEES

	No. of Mtgs	Retainer Cash	Retainer Stock	Member Fee	Meeting Fee	Chairman Fee
Board	6*	$32,000	—	$ —	$ 2,000	$ —
Executive	0	—	—	—	2,000	4,000
Audit	5	—	—	—	2,000	4,000
Organ & Compensation	4	—	—	—	2,000	4,000
Governance	4	—	—	—	2,000	4,000
Finance	1	—	—	—	2,000	4,000

* Includes two teleconference meetings

Same Day Mtg Fees: $2,000/day for attendance at one or more board or committee meetings
Comments: Cash retainer includes a $2,000/year tax allowance.

Average director's annual compensation = $42,000
(assumes all meetings are attended and director sits on the Audit and Compensation committees)

STOCK-BASED COMPENSATION

Grant type(s):	**Restricted**	**Deferred**
Number of shares:	1,570*	500
Frequency:	One-time	Annual
Vesting:	20% per year, beginning at grant	After 6 yrs' service *and* retirement/death/disability/COC
Yr-end stock price:	37.375	Same
Plan type:	Separate	Separate
Plan life:	10 years	10 years
Plan kitty:	25,000	60,000
COC provision	Yes	Yes

* The number of shares includes 570 restricted stock units payable in cash to cover tax liabilities.

COMPENSATION DEFERRAL

Eligible comp: Retainer/meeting
Account types: Cash and/or stock
Interest rate: Variable (set by the Exec Committee)
Payment: After termination

CASH RETIREMENT BENEFITS

Mandatory retirement age: 72
Cash plan terminated 3/97 and replaced with annual restricted stock grants of 500 shares. Accrued benefits were converted to restricted stock.

INSURANCE BENEFITS

None

OTHER BENEFITS

None

CHANGES

None

Ford Motor Company

Industry: Automotive FY97 Revenue (mils): $153,627

BOARD STRUCTURE/FEES

	No. of Mtgs	Retainer Cash	Retainer Stock	Member Fee	Meeting Fee	Chairman Fee
Board	9	$30,000	—	$ —	$ 1,000	$ —
Audit	4	—	—	10,000	—	—
Finance	7	—	—	10,000	—	—
Compensation & Option	8	—	—	10,000	—	—
Org Review & Nominating	8	—	—	10,000	—	—
Environment & Public Policy	2	—	—	10,000	—	—

Comments: 25% of $40,000 total annual retainer is paid in deferred stock units (see STOCK); retired VCOB has agreement for $100,000/yr plus office, secretarial services and security

Average director's annual compensation = $59,000
(assumes all meetings are attended and director sits on the Audit and Compensation committees)

STOCK-BASED COMPENSATION

Grant type(s):	**Restricted**	**Deferred Units**
Number of shares:	2,000	$10,000
Frequency:	5 years	Annual
Vesting:	20% per year	After termination
Year-end stock price:	48.5625	Same
Plan type:	Separate	--
Plan life:	Indefinite	--
Plan kitty:	100,000	--

Comments: 25% of the retainer is mandatorily paid in deferred stock units.

Ownership Guidelines: within 5 years must own five times the annual retainer and committee fees

COMPENSATION DEFERRAL

Eligible comp: Retainer/meeting
Account types: Cash and/or stock
Interest rate: T-bills + 0.75%
Max. installments: 10 years
Payment: After termination

CASH RETIREMENT BENEFITS

Mandatory service: 5 years
Mandatory retirement age: 70
Min retirement age: 55
Basic benefits: $15,000
Payment term Life
Comments: director may receive retirement benefits if life insurance coverage is reduced to $100,000

INSURANCE BENEFITS

Accidental Death/Disability: $500,000
Life: $200,000

Comments: life insurance for a director who retires at 70 or, w/board approval, age 55 w/5 years' service, may be converted to $100,000 + $15,000/year paid for life.

OTHER BENEFITS

Matching Gift Program

Amount: $50,000; payout: Ford pays $2 for each $1 (up to $25,000) that a director contributes to tax-exempt organizations

CHANGES

None

Fortune Brands Inc.

Industry: Consumer Products FY97 Revenue (mils): $7,001

BOARD STRUCTURE/FEES

	No. of Mtgs	Retainer Cash	Retainer Stock	Member Fee	Meeting Fee	Chairman Fee
Board	7	$50,000	482 shrs	$ —	$ —	$ —
Audit	6	—	—	—	—	—
Comp & Stock Option	5	—	—	—	—	—
Nominat & Corp. Governance	3	—	—	—	—	—
Executive	0	—	—	15,000	—	—

Comments: directors receive an annual retainer of $35,000 and $15,000/year for all committee service for an aggregate of $50,000; the COB/CEO is on the Board of an outside director's company.

Average director's annual compensation = $68,105
(assumes all meetings are attended and director sits on the Audit and Compensation committees)

STOCK-BASED COMPENSATION

Grant type(s):	**Stock Award**	**Stock Option**
Number of shares:	482	2,000
Frequency:	Annual	Annual
Vesting:	Immediate	1 year
Year-end stock price:	37.5625	Same
Plan type:	Separate	Separate
Plan life:	5 years	5 years
Plan kitty:	15,000	125,000
COC provision	—	Yes

Comments: stock award is reflected in "Stock Retainer" and "Average Director's Annual Compensation" above.

COMPENSATION DEFERRAL

Eligible comp: Retainer/meeting/stock retainer
Account types: Cash and/or stock
Interest rate: T-bills (avg. quarterly rate)
COC provision Yes
Comments: Annual stock awards also may be deferred.

CASH RETIREMENT BENEFITS

Cash plan terminated 4/97 and replaced with stock option grants (see STOCK). Current directors may elect to continue in plan or receive stock options.

INSURANCE BENEFITS

Travel/Accident
Group Life
Comments: amounts not disclosed.

OTHER BENEFITS

Charitable Award Program: Amount: $500,000; payout: to director selected charity, educational or other qualified organization; insurance funded
Matching Gift Program: company will match 200% of gift up to $15,000

CHANGES Increased stock award by 182 shares

FPL Group, Inc.

Industry: Utilities

FY97 Revenue (mils): $6,369

BOARD STRUCTURE/FEES

	No. of Mtgs	Retainer Cash	Retainer Stock	Member Fee	Meeting Fee	Chairman Fee
Board	10	$27,000	—	$ —	$1,300	$ —
Audit	4	—	—	—	1,300	3,000
Compensation	6	—	—	—	1,300	3,000
Executive	4	—	—	—	1,300	3,000

Comments: Executive Committee functions as Nominating Committee; directors may elect to receive all or a portion of fees in stock.

Average director's annual compensation = $53,000
(assumes all meetings are attended and director sits on the Audit and Compensation committees)

STOCK-BASED COMPENSATION

Grant type(s):	**Stock Award**
Number of shares:	200
Frequency:	One-time
Vesting:	Immediate
Year-end stock price:	59.1875
Plan type:	Separate
Plan life:	10 years
Plan kitty:	300,000
COC provisions:	Yes

COMPENSATION DEFERRAL

None

CASH RETIREMENT BENEFITS

Cash plan terminated 11/96, with accrued benefits converted to share units that are paid out at termination on or after age 65

INSURANCE BENEFITS

Travel/Accident

OTHER BENEFITS

None

CHANGES

- Replaced one-time deferred stock award with the value = retainer with one-time grants of stock

Freeport-McMoran Copper & Gold Inc.

Industry: Chemicals FY97 Revenue (mils): $2,001

BOARD STRUCTURE/FEES

	No. of Mtgs	Retainer Cash	Retainer Stock	Member Fee	Meeting Fee	Chairman Fee
Board	6	$25,000	—	$ —	$1,000	$ —
Audit	3	—	—	—	1,000	2,000
Nominating	2	—	—	—	1,000	2,000
Corp. Personnel	3	—	—	—	1,000	2,000

Comments: Officer directors receive $1,000 for each board meeting attended. Kissinger Associates has an agreement for $250,000 per year. One director consults for $630,000/year in lieu of other board fees.

Average director's annual compensation = $37,000
(assumes all meetings are attended and director sits on the Audit and Compensation committees)

STOCK-BASED COMPENSATION

Grant type(s):	**Stock Option**
Number of shares:	10,000
Frequency:	Annual
Vesting:	25% per year
Year-end stock price:	15.625
Plan type:	Separate
Plan life:	10 years
COC provision	Yes

COMPENSATION DEFERRAL

None

CASH RETIREMENT BENEFITS

Mandatory service: 5 years
Min Retirement Age: 65
Basic benefits: 50–100% of retainer, based on years served
Payment term: Life

INSURANCE BENEFITS

None

OTHER BENEFITS

Matching Gift Program
Annual Maximum: $40,000 contributions up to $1,000 are double matched

CHANGES

None

Fruit of the Loom, Inc.

Industry: Consumer Products

FY97 Revenue (mils): $2,140

BOARD STRUCTURE/FEES

	No. of Mtgs	Retainer Cash	Retainer Stock	Member Fee	Meeting Fee	Chairman Fee
Board	4	$41,000	—	$ —	$1,000	$ —
Executive	0	—	—	—	1,000	—
Audit	5	—	—	—	1,000	—
Compensation	5	—	—	—	1,000	—

Comments: directors may forego half of their annual retainer for a 4-year period and receive 10,000 stock options which vest 25% per year.

Average director's annual compensation = $55,000
(assumes all meetings are attended and director sits on the Audit and Compensation committees)

STOCK-BASED COMPENSATION

Grant type(s):	**Restricted**
Number of shares:	1,850
Frequency:	Annual
Vesting:	2 years
Year-end stock price:	25.625
Plan type:	Separate
Plan life:	Indefinite
Plan kitty:	200,000
COC provision	Yes

Comments: initial grant covers 2,500 shares.

COMPENSATION DEFERRAL

Eligible comp:	Retainer/meeting
Account types:	Stock/stock options
Payment:	Date Specified by director
COC prov:	Yes

CASH RETIREMENT BENEFITS

None

INSURANCE BENEFITS

None

OTHER BENEFITS

None

CHANGES

None

The Gap, Inc.

Industry: Retailing — FY97 Revenue (mils): $6,508

BOARD STRUCTURE/FEES

	No. of Mtgs	Retainer Cash	Retainer Stock	Member Fee	Meeting Fee	Chairman Fee
Board	7	$36,000	—	$ —	$ —	$ —
Audit & Finance	2	—	—	—	—	—
Comp & Stock Option	4	—	—	—	—	—
Corporate Governance	0	—	—	—	—	—

Comments: Directors may elect to receive all or a portion of fees paid in discounted stock options, with a term of 7 years and are immediately exercisable

Attendance Requirements: Retainer is reduced by $2,500 for each Board and/or committee meeting day missed.

Average director's annual compensation = $36,000
(assumes all meetings are attended and director sits on the Audit and Compensation committees)

STOCK-BASED COMPENSATION

Grant type(s):	**Stock Option**
Number of shares:	3,750
Frequency:	Annual
Vesting:	3 years
Year-end stock price:	35.4375
Plan type:	Combined w/ exec.

Comments: initial grant covers 15,000 options; discretionary option grants are also authorized; one director received a discretionary grant of 7,500 discounted options in 1998.

COMPENSATION DEFERRAL

Eligible comp: Retainer
Account types: Stock Options
Comments: directors may elect to receive discounted stock options also

CASH RETIREMENT BENEFITS

Mandatory retirement age: 72
Cash plan terminated in 1996 for future directors. Benefits were frozen for current directors.

INSURANCE BENEFITS

Medical/Dental

OTHER BENEFITS

Discounts on company merchandise

CHANGES

- Increased stock option grant by 1,750 shares, and initial grants by 5,000 shares
- Made a discretionary stock option grant

General Dynamics Corporation

Industry: Aerospace FY97 Revenue (mils): $4,062

BOARD STRUCTURE/FEES

	No. of Mtgs	Retainer Cash	Retainer Stock	Member Fee	Meeting Fee	Chairman Fee
Board	7	$35,000	—	$ —	$2,000	$ —
Audit & Corp. Respon.	7	—	—	—	1,000	10,000
Compensation	2	—	—	—	1,000	10,000
Executive & Nominating	3	—	—	—	1,000	—
Benefit Plans & Investment	3	—	—	—	1,000	10,000

Comments: One director received consulting fees of $100,000 in 1997; the Crown family has contracts with the company and its subsidiaries for an aggregate $1-mil in 1997.

Average director's annual compensation = $58,000
(assumes all meetings are attended and director sits on the Audit and Compensation committees)

STOCK-BASED COMPENSATION

None

COMPENSATION DEFERRAL

None

CASH RETIREMENT BENEFITS

Mandatory service: 5 years
Mandatory retirement age: 72, extendable to 75 for special reasons
Reduced benefit available: Yes
Basic benefits: Average annual income for 3 highest years
Payment term: Life (10 years guaranteed)
Death Benefits: Yes

Comments: retirement before age 75 requires Board approval; for more than 10 years of svc payments are for the number of service years.

INSURANCE BENEFITS

Travel/Accident

OTHER BENEFITS

None

CHANGES

None

General Electric Company

Industry: Conglomerate　　　　FY97 Revenue (mils): $90,840

BOARD STRUCTURE/FEES

	No. of Mtgs	Retainer Cash	Retainer Stock	Member Fee	Meeting Fee	Chairman Fee
Board	11	$50,000	—	$ —	$ 1,400	$ —
Nominating	3	—	—	—	1,400	—
Mgmt Dev & Compensation	9	—	—	—	1,400	—
Audit	4	—	—	—	1,400	—

Comments: One director's company has investment agreements with GE subsidiaries for approximately $2.4-mil per year.

Average director's annual compensation = $83,600

(assumes all meetings are attended and director sits on the Audit and Compensation committees)

STOCK-BASED COMPENSATION

Grant type(s):	**Stock Option**
Number of shares:	6,000
Frequency:	Annual
Vesting:	25% per year
Year-end stock price:	73.375
Plan type:	Separate
Plan life:	7 years
Plan kitty:	350,000

COMPENSATION DEFERRAL

Eligible comp: Retainer/meeting
Account types: Cash and/or stock
Interest rate: long-term government bonds
Payment: After termination
Comments: payouts may be lump sum or installments

CASH RETIREMENT BENEFITS

Mandatory service: 5 years
Mandatory retirement age: 73
Minimum retirement age: 65
Basic Benefits: Retainer
Payment term: Life (+ life of surviving spouse)
Death benefit: Yes (spouse only)
Comments: director may take $450,000 life insurance policy instead

INSURANCE BENEFITS

Life: $150,000
Comments: aggregate amount of $150,000 for group life/accidental death

OTHER BENEFITS

Charitable Award Program

Amount: $1,000,000; payout: made to up to 5 charities; life insurance funded; paid at dir's retirement or death

CHANGES

None

General Mills, Inc.

Industry: Food

FY97 Revenue (mils): $5,609

BOARD STRUCTURE/FEES

	No. of Mtgs	Retainer Cash	Retainer Stock	Member Fee	Meeting Fee	Chairman Fee
Board	8	$35,000	500 shr	$ —	$ 1,000	$ —
Audit	3	—	—	—	1,000	—
Compensation	3	—	—	—	1,000	—
Executive	0	—	—	—	1,000	—
Finance	2	—	—	—	1,000	—
Nominating	0	—	—	—	1,000	—
Public Resonsibility	0	—	—	—	1,000	—

Comments: cash fees may be taken in stock if director elects; stock may be deferred until after termination.

Average director's annual compensation = $84,813
(assumes all meetings are attended and director sits on the Audit and Compensation committees)

STOCK-BASED COMPENSATION

Grant type(s):	**Stock Option**	**Stock Award**
Number of shares:	2,500	500
Frequency:	Annual	Annual
Vesting:	1 year	1 year
Year-end stock price:	71.625	Same
Plan type:	5 years	Same
Plan kitty:	250,000	Same
COC provision	Yes	Same

Comments: stock award is reflected in "Stock Retainer" and "Average Director's Annual Compensation" above

Ownership Guidelines: Five times the annual cash retainer

COMPENSATION DEFERRAL

Eligible comp: Retainer/meeting/stock retainer
Account types: Cash and/or stock
Interest rate: various investment funds

CASH RETIREMENT BENEFITS

Mandatory retirement age: 70; director may not serve for more than 15 years, beyond age 70 or more than 5 years after retirement from principal organization.

Cash plan terminated 2/96 and accrued values converted to 1-time grants of restricted stock units.

INSURANCE BENEFITS

Travel/Accident

OTHER BENEFITS

Charitable Award Program

Amount: $1,000,000; payout: made to one or more qualifying charities; life insurance funded

CHANGES

None

General Motors Corporation

Industry: Automotive FY97 Revenue (mils): $178,174

BOARD STRUCTURE/FEES

	No. of Mtgs	Retainer Cash	Retainer Stock	Member Fee	Meeting Fee	Chairman Fee
Board	12	$26,000	—	$ —	$1,000	$ —
Investment Funds	3	—	—	6,000	750	5,000
Executive Compensation	7	—	—	6,000	750	5,000
Public Policy	6	—	—	6,000	750	5,000
Audit	4	—	—	6,000	750	5,000
Director Affairs	2	—	—	6,000	750	5,000
Capital Stock	5	—	—	6,000	750	5,000
Executive	3	—	—	—	750	200,000

Comments: $1,000/day for services outside normal Board & committee activities; 35% of total retainer value ($40,000) is mandatorily deferred in stock units; the Executive Committee chairman and Compensation Committee member is a former COB; the VCOB is on the Board of a Compensation Committee member's company

Average director's annual compensation = $58,250
(assumes all meetings are attended and director sits on the Audit and Compensation committees)

STOCK-BASED COMPENSATION

Grant type(s):	**Deferred Units**	**Restricted**
Value of award:	$14,000	$10,000
Frequency:	Annual	Annual
Vesting:	After termination & age 70	After 6 years of service
Year-end stock price:	60.75	Same
Plan type:	(deferral plan)	Separate
Plan life:	—	Indefinite

Comments: directors must be age 56 before receiving restricted stock grants. Payment begins following retirement or age 70 in a lump sum or installments. Directors may choose between restricted stock units or 1,000 stock options which are exercisable after 1 year

COMPENSATION DEFERRAL

Eligible comp: Retainer/meeting
Account types: Cash and/or stock
Interest rate: Company rate
Payment: After termination
Comments: rate = average pretax yield of GM's U.S. cash portfolio.

CASH RETIREMENT BENEFITS

Mandatory retirement age: 70
Cash plan terminated 1/96 and replaced with restricted stock unit grants (above). Each outside director required to retire in 15 years or less was credited with one-time units based on projected value of total grants equal to benefit expected under terminated pension plan.

INSURANCE BENEFITS

None

OTHER BENEFITS

None

CHANGES

None

Genuine Parts Company

Industry: Service Industries FY97 Revenue (mils): $6,005

BOARD STRUCTURE/FEES

	No. of Mtgs	Retainer Cash	Retainer Stock	Member Fee	Meeting Fee	Chairman Fee
Board	4	$25,000	—	$ —	$925	$ —
Executive	7	—	—	—	$925	—
Audit	2	—	—	—	$925	3,000
Comp & Stock Option	2	—	—	—	$925	3,000

Comments: the COB/CEO is on the board of a Compensation Committee member's company and the Pres/COO is on the board of another Compensation Committee member's company

Average director's annual compensation = $32,400
(assumes all meetings are attended and director sits on the Audit and Compensation committees)

STOCK-BASED COMPENSATION

None

COMPENSATION DEFERRAL

Eligible comp: Retainer/meeting
Account types: Cash and/or stock
Payment: After at least 2 years
Comments: payout may be in cash or stock.

CASH RETIREMENT BENEFITS

None

INSURANCE BENEFITS

None

OTHER BENEFITS

None

CHANGES

None

The Goodyear Tire & Rubber Company

Industry: Automotive FY97 Revenue (mils): $13,155

BOARD STRUCTURE/FEES

	No. of Mtgs	Retainer Cash	Retainer Stock	Member Fee	Meeting Fee	Chairman Fee
Board	6	$35,000	—	$ —	$1,500	$ —
Audit	3	—	—	—	1,500	—
Compensation	3	—	—	—	1,500	—
Nominating	1	—	—	—	1,500	—
Corp. Responsibility	2	—	—	—	1,500	—

Average director's annual compensation = $53,000
(assumes all meetings are attended and director sits on the Audit and Compensation committees)

STOCK-BASED COMPENSATION

Grant type(s):	**Deferred Units**
Value of award:	$10,000
Frequency:	Annual
Vesting:	After termination
Year-end stock price:	63.625

Comments: these grants are intended to replace the retirement plan. Payout is in cash in lump sum or 10 installments. Benefits may be reduced if director is not age 70 with 5 years of service, or age 65 with 10 years of service.

COMPENSATION DEFERRAL

Eligible comp: Retainer/meeting
Account types: Stock
Payment After termination
Comments: deferrals must be in 25% increments; payouts are in cash

CASH RETIREMENT BENEFITS

Cash plan terminated 2/96 and replaced with stock units (above). Current directors received initial stock unit grants intended to reflect an estimated value commensurate with their accrued plan benefit.

INSURANCE BENEFITS

None

OTHER BENEFITS

Charitable Award Program
Amount: $1,000,000; payout: made to one or more qualifying charities recommended by director; life insurance funded

CHANGES

- Increased annual retainer by $5,000
- Increased deferred stock units by $2,000

GTE Corporation

Industry: Telecommunications FY97 Revenue (mils): $23,260

BOARD STRUCTURE/FEES

	No. of Mtgs	Retainer Cash	Retainer Stock	Member Fee	Meeting Fee	Chairman Fee
Board	12	$60,000	—	$ —	$ —	$ —
Audit	5	—	—	—	1,000	2,500
Exec Comp & Org Structure	10	—	—	—	1,000	2,500
Nominating	4	—	—	—	1,000	2,500
Pension Trust Coord.	1	—	—	—	1,000	2,500
Public Policy	1	—	—	—	1,000	2,500
Strat Issues, Plan & Tech	3	—	—	—	1,000	2,500

Average director's annual compensation = $60,000
(assumes all meetings are attended and director sits on the Audit and Compensation committees)

STOCK-BASED COMPENSATION

Grant type(s):	**Deferred Units**
Number of shares:	1,000
Frequency:	Annual
Vesting:	Termination
Year-end sock price:	52.25
Plan type:	Separate

Comments: payouts may be in cash or stock as elected by director.

COMPENSATION DEFERRAL

Eligible comp: Retainer/meeting
Account types: Cash and/or stock
Payment: Date specified by director
Comments: payouts for deferred stock units may be in cash or stock; payouts for cash amounts are in cash; unpaid balances after retirement may be invested in a variety of investment options.

CASH RETIREMENT BENEFITS

Mandatory retire age: 72
Cash plan terminated 1/1/97; all current directors elected to convert the present value of accrued benefits into a stock unit or cash deferred account.

INSURANCE BENEFITS

None

OTHER BENEFITS

Charitable Award Program
Amount: $1,000,000; payout: made in five annual installments to up to four charities; life insurance funded

CHANGES

None

Hannaford Bros. Company

Industry: Food FY97 Revenue (mils): $3,226

BOARD STRUCTURE/FEES

	No. of Mtgs	Retainer Cash	Retainer Stock	Member Fee	Meeting Fee	Chairman Fee
Board	6	$24,000	—	$ —	$1,000	$76,000
Audit	6	—	—	—	1,000	2,500
Human Resources	5	—	—	—	1,000	2,500
Corp Governance	5	—	—	—	1,000	2,500
Executive	0	—	—	—	1,000	—
Finance	5	—	—	—	1,000	2,500

Comments: Directors may elect to receive stock options in lieu of the annual retainer; the number of options = 3 X retainer + FMV. One director's firm had a consulting contract for $48,800 in 1997. COB fees are in lieu of other retainer/fees.

Average director's annual compensation = $41,000
(assumes all meetings are attended and director sits on the Audit and Compensation committees)

STOCK-BASED COMPENSATION

Grant type(s):	**Deferred Stock**	**Stock Option**
Award value:	Formula	As elected by director
Frequency:	Annual	Annual
Vesting:	5 years	1 year
Year-end stock price:	43.4375	Same
Plan type:	Separate	Same
Plan life:	Indefinite	Same
COC provision	—	Yes

Comments: deferred stock grant is based on projected future stock price; payout depends on actual market performance + dividend equivalents; in 1997 each director received 1,400 performance shares; grants are intended to provide retirement benefits.

Ownership Guidelines: Five times annual retainer; stock options count toward guideline.

COMPENSATION DEFERRAL

Eligible comp: Retainer/meeting
Account types: Cash and/or stock
Interest rate: 5-year T-notes
Payment: After termination
Comments: payout may be in cash or stock

CASH RETIREMENT BENEFITS

Mandatory retirement age: 70

INSURANCE BENEFITS

None

OTHER BENEFITS

None

CHANGES

None

Harcourt General, Inc.

Industry: Conglomerates

FY97 Revenue (mils): $3,692

BOARD STRUCTURE/FEES

	No. of Mtgs	Retainer Cash	Retainer Stock	Member Fee	Meeting Fee	Chairman Fee
Board	6	$22,500	—	$ —	$1,750	$ —
Executive	0	—	—	—	750	—
Audit	3	—	—	—	750	3,000
Compensation	2	—	—	—	750	2,000
Nominating	1	—	—	—	750	500

Comments: Chairman's fee reflects additional $500 per meeting, except Audit and Compensation who receive $1,000 per meeting.

Telephone Mtgs: 50% of regular attendance fee

Misc. fees: Subsidiary Fees Paid; $2,000 for each meeting attended in person or $1,000 by telephone**Average director's annual compensation = $36,750**
(assumes all meetings are attended and director sits on the Audit and Compensation committees)

STOCK-BASED COMPENSATION

None

COMPENSATION DEFERRAL

Eligible comp:	Retainer/meeting
Account types:	Cash and/or stock
Interest rate:	Top rate on 3-month CDs
Payment:	After termination

CASH RETIREMENT BENEFITS

Mandatory service:	10 years
Basic benefits:	Retainer
Payment term	Matching service
Death benefit:	No

Comments: benefits cease if director joins a competitor's board or becomes an employee within 3 years of retirement.

INSURANCE BENEFITS

None

OTHER BENEFITS

None

CHANGES

None

Hewlett-Packard Company

Industry: Office Equipment & Services FY97 Revenue (mils): $42,895

BOARD STRUCTURE/FEES

	No. of Mtgs	Retainer Cash	Retainer Stock	Member Fee	Meeting Fee	Chairman Fee
Board	7	$22,500	$22,500	$ —	$1,500	$ —
Audit	3	—	—	—	1,200	3,000
Compensation	5	—	—	—	1,200	3,000
Org. Review & Nominating	6	—	—	—	1,200	3,000
Executive	4	—	—	—	1,200	3,000
Finance & Investment	5	—	—	—	1,200	3,000

Comments: 50% of total ($45,000) annual retainer mandatorily paid in stock; directors may elect to have more paid in stock, or they may elect to take stock options which vest after 1 year.

Average director's annual compensation = $65,100
(assumes all meetings are attended and director sits on the Audit and Compensation committees)

STOCK-BASED COMPENSATION

Grant type(s):	**Stock Award**
Value of award:	50% of retainer ($22,500)
Frequency:	Annual
Vesting:	6 months
Year-end stock price:	62.375
Plan type:	Separate
Plan life:	10 years
Plan kitty:	1,000,000
COC provision	Yes

Comments: The value of this award is reflected in Stock Retainer and Average Director's Annual Compensation above.

COMPENSATION DEFERRAL

See STOCK comments

CASH RETIREMENT BENEFITS

Cash plan terminated 3/97; amounts previously deferred are paid in a lump sum at termination or death

INSURANCE BENEFITS

None

OTHER BENEFITS

None

CHANGES

None

Honeywell Inc.

Industry: Electronics FY97 Revenue (mils): $8,028

BOARD STRUCTURE/FEES

	No. of Mtgs	Retainer Cash	Retainer Stock	Member Fee	Meeting Fee	Chairman Fee
Board	9	$40,000	—	$ —	$1,200	$ —
Executive	0	—	—	—	1,200	—
Audit	3	—	—	—	1,200	1,800
Personnel	5	—	—	—	1,200	3,000
Nominating & Governance	4	—	—	—	1,200	2,400
Finance	4	—	—	—	1,200	2,400

Comments: Committee chairman fees reflect an additional $600 for each meeting. Directors may elect to receive fees in stock units where amount granted = 110% of fees forgone. The Pres/COO is on the Board of a Compensation Committee member's company.

Average director's annual compensation = $60,400

(assumes all meetings are attended and director sits on the Audit and Compensation committees)

STOCK-BASED COMPENSATION

Grant type(s):	**Deferred Stock**
Number of shares:	Formula
Frequency:	Annual
Vesting:	5 years + approved termination
Year-end stock price:	68.50
Plan type:	Separate
Plan kitty:	300,000
COC provision	Yes

Comments: annual award value equals 50% of prior year's retainer and meeting fees (intended to provide pension) *Note: for analysis purposes a value of $30,200 is used for the deferred stock award.*

Ownership Guidelines: Six times annual retainer

COMPENSATION DEFERRAL

Eligible comp: Retainer/meeting
Account types: Cash and/or stock
Interest rate: Corporate borrowing rate
Payment: After termination

Comments: interest is compounded annually; also may receive 110% of deferred amount if deferred in stock units.

CASH RETIREMENT BENEFITS

Mandatory retirement age: 70 or 15 years of service

INSURANCE BENEFITS

None

OTHER BENEFITS

None

CHANGES

- Increased annual retainer by $8,000

Hormel Foods Corporation

Industry: Food FY97 Revenue (mils): $3,257

BOARD STRUCTURE/FEES

	No. of Mtgs	Retainer Cash	Retainer Stock	Member Fee	Meeting Fee	Chairman Fee
Board	7	$23,000	—	$ —	$ 1,200	$ —
Audit	3	—	—	—	1,000	2,000
Compensation	4	—	—	—	1,000	2,000
Nominating	6	—	—	—	1,000	2,000
Personnel	1	—	—	—	1,000	—
Employee Benefits	3	—	—	—	1,000	—

Comments: Employee directors receive $100 for each meeting attended.

Average director's annual compensation = $38,400
(assumes all meetings are attended and director sits on the Audit and Compensation committees)

STOCK-BASED COMPENSATION

Grant type(s):	**Stock Option**	**Restricted**
Number of shares:	1,000	—
Award value:	—	$5,000
Frequency:	Annual	Annual
Vesting:	6 months	5 years
Year-end stock price:	32.75	Same
Plan type:	Separate	Same
Plan life:	10 years	Same
Plan kitty:	90,000	Same

Comments: options must be exercised in 500-share multiples.

COMPENSATION DEFERRAL

None

CASH RETIREMENT BENEFITS

None

INSURANCE BENEFITS

None

OTHER BENEFITS

None

CHANGES

- Increased committee meeting attendance fee by $500

Houghton Mifflin Company

Industry: Publishing & Broadcasting FY97 Revenue (mils): $797

BOARD STRUCTURE/FEES

	No. of Mtgs	Retainer: Cash	Retainer: Stock	Member Fee	Meeting Fee	Chairman Fee
Board	9	$10,000	1,000 shrs	$ —	$ 700	$ —
Audit	5	—	—	—	500	2,500
Executive	1	—	—	4,000	500	2,500
Compensation & Nominating	3	—	—	—	500	2,500
Finance	3	—	—	—	500	2,500
Employment Practice & Diversity	2	—	—	—	500	2,500

Average director's annual compensation = $58,675
(assumes all meetings are attended and director sits on the Audit and Compensation committees)

STOCK-BASED COMPENSATION

Grant type(s):	**Stock Award**	**Stock Option**
Number of shares:	1,000	2,000
Frequency:	Annual	Annual
Vesting:	Immediate	Undisclosed
Year-end stock price:	38.375	Same
Plan type:	Combined w/ exec.	Same

Comments: Directors also participate in a Stock Purchase Plan and may receive loans from the company to purchase shares

COMPENSATION DEFERRAL

Eligible comp: Retainer/meeting
Account types: Cash
Interest rate: T-bill
Payment: After termination

CASH RETIREMENT BENEFITS

Mandatory retirement age: 72
Basic benefit: 150% of retainer
Payment term: Matching Service

INSURANCE BENEFITS

None

OTHER BENEFITS

Charitable Award Program
Amount: $500,000; payment: After retirement in 20 installments to one or more charitable organizations; life insurance funded

CHANGES

None

Household International

Industry: Conglomerate FY97 Revenue (mils): $5,503

BOARD STRUCTURE/FEES

	No. of Mtgs	Retainer Cash	Retainer Stock	Member Fee	Meeting Fee	Chairman Fee
Board	6	$30,000	—	$ —	$ —	$ —
Audit	4	—	—	4,000	—	5,000
Compensation	3	—	—	4,000	—	5,000
Executive	1	—	—	4,000	—	5,000
Finance	2	—	—	4,000	—	5,000
Nominat & Governance	3	—	—	4,000	—	5,000

Comments: $1,100 paid for other meetings held at request of company. Directors may elect to have fees paid in stock.

Average director's annual compensation = $38,000
(assumes all meetings are attended and director sits on the Audit and Compensation committees)

STOCK-BASED COMPENSATION

Grant type(s):	**Stock Award**	**Stock Option**
Number of shares:	1,000	2,500
Frequency:	One-time	Annual
Vesting:	—	6 months
Year-end stock price:	127.625	Same
Plan type:	Separate	Same
Plan life:	5 years	Same

COMPENSATION DEFERRAL

Eligible comp: Retainer/meeting
Account types: Cash and/or stock
Interest: Company rate
Payment: Date specified by director
Comments: payout is made in shares and may be lump sum or installments.

CASH RETIREMENT BENEFITS

Mandatory retirement age: 72
Cash plan terminated 12/95 and replaced with phantom stock grants. In 1/97 all future benefits were eliminated and future stock contributions ceased

INSURANCE BENEFITS

Death/Disability: $250,000
Personal Excess Liability: $10-mil

OTHER BENEFITS

Matching Gift Program
Amount: up to $10,000 per year
Comments: first $500 of gifts are double matched to educ. org and nonprofits that promote economic development for low income neighborhoods; directors may request Household donate up to $5,000/year to charities that qualify under the philanthropic program.

CHANGES

- Increased stock option grant by 1,000 shares

Huffy Corporation

Industry: Leisure Time Industries FY97 Revenue (mils): $695

BOARD STRUCTURE/FEES

	No. of Mtgs	Retainer Cash	Retainer Stock	Member Fee	Meeting Fee	Chairman Fee
Board	9	$22,500	—	$ —	$ 900	$ —
Audit	4	—	—	—	850	3,000
Compensation	5	—	—	—	850	3,000
Nominating & Governance	3	—	—	—	850	3,000

Misc Fees: $500 paid for plant site visits; $2,500 for retreat meetings; $500 per half day of consulting outside the normal duties as a director

Comments: directors may receive stock options in lieu of cash fees where the number of shares = amount foregone divided by (FMV - $1.00) times 1.5; the exercise price = $1.00 per share; a subsidiary provided services to the Compensation Committee Chairman's firm for $334,800 in 1997.

Average director's annual compensation = $38,250
(assumes all meetings are attended and director sits on the Audit and Compensation committees)

STOCK-BASED COMPENSATION

Grant type(s):	**Stock Option**	**Stock Option**
Number of shares:	2,000	5,625
Frequency:	Annual	3 years
Vesting:	6 months	2 years
Year-end stock price:	13.50	Same
Plan type:	Separate	Same
Plan life:	10 years	Same
COC provision	Yes	Same

Note: for analysis purposes, the every- 3-year grant was annualized and added to the 2,000-share annual grant.

COMPENSATION DEFERRAL

Eligible comp: Retainer/meeting
Account types: Cash and/or stock options

CASH RETIREMENT BENEFITS

Cash plan discontinued 2/96 with benefits frozen for vested directors; benefit was replaced with $4,000 more cash retainer payable only to unvested participants (i.e., those vested receive only $15,000 retainer)

INSURANCE BENEFITS

None

OTHER BENEFITS

None

CHANGES

- Increased annual retainer by $3,500, and chairman's fees by $500
- Added the 1.5 times premium for stock options taken in lieu of cash fees

Idacorp, Inc (Formerly Idaho Power Company)

Industry: Utilities — FY97 Revenue (mils): $749

BOARD STRUCTURE/FEES

	No. of Mtgs	Retainer Cash	Retainer Stock	Member Fee	Meeting Fee	Chairman Fee
Board	6	$19,800	—	$ —	$ 800	$ —
Executive	1	—	—	—	800	2,040
Audit	6	—	—	—	800	2,040
Compensation	3	—	—	—	800	2,040
Finance	0	—	—	—	800	2,040
Investment	3	—	—	—	800	2,040

Comments: One of the Compensation Committee members has a 10-year leasing agreement with Idacorp for $13,425/year

Average director's annual compensation = $31,800
(assumes all meetings are attended and director sits on the Audit and Compensation committees)

STOCK-BASED COMPENSATION

None

COMPENSATION DEFERRAL

Eligible comp: Retainer/meeting
Account types: Cash
Max. Installments: 10 years
Payment: After termination
Comments: payouts may be lump sum or installments

CASH RETIREMENT BENEFITS

Basic benefits: $17,500
Payment term 15 years
Death benefit: Yes
Comments: life insurance funded.

INSURANCE BENEFITS

None

OTHER BENEFITS

None

CHANGES

- Increased annual retainer by $7,800 and all meeting attendance fees by $200
- *Reduced* chairman's fee by $360

IKON Office Solutions, Inc.

Industry: Conglomerate FY97 Revenue (mils): $5,128

BOARD STRUCTURE/FEES

	No. of Mtgs	Retainer Cash	Retainer Stock	Member Fee	Meeting Fee	Chairman Fee
Board	7	$30,000	—	$ —	$ —	$ —
Audit	4	—	—	—	—	3,000
Human Resources	5	—	—	—	—	3,000
Interim	0	—	—	—	—	3,000
Investment	0	—	—	—	—	3,000

Comments: Directors may take discount-priced stock options in lieu of all or a portion of the annual retainer and committee and trustee fees (see STOCK). Trustees for employee benefits plan receive $3,000 per year, $3,000 for chairmanship, and attendance fees of $1,000. Director Hauptfuhrer receives $25,000/yr as Chairman of the Independent Directors, which coordinates the annual evaluation of the CEO and holds periodic meetings of the outside directors. $1,000 fee paid for attendance at special meetings.

Average director's annual compensation = $30,000

(assumes all meetings are attended and director sits on the Audit and Compensation committees)

STOCK-BASED COMPENSATION

Grant type(s):	**Stock Option**	**Restricted**	**Stock Option**	**Discount Option**
Number of shares:	2,000	400	25,000	As elected by director
Frequency:	Annual	Annual	One-time	Annual
Vesting:	Immediate	20% per year	20% per year	One year
Option life:	10 years	–	10 years	20 years
Year-end stock price:	28.125	Same	Same	Same
Plan type:	Separate	Separate	Same	Separate
Plan life:	10 years	–	–	Same

Comments: discount-priced options may be taken in lieu of fees (exercise price =75% of FMV).

COMPENSATION DEFERRAL

Eligible comp: Retainer/chairman fees

Comments: Retainer may be deferred via discount stock options (see STOCK).

CASH RETIREMENT BENEFITS

Mandatory retirement age: 70

Cash plan terminated 5/97 and replaced with annual restricted stock grants. Accrued benefits were converted to restricted stock, paid out upon retirement.

INSURANCE BENEFITS

None

OTHER BENEFITS

None

CHANGES

- Increased annual retainer by $5,000
- Eliminated all meeting attendance fees and committee member fees
- Increased annual stock option grants by 1,200 shares
- Added one-time stock option grants
- Eliminated cash retirement plan and replaced with annual restricted stock grants

Illinois Tool Works Inc.

Industry: Manufacturing FY97 Revenue (mils): $5,220

BOARD STRUCTURE/FEES

	No. of Mtgs	Retainer Cash	Retainer Stock	Member Fee	Meeting Fee	Chairman Fee
Board	5	$25,000	—	$ —	$1,000	$ —
Audit	3	—	—	—	1,000	1,800
Compensation	2	—	—	—	1,000	1,200
Corp. Governance & Nominating	1	—	—	—	1,000	600
Finance	1	—	—	—	1,000	600

Comments: Chairmen fees reflect additional $600 received for each meeting attended; the Chairman of the Executive Committee has a consulting contract for $85,000/year

Average director's annual compensation = $35,000
(assumes all meetings are attended and director sits on the Audit and Compensation committees)

STOCK-BASED COMPENSATION

Grant type(s):	**Restricted**	**Phantom Stock**
Number of shares:	900	1,000
Frequency:	3 years	One-time
Vesting:	1/3 each year	Retirement/approved resignation
Year-end stock price:	60.125	Same
Plan type:	Separate	Same
Plan life:	3 years	Same
COC provision	–	Yes

Comments: director may not sell the restricted shares until 3 years after grant (except after retirement/death); the board may renew the plan for successive 3-yr terms; phantom unit accounts are distributed in cash in a lump sum or up to 10 installments.

COMPENSATION DEFERRAL

Eligible comp: Retainer/meeting
Account types: Cash
Interest: "Current rates"
Payment: After termination

CASH RETIREMENT BENEFITS

Cash plan terminated in 1995 and replaced with phantom stock grants (above); only directors who retired prior to 1995 will receive benefits from the cash plan.

INSURANCE BENEFITS

None

OTHER BENEFITS

None

CHANGES

None

Ingersoll-Rand Company

Industry: Manufacturing

FY97 Revenue (mils): $7,103

BOARD STRUCTURE/FEES

	No. of Mtgs	Retainer Cash	Retainer Stock	Member Fee	Meeting Fee	Chairman Fee
Board	10	$30,000	—	$ —	$1,000	$ —
Audit	4	—	—	—	1,000	4,000
Comp & Nominating	4	—	—	—	1,000	4,000
Corporate Affairs	2	—	—	—	1,000	2,000
Finance	4	—	—	—	1,000	4,000

Comments: Chairmen fees reflect additional $1,000 fee for each meeting attended.

Average director's annual compensation = $48,000
(assumes all meetings are attended and director sits on the Audit and Compensation committees)

STOCK-BASED COMPENSATION

Grant type(s):	**Stock Option**	**Deferred**
Number of shares:	2,250	600
Frequency:	Annual	Annual
Vesting:	1 year	Undisclosed
Year-end stock price:	40.50	Same
Plan type:	Combined w/ exec.	—

COMPENSATION DEFERRAL

Eligible comp: Retainer/meeting
Account types: Stock

Comments: amounts voluntarily deferred are matched 20% by the company; matched amounts vest after 5 years or due to death or normal retirement; payouts are made in shares

CASH RETIREMENT BENEFITS

Mandatory retirement age: 72

Cash plan terminated 4/97 and replaced with annual deferred grants (see STOCK). The value of accrued benefits was converted to deferred stock accounts for current directors.

INSURANCE BENEFITS

None

OTHER BENEFITS

None

CHANGES

None

International Business Machines Corp. (IBM)

Industry: Office Equipment & Services FY97 Revenue (mils): $78,508

BOARD STRUCTURE/FEES

	No. of Mtgs	Retainer Cash	Retainer Stock	Member Fee	Meeting Fee	Chairman Fee
Board	9	$24,000	—	$ —	$ —	$ —
Executive	1	—	—	—	—	5,000
Audit	3	—	—	—	—	5,000
Exec Comp & Mgmt Res	5	—	—	—	—	5,000
Directors & Corp Governance	3	—	—	—	—	5,000

Comments: 60% of the total ($60,000) annual retainer is mandatorily deferred in stock

Average director's annual compensation = $24,000
(assumes all meetings are attended and director sits on the Audit and Compensation committees)

STOCK-BASED COMPENSATION

Grant type(s):	**Stock Option**	**Deferred**
Number of shares:	2,000	60% of Retainer ($36,000)
Frequency:	Annual	Annual
Vesting:	25% per year	After termination
Year-end stock price:	103.125	Same
Plan type:	Separate	(Deferred plan)
Plan life:	Indefinite	—
Plan kitty:	25,000 shares per year	—

Comments: shares acquired upon exercise of options are restricted until retirement, death, disability or termination

COMPENSATION DEFERRAL

Eligible comp: Retainer/meeting
Account types: Cash and/or stock
Interest rate: 6-month T-bill
Payment: After termination

CASH RETIREMENT BENEFITS

Cash plan terminated 1/96 and accrued benefits converted to stock accounts under the deferred compensation plan.

INSURANCE BENEFITS

Group Life = $50,000
Travel/Accident = $300,000

OTHER BENEFITS

Matching Grant Program (same as employees)

CHANGES

None

The Interpublic Group of Companies Inc.

Industry: Service Industries FY97 Revenue (mils): $3,126

BOARD STRUCTURE/FEES

	No. of Mtgs	Retainer Cash	Retainer Stock	Member Fee	Meeting Fee	Chairman Fee
Board	7	$24,000	—	$ —	$1,000	$ —
Finance	13	—	—	2,000	1,000	—
Executive Policy	0	—	—	2,000	1,000	—
Audit	3	—	—	2,000	1,000	2,500
Compensation	6	—	—	2,000	1,000	3,000
Nominating	2	—	—	2,000	1,000	2,500

Average director's annual compensation = $44,000
(assumes all meetings are attended and director sits on the Audit and Compensation committees)

STOCK-BASED COMPENSATION

Grant type(s):	**Stock Option**	**Restricted**
Award Value:	$30,000	3,000 shrs
Frequency:	Annual	5 years
Vesting:	3 years	5 years
Year-end stock price:	49.8125	Same
Plan type:	Separate	Same
Plan life:	10 years	Same
Plan kitty:	200,000	Same

Comments: The Committee may make tax offset payments for restricted awards; directors received 750 stock options in 1997

COMPENSATION DEFERRAL

None

CASH RETIREMENT BENEFITS

Cash plan terminated 12/31/95 and benefits frozen; the restricted stock grants (above) are intended to replace this benefit.

INSURANCE BENEFITS

None

OTHER BENEFITS

None

CHANGES

None

J. C. Penney Company, Inc.

Industry: Retailing FY97 Revenue (mils): $30,546

BOARD STRUCTURE/FEES

	No. of Mtgs	Retainer Cash	Retainer Stock	Member Fee	Meeting Fee	Chairman Fee
Board	9	$26,400	$ —	$ —	$ 1,200	$ —
Audit	4	—	—	—	1,000	4,500
Personnel & Compensation	8	—	—	—	1,000	4,500
Benefit Plans Review	3	—	—	—	1,000	4,000
Directors	6	—	—	—	1,000	4,000
Public Affairs	2	—	—	—	1,000	4,000
Finance	4	—	—	—	1,000	4,000

Misc. Fees: $2,000 paid for subsidiary board and committee meetings

Comments: Outside directors receive $800/day for additional services. Directors who act as representatives under trust agreement with Chase Manhattan Bank are paid $5,000/yr plus $600 per meeting, plus expenses; 3 directors received $400, $400, and $800 for additional services in 1997

Average director's annual compensation = $49,200
(assumes all meetings are attended and director sits on the Audit and Compensation committees)

STOCK-BASED COMPENSATION

Grant type(s):	**Restricted**
Number of shares:	500
Frequency:	Annual
Vesting:	upon "qualifying termination"
Year-end stock price:	60.3125
Plan type:	Separate
Plan life:	5 years
Plan kitty:	90,000
COC provision:	Yes

COMPENSATION DEFERRAL

Eligible comp: Retainter/meeting
Account types: Cash and/or Stock
Interest rate: 1-year T-bill
Max. installments: 10 years
COC provision:: Yes
Comments: rabbi trust must be established upon a COC

CASH RETIREMENT BENEFITS

Mandatory retirement age: 72

Cash plan terminated 2/97 for future directors. Restricted stock grants are 500 shares for new directors or those electing not to continue in retirement plan, and 200 shares for those continuing in plan

INSURANCE BENEFITS

None

OTHER BENEFITS

Charitable Award Program

Amount: \$500,000; payout: utilizes 2nd-to-die policies; \$500,000 is paid out upon the earlier of: 5 years after death of first director or death of second director

CHANGES

- Dropped tandem stock option grants of 800 shares annually (where the lower-value grant, restricted shares, or stock options was canceled)

Johnson & Johnson

Industry: Health Care FY97 Revenue (mils): $22,629

BOARD STRUCTURE/FEES

	No. of Mtgs	Retainer Cash	Retainer Stock	Member Fee	Meeting Fee	Chairman Fee
Board	7	$45,000	—	$ —	$ —	$ —
Audit	3	—	—	5,000	1,500	3,000
Compensation	4	—	—	5,000	1,500	3,000

Same Day Mtg Fees: Meeting fee of $1,500/day for committee meetings held on days other than board meetings.

Comments: $20,000 of total retainer ($65,000) is mandatorily deferred in stock units.

Average director's annual compensation = $55,000
(assumes all meetings are attended and director sits on the Audit and Compensation committees)

STOCK-BASED COMPENSATION

Grant type(s):	Stock Award	Deferred Units	Stock Options
Award Value	$10,000	$20,000	900
Frequency:	One-time	Annual	Annual
Vesting:	—	Upon termination	—
Year-end stock price:	65.875	same	same
Plan Type	—	(deferral plan)	—

Comments: Stock award is granted upon initial election

COMPENSATION DEFERRAL

Eligible comp: Retainter/meeting
Account types: Cash and/or Stock
Payment: After termination

CASH RETIREMENT BENEFITS

Mandatory retirement age: 72
Annual stock unit accruals (see STOCK) are designed to provide retirement benefits.

INSURANCE BENEFITS

None

OTHER BENEFITS

None

CHANGES

- Reduced number of stock options by 200 shares

Kellogg Company

Industry: Food FY97 Revenue (mils): $6,830

BOARD STRUCTURE/FEES

	No. of Mtgs	Retainer Cash	Retainer Stock	Member Fee	Meeting Fee	Chairman Fee
Board	7	$25,000	—	$ —	$1,000	$ —
Executive	1	—	—	—	1,000	4,000
Audit	2	—	—	—	1,000	4,000
Social Responsibility	1	—	—	—	1,000	4,000
Compensation	5	—	—	—	1,000	4,000
Finance	2	—	—	—	1,000	4,000
Nominating & Corp Governance	2	—	—	—	1,000	4,000

Average director's annual compensation = $39,000

(assumes all meetings are attended and director sits on the Audit and Compensation committees)

STOCK-BASED COMPENSATION

Grant type(s):	**Restricted**
Number of shares:	1,000
Frequency:	Annual
Vesting:	After termination
Year-end stock price:	49.625
Plan type:	Separate
Plan life:	10 years
Plan kitty:	187,200
COC provision:	Yes

Comments: shares fully vested at grant but may not be sold or transferred until service terminates; held in a trust

Ownership Guidelines: 10 times annual retainer within 3 years

COMPENSATION DEFERRAL

Eligible comp: Retainter/meeting
Account types: Stock
Max. installments: 10 years
Payment: After termination
Comments: all accounts are denominated in stock units; paid out in cash

CASH RETIREMENT BENEFITS

Cash plan terminated 2/96; accrued benefits were converted to stock and put in a trust (with full vesting assumed for all directors)

INSURANCE BENEFITS

Travel/Accident

OTHER BENEFITS

None

CHANGES

- Added stock ownership guidelines

Kelly Services, Inc.

Industry: Service Industries　　　　FY97 Revenue (mils): $3,853

BOARD STRUCTURE/FEES

	No. of Mtgs	Retainer Cash	Retainer Stock	Member Fee	Meeting Fee	Chairman Fee
Board	4	$21,000	$10,500	$ —	$1,000	$ —
Audit	4	—	—	—	800	—
Compensation	5	—	—	—	800	—

Comments: the value of the stock award = 50% of annual cash retainer

Average director's annual compensation = $42,700
(assumes all meetings are attended and director sits on the Audit and Compensation committees)

STOCK-BASED COMPENSATION

Grant type(s):	**Stock Award**
Number of shares:	50% of annual retainer
Frequency:	Annual
Vesting:	6 months
Year-end stock price:	30.00
Plan type:	Separate
Plan life:	Indefinite
Plan kitty:	0.25% of common outstanding on January 1st each year

Comments: the value of the stock award is reflected in "Stock Retainer" and "Average Director's Annual Compensation" above.

COMPENSATION DEFERRAL

None

CASH RETIREMENT BENEFITS

None

INSURANCE BENEFITS

None

OTHER BENEFITS

None

CHANGES

None

Kimberly-Clark Corporation

Industry: Paper/Forest | FY97 Revenue (mils): $12,547

BOARD STRUCTURE/FEES

	No. of Mtgs	Retainer Cash	Retainer Stock	Member Fee	Meeting Fee	Chairman Fee
Board	8	$30,000	$ —	$ —	$1,200	$ —
Audit	3	—	—	—	1,200	—
Compensation	3	—	—	—	1,200	—
Nominating	1	—	—	—	1,200	—

Same Day Mtg Fees: maximum $3,600/day for same-day board & committee meetings

Comments: one director's firm was paid $1,018,000 for hotel/lodging/car rental by KC in 1997 and property rentals of $649,000; the director's firm paid K-C Aviation $716,000 for airline services in 1997; a K-C Group President serves on the board of a Compensation Committee member's company.

Average director's annual compensation = $46,800
(assumes all meetings are attended and director sits on the Audit and Compensation committees)

STOCK-BASED COMPENSATION

Grant type(s):	**Restricted**
Number of shares:	600
Frequency:	Annual
Vesting: after Termination	After termination
Year-end stock price:	49.3125
Plan type:	Separate
Plan life:	10 years
Plan kitty:	35,000

Comments: dividends are held in interest bearing cash accounts until the shares vest.

COMPENSATION DEFERRAL

Eligible comp: Retainter/meeting
Account types: Cash and/or Stock
Interest rate: 6-month T-bill or 6%, if higher
Max. installments: 20 years
Payment: Date specified by Director
Comments: one-time account transfers permitted; all distributions are in cash

CASH RETIREMENT BENEFITS

None

INSURANCE BENEFITS

None

OTHER BENEFITS

None

CHANGES

- Increased annual retainer by $5,000

Knight-Ridder, Inc.

Industry: Publishing/Broadcasting — FY97 Revenue (mils): $3,139

BOARD STRUCTURE/FEES

	No. of Mtgs	Retainer Cash	Retainer Stock	Member Fee	Meeting Fee	Chairman Fee
Board	7	$15,000	$15,000	$ —	$1,500	$ —
Nominating	2	—	—	—	1,000	5,000
Compensation	5	—	—	—	1,000	5,000
Audit	2	—	—	—	1,000	5,000
Finance	1	—	—	—	1,000	5,000
Environmental Affairs	1	—	—	—	1,000	5,000

Comments: Former CEO has consulting agreement for $150,000 the first year and $100,000 the second year; directors may elect to receive all of the annual retainer in stock

Average director's annual compensation = $47,500

(assumes all meetings are attended and director sits on the Audit and Compensation committees)

STOCK-BASED COMPENSATION

Grant type(s):	**Deferred**	**Stock Option**	**Stock Award**
Number of shares:	600	2,000	$15,000
Frequency:	Annual	Annual	Annual
Year-end stock price:	52.00	same	same

COMPENSATION DEFERRAL

Eligible comp: Retainter/meeting
Account types: Cash
Payment: Date specified by director
Comments: terms are provided under individual agreements

CASH RETIREMENT BENEFITS

Cash plan terminated 4/96. Directors age 65 and over at plan termination continue to be eligible. Other directors now receive 600 shares of deferred stock annually.

INSURANCE BENEFITS

None

OTHER BENEFITS

None

CHANGES

- Now pay 50% of annual retainer in stock (and directors may elect all)
- Increased board meeting attendance fee by $500
- Increased chairman's fee by $2,500

Lee Enterprises, Inc.

Industry: Service Industries FY97 Revenue (mils): $439

BOARD STRUCTURE/FEES

	No. of Mtgs	Retainer Cash	Retainer Stock	Member Fee	Meeting Fee	Chairman Fee
Board	4	$24,400	500	$ —	$1,000	$50,000
Audit	3	—	—	—	700	3,000
Nominating	3	—	—	—	700	3,000
Exec. Compensation	3	—	—	—	700	3,000

Comments: directors may elect to receive 50% or 100% of fees in stock; one director received $165,000 in 1997 for consulting services (rate is $1,500/day); another received $3,000; COB fee is paid in addition to other board fees.

Average director's annual compensation = $47,381
(assumes all meetings are attended and director sits on the Audit and Compensation committees)

STOCK-BASED COMPENSATION

Grant type(s):	**Stock Award**
Number of shares:	500
Frequency:	Annual
Year-end stock price:	29.5625
Plan type:	Separate
Plan life:	Indefinite
Plan kitty:	50,000

Comments: The value of the stock award is reflected in "Stock Retainer" and "Average Director's Annual Compensation" above

COMPENSATION DEFERRAL

Eligible comp: Retainter/meeting
Account types: Cash
Interest rate: Company Rate
Payment: Date specified by director (between ages 60 & 70)
Comments: directors may elect to have deferred compensation credited to a rabbi trust

CASH RETIREMENT BENEFITS

None

INSURANCE BENEFITS

None

OTHER BENEFITS

Matching Gifts: Contributions to charities are matched by the Company up to $5,000 per year

CHANGES

None

Louisiana-Pacific Corporation

Industry: Paper/Forest FY97 Revenue (mils): $2,403

BOARD STRUCTURE/FEES

	No. of Mtgs	Retainer Cash	Retainer Stock	Member Fee	Meeting Fee	Chairman Fee
Board	5*	$20,000	—	$ —	$1,750	$ —
Audit	3*	—	—	—	1,000	750
Nominating	2	—	—	—	1,000	500
Environ. Affairs	2	—	—	—	1,000	500
Compensation	4**	—	—	—	1,000	1,000
Executive	5	—	—	—	1,000	—

* includes one telephone meeting ** includes three telephone meetings

Misc. Fees: Telephone meeting fees: $750 for board meeting, $500 for committee meeting ($750 for chairman)

Comments: chairman fee reflects an additional $250 per meeting attended; one director received $122,000 worth of building materials in exchange for advertising appearances

Average director's annual compensation = $32,750
(assumes all meetings are attended and director sits on the Audit and Compensation committees)

STOCK-BASED COMPENSATION

Grant type(s):	**Discount Stock Option**
Number of shares:	45,000
Frequency:	5 years
Vesting:	20% each year
Year-end stock price:	19.00
Plan type:	Separate
Plan life:	300,000
Plan kitty:	Indefinite
COC provision:	Yes

Comments: option exercise price = 85% of FMV.

COMPENSATION DEFERRAL

Eligible comp: Retainer/meeting
Account types: Cash
Interest rate: Moody's + 2%
Max. installments: 15 years
Payment: After termination
COC provision:: Yes

Comments: payouts are made in lump sum or installments; minimum deferred amount = $2,400/year.

CASH RETIREMENT BENEFITS

Mandatory retirement age: 70
None

INSURANCE BENEFITS

None

OTHER BENEFITS

None

CHANGES

- Changed deferral plan with interest now = Moody's + 2% vs. 90-day high-grade commercial paper before

Manor Care, Inc.

Industry: Health Care

FY97 Revenue (mils): $1,617

BOARD STRUCTURE/FEES

	No. of Mtgs	Retainer Cash	Retainer Stock	Member Fee	Meeting Fee	Chairman Fee
Board	6	$0	—	$ —	$ —	$ —
Finance	3	—	—	—	1,610	—
Audit	2	—	—	—	1,610	—
Comp/Key Exec SO Plan	5	—	—	—	1,610	—
Nominating/Governance	1	—	—	—	1,610	—
Quality Assurance	1	—	—	—	1,610	—
Comp/Key Exec SO Plan #2	1	—	—	—	1,610	—

Same day fees: Committee fees paid only if on a day other than board meeting

Average director's annual compensation = $0

(assumes all meetings are attended and director sits on the Audit and Compensation committees)

STOCK-BASED COMPENSATION

Grant type(s):	**Stock Option**	**Restricted**
Number of Shares:	1,000	$30,000
Frequency:	Annual	Annual
Vesting:	1/3 each yr in years 2-4	1/3 per year
Option Life:	5 years	—
Yr-end Stock Price:	35.00	same
Plan Type:	Separate	Separate
Plan Life:	10 years	—
Plan Kitty:	150,000	40,000
COC provision::	Yes	—

Comments: initial stock option grant covers 5,000 shares; same plan governs elective deferrals in stock (see COMP DEFERRAL) for a maximum of 80,000 shares; restricted shares may be deferred for 2 yrs or more, which is backed by a Rabbi trust

COMPENSATION DEFERRAL

Eligible comp: Committee fees
Account types: Stock
Max. installments: 20 years
Payment: After termination

Comments: minimum amount that may be deferred is 25%; payment may be in lump sum or installments.

CASH RETIREMENT BENEFITS

Cash plan terminated 9/96

INSURANCE BENEFITS

None

OTHER BENEFITS

None

CHANGES

None

Marriott International, Inc.

Industry: Leisure FY97 Revenue (mils): $12,034

BOARD STRUCTURE/FEES

	No. of Mtgs	Retainer Cash	Retainer Stock	Member Fee	Meeting Fee	Chairman Fee
Board	7	$25,000	$12,500	$ —	$1,250	$ —
Executive	0	—	—	—	1,250	1,000
Compensation Policy	5	—	—	—	1,250	1,000
Nominating & Corp Govern	1	—	—	—	1,250	1,000
Audit	3	—	—	—	1,250	1,000

Misc Fees: $1,250 attendance fee for shareholders' meetings; the COB serves on the Compensation Committee of an outside director's firm

Average director's annual compensation = $56,250
(assumes all meetings are attended and director sits on the Audit and Compensation committees)

STOCK-BASED COMPENSATION

Grant type(s):	**Deferred**	**Stock Award**
Number of shares:	250	Value = 50% of cash retainer ($12,500)
Frequency:	Annual	Annual
Vesting:	Immediate (distributed upon retirement)	Immediate
Year-end stock price:	69.25	Same
Plan type:	Separate	Combined with exec
Plan life:	Indefinite	—
Plan kitty:	500,000	—

Comments: Special one-time deferred stock awards were made in 1997 to three directors for 1,500 shares, 2,000 shares, and 3,000 shares

COMPENSATION DEFERRAL

Eligible comp: Retainter/meeting
Account types: Stock/cash
Interest rate: Company
Max. installments: 10 years
Payment: After termination
Comments: payment of accounts is made in shares; fees must be deferred in 25% increments.

CASH RETIREMENT BENEFITS

Mandatory retirement age: 70

Cash plan was terminated and replaced with deferred stock grants. Current directors received between 1,500 and 3,000 shares which vest 10% per year of service (previous service counts).

INSURANCE BENEFITS

None

OTHER BENEFITS

None

CHANGES

- Added annual stock awards and discretionary stock grants

Marsh & McLennan Companies

Industry: Nonbank Financial FY97 Revenue (mils): $6,009

BOARD STRUCTURE/FEES

	No. of Mtgs	Retainer Cash	Retainer Stock	Member Fee	Meeting Fee	Chairman Fee
Board	8	$30,000	$10,000 + 600 shrs	$ —	$1,000	$ —
Executive	0	—	—	2,000	1,000	—
Audit	5	—	—	2,000	1,000	3,000
Compensation	12	—	—	2,000	1,000	3,000

Comments: 25% of $40,000 annual retainer is mandatorily paid in stock; directors may elect to have all or a portion of fees paid in stock; the former COB/CEO received $1,937,500 in consulting fees in 1997.

Average director's annual compensation = $113,738
(assumes all meetings are attended and director sits on the Audit and Compensation committees)

STOCK-BASED COMPENSATION

Grant Type(s):	**Stock Award**	**Stock Award**
Value of Award:	$10,000	600 shares
Frequency:	Annual	Annual
Year-end stock price:	74.5625	Same
Plan type:	Separate	Same
Plan life:	Indefinite	Same
Plan kitty:	250,000	Same
COC provision:	Yes	Same

Comments: the value of the stock awards is reflected in the "Stock Retainer" and "Average Director's Annual Compensation" above.

COMPENSATION DEFERRAL

Eligible comp: Retainter/meeting
Account types: Cash and/or stock
Interest rate: Prime
Payment: Date specified by director
Comments: account transfers are permitted once per quarter.

CASH RETIREMENT BENEFITS

Cash plan terminated 5/97 and directors given a one-time grant of 4,000 shares of deferred stock to replace anticipated benefits

INSURANCE BENEFITS

None

OTHER BENEFITS

None

CHANGES

- Added annual stock award of 600 shares
- Eliminated cash retirement plan and granted current directors 4,000 shares of deferred stock to replace anticipated benefits

The May Dept. Stores Company

Industry: Retailing FY97 Revenue (mils): $12,685

BOARD STRUCTURE/FEES

	No. of Mtgs	Retainer Cash	Retainer Stock	Member Fee	Meeting Fee	Chairman Fee
Board	9	$30,000	—	$ —	$2,000	$ —
Audit	5	—	—	—	1,000	5,000
Exec Comp & Develop	5	—	—	—	1,000	5,000
Nominating	4	—	—	—	1,000	5,000
Executive	0	—	—	—	1,000	—
Finance	2	—	—	—	1,000	5,000

Average director's annual compensation = $58,000
(assumes all meetings are attended and director sits on the Audit and Compensation committees)

STOCK-BASED COMPENSATION

Grant type(s):	**Restricted**
Value of award	$45,000
Frequency:	Annual
Vesting:	Termination
Year-end stock price:	52.6875
Plan type:	Separate
Plan kitty:	100,000

Comments: initial grants upon election to the board cover 2,000 shares.

COMPENSATION DEFERRAL

Eligible comp: Retainter/meeting
Account Type: Cash or stock
Comments: no additional information disclosed

CASH RETIREMENT BENEFITS

Cash plan terminated as of 1/1/96 and accrued benefits transferred to deferral accounts.

INSURANCE BENEFITS

None

OTHER BENEFITS

None

CHANGES

- increased restricted stock grants by $5,000

McDermott International, Inc.

Industry: Service Industries FY97 Revenue (mils): $3,308

BOARD STRUCTURE/FEES

	No. of Mtgs	Retainer Cash	Retainer Stock	Member Fee	Meeting Fee	Chairman Fee
Board	6	$28,000	$ —	$ —	$2,500	$ —
Audit	2	—	—	2,000	1,650	1,000
Directors/Nominating & Govern.	1	—	—	1,750	1,650	750
Compensation	6	—	—	1,750	1,650	750

Misc Fees: Telephone Meetings: $1,000

Average director's annual compensation = $59,950
(assumes all meetings are attended and director sits on the Audit and Compensation committees)

STOCK-BASED COMPENSATION

Grant type(s):	**Stock Option**	**Restricted**
Number of shares:	900; 300; 300*	450; 150; 150**
Frequency:	Annual	Annual
Vesting:	6 months	end of 3-year term
Year-end stock price:	36.625	Same
Plan type:	Separate	Same
Plan life:	10 years	Same
Plan kitty:	100,000	Same
COC provision:	Yes	Same

* number of shares/options granted on 1st, 2nd, and 3rd year of director's term

** restricted stock is purchased at par value ($1.00/sh)

COMPENSATION DEFERRAL

None

CASH RETIREMENT BENEFITS

Mandatory retirement age: 76
Basic benefits: greater of: (1) 50% of 3-year average compensation or (2) the annual retainer
Payment term: Matching Service
Death benefit: Yes

INSURANCE BENEFITS

Medical/dental
Comments: directors participate in health care plan under the same terms as employees.

OTHER BENEFITS

None

CHANGES

None

McDonald's Corporation

Industry: Leisure FY97 Revenue (mils): $11,409

BOARD STRUCTURE/FEES

	No. of Mtgs	Retainer Cash	Retainer Stock	Member Fee	Meeting Fee	Chairman Fee
Board	6	$35,000	$ —	$ —	$2,000	$ —
Audit	7	—	—	—	1,000	—
Compensation	5	—	—	—	1,000	—
Executive	0	—	—	—	1,000	—
Nominating & Corp. Govern.	6	—	—	—	1,000	—

Comments: The VCOB is on the Compensation Committee of an outside director's firm that sold $12.3-mil of cartons/paper products to McDonald's subsidiaries; another director's firms sold approximately $8.5-mil of paper and other products to subsidiaries

Average director's annual compensation = $59,000
(assumes all meetings are attended and director sits on the Audit and Compensation committees)

STOCK-BASED COMPENSATION

Grant type(s):	**Stock Option**	**Deferred**
Number of shares:	1,000	$17,500
Frequency:	Annual	Annual (max. 10)
Vesting:	1/3 per year	Retirement or death
Year-end stock price:	47.75	Same
Plan type:	Separate	—
Plan life:	10 years	—
Plan kitty:	150,000	—

Ownership Guidelines: Five times annual retainer within 5 years

COMPENSATION DEFERRAL

Eligible comp:	Retainter/meeting
Account types:	Stock
Interest rate:	Stock fund

CASH RETIREMENT BENEFITS

Cash plan terminated and replaced with deferred stock grants (above). Current directors received initial credits of $17,500 for each year of previous service.

INSURANCE BENEFITS

None

OTHER BENEFITS

Two directors received use of a company car (value = $10,250 and $5,125 in 1997)

CHANGES

- Added stock ownership guidelines

McGraw-Hill, Inc.

Industry: Publishing/Broadcasting FY97 Revenue (mils): $3,534

BOARD STRUCTURE/FEES

	No. of Mtgs	Retainer Cash	Retainer Stock	Member Fee	Meeting Fee	Chairman Fee
Board	8	$17,000	$ —	$ —	$1,200	$ —
Audit	3	—	—	—	1,000	—
Compensation	5	—	—	—	1,000	—
Nomin & Corp. Governance	3	—	—	—	1,000	—
Executive	0	—	—	—	1,000	—
Financial Policy	0	—	—	—	1,000	—

Comments: directors may elect to receive all or a portion of fees paid in stock

Average director's annual compensation = $34,600
(assumes all meetings are attended and director sits on the Audit and Compensation committees)

STOCK-BASED COMPENSATION

Grant type(s):	**Deferred**
Value of award	50% of total compensation ($17,000)
Frequency:	Annual
Vesting:	After termination
Year-end stock price:	74.00
Plan type:	Separate
Plan life:	Indefinite
Plan kitty:	80,000
COC provision:	Yes

COMPENSATION DEFERRAL

Eligible comp: Retainter/meeting
Account types: Cash or deferred stock
Interest rate: Moody's + 2%
COC provision:: Yes
Comments: maximum rate equals 150% of Moody's Bond Index; no premium is applied the interest rate after director attains age 70.

CASH RETIREMENT BENEFITS

Mandatory retirement age: 70
Cash plan terminated in 1996 and replaced with deferred stock plan; no additional benefits accrue for current directors

INSURANCE BENEFITS

None

OTHER BENEFITS

None

CHANGES

- Increased cash retainer by $2,000, and all meeting attendance fees by $200
- Changed deferred stock grants from the greater of $30,000 or 50% of total prior year compensation to 50% of total compensation

The Mead Corporation

Industry: Paper/Forest FY97 Revenue (mils): $5,077

BOARD STRUCTURE/FEES

	No. of Mtgs	Retainer Cash	Retainer Stock	Member Fee	Meeting Fee	Chairman Fee
Board	7	$20,500	$ —	$ —	$1,200	$ —
Audit	2	—	—	—	1,200	—
Compensation	3	—	—	—	1,200	—
Corp. Objectives	3	—	—	—	1,200	—
Corp. Responsibility	2	—	—	—	1,200	—
Executive	0	—	—	—	1,200	—
Finance	2	—	—	—	1,200	—
Nominating & Organization	2	—	—	—	1,200	—

Comments: directors may defer all or part of retainer in restricted shares vesting at termination

Average director's annual compensation = $34,900
(assumes all meetings are attended and director sits on the Audit and Compensation committees)

STOCK-BASED COMPENSATION

Grant type(s):	**Restricted**	**Restricted**	**Stock Option**
Award value	$7,500	Formula	Formula
Frequency:	Annual	Annual	Annual
Vesting:	5 years	as determined by Comm.	Age 55
Year-end stock price:	28.00	Same	Same
Plan type:	Combined w/ exec.	Same	Separate
COC provision:	Yes	Same	Yes

Comments: Option grants = 300 shares X (the avg. total comp. paid to directors at companies with sales > $4-billion ÷ $36,246 [the avg. total comp for the same group in 1994]). Annual restricted stock grants = $5,000 X (the same as above). For 1997 stock options = 620 shares ($18,115 FMV) and restricted stock = $5,085.

COMPENSATION DEFERRAL

Eligible comp: Retainter/meeting
Account types: Cash or restricted stock
Payment: After termination

CASH RETIREMENT BENEFITS

Mandatory retirement age: 70
Cash plan terminated 10/95 and no further benefits accrue; stock option grants are intended to replace it

INSURANCE BENEFITS

None

OTHER BENEFITS

None

CHANGES

- Changed from restricted stock grants of $37,500 every 5 years to $7,500 annually

Media General, Inc.

Industry: Leisure FY97 Revenue (mils): $910

BOARD STRUCTURE/FEES

	No. of Mtgs	Retainer Cash	Retainer Stock	Member Fee	Meeting Fee	Chairman Fee
Board	7	$27,500	—	$ —	$ —	$ —
Executive	6	—	—	—	—	—
Audit	2	—	—	—	—	—
Compensation & Organization	2	—	—	—	—	—

Comments: 50% of total retainer value ($55,000) is mandatorily deferred in stock units

Average director's annual compensation = $27,500
(assumes all meetings are attended and director sits on the Audit and Compensation committees)

STOCK-BASED COMPENSATION

Grant type(s):	**Deferred**
Value of award	50% of retainer ($27,500)
Frequency:	Annual
Vesting:	Undisclosed
Year-end stock price:	41.8125
Plan type:	Separate

COMPENSATION DEFERRAL

None

CASH RETIREMENT BENEFITS

Cash plan terminated 1/97 and the present value of accrued benefits converted to deferred stock units.

INSURANCE BENEFITS

None

OTHER BENEFITS

None

CHANGES

None

Mentor Graphics Corporation

Industry: Office Equipment & Services — FY97 Revenue (mils): $455

BOARD STRUCTURE/FEES

	No. of Mtgs	Retainer Cash	Retainer Stock	Member Fee	Meeting Fee	Chairman Fee
Board	5	$20,000	—	$ —	$ —	$10,000
Audit	4	—	—	—	—	—
Compensation	6	—	—	—	—	—
Nominating	1	—	—	—	—	—

Comments: COB fee is in addition to other fees

Average director's annual compensation = $20,000
(assumes all meetings are attended and director sits on the Audit and Compensation committees)

STOCK-BASED COMPENSATION

Grant type(s):	**Stock Option**
Number of shares:	10,000
Frequency:	Annual
Vesting:	20% per year
Year-end stock price:	9.6875
Plan type:	Separate
Plan kitty:	1,100,000

Comments: The outside COB is granted an additional 12,500 options annually.

COMPENSATION DEFERRAL

None

CASH RETIREMENT BENEFITS

None

INSURANCE BENEFITS

None

OTHER BENEFITS

None

CHANGES

None

Merck & Co., Inc.

Industry: Health Care

FY97 Revenue (mils): $23,637

BOARD STRUCTURE/FEES

	No. of Mtgs	Retainer Cash	Retainer Stock	Member Fee	Meeting Fee	Chairman Fee
Board	9	$38,000	$ —	$ —	$1,200	$ —
Executive	0	—	—	—	1,200	—
Audit	3	—	—	—	1,200	3,000
Compensation & Benefits	4	—	—	—	1,200	3,000
Directors	2	—	—	—	1,200	3,000
Finance	2	—	—	—	1,200	3,000

Average director's annual compensation = $57,200
(assumes all meetings are attended and director sits on the Audit and Compensation committees)

STOCK-BASED COMPENSATION

Grant type(s):	**Stock Option**	**Deferred**
Number of shares:	1,000	$15,000
Frequency:	Annual	Annual
Vesting:	5 years after grant	After termination
Year-end stock price:	106.00	Same
Plan type:	Separate	(deferral plan)
Plan life:	4 years	—
Plan kitty:	225,000	—

COMPENSATION DEFERRAL

Eligible comp: Retainter/meeting
Account types: Cash and/or stock
Interest rate: 18 investment options
Payment: After termination
Comments: payments may be in lump sum or installments.

CASH RETIREMENT BENEFITS

Cash plan terminated with respect to directors elected after 12/31/95; new directors receive $15,000 deferred compensation annually

INSURANCE BENEFITS

None

OTHER BENEFITS

None

CHANGES

None

Merrill Lynch & Co., Inc.

Industry: Nonbank Financial FY97 Revenue (mils): $31,731

BOARD STRUCTURE/FEES

	No. of Mtgs	Retainer Cash	Retainer Stock	Member Fee	Meeting Fee	Chairman Fee
Board	9	$35,000	—	$ —	$ —	$ —
Audit & Finance	7	—	—	15,000	—	10,000
Mgmt Devel & Comp	9	—	—	15,000	—	10,000
Nominating	0	—	—	—	—	6,000
Executive	0	—	—	—	—	—

Average director's annual compensation = $65,000
(assumes all meetings are attended and director sits on the Audit and Compensation committees)

STOCK-BASED COMPENSATION

Grant type(s):	**Deferred Units**	**Deferred Stock**
Award value	$50,000	$50,000
Frequency:	5 years	5 years
Vesting:	5 years	5 years
Year-end stock price:	72.9375	Same
Plan type:	Separate	Same

Comments: deferred units are paid out in cash and deferred stock is paid out in stock

COMPENSATION DEFERRAL

Eligible comp: Retainter/meeting
Account type: Cash or stock
Interest: Return on selected mutual funds
Payment: Date specified by director
Comments: payout is in cash.

CASH RETIREMENT BENEFITS

Mandatory Service: 5 years
Reduced benefit avail: Yes
Basic benefits: Retainer + $20,000
Payment term: Matching service
Death benefit: Yes (if director dies while serving)
Comments: benefits are payable after 5 yrs' service *or* age 65 with 1 year service; formula benefit is determined at time of entitlement based on director's age and tenure.

INSURANCE BENEFITS

Travel/Accident
Life
Medical/Dental
Comments: life insurance is contributory.

OTHER BENEFITS

Outside directors have opportunities to invest personal funds in ML&Co-sponsored employee partnerships.

CHANGES

None

MGM Grand, Inc.

Industry: Leisure

FY97 Revenue (mils): $828

BOARD STRUCTURE/FEES

	No. of Mtgs	Retainer Cash	Retainer Stock	Member Fee	Meeting Fee	Chairman Fee
Board	4	$26,000	$ —	$ —	$ —	$ —
Audit	3	—	—	—	1,500	—
Compensation & Stock Option	13	—	—	3,000	—	—
Executive	16	—	—	—	750	—

Comments: Audit committee meeting attendance fees are capped at $6,000/yr. One director has a consulting contract for $50,000/year.

Average director's annual compensation = $33,500
(assumes all meetings are attended and director sits on the Audit and Compensation committees)

STOCK-BASED COMPENSATION

Grant type(s):	**Stock Option**
Number of shares:	1,000
Frequency:	Annual
Vesting:	20% per year
Year-end stock price:	36.125
Plan type:	Combined with exec.

Comments: initial grant covers 5,000 options.

COMPENSATION DEFERRAL

None

CASH RETIREMENT BENEFITS

None

INSURANCE BENEFITS

None

OTHER BENEFITS

None

CHANGES

None

MicroAge, Inc.

Industry: Service Industries FY97 Revenue (mils): $4,446

BOARD STRUCTURE/FEES

	No. of Mtgs	Retainer Cash	Retainer Stock	Member Fee	Meeting Fee	Chairman Fee
Board	6	$18,000	$—	$—	$1,500	$—
Audit	2	—	—	—	1,000	3,000
Compensation	6	—	—	—	1,000	3,000
Corporate Governance	3	—	—	—	1,000	3,000

Comments: $1,000 fee paid for special board meetings.

Average director's annual compensation = $35,000
(assumes all meetings are attended and director sits on the Audit and Compensation committees)

STOCK-BASED COMPENSATION

Grant type(s):	**Stock Option**	**Restricted**
Number of shares:	2,500	1,000
Frequency:	Annual	Annual
Vesting:	1/3 per year if stock price goals are met	Same
Year-end stock price:	15.0625	Same
Plan type:	Separate	Same
Plan life:	10 years	Same
Plan kitty:	250,000	Same
COC provision:	Yes	Same

Comments: Initial option grant covers 2,500 shares and initial restricted stock grant = 1,000 shares; the stock price goals are 110% increase over previous price for 3 years (e.g., grant price = $22.00, one year later goal = $24.20, two years later goal = $26.62, etc.) if price targets are not met options vest after 9 years; additional options and restricted stock may be granted at the board's discretion

COMPENSATION DEFERRAL

None

CASH RETIREMENT BENEFITS

None

INSURANCE BENEFITS

None

OTHER BENEFITS

None

CHANGES

- Increased stock plan kitty by 170,000 shares
- Increased stock option grants by 1,500 shares

Millipore Corporation

Industry: Electronics FY97 Revenue (mils): $619

BOARD STRUCTURE/FEES

	No. of Mtgs	Retainer Cash	Retainer Stock	Member Fee	Meeting Fee	Chairman Fee
Board	5	$19,000	—	$ —	$1,000	$ —
Audit & Finance	3	—	—	—	—	2,500
Mgmt Development & Comp	4	—	—	—	—	2,500
Org. Nom. & Public Policy	4	—	—	—	—	2,500

Comments: one director received $13,000 in consulting fees, and another received $1,000

Average director's annual compensation = $24,000
(assumes all meetings are attended and director sits on the Audit and Compensation committees)

STOCK-BASED COMPENSATION

Grant type(s):	**Stock Option**
Number of shares:	2,000
Frequency:	Annual
Vesting:	25% per year
Year-end stock price:	33.9375
Plan type:	Separate

Comments: initial grant covers 4,000 shares.

COMPENSATION DEFERRAL

Eligible comp: Retainter/meeting
Account types: Stock
Payment: After retirement
Max. installments: 10 years
Comments: payouts are in cash in installments or lump sum in the case of death prior to retirement.

CASH RETIREMENT BENEFITS

Mandatory retirement age: 70

INSURANCE BENEFITS

None

OTHER BENEFITS

None

CHANGES

- Appear to have eliminated committee meeting fees of $1,000

Minnesota Mining & Manufacturing Company (3m)

Industry: Manufacturing FY97 Revenue (mils): $15,070

BOARD STRUCTURE/FEES

	No. of Mtgs	Retainer Cash	Retainer Stock	Member Fee	Meeting Fee	Chairman Fee
Board	6	$25,000	$35,000	$ —	$1,800	$ —
Audit	4	—	—	—	1,200	5,500
Compensation	4	—	—	—	1,200	5,500
Board Organization	3	—	—	—	1,200	—

Comments: Directors may elect to receive all fees in shares rather than cash.

Average director's annual compensation = $80,400
(assumes all meetings are attended and director sits on the Audit and Compensation committees)

STOCK-BASED COMPENSATION

Grant type(s):	**Stock Award**
Value of Award:	$35,000
Frequency:	Annual
Yr-end stock price:	82.0625

Comments: The value of the award is reflected in "Stock Retainer" and "Average Director's Annual Compensation" above

COMPENSATION DEFERRAL

Eligible comp: Retainter/meeting
Account types: Cash and/or stock
COC provision:: Yes
Comments: may be paid out in shares.

CASH RETIREMENT BENEFITS

Cash plan terminated 5/96 and replaced with additional shares of stock.

INSURANCE BENEFITS

None

OTHER BENEFITS

None

CHANGES

None

Mobil Corporation

Industry: Fuel FY97 Revenue (mils): $59,978

BOARD STRUCTURE/FEES

	No. of Mtgs	Retainer Cash	Retainer Stock	Member Fee	Meeting Fee	Chairman Fee
Board	11	$36,000	—	$ —	$1,250	$ —
Directors & Board Affairs	3	—	—	—	1,250	8,000
Audit	3	—	—	—	1,250	8,000
Mgmt Comp & Organization	5	—	—	—	1,250	8,000
Finance	(new)	—	—	—	1,250	8,000
Public Issues	3	—	—	—	1,250	8,000

Comments: a portion of retainer is paid in the form of stock equivalents (see STOCK).

Average director's annual compensation = $59,750
(assumes all meetings are attended and director sits on the Audit and Compensation committees)

STOCK-BASED COMPENSATION

Grant type(s):	**Deferred**
Number of shares:	600
Frequency:	Annual
Vesting:	Termination
Year-end stock price:	72.1875

COMPENSATION DEFERRAL

Eligible comp: Retainter/meeting
Account types: Cash and/or stock
Interest rate: 10-year T-note + 1%
Payment: After retirement
COC provision:: Yes

CASH RETIREMENT BENEFITS

Mandatory retirement age: 72

Cash plan terminated and additional 200 shares of deferred stock is granted annually. Current directors could elect to have accrued benefits paid out according to the plan after retirement or credited to a deferred account.

INSURANCE BENEFITS

Travel/Accident: $500,000
Group Life: $100,000
Comments: accident insurance covers time spent on Mobil business.

OTHER BENEFITS

None

CHANGES

None

Monsanto Company

Industry: Chemicals FY97 Revenue (mils): $9,457

BOARD STRUCTURE/FEES

	No. of Mtgs	Retainer Cash	Retainer Stock	Member Fee	Meeting Fee	Chairman Fee
Board	8	$45,000	—	$ —	$ —	$ —
Audit	3	—	—	—	—	10,000
Corp. Social Responsibility	4	—	—	—	—	10,000
Executive	0	—	—	—	—	10,000
Exec Comp & Development	5	—	—	—	—	10,000
Finance	4	—	—	—	—	10,000
Nominating	2	—	—	—	—	10,000
Pension & Savings Funds	2	—	—	—	—	10,000
Special	3	—	—	—	—	10,000

Comments: 50% of chairman's fees paid in stock options; one director has consulting agreement and received $134,172 in 1997; one director serves on a subsidiary board and received 15,000 shares of subsidiary stock in addition to other subsidiary director fees; directors may elect to have cash retainer paid in deferred stock, additional options, or restricted stock, which vests 1/3 per year

Average director's annual compensation = $45,000
(assumes all meetings are attended and director sits on the Audit and Compensation committees)

STOCK-BASED COMPENSATION

Grant type(s):	**Stock Options**
Award value	$45,000
Frequency:	Annual
Vesting:	1/3 per year
Year-end stock price:	42.00

Comments: Options are calculated using Black-Scholes valuation methodology.
Ownership Guidelines: Three times the annual retainer by the 5th year after election.

COMPENSATION DEFERRAL

Eligible comp: Retainer
Account types: Cash and/or stock
Interest: Moody's
Payment: After termination
Comments: Payout may be lump sum or installments

CASH RETIREMENT BENEFITS

Mandatory retirement age: 70
Cash plan terminated in 1997 with accrued benefits either (1) paid out in a lump sum or (2) deferred

INSURANCE BENEFITS

Travel/Accident

OTHER BENEFITS

None

CHANGES

- Eliminated committee member fees of $3,000 and meeting attendance fees of $1,300
- Increased annual retainer by $25,000
- Increased committee chairman's fees by $8,000–$9,000
- Eliminated the cash retirement plan, with accrued benefits either paid out or deferred
- Eliminated the Charitable Award program for future directors
- Added deferral plan
- Eliminated restricted stock grants of $50,000 every 5 years

The Montana Power Company

Industry: Utility — FY97 Revenue (mils): $1,024

BOARD STRUCTURE/FEES

	No. of Mtgs	Retainer Cash	Retainer Stock	Member Fee	Meeting Fee	Chairman Fee
Board	9	$19,600	480 shrs	$ —	$ —	$ —
Audit	3	—	—	—	500	—
Personnel	7	—	—	—	500	—
Nominating	5	—	—	—	500	—
Executive	0	—	—	—	500	—
Contributions	0	—	—	—	500	—
Environment & Safety	0	—	—	—	500	—
Finance	0	—	—	—	500	—
Mergers & Acquisitions	0	—	—	—	500	—

Same day fees: no committee meeting fee paid for meeting on same day as board

Comments: Directors may elect to have all fees paid in stock; $850 paid for special board meetings.

Average director's annual compensation = $34,840
(assumes all meetings are attended and director sits on the Audit and Compensation committees)

STOCK-BASED COMPENSATION

Grant type(s):	**Stock Award**
Number of shares:	480
Frequency:	Annual
Year-end stock price:	31.75
Plan type:	Separate

Comments: the value of this award is reflected in Stock Retainer and Average Director's Annual Comp above

COMPENSATION DEFERRAL

Eligible comp: Retainter/meeting/stock
Account types: Cash and/or stock
Interest rate: Moody's Avg. Baa Corp. Bond rate
Payment: After termination
Comments: stock payment may be deferred and will be paid out in cash or stock.

CASH RETIREMENT BENEFITS

Cash plan frozen 12/31/97 and replaced with annual stock grants (above)

INSURANCE BENEFITS

None

OTHER BENEFITS

None

CHANGES

- Removed requirement for 25% of annual retainer to be paid in stock
- Eliminated cash retirement plan, freezing all benefits for current directors; annual stock awards replace this benefit

Morton International Inc.

Industry: Chemicals FY97 Revenue (mils): $3,637

BOARD STRUCTURE/FEES

	No. of Mtgs	Retainer Cash	Retainer Stock	Member Fee	Meeting Fee	Chairman Fee
Board	8	$28,000	500 shr	$ —	$1,500	$ —
Audit	2	—	—	—	750	2,500
Compensation	3	—	—	—	750	2,500
Nominat & Organization	1	—	—	—	750	1,500
Executive	0	—	—	—	750	—

Average director's annual compensation = $60,938
(assumes all meetings are attended and director sits on the Audit and Compensation committees)

STOCK-BASED COMPENSATION

Grant type(s):	**Stock Award**
Number of shares:	500
Frequency:	Annual
Vesting:	6 months
Year-end stock price:	34.375
Plan type:	Separate
Plan kitty:	100,000

Comments: the value of these shares is reflected in the "Average Director's Annual Comp" above

COMPENSATION DEFERRAL

Eligible comp: Cash Retainter/meeting
Account types: Stock
Payment: After termination
COC provision:: Yes
Comments: payouts are made in cash.

CASH RETIREMENT BENEFITS

None

INSURANCE BENEFITS

None

OTHER BENEFITS

None

CHANGES

None

Motorola, Inc.

Industry: Electronics FY97 Revenue (mils): $29,794

BOARD STRUCTURE/FEES

	No. of Mtgs	Retainer Cash	Retainer Stock	Member Fee	Meeting Fee	Chairman Fee
Board	8	$40,000	$ —	$ —	$1,500	$ —
Audit & Legal	3	—	—	1,500	1,000	4,000
Compensation	6	—	—	—	1,000	4,000
Nominating	3	—	—	—	1,000	4,000
Executive	0	—	—	—	1,000	4,000
Finance	4	—	—	—	1,000	4,000
Management Development	3	—	—	—	1,000	4,000
Technology	5	—	—	—	1,000	4,000

Same Day Mtg Fees: $500/day for committee meetings held in conjunction with board meetings

Comments: $1,500/day for assigned work on behalf of board comm. or other services; directors may elect to receive shares in lieu of cash; one director consulted for $290,400 in 1997

Average director's annual compensation = $58,000
(assumes all meetings are attended and director sits on the Audit and Compensation committees)

STOCK-BASED COMPENSATION

Grant type(s):	**Stock Option**
Number of shares:	2,500
Frequency:	Annual
Vesting:	1 year
Year-end stock price:	57.1875
Plan type:	Combined w/ exec
COC provision:	Yes

COMPENSATION DEFERRAL

Eligible comp: Retainter/meeting
Account types: Cash
Interest rate: 3-month T-bill
Max. installments: 10 years
Payment: After termination
Comments: payout is in lump sum or installments.

CASH RETIREMENT BENEFITS

Cash plan terminated 2/96 and current accrued benefits are frozen.

INSURANCE BENEFITS

Accidental Death/Dismemberment: $500,000
Comments: spouse is also covered when traveling on business trips.

OTHER BENEFITS

Company reimburses travel and lodging expenses of spouse traveling with director on company business

CHANGES

- Increased stock option grant by 1,500 shares
- Eliminated COB fee of $330,000

The Neiman Marcus Group, Inc.

Industry: Retailing FY97 Revenue (mils): $2,210

BOARD STRUCTURE/FEES

	No. of Mtgs	Retainer Cash	Retainer Stock	Member Fee	Meeting Fee	Chairman Fee
Board	5	$20,000	—	$ —	$2,000	$ —
Special Review	3	—	—	—	750	2,250
Audit	3	—	—	—	750	2,250
Compensation	1	—	—	—	750	750
Executive	0	—	—	—	750	—
Nominating	1	—	—	—	750	750

Misc. Fees: 50% of customary fees for telephone meeting participation.

Comments: Chairmen fees reflect additional $750 per committee meeting attended.

Average director's annual compensation = $33,000
(assumes all meetings are attended and director sits on the Audit and Compensation committees)

STOCK-BASED COMPENSATION

Comments: Shareholders approved the 1997 Incentive Plan, which provides for unspecified discretionary grants to members of the board.

COMPENSATION DEFERRAL

Eligible comp:	Retainter/meeting
Account types:	Cash and/or stock
Interest rate:	90-day certificate of deposit

CASH RETIREMENT BENEFITS

None

INSURANCE BENEFITS

None

OTHER BENEFITS

None

CHANGES

- Increased board meeting attendance fee by $500, committee meeting attendance fees by $250, and committee chairman's fees by $250 per meeting
- Added alternative for directors to defer in stock accounts

Nike, Inc.

Industry: Consumer Products FY97 Revenue (mils): $9,187

BOARD STRUCTURE/FEES

	No. of Mtgs	Retainer Cash	Retainer Stock	Member Fee	Meeting Fee	Chairman Fee
Board	5	$18,000	—	$ —	$2,000	$ —
Executive	0	—	—	—	1,000	—
Audit	2	—	—	—	1,000	—
Personnel	3	—	—	—	1,000	—
Finance	5	—	—	—	1,000	—

Comments: One director on the Personnel Committee received $367,713 in 1997 pursuant to an endorsement contract.

Average director's annual compensation = $33,000
(assumes all meetings are attended and director sits on the Audit and Compensation committees)

STOCK-BASED COMPENSATION

Grant type(s):	**Stock Option**
Number of shares:	30,000
Frequency:	One-time
Vesting:	20% per year
Year-end stock price:	39.0625

Comments: options are granted to directors "from time to time" (none granted in 1997).

COMPENSATION DEFERRAL

None

CASH RETIREMENT BENEFITS

Mandatory service: 5 years
Mandatory retirement age: 72
Basic benefits: Retainer
Payment term: Life

Comments: benefits = sliding percentage from 50% for 5 yrs service up to 100% for 10 yrs or more of service; life and medical insurance are also provided for life to directors who retire with at least 10 years service

INSURANCE BENEFITS

Life: $500,000
Medical/Dental

OTHER BENEFITS

None

CHANGES

None

Nordstrom, Inc.

Industry: Retailing

FY97 Revenue (mils): $4,852

BOARD STRUCTURE/FEES

	No. of Mtgs	Retainer Cash	Retainer Stock	Member Fee	Meeting Fee	Chairman Fee
Board	4	$19,000	$10,000	$ —	$1,000	$ —
Audit	4	—	—	—	1,000	—
Comp & Stock Option	5	—	—	—	1,000	—
Corp Governance & Nominating	5	—	—	—	1,000	—

Comments: the "Cash Retainer" includes a $4,000/year payment to offset tax liabilities for the stock award.

Average director's annual compensation = $42,000
(assumes all meetings are attended and director sits on the Audit and Compensation committees)

STOCK-BASED COMPENSATION

Grant type(s):	**Stock Award**
Award value	$10,000
Frequency:	Annual
Vesting:	6 months
Year-end stock price:	60.375
Plan type:	Separate
Plan life:	10 years
Plan kitty:	25,000
COC provision:	Yes

Comments: Directors also receive cash payment of $4,000/yr to offset tax liabilities; award is reflected under "Stock Retainer" and "Average Director's Annual Comp" above.

COMPENSATION DEFERRAL

None

CASH RETIREMENT BENEFITS

None

INSURANCE BENEFITS

None

OTHER BENEFITS

None

CHANGES

None

Norfolk Southern Corporation

Industry: Transportation FY97 Revenue (mils): $5,165

BOARD STRUCTURE/FEES

		Retainer				
	No. of Mtgs	**Cash**	**Stock**	**Member Fee**	**Meeting Fee**	**Chairman Fee**
Board	7	$32,000	—	$ —	$1,800	$ —
Audit	6	—	—	—	1,800	—
Compensation & Nominating	6	—	—	—	1,800	—
Executive	3	—	—	—	1,800	—
Pension	5	—	—	—	1,800	—

Comments: One director's company has leases with a NS subsidiary and paid rent/royalties of $3.7-mil in 1997

Average director's annual compensation = $66,200
(assumes all meetings are attended and director sits on the Audit and Compensation committees)

STOCK-BASED COMPENSATION

Grant type(s):	**Restricted**	**Deferred Stock Units**
Number of shares:	3,000	1,000
Frequency:	One-time	Annual
Vesting:	Retirement, death or disability	Termination
Year-end stock price:	30.50	same
Plan type:	Separate	Separate

Comments: deferred stock units receive dividend equivalents; payment is in cash, in a lump sum or 10 installments; initial grant in 1996 equaled 600 units; future annual grants may be given to ensure competitive pay for the directors.

COMPENSATION DEFERRAL

Eligible comp: Retainter/meeting
Account types: Cash
Max. installments: 10 years
Payment: After termination

Comments: interest rate is based on age at time of deferral: <age 45 = 7%; age 45–54 = 10%; age 55–60 = 11%; >age 60 = 12%; funded by company-owned life insurance

CASH RETIREMENT BENEFITS

Mandatory retirement age: 72

Cash plan terminated 6/1/96 and the present value of projected benefits converted over to the stock unit program.

INSURANCE BENEFITS

None

OTHER BENEFITS

Charitable Award Program

Amount: $1,000,000; payout: $500,000 to one or more tax exempt organizations and $500,000 to N.S. Foundation; paid in five installments; insurance funded

CHANGES

- Increased deferred stock unit award by 250 shares

Northrop Grumman Corporation

Industry: Aerospace FY97 Revenue (mils): $9,153

BOARD STRUCTURE/FEES

	No. of Mtgs	Retainer Cash	Retainer Stock	Member Fee	Meeting Fee	Chairman Fee
Board	12	$19,600	$8,400	$ —	$1,000	$ —
Audit	6	—	—	—	1,000	3,000
Compen & Mgmt Develop	8	—	—	—	1,000	3,000
Executive & Public Policy	7	—	—	—	1,000	3,000
Finance	6	—	—	—	1,000	3,000
Nominating	3	—	—	—	1,000	3,000

Comments: 30% of retainer is paid in stock issued at the end of the fiscal year and directors may elect to receive additional fees in such stock; directors are paid $1,000/day for special services; the COB/CEO is on the board of an outside director's firm that paid $19.9-mil to Northrop for a contract in Puerto Rico

Average director's annual compensation = $54,000
(assumes all meetings are attended and director sits on the Audit and Compensation committees)

STOCK-BASED COMPENSATION

Grant type(s):	Stock Award	Stock Option	Deferred Units
Value of award	30% of retainer ($8,400)	1,500 shares	Value = 50% of retainer ($14,000)
Frequency:	Annual	Annual	Annual
Vesting:	Immediate	Immediate	After termination
Year-end stock price:	115.00	Same	Same
Plan type:	Separate	Separate	Separate
Plan life:	Indefinite	Indefinite	Indefinite
Plan kitty:	50,000	300,000	undisclosed

Ownership Guidelines: 3 x retainer within 5 years

COMPENSATION DEFERRAL

Eligible comp: Retainter/meeting
Account types: Stock
Payment: Date specified by director
Comments: amounts must be deferred for at least 2 years.

CASH RETIREMENT BENEFITS

Mandatory retirement age: 70
Cash plan terminated 3/97 for future directors. Current directors may elect to have the present value of accrued benefits converted to stock units.

INSURANCE BENEFITS

None

OTHER BENEFITS

None

CHANGES

None

Old Kent Financial Corporation

Industry: Banks FY97 Revenue (mils): $1,306

BOARD STRUCTURE/FEES

	No. of Mtgs	Retainer Cash	Retainer Stock	Member Fee	Meeting Fee	Chairman Fee
Board	7	$8,500	$ —	$ —	$1,000	$ —
Executive	1	—	—	—	1,000	4,000
Audit	4	—	—	—	1,000	4,000
Compensation	3	—	—	—	1,000	4,000
Directors (Nominating)	2	—	—	—	1,000	4,000

Comments: 50% of total retainer value ($17,000) is mandatorily deferred in stock

Average director's annual compensation = $22,500
(assumes all meetings are attended and director sits on the Audit and Compensation committees)

STOCK-BASED COMPENSATION

Grant type(s):	**Deferred**
Value of award:	$8,500
Frequency:	Annual
Yr-end stock price:	39.625
Plan type:	(Deferral plan)

Comments: 50% of retainer value is deferred in stock.

COMPENSATION DEFERRAL

Eligible comp: Retainter/meeting
Account types: Cash
Interest rate: 5 Fund Alternatives
Max. installments: 10 years
Payment: After termination
Comments: payout may be in lump sum or installments; 50% of retainer value is mandatorily deferred in stock.

CASH RETIREMENT BENEFITS

None

INSURANCE BENEFITS

None

OTHER BENEFITS

None

CHANGES

- Now require 50% of retainer to be deferred in stock

Omnicom Group Inc.

Industry: Service FY97 Revenue (mils): $3,125

BOARD STRUCTURE/FEES

	No. of Mtgs	Retainer Cash	Retainer Stock	Member Fee	Meeting Fee	Chairman Fee
Board	6	$18,000	$ —	$ —	$2,000	$ —
Audit	3	—	—	—	2,000	—
Nominating	3	—	—	—	2,000	—
Compensation	3	—	—	—	2,000	—

Same Day Mtg Fees: $1,500 paid for second meeting on any day

Average director's annual compensation = $39,000
(assumes all meetings are attended and director sits on the Audit and Compensation committees)

STOCK-BASED COMPENSATION

None

COMPENSATION DEFERRAL

None

CASH RETIREMENT BENEFITS

None

INSURANCE BENEFITS

None

OTHER BENEFITS

None

CHANGES

None

Oryx Energy Company

Industry: Fuel

FY97 Revenue (mils): $1,197

BOARD STRUCTURE/FEES

	No. of Mtgs	Retainer Cash	Retainer Stock	Member Fee	Meeting Fee	Chairman Fee
Board	8	$12,000	$12,000	$ —	$1,00 0	$ —
Executive	0	—	+500 shr	2,500	1,000	—
Audit	3	—	—	2,500	1,000	1,500
Compensation	3	—	—	2,500	1,000	1,500
Board Policy & Nominating	3	—	—	2,500	1,000	1,500
MLP	4	—	—	2,500	1,000	1,500

Comments: Directors may elect to receive all or a portion of fees paid in stock; stock may be restricted until termination if elected by director, with the number of shares = 130% of those deferred

Average director's annual compensation = $55,750
(assumes all meetings are attended and director sits on the Audit and Compensation committees)

STOCK-BASED COMPENSATION

Grant type(s):	**Stock Award**	**Stock Award**	**Stock Option**
Number of shares:	50% of retainer ($12,000)	500	9,000
Frequency:	Annual	Annual	3 years
Vesting:	Immediate	Immediate	3 years
Year-end stock price:	25.50	Same	Same
Plan type:	Separate	Same	Same

Comments: Initial stock award covers 5,000 shares; the value of both stock awards is reflected in "Stock Retainer" and "Average Director's Annual Compensation" above.

Ownership Guidelines: Three times annual retainer within 3 years

COMPENSATION DEFERRAL

Eligible comp:	Retainter/meeting
Account types:	Cash
Interest rate:	Company
Payment:	Date specified by director

CASH RETIREMENT BENEFITS

Cash plan terminated 7/96 and replaced with annual stock grants of 500 shares; accrued benefits were converted to common stock

INSURANCE BENEFITS

None

OTHER BENEFITS

None

CHANGES

- Added the alternative for elective stock to be restricted and thus would be increased by 30%
- Added stock option grants

Oshkosh B'Gosh, Inc.

Industry: Consumer Products FY97 Revenue (mils): $395

BOARD STRUCTURE/FEES

	No. of Mtgs*	Retainer Cash	Retainer Stock	Member Fee	Meeting Fee	Chairman Fee
Board	5	$18,000	$ —	$ —	$1,000	$ —
Audit	2	—	—	—	800	—
Executive	1	—	—	—	800	—
Compensation	1	—	—	—	800	—
Nominating	1	—	—	—	800	—
Retirement Plan	1	—	—	—	800	—

* actual meetings not available, by policy each meets as indicated above

Same Day Mtg Fees: $800 paid for meetings on a day other than a regular board meeting

Misc. fees: Telephone fees: $1,000 fee for conference of 1 hour or more, $600 for up to 1 hour in length

Average director's annual compensation = $23,000
(assumes all meetings are attended and director sits on the Audit and Compensation committees)

STOCK-BASED COMPENSATION

Grant type(s):	**Stock Option**
Number of shares::	3,000
Frequency:	Annual
Vesting:	6 months
Yr-end stock price:	33.00
Plan type:	Separate
Plan life::	10 years
Plan kitty::	70,000
COC provision::	Yes

COMPENSATION DEFERRAL

None

CASH RETIREMENT BENEFITS

None

INSURANCE BENEFITS

None

OTHER BENEFITS

None

CHANGES

None

Owens-Corning Fiberglas Corporation

Industry: Housing FY97 Revenue (mils): $4,373

BOARD STRUCTURE/FEES

	No. of Mtgs	Retainer Cash	Retainer Stock	Member Fee	Meeting Fee	Chairman Fee
Board	9	$25,000	500 shr	$ —	$1,000	$ —
Audit	3	—	—	—	1,000	4,000
Compensation	4	—	—	—	1,000	4,000
Executive	1	—	—	—	1,000	4,000
Finance	2	—	—	—	1,000	4,000
Corporate Governance	2	—	—	—	1,000	4,000

Same Day Mtg Fees: $1,000 for one or more board mtgs or one or more comm. mtgs on same day

Comments: $1,000 per diem for functions which director is specifically requested to attend; the former SrVP/General Counsel/Secretary has a consulting agreement for $175,000 per year; one director's firm sold Owens approximately $5-mil of materials.

Average director's annual compensation = $51,063
(assumes all meetings are attended and director sits on the Audit and Compensation committees)

STOCK-BASED COMPENSATION

Grant type(s):	Stock Option	Stock Award
Number of shares::	10,000	500
Frequency:	One-time	Annual
Vesting:	20% per year	Immediate
Year-end stock price::	34.125	Same
Plan type:	Separate	Same
Plan life::	10 years	Same
Plan kitty::	600,000	Same
COC provision::	Yes	Same

Comments: no award is made in the year a director receives the one-time option grant; director may defer receipt of annual awards; stock award is reflected under "Stock Retainer" and "Average Director's Annual Comp" above.

COMPENSATION DEFERRAL

Eligible comp: Retainter/meeting
Account types: Stock
Max. installments: 10 years
Payment: After termination
COC provision:: Yes
Comments: payout is in cash.

CASH RETIREMENT BENEFITS

None

INSURANCE BENEFITS

None

OTHER BENEFITS

Charitable Award Program
Amount: $1,000,000; payout: to up to two charities selected by director; life insurance funded

CHANGES

None

Pacific Enterprises

Industry: Utilities FY97 Revenue (mils): $2,777

BOARD STRUCTURE/FEES

	No. of Mtgs	Retainer Cash	Retainer Stock	Member Fee	Meeting Fee	Chairman Fee
Board	16	$25,000	—	$ —	$ 900	$ —
Audit	3	—	—	—	900	3,000
Compensation	5	—	—	—	900	3,000
Public Policy	3	—	—	—	900	3,000
Executive	1	—	—	—	900	3,000
Nominating	2	—	—	—	900	3,000

Average director's annual compensation = $46,600
(assumes all meetings are attended and director sits on the Audit and Compensation committees)

STOCK-BASED COMPENSATION

None

COMPENSATION DEFERRAL

Eligible comp: Retainter/meeting
Account types: Cash
Comments: no additional information disclosed.

CASH RETIREMENT BENEFITS

Mandatory service: 5 years
Basic benefits: Retainer + board mtg fees x 10
Payment term: Matching service
Comments: benefit is based on retainer + 10x the number of board meeting fees; benefits begin at later of retirement or age 65.

INSURANCE BENEFITS

None

OTHER BENEFITS

None

CHANGES

None

Paine Webber Group, Inc.

Industry: Nonbank Financial | FY97 Revenue (mils): $6,657

BOARD STRUCTURE/FEES

	No. of Mtgs	Retainer Cash	Retainer Stock	Member Fee	Meeting Fee	Chairman Fee
Board	8	$40,000	1,162 shrs	$ —	$1,200	$ —
Executive	2	—	—	—	1,200	15,000
Audit	4	—	—	—	1,200	15,000
Nominating	3	—	—	—	1,200	15,000
Compensation	6	—	—	—	1,200	15,000
Public Policy	3	—	—	—	1,200	15,000

Comments: PWI paid 2 directors' firm $3.2-mil in rent in 1997; a Compensation Committee member's son is a manager of a limited partnership with a PWI subsidiary committed to invest $5-mil in the partnership.

Average director's annual compensation = $101,762
(assumes all meetings are attended and director sits on the Audit and Compensation committees)

STOCK-BASED COMPENSATION

Grant type(s):	**Stock Option**	**Stock Award**
Number of shares:	22,500	1,162
Frequency:	5 years	Annual
Vesting:	100% after 3 years	None
Year-end stock price:	34.5625	Same
Plan type:	Separate	Same
Plan life:	Indefinite	Same
Plan kitty:	600,000	Same
COC provision:	Yes	Same

Comments: Same plan authorizes options, stock awards, and stock-denominated deferred compensation accounts; stock award is reflected under "Stock Retainer" and "Average Director's Annual Comp" above.

COMPENSATION DEFERRAL

Eligible comp: Retainter/meeting
Account types: Cash and/or stock
Interest rate: T-bills
Payment: After termination
Comments: stock accounts are 100% vested; lump sum payouts

CASH RETIREMENT BENEFITS

Terminated cash retirement plan 5/97 with accrued benefits either paid in cash or deferred; annual stock grants were increased by 600 shares in lieu of future benefits

INSURANCE BENEFITS

Medical benefits

OTHER BENEFITS

None

CHANGES

- Eliminated cash retirement plan, with accrued benefits either paid in cash or deferred

PepsiCo

Industry: Consumer Products FY97 Revenue (mils): $29,292

BOARD STRUCTURE/FEES

	No. of Mtgs	Retainer Cash	Retainer Stock	Member Fee	Meeting Fee	Chairman Fee
Board	7*	$70,000	$—	$—	$—	$—
Audit	3*	—	—	—	—	—
Compensation	6	—	—	—	—	—
Nominating	1	—	—	—	—	—

* includes one telephone meeting

Comments: The former COB/CEO received consulting fees of $500,000, a bonus of $1.5-mil and a one-time payment of $2-mil in 1997.

Average director's annual compensation = $70,000
(assumes all meetings are attended and director sits on the Audit and Compensation committees)

STOCK-BASED COMPENSATION

Grant type(s):	**Stock Option**
Award value	$120,000
Frequency:	Annual
Year-end stock price:	36.25

Comments: up to $90,000 of the options may be converted to capital stock at a ratio of three options per one share; stock may be deferred

COMPENSATION DEFERRAL

Eligible comp: Retainer/stock grants
Account types: Stock
Payment: Date specified by director
Comments: stock grant deferrals must be made in PepsiCo Capital Stock equivalents, payable only in cash.

CASH RETIREMENT BENEFITS

Mandatory retirement age: 70
None

INSURANCE BENEFITS

None

OTHER BENEFITS

None

CHANGES

None

Pfizer Inc.

Industry: Health Care FY97 Revenue (mils): $12,504

BOARD STRUCTURE/FEES

	No. of Mtgs	Retainer Cash	Retainer Stock	Member Fee	Meeting Fee	Chairman Fee
Board	10	$26,000	—	$ —	$1,500	$ —
Executive Compensation	12	—	—	4,000	1,500	2,000
Corp. Governance	5	—	—	4,000	1,500	2,000
Audit	6	—	—	4,000	1,500	2,000
Executive	0	—	—	—	1,500	—

Comments: $1,500/day paid for visits to company/subsidiary plant or office; $4,000 committee fee covers one or more committees; one director consulted for $64,000 in 1997; personal use of company transportation for three outside directors totaled $22,487 in 1997.

Average director's annual compensation = $72,000
(assumes all meetings are attended and director sits on the Audit and Compensation committees)

STOCK-BASED COMPENSATION

Grant type(s):	**Deferred Units**	**Deferred Units**
Number of shares:	1,200	Value = Retainer ($26,000)
Frequency:	Annual	Annual
Vesting:	6 months after termination of service	Same
Year-end stock price:	74.5625	Same
Plan type:	Separate	Same
Plan kitty:	50,000	Same
COC provision:	Yes	Same

Comments: deferred units are paid out in cash; the number of shares covering the retainer value for 1997 was 606.

COMPENSATION DEFERRAL

Eligible comp: Retainter/meeting
Account types: Cash and/or stock
Interest rate: Company rate
Payment: After termination
Comments: restricted stock dividends may be deferred; payouts are made in cash.

CASH RETIREMENT BENEFITS

Cash plan terminated 10/95 and existing benefits vested.

INSURANCE BENEFITS

None

OTHER BENEFITS

None

CHANGES

None

PG&E Corporation

Industry: Utilities

FY97 Revenue (mils): $15,400

BOARD STRUCTURE/FEES

	No. of Mtgs	Retainer Cash	Retainer Stock	Member Fee	Meeting Fee	Chairman Fee
Board	14	$30,000	—	$ —	$1,000	$ —
Executive	0	—	—	—	1,000	2,500
Nominating & Compensation	8	—	—	—	1,000	2,500
Audit	4	—	—	—	1,000	2,500
Finance	4	—	—	—	1,000	2,500
Public Policy	2	—	—	—	1,000	2,500

Comments: PG&E provided $100,000 support to one director's nonprofit organization in 1997.

Misc fees: Fees cover service on both PG&E and Pacific Gas & Electric Company

Average director's annual compensation = $56,000
(assumes all meetings are attended and director sits on the Audit and Compensation committees)

STOCK-BASED COMPENSATION

Grant type(s):	**Restricted**	**Stock Options**	**Deferred**
Value of award	$10,000	$10,000*	$10,000*
Frequency:	Annual	Annual	Annual
Vesting:	20% per year	Same	After retirement
Year-end stock price:	30.3125	Same	Same
Plan type:	Separate	Same	Same
COC provision:	Yes	Same	Same

* the combined value of options and deferred = $20,000; for valuation purposes, we used $10,000 each

COMPENSATION DEFERRAL

Eligible comp: Retainter/meeting
Account types: Cash and/or stock
Interest rate: Moody's
Max. installments: 10 years
Comments: indemnity policies protect benefits.

CASH RETIREMENT BENEFITS

Mandatory retirement age: 70
Cash plan terminated 1/97 for future directors

INSURANCE BENEFITS

None

OTHER BENEFITS

None

CHANGES

- Increased retainer value by $8,000
- Added stock options and deferred stock grants

Pharmacia & Upjohn, Inc.

Industry: Health FY97 Revenue (mils): $6,710

BOARD STRUCTURE/FEES

	No. of Mtgs	Retainer Cash	Retainer Stock	Member Fee	Meeting Fee	Chairman Fee
Board	7	$50,000	500 shr	$ —	$ —	$100,000
Audit	5	—	—	—	—	5,000
Compensation	5	—	—	—	—	5,000
Nominating & Corp. Govern.	7	—	—	—	—	5,000

Comments: directors selecting new President/CEO receive $1,500 for each meeting attended and committee chairman receives additional $5,000/year.; the COB's fee is in lieu of the $50,000 cash retainer.

Average director's annual compensation = $68,313
(assumes all meetings are attended and director sits on the Audit and Compensation committees)

STOCK-BASED COMPENSATION

Grant type(s):	**Stock Award**
Number of shares:	500
Frequency:	Annual
Year-end stock price:	36.625

Comments: the value of these shares is reflected in "Average Director's Annual Comp" above.

COMPENSATION DEFERRAL

None

CASH RETIREMENT BENEFITS

Cash plan terminated at time of merger.

INSURANCE BENEFITS

None

OTHER BENEFITS

None

CHANGES

None

Phelps Dodge Corporation

Industry: Metal/Mining FY97 Revenue (mils): $3,914

BOARD STRUCTURE/FEES

	No. of Mtgs	Retainer Cash	Retainer Stock	Member Fee	Meeting Fee	Chairman Fee
Board	8	$25,000	—	$ —	$1,000	$ —
Audit	4	—	—	—	1,000	3,000
Comp & Mgmt Develop	5	—	—	—	1,000	3,000
Directors (Nominating)	2	—	—	—	1,000	3,000
Environ, Health & Safety	3	—	—	—	1,000	3,000

Average director's annual compensation = $42,000
(assumes all meetings are attended and director sits on the Audit and Compensation committees)

STOCK-BASED COMPENSATION

Grant type(s):	**Deferred Units**
Number of shares:	450
Frequency:	Annual
Vesting:	At termination
Year-end stock price:	62.25
Plan type:	Separate
Plan life:	10 years
COC provision:	Yes

Ownership Guidelines: must own 2,000 shares

COMPENSATION DEFERRAL

Eligible comp: Retainter/meeting
Account types: Cash/stock/mutual funds
Interest rate: Market rate
Payment: Date specified by director

CASH RETIREMENT BENEFITS

Cash plan terminated 12/31/97, with accrued benefits converted to deferred stock units; an additional 150 deferred units are now granted each year

INSURANCE BENEFITS

Life: $50,000
Comments: $25,000 for retired directors.

OTHER BENEFITS

Matching Gift Program: up to $10,000 per year

CHANGES

- Added stock ownership guidelines
- Eliminated cash retirement plan, converting accrued benefits to deferred stock units, and adding 150 additional deferred units to annual grants of 300 shares
- Added matching gift program

Philip Morris Companies Inc.

Industry: Consumer Products FY97 Revenue (mils): $56,114

BOARD STRUCTURE/FEES

	No. of Mtgs	Retainer Cash	Retainer Stock	Member Fee	Meeting Fee	Chairman Fee
Board	11	$40,000	932 shrs	$ —	$1,500	$ —
Audit	6	—	—	—	1,500	16,000
Public Affairs & Soc Respon	4	—	—	—	1,500	9,000
Compensation	6	—	—	—	1,500	16,000
Corp Empl Plans Investment	3	—	—	—	1,500	8,000
Executive	0	—	—	—	1,500	—
Finance	4	—	—	—	1,500	9,000
Nominating & Corp Govern	3	—	—	—	1,500	8,000

Comments: Chairmen receive a fee of $5,000/yr ($10,000 for Audit and Compensation) *and* an additional $1,000 per mtg attended; $500 paid for other committee meetings attended ($1,000 for chairman)

Average director's annual compensation = $116,673
(assumes all meetings are attended and director sits on the Audit and Compensation committees)

STOCK-BASED COMPENSATION

Grant type(s):	**Stock Award**
Number of shares:	Formula*
Frequency:	Annual
Year-end stock price:	45.25
Plan type:	Separate
Plan life:	10 years
Plan kitty:	200,000
COC provision:	Yes

* award = lesser of 1,200 shares or value of current retainer (for 1997, they received 932 shares);

Comments: award is reflected under "Stock Retainer" and Average Director's Annual Comp" above.

COMPENSATION DEFERRAL

Eligible comp:	Retainter/meeting
Account types:	Cash and/or stock
Interest rate:	7 investment choices
Payment:	Date specified by director

Comments: lump sum or installments payouts.

CASH RETIREMENT BENEFITS

Cash plan terminated 1/96 and each director received 3,150 stock units, with the option to have 50% of these put in a deferred fixed income account.

INSURANCE BENEFITS

None

OTHER BENEFITS

None

CHANGES

- Increased meeting attendance fees by $500
- Changed from a variable interest rate on deferred accounts to seven different investment choices

Pioneer Hi-Bred International, Inc.

Industry: Food FY97 Revenue (mils): $1,784

BOARD STRUCTURE/FEES

	No. of Mtgs	Retainer Cash	Retainer Stock	Member Fee	Meeting Fee	Chairman Fee
Board	6	$18,000	—	$ —	$4,000	$—
Audit	4	—	—	—	—	2,000
Compensation	3	—	—	—	—	1,500
Nominating	2	—	—	—	—	1,000

Comments: One director is paid $25,000/year for consulting services for a 3-year period beginning in July 1995; directors may elect to receive restricted stock in lieu of fees (the value = 105% of foregone compensation for next 3 years; quarterly meeting fee shares vest upon attendance of meeting; annual retainer shares vest at year-end); chair fees reflect additional $500 per meeting.

Misc. Fees: $1,000 is paid for certain special meetings

Attendance Requirements: if fees are elected to be paid in restricted stock and director misses quarterly meeting, those shares are forfeited

Average director's annual compensation = $42,000
(assumes all meetings are attended and director sits on the Audit and Compensation committees)

STOCK-BASED COMPENSATION

Grant type(s):	**Restricted**
Number of shares::	As elected by director
Frequency:	Annual
Vesting:	Upon attendance at quarterly meeting or at year-end
Year-end stock price::	107.4375
Plan type:	Separate
COC provision::	Yes

COMPENSATION DEFERRAL

None

CASH RETIREMENT BENEFITS

None

INSURANCE BENEFITS

None

OTHER BENEFITS

None

CHANGES

- Increased annual retainer by $6,000, and board meeting fee by $500
- Eliminated COB fee of $310,000
- Added chairman's fee of $500 per meeting
- Added alternative for directors to have fees paid in restricted stock, with a 5% premium

The Pittston Company

Industry: Fuel FY97 Revenue (mils): $3,394

BOARD STRUCTURE/FEES

	No. of Mtgs	Retainer Cash	Retainer Stock	Member Fee	Meeting Fee	Chairman Fee
Board	7	$18,000	—	$ —	$1,200	$ —
Audit & Ethics	4	—	—	—	1,200	—
Compensation & Benefits	6	—	—	—	1,200	—
Executive	0	—	—	—	1,200	—
Nominating	3	—	—	—	1,200	—
Finance	4	—	—	—	1,200	—
Pension	4	—	—	—	1,200	—

Comments: $1,200/day paid for special assignments

Average director's annual compensation = $38,400
(assumes all meetings are attended and director sits on the Audit and Compensation committees)

STOCK-BASED COMPENSATION

Grant type(s):	Stock Option	Deferred
Number of shares:	1,700*	50% of retainer if <8 years' service 25% of retainer if >8 years' service
Frequency:	Annual	Annual
Vesting:	6 months	After approved termination with at least 5 years service
Year-end stock price:	40.25(Brinks), 7.50 (Minerals), 26.25 (Burlington)	Same
Plan type:	Separate	Separate
Plan life:	10 years	—
Plan kitty:	510,000	125,000
COC provision:	—	Yes

* 1,000 shares of Brinks Stock, 200 shares of Minerals Stock and 500 shares of Burlington Stock

Comments: initial stock option grant covers 10,000 shares of Brinks stock, 2,000 shares of Minerals stock and 5,000 shares of Burlington stock, which vests 1/3 immediately and 1/3 for the next 2 years.

COMPENSATION DEFERRAL

Eligible comp: Retainter/meeting
Account types: Cash
Interest rate: Prime
Comments: interest is compounded quarterly

CASH RETIREMENT BENEFITS

Cash plan terminated 5/96 and replaced with deferred stock plan (above). Accrued benefits were converted to deferred stock accounts.

INSURANCE BENEFITS

None

OTHER BENEFITS

Charitable Award Program
Amount: $1,100,000; payout: $100,000 paid to co. selected charity and $1-mil paid to director-selected; life insurance funded

CHANGES

None

Policy Management Systems Corporation

Industry: Office Equipment & Services FY97 Revenue (mils): $583

BOARD STRUCTURE/FEES

	No. of Mtgs	Retainer Cash	Retainer Stock	Member Fee	Meeting Fee	Chairman Fee
Board	9	$18,000	$ —	$ —	$2,000	$ —
Audit	7	—	—	—	1,000	—
Compensation	5	—	—	—	1,000	—
Corporate Governance	2	—	—	—	1,000	—

Comments: $1,000 per day for attendance at any other company meeting required

Same day fees: $1,000 committee meeting fee paid only if on a different day than a board meeting

Misc fees: Telephone fees: $500 paid for 1 hour meetings, $250 paid per additional hour, up to $1,000 total

Average director's annual compensation = $36,000
(assumes all meetings are attended and director sits on the Audit and Compensation committees)

STOCK-BASED COMPENSATION

None

COMPENSATION DEFERRAL

None

CASH RETIREMENT BENEFITS

None

INSURANCE BENEFITS

None

OTHER BENEFITS

None

CHANGES

- Increased annual retainer by $3,000
- Increased telephone meeting fee by $250

PPG Industries, Inc.

Industry: Housing — FY97 Revenue (mils): $7,379

BOARD STRUCTURE/FEES

	No. of Mtgs	Retainer Cash	Retainer Stock	Member Fee	Meeting Fee	Chairman Fee
Board	9	$20,000	$ —	$ —	$1,000	$ —
Audit	3	—	—	4,000	1,000	1,000
Nominating & Governance	5	—	—	3,000	1,000	1,000
Officers-Directors Comp	3	—	—	3,000	1,000	1,000

Comments: 1/3 of the $30,000 annual retainer is mandatorily deferred (see STOCK); directors may elect to have all fees deferred in stock

Average director's annual compensation = $42,000
(assumes all meetings are attended and director sits on the Audit and Compensation committees)

STOCK-BASED COMPENSATION

Grant type(s):	**Deferred**	**Deferred**
Award value	1/3 of retainer ($10,000)	Value = 1/2 of retainer ($15,000)
Frequency:	Annual	Annual, maximum 10
Vesting:	Undisclosed	After termination
Year-end stock price:	57.125	same

Comments: $15,000 annual grant is intended to be a retirement benefit; payout will be to director or surviving spouse in cash of up to 10 installments.

COMPENSATION DEFERRAL

Eligible comp: Retainter/meeting
Account types: Stock equivalents
Payment: Stock
COC provision:: Yes
Comments: 1/3 of the retainer is mandatorily deferred; payouts are in stock.

CASH RETIREMENT BENEFITS

see STOCK above

INSURANCE BENEFITS

None

OTHER BENEFITS

Charitable Award Program

Amount: $1,000,000; payout: to one or more charities designated by director; life insurance funded

CHANGES

None

Premark International, Inc.

Industry: Consumer Products FY97 Revenue (mils): $2,407

BOARD STRUCTURE/FEES

	No. of Mtgs	Retainer Cash	Retainer Stock	Member Fee	Meeting Fee	Chairman Fee
Board	6	$26,000	$ —	$ —	$1,500	$ —
Audit & Corp Responsibility	4	—	—	2,000	1,500	2,000
Comp & Directors (Nominat)	4	—	—	2,000	1,500	2,000
Executive	0	—	—	—	1,500	—

Comments: directors may elect to receive retainer and committee member fees in stock or discount-priced stock options

Average director's annual compensation = $51,000
(assumes all meetings are attended and director sits on the Audit and Compensation committees)

STOCK-BASED COMPENSATION

Grant type(s):	**Stock Award**
Number of shares:	1,000
Frequency:	One-time
Year-end stock price:	29.00
Plan type:	Separate

Comments: One-time issuance after three months of service.

COMPENSATION DEFERRAL

Eligible comp: Retainter/meeting
Account types: Cash
Interest rate: Prime

CASH RETIREMENT BENEFITS

Mandatory retirement age: 70
None

INSURANCE BENEFITS

None

OTHER BENEFITS

None

CHANGES

None

The Procter & Gamble Company

Industry: Consumer Products FY97 Revenue (mils): $35,764

BOARD STRUCTURE/FEES

	No. of Mtgs	Retainer Cash	Retainer Stock	Member Fee	Meeting Fee	Chairman Fee
Board	9	$55,000	$ —	$ —	$ —	$ —
Executive	0	—	—	—	—	—
Audit	3	—	—	—	—	—
Board Org & Nominating	2	—	—	—	—	—
Compensation	4	—	—	—	—	—
Finance	3	—	—	—	—	—
Public Policy	3	—	—	—	—	—

Comments: directors may elect to have all or a portion of fees paid in stock.

Attendance requirements: The fourth quarter retainer payment is contingent on 75% attendance level at board meetings

Average director's annual compensation = $55,000
(assumes all meetings are attended and director sits on the Audit and Compensation committees)

STOCK-BASED COMPENSATION

Grant type(s):	**Stock Option**	**Restricted**
Number of shares:	1,000	$20,000
Frequency:	Annual	Annual
Vesting:	1 year	Termination
Year-end stock price:	79.8125	Same
Plan type:	Separate	—
Plan life:	10 years	—
Plan kitty:	35,000 each year	—

COMPENSATION DEFERRAL

Eligible comp: Retainter/meeting
Account types: Cash
Interest rate: Prime
Payment: Date specified by director
Comments: interest is credited monthly.

CASH RETIREMENT BENEFITS

Cash plan terminated 1/97 and the present value of benefits converted to restricted stock

INSURANCE BENEFITS

Accident Insurance: $750,000

OTHER BENEFITS

Charitable Award Program
Amount: $1,000,000; payout: up to five charities designated by director; life insurance funded

CHANGES

None

Public Service Enterprise Group Inc.

Industry: Utilities | FY97 Revenue (mils): $6,370

BOARD STRUCTURE/FEES

	No. of Mtgs	Retainer Cash	Retainer Stock	Member Fee	Meeting Fee	Chairman Fee
Board	14	$11,000	$11,000	$ —	$1,200	$ —
Audit	4	—	—	—	1,200	—
Executive	0	—	—	—	1,200	—
Finance	4	—	—	—	1,200	—
Nominating	1	—	—	—	1,200	—
Organ & Compensation	4	—	—	—	1,200	—
Nuclear	8	—	—	—	1,200	—

Comments: $1,200 paid for inspection trips, conferences, etc.; the Pres/COO sits on the board of a Compensation Committee member's company.

Average director's annual compensation = $48,400
(assumes all meetings are attended and director sits on the Audit and Compensation committees)

STOCK-BASED COMPENSATION

Grant type(s):	**Stock Award**	**Restricted**
Number of shares:	50% of retainer ($11,000)	300
Frequency:	Annual	Annual
Vesting:	—	Annual mtg following age 70
Year-end stock price:	31.8125	Same
COC provision:	—	Yes

Comments: vesting requirement may be waived in good cause situations; the value of the stock award is reflected in "Stock Retainer" and "Average Director's Annual Compensation" above.

COMPENSATION DEFERRAL

None

CASH RETIREMENT BENEFITS

Mandatory retirement age: 70

Cash plan terminated 12/95 and replaced with restricted stock grants (above). Current directors with >10 years of service had accrued benefits converted to restricted stock; others received 300 shares per year of service

INSURANCE BENEFITS

None

OTHER BENEFITS

None

CHANGES

None

The Quaker Oats Company

Industry: Food

FY97 Revenue (mils): $5,016

BOARD STRUCTURE/FEES

	No. of Mtgs	Retainer Cash	Retainer Stock	Member Fee	Meeting Fee	Chairman Fee
Board	14*	$45,000	$ —	$ —	$1,000	$ —
Executive	1	—	—	—	1,000	5,000
Audit	4	—	—	—	1,000	5,000
Compensation	5	—	—	—	1,000	5,000
Finance	6	—	—	—	1,000	5,000
Nominating	1	—	—	—	1,000	5,000
Public Responsibility	2	—	—	—	1,000	5,000

* includes two actions taken by unanimous written consent, for which directors receive $1,000

Average director's annual compensation = $68,000
(assumes all meetings are attended and director sits on the Audit and Compensation committees)

STOCK-BASED COMPENSATION

Grant type(s):	**Deferred**
Number of shares::	800
Frequency:	Annual
Vesting:	After termination
Year-end stock price::	52.75

COMPENSATION DEFERRAL

Eligible comp: Retainter/meeting
Account types: Cash/stock
Payment: After termination
Max. installments: 15 years
Comments: payments begin at the later of January 1st following (1) age 55 or (2) termination and are made in cash

CASH RETIREMENT BENEFITS

None

INSURANCE BENEFITS

None

OTHER BENEFITS

None

CHANGES

None

Qualcomm, Inc.

Industry: Electrical & Electronics | FY97 Revenue (mils): $2,036

BOARD STRUCTURE/FEES

	No. of Mtgs	Retainer Cash	Retainer Stock	Member Fee	Meeting Fee	Chairman Fee
Board	10	$ —	—	$ —	$1,000	$ —
Audit	6	—	—	—	1,000	2,500
Compensation	7	—	—	—	1,000	2,500
Nominating	2	—	—	—	1,000	—
Stock Option	5	—	—	—	1,000	2,500

Same day fees: no committee meeting fee paid if on the same day as board meeting

Misc. Fees: $500 telephone meeting fee

Average director's annual compensation = $10,000
(assumes all meetings are attended and director sits on the Audit and Compensation committees)

STOCK-BASED COMPENSATION

Grant type(s):	**Stock Option**
Number of shares:	10,000
Frequency:	Annual
Vesting:	20% per year
Year-end stock price:	50.50
Plan type:	Separate
Plan kitty:	500,000
Plan life:	15 years
COC provision:	Yes

Comments: initial option grants = 20,000 shares; directors may also participate in the executive stock option plan.

COMPENSATION DEFERRAL

None

CASH RETIREMENT BENEFITS

None

INSURANCE BENEFITS

None

OTHER BENEFITS

None

CHANGES

- Decreased board meeting fees by $500
- Increased committee meeting fees by $250
- Reduced board telephone fee by $250 and increased committee telephone fee by $100
- Refueled plan kitty with 470,000 additional shares
- Added committee chairman's fees
- Changed from one-time 60,000 stock option grant to annual grants (above)

Questar Corporation

Industry: Utilities FY97 Revenue (mils): $933

BOARD STRUCTURE/FEES

	No. of Mtgs	Retainer Cash	Retainer Stock	Member Fee	Meeting Fee	Chairman Fee
Board	4	$14,400	$ —	$ —	$900	$ —
Executive	1	—	—	—	700	12,100
Finance & Audit	2	—	—	—	700	12,300
Mgmt Performance	2	—	—	—	700	12,300
Nominating	1	—	—	—	700	12,100

Comments: chairmen fees reflect additional $200 per meeting attended and 800 additional stock options (for analysis purposes these are valued at $11,900); directors may elect to receive fees paid in stock; one director's firm paid $2.1-mil to a Questar subsidiary for gas supplies in 1997; another director's firm (BCGas) paid $5-mil to a Questar subsidiary and they paid BCG $4.8-mil for gas deliveries; BCG also paid $2.7-mil for storage services to a Questar subsidiary.

Average director's annual compensation = $20,800
(assumes all meetings are attended and director sits on the Audit and Compensation committees)

STOCK-BASED COMPENSATION

Grant type(s):	**Stock Option**
Number of shares:	3,200
Frequency:	Annual
Vesting:	6 months
Year-end stock price:	44.625
Plan type:	Separate
Plan life:	14 years
Plan kitty:	470,000
COC provision:	Yes

Comments: committee chairmen receive additional 800 options each year.

COMPENSATION DEFERRAL

Eligible comp: Retainter/meeting
Account types: Cash and/or stock
Interest rate: Long-term cert. of deposit
Payment: After termination
Comments: payouts are in cash

CASH RETIREMENT BENEFITS

None
Mandatory retirement age: 72

INSURANCE BENEFITS

None

OTHER BENEFITS

None

CHANGES

None

Reebok International Ltd.

Industry: Consumer Products FY97 Revenue (mils): $3,637

BOARD STRUCTURE/FEES

	No. of Mtgs	Retainer Cash	Retainer Stock	Member Fee	Meeting Fee	Chairman Fee
Board	5	$15,000	$10,000	$ —	$2,000	$ —
Audit	3	—	—	—	1,000	2,000
Compensation	3	—	—	—	1,000	2,000
Executive	0	—	—	—	1,000	—
Board Affairs	3	—	—	—	1,000	2,000

Comments: one director's sports team has a 3-yr sponsorship agreement for a minimum royalty payment of $200,000/year and Reebok provides products to the basketball team for up to $140,000/year.

Average director's annual compensation = $41,000
(assumes all meetings are attended and director sits on the Audit and Compensation committees)

STOCK-BASED COMPENSATION

Grant type(s):	**Stock Option**	**Stock Award**
Grant value:	3x avg. annual comp. in prior yr	$10,000
Frequency:	Annual	Annual
Vesting:	1/3 per year	Immediate
Year-end stock price:	28.8125	Same
Plan type:	Separate	—
Plan kitty:	300,000	—
COC provision:	Yes	—

Comments: initial grants are for a value of 6x the average annual cash compensation of all directors in prior year; directors who hold more than 5% of common are not eligible to receive grants; directors received 3,189 shares in 1997; the value of the stock award is reflected in "Stock Retainer" and "Average Director's Annual Compensation" above.

Ownership Guidelines: 4 times annual retainer within 5 years

COMPENSATION DEFERRAL

Eligible comp: Retainter/meeting
Account types: Cash/stock
Interest rate: Merrill Lynch Corp Bond Rate
Payment: Date specified by director
Comments: payout is in lump sum or installments; cash accounts paid in cash; stock accounts paid out in stock

CASH RETIREMENT BENEFITS

None
Mandatory retirement age: 4 full terms (3 years each)

INSURANCE BENEFITS

None

OTHER BENEFITS

None

CHANGES

- Now pay at least 40% of total retainer in stock
- Added stock ownership guidelines

Reynolds Metals Company

Industry: Metals/Mining

FY97 Revenue (mils): $6,900

BOARD STRUCTURE/FEES

	No. of Mtgs	Retainer Cash	Retainer Stock	Member Fee	Meeting Fee	Chairman Fee
Board	9	$30,000	$ —	$ —	$1,000	$ —
Executive	0	—	—	—	1,000	3,000
Audit	3	—	—	—	1,000	4,000
Compensation	4	—	—	—	1,000	4,000
Pension & Finance	3	—	—	—	1,000	3,000
Directors	2	—	—	—	1,000	3,000

Comments: the former COB/CEO has an agreement for $100,000/year plus office, secretarial services and a car.

Average director's annual compensation = $46,000
(assumes all meetings are attended and director sits on the Audit and Compensation committees)

STOCK-BASED COMPENSATION

Grant type(s):	**Restricted**	**Deferred**
Number of shares:	1,000	225
Frequency:	5 years	Annual
Vesting:	200 shares per year	After termination
Year-end stock price:	60.00	Same
Plan type:	Separate	—
COC provision:	Yes	Yes

Comments: payouts of deferred phantom stock are made in shares in lump sum or five installments.

Ownership Guidelines: 1,500 shares

COMPENSATION DEFERRAL

Eligible comp: Retainter/meeting
Account types: Cash and/or stock
Interest rate: Variable (set by board)
Max. installments: 10 years
Payment: Date specified by director except stock accounts (which are after termination)
Comments: payouts are in cash, in lump sum or annual installments

CASH RETIREMENT BENEFITS

Mandatory retirement age: 70
Cash plan terminated 1/97 and replaced with deferred stock; the value of accrued benefits was converted to deferred phantom stock

INSURANCE BENEFITS

Death/Disability: $50,000
Comments: benefit continues after retirement if the director serves until age 65

OTHER BENEFITS

None

CHANGES

None

The Rouse Company

Industry: Housing FY97 Revenue (mils): $930

BOARD STRUCTURE/FEES

	No. of Mtgs	Retainer: Cash	Retainer: Stock	Member Fee	Meeting Fee	Chairman Fee
Board	8	$27,500	$—	$ —	$1,250	$—
Audit	4	—	—	—	1,000	3,000
Executive	0	—	—	—	1,000	3,000
Personnel	4	—	—	—	1,000	3,000

Comments: $1,000 is paid for special assignments; former COB receives $100,000 in lieu of other fees

Average director's annual compensation = $45,500
(assumes all meetings are attended and director sits on the Audit and Compensation committees)

STOCK-BASED COMPENSATION

Grant type(s):	**Stock Option**	**Deferred Units**
Number of shares:	1,000	Value = 10% of retainer ($2,750)
Frequency:	Annual	Annual
Vesting:	6 months	At retirement
Year-end stock price:	32.75	Same
Plan type:	Combined w/ exec.	(Deferral plan)

Comments: initial grants of 5,000 options given to newly elected directors.

COMPENSATION DEFERRAL

(See deferred units above)

CASH RETIREMENT BENEFITS

Cash plan terminated 2/96 and replaced with deferred stock units (10% per year of service). Current directors guaranteed a benefit not less than that under the terminated plan.

INSURANCE BENEFITS

None

OTHER BENEFITS

None

CHANGES

None

Rubbermaid Inc.

Industry: Manufacturing — FY97 Revenue (mils): $2,400

BOARD STRUCTURE/FEES

	No. of Mtgs	Retainer Cash	Retainer Stock	Member Fee	Meeting Fee	Chairman Fee
Board	7	$13,500	—	$ —	$1,100	$ —
Audit & Environmental	2	—	—	—	1,100	3,000
Comp & Mgmt Develop	7	—	—	—	1,100	3,000
Nominating & Dir Activity	3	—	—	—	1,100	3,000

Same Day Mtg Fees: $550 fee for second meeting on same day as board or other committee meeting

Comments: 50% of all fees are mandatorily deferred in stock account (see DEFERRAL and STOCK).

Average director's annual compensation = $26,150
(assumes all meetings are attended and director sits on the Audit and Compensation committees)

STOCK-BASED COMPENSATION

Grant type(s):	**Deferred**
Value of award:	50% of retainer ($13,500)
Frequency:	Annual
Payout	After termination
Year-end stock price:	25.00
Plan type:	(Deferral plan)

Comments: shareholders approved an amendment to the Stock Incentive and Option Plan which provides for participation by outside directors; but the grants are unspecified.

COMPENSATION DEFERRAL

Eligible comp: Retainter/meeting
Account types: Cash/stock
Interest rate: 120% of Federal Test Rate
Payment: After termination
Max. installments: 10 years

Comments: 50% of fees are mandatorily deferred in stock; payout is made in lump sum or installments beginning at earlier of age 70 or termination.

CASH RETIREMENT BENEFITS

Mandatory retirement age: 70
None

INSURANCE BENEFITS

Accidental Death/Disability: $250,000

OTHER BENEFITS

Charitable Award Program
Amount: $500,000; payout: to up to 2 educational institutions; 3 years' service required; insurance funded

CHANGES

- Increased total annual retainer value by $1,000 ($500 in cash and $500 in deferred stock)

Russell Corporation

Industry: Consumer Products FY97 Revenue (mils): $1,228

BOARD STRUCTURE/FEES

	No. of Mtgs	Retainer Cash	Retainer Stock	Member Fee	Meeting Fee	Chairman Fee
Board	4	$15,000	$5,000	$ —	$1,000	$ —
Executive	8	—	—	2,600	—	2,600
Audit	1	—	—	2,600	—	2,600
Exec. Compensation	2	—	—	2,600	—	2,600
Nominating	1	—	—	2,600	—	2,600

Comments: Stock may be deferred.

Average director's annual compensation = $29,200
(assumes all meetings are attended and director sits on the Audit and Compensation committees)

STOCK-BASED COMPENSATION

Grant type(s):	**Stock Award**	**Stock Option**
Value of award:	$5,000	$5,000
Frequency:	Annual	Annual
Vesting:	Immediate	Undisclosed
Yr-end stock price:	26.5625	Same
Plan type:	Separate	Same
Plan kitty:	200,000	Same

Comments: The value of the stock award is reflected in "Stock Retainer" and "Average Director's Annual Compensation" above

COMPENSATION DEFERRAL

Eligible comp: Retainer/meeting/stock
Account types: Cash and/or stock

CASH RETIREMENT BENEFITS

Cash plan terminated in 1997 with accrued benefits converted to deferred "phantom units"

INSURANCE BENEFITS

None

OTHER BENEFITS

None

CHANGES

- Added $5,000 stock awards and $5,000 stock option grants
- Added deferral plan
- Eliminated cash retirement plan and converted accrued benefits to deferred stock units

Ryder System, Inc.

Industry: Transportation FY97 Revenue (mils): $5,351

BOARD STRUCTURE/FEES

	No. of Mtgs	Retainer Cash	Retainer Stock	Member Fee	Meeting Fee	Chairman Fee
Board	8	$21,500	$ —	$ —	$2,200	$ —
Audit	6	—	—	3,500	1,100	4,500
Directors & Public Resp	6	—	—	3,500	1,100	4,500
Compensation	6	—	—	3,500	1,100	4,500
Finance	7	—	—	3,500	1,100	4,500

Misc. Fees: Telephone Meeting Fee = $1,100

Comments: Director may elect to receive $15,000 worth of shares restricted until 6 months after service termination and $11,500 in cash (total value: $26,500) in lieu of the annual retainer.

Average director's annual compensation = $59,300
(assumes all meetings are attended and director sits on the Audit and Compensation committees)

STOCK-BASED COMPENSATION

Grant type(s):	**Stock Option**
Number of shares:	1,000
Frequency:	Annual
Vesting:	1/3 per year
Year-end stock price:	32.75
Plan type:	Separate
Plan life:	10 years
Plan kitty:	200,000
COC provision:	Yes

COMPENSATION DEFERRAL

Eligible comp:	Retainter/meeting
Account types:	Cash and/or stock
Interest rate:	Various investment options
Max. installments:	10 years
Payment:	Date specified by director
COC provision::	Yes

CASH RETIREMENT BENEFITS

Cash plan terminated 2/97 and current directors received restricted stock units equal to the prior retirement benefit

INSURANCE BENEFITS

Accidental Death/Disability: $100,000
Group Term Life: $100,000
Medical/Dental (optional)
Long-term Disability Insurance

OTHER BENEFITS

Charitable Award Program
Amount: $500,000; payout: made in 10 annual installments to up to two charities; life insurance funded

CHANGES

None

Sara Lee Corporation

Industry: Food

FY97 Revenue (mils): $19,734

BOARD STRUCTURE/FEES

	No. of Mtgs	Retainer Cash	Retainer Stock	Member Fee	Meeting Fee	Chairman Fee
Board	6	$62,500	$ —	$ —	$ —	$ —
Audit	4	—	—	—	—	9,385
Comp & Employee Benefits	3	—	—	—	—	9,385
Board Affairs & Corp Governance	1	—	—	—	—	9,385
Executive	1	—	—	—	—	9,385
Finance	4	—	—	—	—	9,385
Empl. & Public Respon.	3	—	—	—	—	9,385

Comments: Directors may elect to receive all or a portion of fees in stock or stock options; if options are elected, the value forgone is multiplied by 4 and then divided by FMV to determine the number of options; chairman's fee reflects the value of 500 additional options.

Average director's annual compensation = $62,500
(assumes all meetings are attended and director sits on the Audit and Compensation committees)

STOCK-BASED COMPENSATION

Grant type(s):	**Stock Option**
Number of shares:	5,000
Frequency:	Annual
Vesting:	6 months
Year-end stock price:	56.3125
Plan type:	Separate
Plan kitty:	500,000
COC provision:	Yes

Comments: committee chairmen receive an additional 500 options each year.

COMPENSATION DEFERRAL

Eligible comp:	Retainter/meeting
Account types:	Cash and/or stock
Payment:	Date specified by director

CASH RETIREMENT BENEFITS

None

INSURANCE BENEFITS

None

OTHER BENEFITS

None

CHANGES

None

SBC Communications Inc.

Industry: Telecommunications FY97 Revenue (mils): $24,856

BOARD STRUCTURE/FEES

		Retainer				
	No. of Mtgs	**Cash**	**Stock**	**Member Fee**	**Meeting Fee**	**Chairman Fee**
Board	9	$35,000	$ —	$ —	$1,500	$ —
Audit	3	—	—	—	1,200	5,000
Corp. Development	5	—	—	—	1,200	5,000
Corp Public Policy & Env	3	—	—	—	1,200	5,000
Executive	0	—	—	—	1,200	5,000
Finance/Pension	6	—	—	—	1,200	5,000
Human Resources	8	—	—	—	1,200	5,000

Comments: Directors may elect to receive fees in stock; advisory directors receive the same fees as regular directors; the COB/CEO serves on a Compensation Committee member's board.

Average director's annual compensation = $61,700
(assumes all meetings are attended and director sits on the Audit and Compensation committees)

STOCK-BASED COMPENSATION

Grant type(s):	**Deferred Stock Units**	**Deferred Stock Units**
Award value	Value = 50% of retainer ($17,500)	$13,000
Frequency:	Annual	Annual
Year-end stock price:	73.25	Same
Plan type:	(Deferral plan)	Same

Comments: the grants = $13,000 replace cash retirement benefits.

COMPENSATION DEFERRAL

Eligible comp: Retainter/meeting
Account types: Cash and/or stock
Interest rate: Moody's
Payment: After termination
Max installments: 15 years

CASH RETIREMENT BENEFITS

Cash plan terminated 11/97 for new directors; current directors continue in plan; new directors now receive up to 10 annual grants of $13,000 of stock units

INSURANCE BENEFITS

Travel/Accident
Group Life: $100,000

OTHER BENEFITS

Company Products: directors receive telecommunications services & equipment from a subsidiary plus tax gross-ups; in 1997 this averaged $7,576 per director

CHANGES

- Added annual stock grants
- Added elective payment of fees in stock
- Added deferral in stock alternative to deferral plan
- Eliminated cash retirement plan for future directors and replaced with 10 annual grants of $13,000 deferred stock units

Schering-Plough Corporation

Industry: Health Care | FY97 Revenue (mils): $6,778

BOARD STRUCTURE/FEES

	No. of Mtgs	Retainer Cash	Retainer Stock	Member Fee	Meeting Fee	Chairman Fee
Board	9	$39,000	1,100 shrs	$ —	$1,000	$ —
Finance, Compliance & Audit	5	—	—	—	1,000	5,000
Exec Compens & Organiz	4	—	—	—	1,000	4,000
Nominating & Corp Governance	3	—	—	—	1,000	3,000
Pension	3	—	—	—	1,000	3,000

Comments: $1,000 per diem for special assignments. Chairman fees reflect additional $1,000 paid for attendance at committee meetings.

Average director's annual compensation = $125,338
(assumes all meetings are attended and director sits on the Audit and Compensation committees)

STOCK-BASED COMPENSATION

Grant type(s):	**Stock Award**	**Deferred Units**
Number of shares:	1,100	$25,000
Frequency:	Annual	Annual
Year-end stock price:	62.125	same
Plan type:	Separate	(Deferred plan)

Comments: Stock award is reflected under "Stock Retainer" and "Average Director's Annual Comp" above.

COMPENSATION DEFERRAL

Eligible comp: Retainter/meeting
Account types: Cash and/or stock
Max. installments: 10 years
Payment: After termination
Comments: payouts may be in lump sum or installments; payment is in cash.

CASH RETIREMENT BENEFITS

Mandatory retirement age: 72
Cash plan terminated 12/31/96 with the value of accrued benefits transferred to deferred stock accounts; in the future, directors will receive $25,000 per year deferred in stock equivalent accounts

INSURANCE BENEFITS

None

OTHER BENEFITS

None

CHANGES

- changed from stock award grants at the beginning of each 3-year term to annual grants

Sears, Roebuck & Company

Industry: Retailing FY97 Revenue (mils): $41,296

BOARD STRUCTURE/FEES

	No. of Mtgs	Retainer Cash	Retainer Stock	Member Fee	Meeting Fee	Chairman Fee
Board	7	$30,000	—	$ —	$ —	$ —
Audit	4	—	—	—	—	5,000
Compensation	6	—	—	—	—	5,000
Executive	0	—	—	—	—	—
Nominating	5	—	—	—	—	5,000

Average director's annual compensation = $30,000
(assumes all meetings are attended and director sits on the Audit and Compensation committees)

STOCK-BASED COMPENSATION

Grant type(s):	**Deferred**	**Stock Option**
Value of shares:	$30,000	$30,000
Frequency:	Annual	Annual
Vesting:	At termination	1 year
Year-end stock price:	45.25	Same
Plan type:	Separate	Same
Plan life:	10 years	Same
Plan kitty:	0.1% of outstanding common each yr	Same
COC provision:	Yes	Same

Comments: deferred shares are paid out in stock; number of options granted is based on dividing $30,000 by 1/3 of FMV on the grant date (for 1997 directors received 600 deferred shares and 1,800 stock options).

Ownership Guidelines: director must own shares and deferred stock = 5 times annual retainer, within 5 years

COMPENSATION DEFERRAL

Eligible comp: Retainter/meeting
Account types: Cash and/or stock
Interest rate: Variable
Max. installments: 10 years
Payment: Lump sum or up to 10 annual installations.

Comments: Four invest. choices: Lehman Brothers Bond Index, Sears Stock Index, S&P 500 Stock Price Index, or avg. interest on commercial paper issued by Sears Acceptance; account transfers permitted

CASH RETIREMENT BENEFITS

Mandatory retirement age: 70
Cash plan terminated and accrued benefits frozen; benefits replaced with stock option grants (above)

INSURANCE BENEFITS

None

OTHER BENEFITS

None

CHANGES

- Eliminated life insurance of $150,000

The Sherwin-Williams Company

Industry: Housing FY97 Revenue (mils): $4,881

BOARD STRUCTURE/FEES

	No. of Mtgs	Retainer Cash	Retainer Stock	Member Fee	Meeting Fee	Chairman Fee
Board	5	$30,000	—	$ —	$1,750	$ —
Audit	2	—	—	—	1,750	500
Board Composition	1	—	—	—	1,750	250
Comp & Mgmt Develop	3	—	—	—	1,750	750

Comments: chairmen fees reflect an additional $250 received per committee meeting attended; the COB/CEO serves on the Compensation Committee of a director on Sherwin-Williams' Comp. Committee

Average director's annual compensation = $47,500
(assumes all meetings are attended and director sits on the Audit and Compensation committees)

STOCK-BASED COMPENSATION

Grant type(s):	**Stock Option**
Number of shares:	2,000
Frequency:	Annual
Vesting:	Undisclosed
Year-end stock price:	27.75
Plan type:	Separate
Plan life:	10 years
Plan kitty:	400,000

Comments: the plan also authorizes restricted stock grants, although none were granted in 1997.

COMPENSATION DEFERRAL

Eligible comp:	Retainter/meeting
Account types:	Cash and/or stock
Interest rate:	Prime
Maximum installments:	10 years
COC provision::	Yes

CASH RETIREMENT BENEFITS

None

INSURANCE BENEFITS

None

OTHER

None

CHANGES

- Increased annual retainer by $5,000

Shoney's Inc.

Industry: Leisure FY97 Revenue (mils): $1,203

BOARD STRUCTURE/FEES

	No. of Mtgs	Retainer Cash	Retainer Stock	Member Fee	Meeting Fee	Chairman Fee
Board	18	$16,000	$ —	$ —	$1,000	$ —
Audit	3	—	—	—	1,000	—
Human Resources & Comp	8	—	—	—	1,000	—
Nominating	4	—	—	—	1,000	—
Executive	1	—	—	—	1,000	—
Franchise Relations	1	—	—	—	1,000	—
Special	7	—	—	—	1,000	—

Comments: The chairman of Audit, HRC, and Special Committees received $10,000 each in 1997 and another director received $10,000 for assisting with strategic review of company operations in 1997

Average director's annual compensation = $45,000
(assumes all meetings are attended and director sits on the Audit and Compensation committees)

STOCK-BASED COMPENSATION

Grant type(s):	**Stock Option**
Number of shares:	5,000
Frequency:	5 years
Vesting:	20% per year
Year-end stock price:	3.25
Plan type:	Separate
Plan life:	10 years
Plan kitty:	200,000
COC provision:	Yes

Comments: A new 1998 Stock Plan provides for discretionary grants of restricted stock or other stock-based awards to outside directors.

COMPENSATION DEFERRAL

None

CASH RETIREMENT BENEFITS

None

INSURANCE BENEFITS

None

OTHER BENEFITS

None

CHANGES

- The new 1998 Stock Plan provides for discretionary grants to directors

Silicon Graphics, Inc.

Industry: Office Equipment & Services FY97 Revenue (mils): $3,663

BOARD STRUCTURE/FEES

	No. of Mtgs	Retainer Cash	Retainer Stock	Member Fee	Meeting Fee	Chairman Fee
Board	4	$20,000	$ —	$ —	$1,000	$ —
Compensation & Human Resources	4	—	—	—	1,000	4,000
Audit	7	—	—	—	1,000	7,000

Comments: Chairmen fees reflect additional $1,000 per meeting attended; the company sold $38,831,554 of products to Tandem Computers Inc. whose former CEO is a director.

Average director's annual compensation = $35,000
(assumes all meetings are attended and director sits on the Audit and Compensation committees)

STOCK-BASED COMPENSATION

Grant type(s):	**Stock Option**
Number of shares:	10,000
Frequency:	Annual
Vesting:	1/3 each year
Year-end stock price:	12.3125
Plan type:	Separate
Plan kitty:	1,000,000

Comments: initial grant upon election to board covers 30,000 stock options.

COMPENSATION DEFERRAL

Eligible comp: Retainter/meeting
Account types: Cash and/or stock
Interest rate: Various mutual funds
Max. installments: 10 years
Payment: After termination
Comments: payouts are in lump sum or installments except stock accounts, which are lump sum.

CASH RETIREMENT BENEFITS

None

INSURANCE BENEFITS

None

OTHER BENEFITS

None

CHANGES

None

Snap-On Inc.

Industry: Manufacturing FY97 Revenue (mils): $1,672

BOARD STRUCTURE/FEES

	No. of Mtgs	Retainer Cash	Retainer Stock	Member Fee	Meeting Fee	Chairman Fee
Board	6	$19,500	$6,500	$ —	$1,250	$ —
Executive	1	—	—	—	1,250	4,000
Organ & Exec Comp	3	—	—	—	1,250	4,000
Audit	4	—	—	—	1,250	4,000
Board Affairs & Nominat	2	—	—	—	1,250	4,000
Finance	5	—	—	—	1,250	4,000

Misc. Fees: Telephone Meeting Fee: $1,250

Comments: Mandatory 25% of $26,000 annual retainer and fees paid in stock; directors may elect up to 100% paid in shares, which may be deferred.

Average director's annual compensation = $42,250
(assumes all meetings are attended and director sits on the Audit and Compensation committees)

STOCK-BASED COMPENSATION

Grant type(s):	Stock Option	Stock Award
Number of shares:	3,000	$6,500
Frequency:	Annual	Annual
Vesting:	Immediate	Same
Year-end stock price:	43.625	Same
Plan type:	Combined w/ exec.	—
COC provision:	Yes	—

COMPENSATION DEFERRAL

Eligible comp: Retainter/meeting/shares
Account types: Cash/stock
Interest rate: Various investment options

CASH RETIREMENT BENEFITS

None

INSURANCE BENEFITS

Accidental Death/Disability
Life

OTHER BENEFITS

None

CHANGES

- Increased committee meeting fee and telephone fee by $250 each

Sonoco Products Company

Industry: Containers & Packaging FY97 Revenue (mils): $2,848

BOARD STRUCTURE/FEES

	No. of Mtgs	Retainer Cash	Retainer Stock	Member Fee	Meeting Fee	Chairman Fee
Board	6*	$42,000	—	$ —	$ —	$ —
Audit	3	—	—	—	—	—
Executive Compensation	5	—	—	—	—	—
Nominating	2	—	—	—	—	—
Finance	2	—	—	—	—	—
Executive	3	—	—	—	—	—
Employee/Public Responsibility	1	—	—	—	—	—

* includes two special meetings

Comments: $1,000 paid for special meetings; directors may elect to have all or a portion of fees paid in deferred stock options with an exercise price = 100% of FMV; total purchase price = 4 times amount deferred; option life = 5 years after termination; optionees credited with partial dividend equivalents; the COB/CEO is on the Compensation Committee of an outside director's company; the Pres/COO is a director at a Compensation Committee member's company; the company purchased lumber/timber from 3 director's companies for a total of $2.1-mil in 1997; the company sold timber to a director's firm for $904,000.

Average director's annual compensation = $44,000
(assumes all meetings are attended and director sits on the Audit and Compensation committees)

STOCK-BASED COMPENSATION

Grant type(s):	**Stock Option**
Number of shares:	2,000
Frequency:	Annual
Vesting:	6 months
Year-end stock price:	34.6875
Plan type:	Separate
Plan life:	Indefinite
Plan kitty:	125,000 each year
COC provision:	Yes

Comments: Grants include reload options; the number granted annually may be increased up to 10,000 without shareholder approval.

COMPENSATION DEFERRAL

Eligible comp:	Retainter/meeting
Account types:	Cash and/or stock
Interest rate:	Market rate
Max. installments:	15 years
Payment:	After termination

Comments: payout is in annual installments.

CASH RETIREMENT BENEFITS

None

INSURANCE BENEFITS

None

OTHER BENEFITS

None

CHANGES

None

Southern Company

Industry: Utilities

FY97 Revenue (mils): $12,611

BOARD STRUCTURE/FEES

	No. of Mtgs	Retainer Cash	Retainer Stock	Member Fee	Meeting Fee	Chairman Fee
Board	8	$30,000	$ —	$ —	$1,250	$ —
Audit	5	—	—	—	1,000	5,000
Comp & Mgmt Succession	3	—	—	—	1,000	5,000
Governance	2	—	—	—	1,000	5,000

Comments: $19,000 of $49,000 total annual retainer is mandatorily deferred in stock; directors may elect to receive up to 100% of retainer in shares

Average director's annual compensation = $48,000
(assumes all meetings are attended and director sits on the Audit and Compensation committees)

STOCK-BASED COMPENSATION

Grant type(s):	**Deferred**
Value of award:	$19,000
Frequency:	Annual
Vesting:	After termination
Year-end stock price:	25.875
Plan type:	(Deferral plan)

COMPENSATION DEFERRAL

Eligible comp: Retainter/meeting (cash fees only)
Payment: After termination
Comments: no additional information disclosed.

CASH RETIREMENT BENEFITS

Cash plan terminated 1/97 and benefits frozen; current directors could elect to defer the present value of benefits or to continue in the plan at frozen level

INSURANCE BENEFITS

None

OTHER BENEFITS

None

CHANGES

- Increased total retainer value by $9,000, with all this amount being deferred

Southern New England Telecommunications Corporation

Industry: Telecommunications — FY97 Revenue (mils): $2,022

BOARD STRUCTURE/FEES

	No. of Mtgs	Retainer Cash	Retainer Stock	Member Fee	Meeting Fee	Chairman Fee
Board	9	$13,500	—	$ —	$1,000	$ —
Audit	5	—	—	—	1,000	2,500
Board Affairs & Public Policy	3	—	—	—	1,000	2,500
Executive	0	—	—	—	1,000	2,500
Employee Benefits	4	—	—	—	1,000	2,500
Financial Resources	4	—	—	—	1,000	2,500
Personnel & Board Affairs	5	—	—	—	1,000	2,500

Comments: directors may elect to receive up to 100% of retainers in shares, which are restricted for 6 months.

Average director's annual compensation = $32,500
(assumes all meetings are attended and director sits on the Audit and Compensation committees)

STOCK-BASED COMPENSATION

Grant type(s):	**Restricted**
Number of shares:	300
Frequency:	Annual
Vesting:	Termination
Year-end stock price:	50.3125
Plan type:	Separate
Plan life:	10 years
Plan kitty:	200,000
COC provision:	Yes

COMPENSATION DEFERRAL

Eligible comp: Retainter/meeting (cash only)
Account types: Cash
Interest rate: Variable
Comments: interest based on applicable Federal Rate.

CASH RETIREMENT BENEFITS

Cash plan was terminated and accrued benefits frozen; stock plan is intended to replace it

INSURANCE BENEFITS

Accidental Death/Disability
Life

OTHER BENEFITS

Company Products: Telephone service concession

CHANGES

- Eliminated travel/accident insurance

Springs Industries, Inc.

Industry: Manufacturing FY97 Revenue (mils): $2,226

BOARD STRUCTURE/FEES

	No. of Mtgs	Retainer Cash	Retainer Stock	Member Fee	Meeting Fee	Chairman Fee
Board	7	$18,000	$ —	$ —	$ —	$ —
Audit	3	—	—	—	—	1,000
Mgmt Comp & Organ	5	—	—	—	—	1,000
Executive	0	—	—	—	—	1,000
Finance	2	—	—	—	—	1,000
Springs of Achievement	1	—	—	—	—	1,000

Misc. Fees: Telephone Meeting Fee: $1,000 for special board meetings

Comments: $2,500 paid for attendance at each special board meeting. One director received $59,000 for consulting services.

Average director's annual compensation = $18,000
(assumes all meetings are attended and director sits on the Audit and Compensation committees)

STOCK-BASED COMPENSATION

Grant type(s):	**Restricted**
Award value:	$18,000
Frequency:	Annual
Vesting:	Upon approved termination
Year-end stock price:	52.00
Plan type:	Separate
Plan kitty:	100,000

Comments: Approved termination includes death/disability/retirement, hardship, government service, etc.; annual stock award has value equal to the prior year's annual retainer earned by the director.

COMPENSATION DEFERRAL

Eligible comp: Retainter/meeting
Account types: Cash and/or stock
Interest rate: Prime, or company investment fund
Max. installments: 10 years
Payment: After termination

Comments: accounts denominated in company shares receive quarterly dividend equivalents; dividend equivalents earn quarterly interest at the prime rate; payouts are made in stock or cash.

CASH RETIREMENT BENEFITS

Mandatory retirement age: 70
None

INSURANCE BENEFITS

None

OTHER BENEFITS

None

CHANGES

None

Sprint Corporation

Industry: Telecommunications FY97 Revenue (mils): $14,874

BOARD STRUCTURE/FEES

	No. of Mtgs	Retainer Cash	Retainer Stock	Member Fee	Meeting Fee	Chairman Fee
Board	7	$35,000	$ —	$ —	$1,250	$ —
Audit	2	—	—	—	1,000	—
Org., Compen. & Nominating	7	—	—	—	1,000	—
Executive	0	—	—	—	1,000	—

Misc. Fees: Subsidiary Fees Paid

Comments: directors may elect to receive stock in lieu of fees; stock may also be deferred.

Average director's annual compensation = $52,750
(assumes all meetings are attended and director sits on the Audit and Compensation committees)

STOCK-BASED COMPENSATION

Grant type(s):	**Stock Option**	**Deferred Units**
Number of shares:	2,000	2,500
Frequency:	Annual	One-time
Vesting:	25% per year	50% after 5 years & 10% per year thereafter
Year-end stock price:	58.625	Same
Plan type:	Combined w/ exec.	(Deferred plan)
COC provision:	Yes	—

Comments: Deferred grants replace former cash retirement plan

COMPENSATION DEFERRAL

Eligible comp: Retainter/meeting

Comments: no additional information disclosed

CASH RETIREMENT BENEFITS

Cash plan terminated 12/96 for unvested directors (5 years of service); unvested and new directors receive one-time grant of deferred stock (see STOCK)

INSURANCE BENEFITS

None

OTHER BENEFITS

Residential long distance service with a value between $700 and $4,961

CHANGES

None

SPX Corporation

Industry: Automotive

FY97 Revenue (mils): $922

BOARD STRUCTURE/FEES

	No. of Mtgs	Retainer Cash	Retainer Stock	Member Fee	Meeting Fee	Chairman Fee
Board	6	$43,597*	$ —	$ —	$ —	$ —
Executive	0	—	—	—	—	—
Audit	3	—	—	—	—	—
Compensation	2	—	—	—	—	—
Governance	1	—	—	—	—	—
Retirement Funds	3	—	—	—	—	—

* includes $25,500 annual retainer and a bonus of $18,097; the bonus each year equals $5,000 times the multiple of target award earned by the CEO under the EVA Plan; $8,731 is put in their reserve account

Average director's annual compensation = $43,597
(assumes all meetings are attended and director sits on the Audit and Compensation committees)

STOCK-BASED COMPENSATION

Grant type(s):	**Stock Option**
Value of award	1,500
Frequency:	Annual
Vesting:	6 months
Year-end stock price:	69.00
Plan type:	Separate
Plan life:	2 years
Plan kitty:	75,000
COC provision:	Yes

Ownership Guidelines: 1 times the retainer

COMPENSATION DEFERRAL

Eligible comp: Retainer/bonus
Comments: no additional information disclosed.

CASH RETIREMENT BENEFITS

Cash plan terminated 12/96 and 115% of the present value of accrued benefits was converted to a deferred account

INSURANCE BENEFITS

None

OTHER BENEFITS

None

CHANGES

- The retainer includes the first bonus payment under the compensation program approved in 1997

St. Joe Corporation

Industry: Paper/Forest FY97 Revenue (mils): $346

BOARD STRUCTURE/FEES

	No. of Mtgs	Retainer Cash	Retainer Stock	Member Fee	Meeting Fee	Chairman Fee
Board	10	$25,000	$ —	$ —	$1,250	$ —
Audit	4	—	—	—	1,250	—
Compensation	6	—	—	—	1,250	—
Nominating	1	—	—	—	1,250	—
Finance	5	—	—	—	1,250	—

Comments: Employee directors receive $200 for attendance at board meetings; two former COB/CEOs have consulting agreements for $100,000 and $112,000; the Compensation Committee chairman was owner of 10% of a company bought out by St. Joe

Average director's annual compensation = $50,000
(assumes all meetings are attended and director sits on the Audit and Compensation committees)

STOCK-BASED COMPENSATION

A new 1998 Stock Incentive Plan authorizes discretionary stock option grants to outside directors (no specific awards are disclosed).

COMPENSATION DEFERRAL

None

CASH RETIREMENT BENEFITS

None

INSURANCE BENEFITS

None

OTHER BENEFITS

None

CHANGES

None

St. Jude Medical, Inc.

Industry: Health Care

FY97 Revenue (mils): $809

BOARD STRUCTURE/FEES

	No. of Mtgs	Retainer Cash	Retainer Stock	Member Fee	Meeting Fee	Chairman Fee
Board	8	$30,000	$ —	$ —	$1,000	$ —
Audit	4	—	—	—	—	—
Compensation	2	—	—	—	—	—
Governance & Nominating	2	—	—	—	—	—

Comments: Directors may elect to receive 50% or 100% of their fees in stock (restricted for 6 months).

Average director's annual compensation = $38,000
(assumes all meetings are attended and director sits on the Audit and Compensation committees)

STOCK-BASED COMPENSATION

Grant type(s):	**Stock Option**
Number of shares:	3,000
Frequency:	Annual
Vesting:	6 months
Yr-end stock price:	30.50
Plan type:	Combined with exec

Comments: directors may receive additional discretionary option grants, not to exceed 5,000 shares per year.

COMPENSATION DEFERRAL

None

CASH RETIREMENT BENEFITS

Cash plan frozen 3/96

INSURANCE BENEFITS

None

OTHER BENEFITS

None

CHANGES

None

The St. Paul Companies, Inc.

Industry: Nonbank Financial FY97 Revenue (mils): $6,219

BOARD STRUCTURE/FEES

	No. of Mtgs	Retainer Cash	Retainer Stock	Member Fee	Meeting Fee	Chairman Fee
Board	5	$20,500	$ —	$ —	$1,000	$ —
Executive	2	—	—	—	1,000	4,000
Audit	4	—	—	—	1,000	4,000
Personnel & Compensation	4	—	—	—	1,000	4,000
Finance	4	—	—	—	1,000	4,000
Board Governance	4	—	—	—	1,000	4,000

Directors may elect to receive all or a portion of annual retainer in stock, restricted for 5 years; the value received = 110% of the amount foregone; restricted shares are forfeited if service terminates for other than death, disability or retirement before vesting. The board adopted a policy that the company not hire a director or their firm except in exceptional circumstances with the Governance Committee's consent.

Average director's annual compensation = $33,500
(assumes all meetings are attended and director sits on the Audit and Compensation committees)

STOCK-BASED COMPENSATION

Grant type(s):	**Stock Option**
Number of shares:	1,500
Frequency:	Annual
Vesting:	1 year
Year-end stock price:	82.0625
Plan type:	Combined w/ exec.
COC provision:	Yes

Ownership Guidelines: Five times the annual retainer within 5 years

COMPENSATION DEFERRAL

Eligible comp: Retainter/meeting
Account types: Cash and/or stock
Interest: 9 phantom mutual funds
Payment: After termination
Comments: benefits backed by a grantor trust.

CASH RETIREMENT BENEFITS

Mandatory Service: 2 years
Mandatory retirement age: after 15 years' service
Basic benefits: Retainer + stock option value
Payment term: Matching service, up to 15 years
Death benefit: Yes (spouse only)
COC provision:: Yes
Comments: payment may be in discounted lump sum; backed by grantor trust.

INSURANCE BENEFITS

Group Term Life: $100,000
Travel/Accident: $200,000

OTHER BENEFITS

Charitable Award Program

Amount: $1,000,000; payout: over 10 years to up to four charities; life insurance funded; directors vest in 20% increments in years 3–7 or at death, disability, or retirement at age 70

CHANGES

- Increased stock option grant by 500 shares
- Changed deferral plan interest from Prime to mutual funds

The Standard Register Company

Industry: Office Equipment & Services

FY97 Revenue (mils): $966

BOARD STRUCTURE/FEES

	No. of Mtgs	Retainer Cash	Retainer Stock	Member Fee	Meeting Fee	Chairman Fee
Board	6	$20,000	$ —	$ —	$1,000	$ —
Audit	2	—	—	5,500	—	2,000
Compensation	3	—	—	5,500	—	2,000
Pension Advisory	3	—	—	5,500	—	2,000
Executive	(new)	—	—	—	1,000	—

Average director's annual compensation = $37,000
(assumes all meetings are attended and director sits on the Audit and Compensation committees)

STOCK-BASED COMPENSATION
None

COMPENSATION DEFERRAL
None

CASH RETIREMENT BENEFITS
None

INSURANCE BENEFITS
None

OTHER BENEFITS
None

CHANGES
- Increased Audit and Compensation Committees' member fees by $2,500 and their chairman's fees by $1,000

The Stanley Works

Industry: Manufacturing FY97 Revenue (mils): $2,670

BOARD STRUCTURE/FEES

	No. of Mtgs	Retainer Cash	Retainer Stock	Member Fee	Meeting Fee	Chairman Fee
Board	11	$21,000	$ —	$ —	$1,000	$ —
Executive	0	—	—	—	1,000	2,000
Audit	4	—	—	—	1,000	2,000
Board Affairs & Public Policy	3	—	—	—	1,000	2,000
Finance & Pension	3	—	—	—	1,000	2,000
Compensation & Organiz	8	—	—	—	1,000	2,000

Misc. Fees: Telephone Meeting Fees: $200

Average director's annual compensation = $44,000
(assumes all meetings are attended and director sits on the Audit and Compensation committees)

STOCK-BASED COMPENSATION

Grant type(s):	**Stock Option**
Number of shares:	2,000
Frequency:	Annual
Vesting:	1 year
Year-end stock price:	47.1875
Plan type:	Separate
Plan life:	10 years
Plan kitty:	100,000

Ownership Guidelines: a director must defer fees in stock until he owns 5,000 shares

COMPENSATION DEFERRAL

Eligible comp: Retainter/meeting
Account types: Cash and/or stock
Interest rate: T-bills
Max. installments: 10 years
COC provision:: Yes
Comments: directors are required to defer fees in stock until he/she owns 5,000 shares.

CASH RETIREMENT BENEFITS

Mandatory retirement age: 70
None

INSURANCE BENEFITS

None

OTHER BENEFITS

None

CHANGES

- Increased chairman's fee by $1,000
- Changed from granting 1,000 options every 2 years to annual grants of 2,000 shares
- Added ownership guidelines

Stone & Webster, Inc.

Industry: Service Industries FY97 Revenue (mils): $1,323

BOARD STRUCTURE/FEES

	No. of Mtgs	Retainer Cash	Retainer Stock	Member Fee	Meeting Fee	Chairman Fee
Board	10	$8,000	400 shrs	$ —	$2,000	$ —
Audit	3	—	—	—	1,000	3,000
Compensation	8	—	—	—	1,000	8,000
Governance	5	—	—	—	1,000	5,000
Employee Benefits	3	—	—	—	1,000	3,000

Comments: Chairmen fees reflect an additional $1,000 per meeting. Directors may elect to receive meeting and/or chairman fees in stock; the Lead Director receives $10,000 per year and received a prorated amount based on $50,000/year while interim COB; he also received a bonus of $50,000 and 1,000 shares of stock; all directors received special fees in 1997 ranging from $1,000 to $4,000 and an additional $3,000 for special corporate governance meetings (3 days).

Misc. fees: one director receives $4,177 for serving on a subsidiary board

Average director's annual compensation = $57,750
(assumes all meetings are attended and director sits on the Audit and Compensation committees)

STOCK-BASED COMPENSATION

Grant type(s):	**Stock Option**	**Stock Award**
Number of shares:	1,000	400
Frequency:	Annual	Annual
Vesting:	6 months	—
Year-end stock price:	46.875	same
Plan type:	Combined w/ exec	Separate
Plan life:	—	Indefinite
Plan kitty:	—	100,000
COC provision:	Yes	—

Comments: The value of stock award is reflected in Avg. Director's Annual Comp above. Initial stock option grants cover 2,000 shares; the plan also provides for "reload options," restricted stock grants, and performance shares/units

COMPENSATION DEFERRAL

Eligible comp: Retainer/meeting (cash only)
Account types: Cash and/or stock
Interest rate: Prime + 1%

CASH RETIREMENT BENEFITS

None

INSURANCE BENEFITS

None

OTHER BENEFITS

None

CHANGES

- Added deferral plan

Sun Company, Inc.

Industry: Fuel FY97 Revenue (mils): $8,968

BOARD STRUCTURE/FEES

	No. of Mtgs	Retainer Cash	Retainer Stock	Member Fee	Meeting Fee	Chairman Fee
Board	9	$8,520	$19,880	$ —	$1,250	$ —
Audit	6	—	—	—	1,250	2,000
Governance	5	—	—	—	1,250	2,000
Compensation	7	—	—	—	1,250	2,000
Executive	1	—	—	—	1,250	2,000
Public Affairs	3	—	—	—	1,250	2,000

Comments: $1,250/day for special assignments. 70% of the annual retainer is paid in stock; maximum value of stock retainer portion is $40,000 under plan.

Average director's annual compensation = $55,900
(assumes all meetings are attended and director sits on the Audit and Compensation committees)

STOCK-BASED COMPENSATION

Grant type(s):	**Deferred Units**	**Stock Award**
Value of award:	$10,000	70% of Retainer ($19,880)
Frequency:	Annual	Annual
Vesting:	At termination	—
Year-end stock price:	42.0625	same

Comments: Deferred units intended to compensate for discontinued pension plan; stock award is reflected in Stock Retainer and "Average Director's Annual Compensation" above.

Ownership Guidelines: Three times average annual compensation (retainer and fees), which is currently approximately $200,000, within 5 years

COMPENSATION DEFERRAL

Eligible comp: Retainter/meeting/stock
Account types: Cash and/or Stock
Interest rate: Set by committee, but based on T-bill
Payment: Date specified by director, must begin no later than age 73

CASH RETIREMENT BENEFITS

Mandatory retirement age: 72
Cash plan terminated 2/96 and accrued benefits converted to deferred restricted share units; in lieu of future accruals, $10,000 is credited annually to directors' deferred stock unit accounts.

INSURANCE BENEFITS

None

OTHER BENEFITS

None

CHANGES

- Added stock ownership guidelines
- Increased mandatory retirement age from 70 to 72

SunAmerica Inc.

Industry: Nonbank Financial | FY97 Revenue (mils): $2,084

BOARD STRUCTURE/FEES

	No. of Mtgs	Retainer Cash	Retainer Stock	Member Fee	Meeting Fee	Chairman Fee
Board	5	$25,000	—	$ —	$1,000	$ —
Audit & Compliance	2	—	—	—	1,000	5,000
Personnel, Comp & Stock Plan	3	—	—	—	1,000	5,000
Nominating	1	—	—	—	1,000	5,000

Same Day fees: $500 is paid for the second meeting in a day

Comments: directors may take stock options in lieu of fees, with the number = 2.5 times forgone amount divided by FMV; they are exercisable 25% per year.

Average director's annual compensation = $32,500
(assumes all meetings are attended and director sits on the Audit and Compensation committees)

STOCK-BASED COMPENSATION

Grant type(s):	**Stock Option**
Number of shares:	1,500
Frequency:	Annual
Vesting:	1/3 per year
Year-end stock price:	42.75
Plan type:	Separate
Plan life:	Indefinite
Plan kitty:	250,000

COMPENSATION DEFERRAL

Eligible comp: Retainter/meeting
Account types: Cash
Payment: Date specified by director

CASH RETIREMENT BENEFITS

Mandatory service: 3 years
Basic benefit: 50% of retainer
Payment term: Matching service, up to 10 yrs

INSURANCE BENEFITS

None

OTHER BENEFITS

Charitable Award Program
Amount: $500,000; payout: up to five charities

CHANGES

None

The Talbots, Inc.

Industry: Discount & Fashion Retailing FY97 Revenue (mils): $1,054

BOARD STRUCTURE/FEES

	No. of Mtgs	Retainer Cash	Retainer Stock	Member Fee	Meeting Fee	Chairman Fee
Board	4	$23,000	—	$ —	$ —	$50,000
Audit	2	—	—	—	—	5,000
Compensation	2	—	—	—	—	5,000

Comments: COB fee is in lieu of other fees.

Average director's annual compensation = $23,000
(assumes all meetings are attended and director sits on the Audit and Compensation committees)

STOCK-BASED COMPENSATION

Grant type(s):	**Stock Option**
Number of shares:	3,000 - 5,000
Frequency:	Annual
Year-end stock price:	18.125

Comments: No additional information disclosed; (4,000 shares used for stock valuation analyses in this study).

COMPENSATION DEFERRAL

None

CASH RETIREMENT BENEFITS

None

INSURANCE BENEFITS

None

OTHER BENEFITS

None

CHANGES

None

Temple-Inland, Inc.

Industry: Containers & Packaging FY97 Revenue (mils): $3,625

BOARD STRUCTURE/FEES

	No. of Mtgs	Retainer Cash	Retainer Stock	Member Fee	Meeting Fee	Chairman Fee
Board	4	$35,000	—	$ —	$2,000	$ —
Audit	3	—	—	—	2,000	2,500
Executive	0	—	—	—	2,000	2,500
Finance	3	—	—	—	2,000	2,500
Mgmt Develop & Exec Comp	3	—	—	—	2,000	2,500
Nominating	2	—	—	—	2,000	2,500
Public Policy/Environmental	2	—	—	—	2,000	2,500

Same Day Mtg Fees: $1,000 paid for attendance at committee meeting held on same day as board

Comments: Directors may elect to receive discount-priced stock options in lieu of annual retainer; a Compensation Committee member's company performed repair services for a Temple-Inland subsidiary for $121,147 in 1997.

Average director's annual compensation = $49,000
(assumes all meetings are attended and director sits on the Audit and Compensation committees)

STOCK-BASED COMPENSATION

Grant type(s):	**Stock Option**	**Discount Options**
Number of shares:	10,000	2,000
Frequency:	One-time	As elected by director
Vesting:	25% per year after 4-yrs service	1 year
Option life	10 years	15 years
Year-end stock price:	52.3125	same
Plan type:	Combined w/ exec.	same
COC provision:	Yes	same

Comments: Exercise price of discount options = FMV price minus (Retainer + 2,000); newly approved plan allows for discretionary option grants to directors in the future.

COMPENSATION DEFERRAL

Eligible comp: Retainter/meeting
Account types: Cash
Interest rate: Prime
Payment: After termination

CASH RETIREMENT BENEFITS

Mandatory service: 10 years
Min. retirement age: 65
Basic benefits: Retainer
Payment term: Matching service, with 5 years guaranteed
Death benefit: Yes (spouse only)
COC provision: Yes

Comments: 10 years *or* age 65; lump sum payout for termination within two years after a COC (plus excise tax gross-up, if applicable.)

INSURANCE BENEFITS

None

OTHER BENEFITS

None

CHANGES

None

Tenet Healthcare Corporation

Industry: Health Care FY97 Revenue (mils): $8,691

BOARD STRUCTURE/FEES

	No. of Mtgs	Retainer Cash	Retainer Stock	Member Fee	Meeting Fee	Chairman Fee
Board	8	$50,000	$ —	$ —	$1,000	$ —
Executive	4	—	—	—	1,200	4,000
Audit	5	—	—	—	1,200	4,000
Compens & Stock Option	11	—	—	—	1,200	4,000
Nominating	2	—	—	—	1,200	4,000
Ethics & Quality Assurance	3	—	—	—	1,200	4,000
Pension	3	—	—	—	1,200	4,000

Comments: One director received $1,000/month for serving as a Compensation Committee advisor in 1997.

Average director's annual compensation = $77,200
(assumes all meetings are attended and director sits on the Audit and Compensation committees)

STOCK-BASED COMPENSATION

Grant type(s):	**Stock Option**
Number of shares:	7,500
Frequency:	Annual
Vesting:	1 year
Year-end stock price:	33.125
Plan type:	Separate
Plan kitty:	500,000
Plan life:	10 years
COC provision:	Yes

COMPENSATION DEFERRAL

None

CASH RETIREMENT BENEFITS

Mandatory Service: 10 years
Reduced Benefit Avail: Yes
Basic benefits: Retainer
Payment term: 10 years
Death benefit: Yes (surviving spouse or dependents)
COC provision:: Yes

Comments: max. benefit = $25,000 compounded at 6% per annum from 1985. In 1994, plan amended to allow former employees to participate (service years are measured from the date employment terminates).

INSURANCE BENEFITS

Split dollar second-to-die life insurance with death ben. up to $1-mil for director's beneficiary. Participant pays the cost of pure term insurance & Tenet pays balance

OTHER BENEFITS

One director used company airplane for personal use at a cost of $24,336

CHANGES

- Increased annual retainer by $10,000
- Increased stock option grants by 2,500 shares

Texaco Inc.

Industry: Fuel

FY97 Revenue (mils): $45,187

BOARD STRUCTURE/FEES

	No. of Mtgs	Retainer Cash	Retainer Stock	Member Fee	Meeting Fee	Chairman Fee
Board	11	$15,000	$15,000	$ —	$1,250	$ —
Audit	2	—	—	—	1,250	7,000
Compensation	5	—	—	—	1,250	7,000
Finance	3	—	—	—	1,250	—
Dir & Board Governance	3	—	—	—	1,250	7,000
Non-Management Directors	2	—	—	—	1,250	7,000
Pension	3	—	—	—	1,250	7,000
Public Responsibility	3	—	—	—	1,250	7,000
Executive	1	—	—	—	1,250	7,000

Comments: Directors may elect to receive all or a portion of fees in stock; 50% of annual retainer is paid in stock or restricted stock units; Texaco paid $274,924 for oil barge services to a director's subsidiary company.

Average director's annual compensation = $52,500
(assumes all meetings are attended and director sits on the Audit and Compensation committees)

STOCK-BASED COMPENSATION

Grant type(s):	**Deferred Units**	**Stock Award**
Number of shares:	900	50% of Retainer ($15,000)
Frequency:	Annual	Annual
Vesting:	5 years of board service	—
Year-end stock price:	54.375	same
Payment	Later of retirement or age 65	—
COC provision:	Yes	—

Comments: Units are forfeited if retired director engages in conduct detrimental to the company.

COMPENSATION DEFERRAL

Eligible comp: Retainter/meeting
Account types: Cash, stock, or restricted units
Comments: no additional information disclosed.

CASH RETIREMENT BENEFITS

Mandatory retirement age: 72
Cash plan terminated 10/95, with accrued benefits fully vested and frozen; replaced with restricted stock unit grants (above).

INSURANCE BENEFITS

Group Personal liability and property damage

OTHER BENEFITS

Charitable Award Program
Amount: $1,000,000; payout: made to one or more charities; life insurance funded

CHANGES

None

Texas Instruments Inc.

Industry: Telecommunications FY97 Revenue (mils): $10,562

BOARD STRUCTURE/FEES

	No. of Mtgs	Retainer Cash	Retainer Stock	Member Fee	Meeting Fee	Chairman Fee
Board	12	$20,000	$ —	$ —	$ —	$ —
Audit	6	—	—	7,500	—	2,500
Compensation	6	—	—	7,500	—	2,500
Board Org & Nominating	7	—	—	7,500	—	2,500
Benefit Plans	4	—	—	7,500	—	2,500
Finance	5	—	—	7,500	—	2,500
Stockholder Rel & Public Policy	5	—	—	7,500	—	2,500
Trust Review	3	—	—	10,000	—	2,500

Comments: half of the annual retainer ($40,000) is paid in restricted stock units

Misc. Fees: $2,500 for attendance at Strategic Planning conference, and annual planning conference; $1,000/day paid for other visits or company activities

Average director's annual compensation = $35,000
(assumes all meetings are attended and director sits on the Audit and Compensation committees)

STOCK-BASED COMPENSATION

Grant type(s):	**Restricted Units**	**Restricted Units**
Number of shares:	$20,000	1,000
Frequency:	Annual	One-time
Vesting:	Termination	Termination (after 8 years service)
Year-end stock price:	45.00	Same
Plan type:	Separate	Same

COMPENSATION DEFERRAL

Eligible comp: Retainter/meeting
Account types: Cash and/or stock
Interest rate: Corp. bonds
Payment: Date specified by director
Comments: payout may be in lump sum or installments.

CASH RETIREMENT BENEFITS

Cash plan terminated 6/95 and replaced with restricted stock unit plan (above). Current directors received 1,000 restricted units to replace accrued benefits

INSURANCE BENEFITS

Life
Medical/Dental
Travel/Accident

OTHER BENEFITS

Charitable Award Program

Amount: $500,000; payout: in five installments to up to three educational institutions or approved charities; requires 5 years' service

CHANGES

- Added stock alternative to deferral plan

Textron Inc.

Industry: Conglomerate FY97 Revenue (mils): $10,544

BOARD STRUCTURE/FEES

	No. of Mtgs	Retainer Cash	Retainer Stock	Member Fee	Meeting Fee	Chairman Fee
Board	8	$25,000	$ —	$ —	$1,200	$ —
Executive	0	—	—	—	1,200	5,000
Audit	5	—	—	—	1,200	5,000
Nominating & Board Affairs	4	—	—	—	1,200	5,000
Organ. & Compensation	5	—	—	—	1,200	5,000
Pension	2	—	—	—	1,200	5,000

Comments: $16,000 of the total annual retainer ($41,000) is mandatorily deferred in stock units; Textron matches 25% of that and any additional amounts a director elects to defer into stock units.

Average director's annual compensation = $46,600
(assumes all meetings are attended and director sits on the Audit and Compensation committees)

STOCK-BASED COMPENSATION

Grant type(s):	**Restricted**	**Deferred Units**	**Deferred Units**
Number of shares:	1,000	$20,000	Value = 20% of retainer ($8,200)
Frequency:	One-time	Annual	Annual
Vesting:	Retirement	Termination	Same
Year-end stock price:	62.50	Same	Same
COC provision:	Yes	—	—

Comments: the $20,000 deferred stock represents the portion of the annual retainer mandatorily deferred, plus Textron's 25% match; the $8,200 is in addition to the retainer, in lieu of retirement benefits.

COMPENSATION DEFERRAL

Eligible comp: Retainter/meeting
Account types: Cash and/or stock
Payment: After termination

Comments: $16,000 of the retainer is mandatorily deferred in stock; stock unit deferrals are matched 25% by Textron and earn dividend equivalents; the matched shares vest 50% at year-end and 50% 1 year after that.

CASH RETIREMENT BENEFITS

Cash plan apparently terminated and replaced with deferred stock = 20% of annual retainer

INSURANCE BENEFITS

None

OTHER BENEFITS

Charitable Award Program

Amount: $1,000,000; payout: 50% to up to five charities selected by director and 50% to Textron Charitable Trust; life insurance funded

CHANGES

- Added charitable award program

Time Warner Inc.

Industry: Publishing/Broadcasting FY97 Revenue (mils): $13,294

BOARD STRUCTURE/FEES

	No. of Mtgs	Retainer Cash	Retainer Stock	Member Fee	Meeting Fee	Chairman Fee
Board	7	$30,000	$ —	$ —	$ —	$ —
Finance	4	—	—	—	—	—
Audit	3	—	—	—	—	—
Nominating & Governance	5	—	—	—	—	—
Compensation	6	—	—	—	—	—

Average director's annual compensation = $30,000
(assumes all meetings are attended and director sits on the Audit and Compensation committees)

STOCK-BASED COMPENSATION

Grant type(s):	**Restricted**	**Stock Option**
Number of shares:	$30,000	1,500
Frequency:	Annual	Annual
Vesting:	"Qualified" termination	1/3 each year
Year-end stock price:	62.00	Same
Plan type:	Separate	Separate
Plan kitty:	37,000	250,000
COC provision:	Yes	Yes

Comments: Restricted stock is granted as half of retainer; qualified termination includes death/disability/mandatory retirement/failure to be elected; directors received 665 restricted shares in 1997.

COMPENSATION DEFERRAL

Eligible comp: Retainter/meeting
Account types: Cash or stock
Interest rate: Variable
Payment: After termination or age 70

Comments: deferrals must be in 25% increments; payouts may be lump sum or installments; deferred accounts are based on either cash *or* stock, whichever yields the higher value at distribution.

CASH RETIREMENT BENEFITS

Mandatory retirement age: 70
Cash plan terminated with accrued benefits frozen, and replaced with stock options (above)

INSURANCE BENEFITS

None

OTHER BENEFITS

None

CHANGES

None

The TJX Companies, Inc.

Industry: Retailing FY97 Revenue (mils): $7,389

BOARD STRUCTURE/FEES

	No. of Mtgs	Retainer Cash	Retainer Stock	Member Fee	Meeting Fee	Chairman Fee
Board	7	$25,000	$ —	$ —	$1,250	$225,000
Audit	4	—	—	—	1,000	3,500
Executive Compensation	4	—	—	—	1,000	3,500
Executive	2	—	—	—	—	—
Finance	7	—	—	—	1,000	3,500
Dir. & Corp. Governance	9	—	—	—	1,000	3,500

Comments: the COB fee is in addition to regular board fees.

Average director's annual compensation = $41,750
(assumes all meetings are attended and director sits on the Audit and Compensation committees)

STOCK-BASED COMPENSATION

Grant type(s):	**Stock Option**	**Deferred**
Number of shares:	2,000	$10,000
Frequency:	Annual	Annual
Vesting:	1 year	Termination
Year-end stock price:	34.375	Same
Plan type:	Separate	Separate
Plan life:	10 years	—
Plan kitty:	50,000	—
COC provision:	Yes	—

Note: for analysis purposes, the pre-split stock option grant of 1,000 shares is used.

COMPENSATION DEFERRAL

Eligible comp: Retainter/meeting
Account types: Cash
Comments: directors may participate in company's general deferred compensation plan.

CASH RETIREMENT BENEFITS

Cash plan terminated 1/98 and replaced with deferred stock grants; the present value of accrued benefits was converted to deferred stock

INSURANCE BENEFITS

None

OTHER BENEFITS

None

CHANGES

- Increased annual retainer by $5,000, committee meeting attendance fees by $250, and chairman's fees by $1,000
- Increased stock option grant by 1,000 shares per year
- Eliminated cash retirement plan and replaced with deferred stock grants; accrued benefits were converted to deferred stock

Tootsie Roll Industries, Inc.

Industry: Food

FY97 Revenue (mils): $376

BOARD STRUCTURE/FEES

	No. of Mtgs	Retainer Cash	Retainer Stock	Member Fee	Meeting Fee	Chairman Fee
Board	5	$19,000	$—	$—	$1,250	$—
Audit	2	—	—	—	1,250	5,500
Executive	4	—	—	3,000	—	—
Compensation	1	—	—	—	1,250	—

Comments: Employee directors (excluding the COB/CEO and Pres/COO) receive the same fees as outside directors.

Average director's annual compensation = $29,000
(assumes all meetings are attended and director sits on the Audit and Compensation committees)

STOCK-BASED COMPENSATION
None

COMPENSATION DEFERRAL
None

CASH RETIREMENT BENEFITS
None

INSURANCE BENEFITS
None

OTHER BENEFITS
None

CHANGES
- Increased annual retainer by $1,500

Transamerica Corporation

Industry: Nonbank Financial — FY97 Revenue (mils): $6,486

BOARD STRUCTURE/FEES

	No. of Mtgs	Retainer Cash	Retainer Stock	Member Fee	Meeting Fee	Chairman Fee
Board	8	$30,000	$ —	$ —	$1,000	$ —
Corporate Audit	4	—	—	—	1,000	5,000
Nominating	1	—	—	—	1,000	5,000
Mgmt Devel & Compens	6	—	—	—	1,000	5,000
Executive	0	—	—	—	1,000	5,000

Average director's annual compensation = $48,000
(assumes all meetings are attended and director sits on the Audit and Compensation committees)

STOCK-BASED COMPENSATION

Grant type(s):	**Stock Option**	**Phantom Restricted**
Number of shares:	1,500	Value = 50% of retainer ($15,000)
Frequency:	Annual	Annual
Vesting:	6 months	Termination
Year-end stock price:	106.50	same
Plan type:	Combined w/ exec.	—
COC provision:	—	Yes

COMPENSATION DEFERRAL

Eligible comp: Retainter/meeting
Account types: Cash
Interest rate: 10-year T-note + 0-3%
Max. installments: 20 years
Payment: Date specified by director
Comments: T-bill interest for 5-year deferrals; Moody's plus up to 4% for longer deferrals.

CASH RETIREMENT BENEFITS

Mandatory retirement age: 72
Cash plan terminated 3/97; current directors may elect to have accrued benefits converted to phantom restricted stock

INSURANCE BENEFITS

None

OTHER BENEFITS

None

CHANGES

None

The Travelers Group Inc.

Industry: Nonbank Financial — FY97 Revenue (mils): $37,609

BOARD STRUCTURE/FEES

	No. of Mtgs	Retainer Cash	Retainer Stock	Member Fee	Meeting Fee	Chairman Fee
Board	8	$ —	$100,000	$ —	$ —	$ —
Executive	4	—	—	—	—	—
Audit	6	—	—	—	—	—
Nominat, Comp & Corp Gov.	8	—	—	—	—	—
Ethics & Public Affairs	3	—	—	—	—	—
Finance	3	—	—	—	—	—

Comments: Entire retainer is paid in stock except cash to cover tax liabilities.

Average director's annual compensation = $100,000
(assumes all meetings are attended and director sits on the Audit and Compensation committees)

STOCK-BASED COMPENSATION

Grant type(s):	**Stock Award**
Award value:	$100,000
Frequency:	Annual
Year-end stock price:	53.875

Comments: The value of this award is reflected in "Stock Retainer" and "Average Director's Annual Compensation" above.

COMPENSATION DEFERRAL

Eligible comp: Retainer

Comments: director may "defer" retainer by taking deferred shares.

CASH RETIREMENT BENEFITS

None

INSURANCE BENEFITS

None

OTHER BENEFITS

None

CHANGES

None

TRW Inc.

Industry: Conglomerate FY97 Revenue (mils): $10,831

BOARD STRUCTURE/FEES

	No. of Mtgs	Retainer Cash	Retainer Stock	Member Fee	Meeting Fee	Chairman Fee
Board	7	$35,000	$ —	$ —	$ —	$ —
Audit	4	—	—	—	—	5,000
Compens & Stock Option	3	—	—	—	—	5,000
Retirement Funding	2	—	—	—	—	3,000
Public Policy	3	—	—	—	—	3,000
Nominating	1	—	—	—	—	3,000
Executive	0	—	—	—	—	3,000

Comments: 50% of $70,000 total retainer value is mandatorily deferred in stock; one director has a consulting contract for $210,000 per year.

Average director's annual compensation = $35,000
(assumes all meetings are attended and director sits on the Audit and Compensation committees)

STOCK-BASED COMPENSATION

Grant type(s):	**Deferred**	**Stock Option**
Number of shares:	$35,000	1,500
Frequency:	Annual	Annual
Vesting:	After termination	Undisclosed
Year-end stock price:	53.375	Same
Plan type:	(Deferral plan)	Combined with exec.

Comments: The 1997 Long-Term Incentive Plan permits discretionary grants to directors.

COMPENSATION DEFERRAL

Eligible comp: Retainter/meeting
Account types: Cash and/or stock
Interest rate: Company rate
Payment: Date specified by director
Comments: must be deferred at least 2 years; earnings based on an equity fund or co. Savings Plan rate.

CASH RETIREMENT BENEFITS

Mandatory retirement age: 72
Cash plan was frozen effective 6/30/97

INSURANCE BENEFITS

None

OTHER BENEFITS

None

CHANGES

None

Unicom Corporation

Industry: Utilities — FY97 Revenue (mils): $7,083

BOARD STRUCTURE/FEES

	No. of Mtgs	Retainer Cash	Retainer Stock	Member Fee	Meeting Fee	Chairman Fee
Board	9	$ —	$36,200	$ —	$1,000	$—
Executive	1	—	—	—	1,000	2,500
Audit	3	—	—	—	1,000	2,500
Corp Govern & Comp	4	—	—	—	1,000	2,500
Finance	2	—	—	—	1,000	2,500
Nominating	3	—	—	—	1,000	2,500

Comments: Fees cover board service for both Unicom and ComEd. Directors may elect to have all cash fees paid in stock; one director received $120,000 for consulting in 1997.

Misc. Fees: $1,000 paid for special board meetings

Average director's annual compensation = $52,200
(assumes all meetings are attended and director sits on the Audit and Compensation committees)

STOCK-BASED COMPENSATION

Grant type(s):	**Stock Award**
Value of award:	$36,200
Frequency:	Annual
Year-end stock price:	30.75
Plan type:	Separate
Plan life:	Indefinite
Plan kitty:	200,000

Comments: The value of this award is reflected in "Stock Retainer" and "Average Director's Annual Compensation" above.

COMPENSATION DEFERRAL

Eligible comp: Cash fees only
Account types: Cash
Interest rate: Company rate

CASH RETIREMENT BENEFITS

Mandatory retirement age: 72

Cash plan terminated 1/97 with accrued benefits converted to deferred cash or stock ; the annual stock retainer was increased by $6,200 in lieu of future benefits

INSURANCE BENEFITS

None

OTHER BENEFITS

None

CHANGES

None

Union Pacific Corporation

Industry: Transportation — FY97 Revenue (mils): $11,014

BOARD STRUCTURE/FEES

	No. of Mtgs	Retainer Cash	Retainer Stock	Member Fee	Meeting Fee	Chairman Fee
Board	8	$30,000	$ —	$ —	$ —	$ —
Executive	0	—	—	—	—	6,000
Audit	3	—	—	—	—	6,000
Finance	4	—	—	—	—	6,000
Compensation & Benefits	3	—	—	—	—	6,000
Corp. Governance & Nominating	3	—	—	—	—	6,000

Comments: $30,000 of $60,000 annual retainer is mandatorily deferred in stock unit account; one director's firm provided services to UP for $885,600 in 1997.

Average director's annual compensation = $30,000
(assumes all meetings are attended and director sits on the Audit and Compensation committees)

STOCK-BASED COMPENSATION

Grant type(s):	**Restricted**	**Deferred**
Number of shares:/value	1,785	$30,000
Frequency:	One-time	Annual
Vesting:	Death, disability or retirement	After termination
Year-end stock price:	62.625	Same
Plan type:	Separate	—
Plan life:	10 years	—
Plan kitty:	50,000	—
COC provision:	Yes	—

Comments: 50% of annual retainer is mandatorily deferred in stock unit account.

Ownership Guidelines: Three times annual retainer within 5 years

COMPENSATION DEFERRAL

Eligible comp: Retainter/meeting
Account types: Cash or stock
Interest rate: Company rate
Max. installments: 10 years
Payment: After termination or cessation of primary employment
Comments: payout may be lump sum or installments.

CASH RETIREMENT BENEFITS

Mandatory retirement age: 73
Cash plan terminated 1/96 for future directors; current directors continue to be eligible for a $36,000 lifetime benefit or could have chosen to have $6,000 of this converted to deferred unit account; the amount is based on age, retirement date and mortality assumptions

INSURANCE BENEFITS

Excess Liability: $10,000,000
Term Life: $100,000
Medical/Dental
Comments: medical/dental benefits paid only after payment from any other plan.

OTHER BENEFITS

Charitable Award Program

Amount: $1,000,000; payout: $500,000 to company foundation; $500,000 to director's choice of 1 or more org; life insurance funded; directors vest 20% per year in this benefit

CHANGES

- Changed from requiring 10% of retainer to be deferred to 50%

Unisys Corporation

Industry: Office Equipment & Services FY97 Revenue (mils): $6,636

BOARD STRUCTURE/FEES

	No. of Mtgs	Retainer Cash	Retainer Stock	Member Fee	Meeting Fee	Chairman Fee
Board	15	$22,500	$ —	$ —	$1,000	$ —
Audit	4	—	—	—	1,000	—
Compensation & Organiz	6	—	—	—	1,000	—
Nominating	3	—	—	—	1,000	—
Finance	0	—	—	—	1,000	—

Comments: directors may elect to have fees paid in stock units.

Same day fees: $1,000 meeting fee paid for meetings not held on regularly scheduled meeting days

Average director's annual compensation = $37,500
(assumes all meetings are attended and director sits on the Audit and Compensation committees)

STOCK-BASED COMPENSATION

Grant type(s):	**Deferred**
Value of award	$22,500
Frequency:	Annual
Vesting:	5 years
Year-end stock price:	13.875

Comments: Payout is at termination or at least 5 years after grant, in cash or stock as elected by director

COMPENSATION DEFERRAL

Eligible comp: Retainter/meeting
Account types: Cash/stock
Maximum installments: 10 years
Payout: Date specified by director (at least 5 years after grant)
Comments: payout may be cash or stock as elected by director.

CASH RETIREMENT BENEFITS

Mandatory retirement age: 70
None

INSURANCE BENEFITS

None

OTHER BENEFITS

None

CHANGES

- Replaced $750 per meeting attendance fee with a $10,000 annual fee (50% paid in cash and 50% paid in deferred stock)
- Thus, total retainer value increased from $27,000 to $45,000

United Healthcare Corporation

Industry: Health Care FY97 Revenue (mils): $11,794

BOARD STRUCTURE/FEES

	No. of Mtgs	Retainer Cash	Retainer Stock	Member Fee	Meeting Fee	Chairman Fee
Board	4	$20,000	—	$ —	$1,500	$ —
Executive	1	—	—	—	—	—
Audit	4	—	—	—	—	5,000
Compensation & Human Resources	4	—	—	—	—	5,000
Nominating	3	—	—	—	—	—

Average director's annual compensation = $26,000
(assumes all meetings are attended and director sits on the Audit and Compensation committees)

STOCK-BASED COMPENSATION

Grant type(s):	**Stock Option**
Number of shares:	4,000
Frequency:	Annual
Vesting:	6 months
Year-end stock price:	49.6875
Plan type:	Separate
Plan life:	10 years
Plan kitty:	350,000

Comments: Initial grants cover 9,000 shares which vest 1/3 per year.

COMPENSATION DEFERRAL

None

CASH RETIREMENT BENEFITS

None

INSURANCE BENEFITS

Medical/Dental

OTHER BENEFITS

None

CHANGES

None

United Technologies Corporation

Industry: Aerospace FY97 Revenue (mils): $24,713

BOARD STRUCTURE/FEES

	No. of Mtgs	Retainer Cash	Retainer Stock	Member Fee	Meeting Fee	Chairman Fee
Board	7	$24,000	$ —	$ —	$ —	$ —
Executive	0	—	—	—	—	5,000
Audit Review	4	—	—	—	—	5,000
Comp & Exec Develop	8	—	—	—	—	5,000
Finance	5	—	—	—	—	5,000
Nominating	4	—	—	—	—	5,000
Public Issues Review	4	—	—	—	—	5,000

Comments: 60% of $60,000 total annual retainer mandatorily deferred in stock units; directors may elect to receive all fees in deferred units.

Average director's annual compensation = $24,000
(assumes all meetings are attended and director sits on the Audit and Compensation committees)

STOCK-BASED COMPENSATION

Grant type(s):	**Restricted**	**Deferred Units**	**Stock Option**
Number of shares:/value	2,000	$36,000	2,000
Frequency:	One-time	Annual	Annual
Vesting:	20% per year	After termination	3 years
Year-end stock price:	72.8125	Same	Same
Plan type:	Separate	(deferral plan)	Separate
Plan life:	—	—	Indefinite
COC provision:	Yes	Same	Yes

Comments: foreign nationals receive one-time restricted stock unit award instead of restricted shares (vesting as above, paid out in cash).

COMPENSATION DEFERRAL

Eligible comp: Retainter/meeting
Account types: Cash or stock
Interest rate: Company rate
Payment: After termination

Comments: interest rate matches savings plan; payouts are in cash, in lump sum or installments.

CASH RETIREMENT BENEFITS

Cash plan terminated 12/31/95 and accrued benefits converted to deferred stock units.

INSURANCE BENEFITS

None

OTHER BENEFITS

Charitable Award Program

Amount: $1,000,000; payout: to up to four charities; life insurance funded

CHANGES

None

Universal Foods Corporation

Industry: Food

FY97 Revenue (mils): $826

BOARD STRUCTURE/FEES

	No. of Mtgs	Retainer Cash	Retainer Stock	Member Fee	Meeting Fee	Chairman Fee
Board	5	$16,500	$5,500	$—	$1,000	$—
Executive	2	—	—	—	1,000	1,000
Audit	2	—	—	—	1,000	1,000
Compensation & Develop	4	—	—	—	1,000	1,000
Nominating	2	—	—	—	1,000	1,000
Scientific Advisory	2	—	—	—	1,000	1,000
Finance	2	—	—	—	1,000	1,000

Comments: shares are restricted for 6 months; board sets annual stock retainer amount, between $3,000 and $10,000.

Average director's annual compensation = $33,000
(assumes all meetings are attended and director sits on the Audit and Compensation committees)

STOCK-BASED COMPENSATION

Grant type(s):	**Stock Award**
Value of award:	$5,500
Frequency:	Annual
Year-end stock price:	42.25

COMPENSATION DEFERRAL

Eligible comp: Cash retainter/meeting
Account types: Cash
Interest rate: 6.5%
Max. installments: 5 years
Payment: After termination
Comments: payout may be in lump sum or installments.

CASH RETIREMENT BENEFITS

Mandatory service: 3 years
Basic benefits: Retainer
Payment term: Matching Service
Death benefit: No
Comments: directors must be available for consulting; funded by a rabbi trust.

INSURANCE BENEFITS

None

OTHER BENEFITS

None

CHANGES

None

UNOCAL Corporation

Industry: Fuel

FY97 Revenue (mils): $6,064

BOARD STRUCTURE/FEES

	No. of Mtgs	Retainer Cash	Retainer Stock	Member Fee	Meeting Fee	Chairman Fee
Board	8	$25,000	$—	$—	$3,000	$—
Actg., Auditing & Ethics	6	—	—	—	1,000	6,000
Mgmt Develop & Comp	5	—	—	—	1,000	6,000
Executive	1	—	—	—	1,000	—
Health, Environ & Safety	5	—	—	—	1,000	6,000
Retirement Plan	4	—	—	—	1,000	6,000
Board Governance	4	—	—	—	1,000	6,000
Management	50	—	—	—	—	—

Comments: directors may take restricted stock units (with value = 120% of amount deferred) in lieu of cash comp (in addition to annual restricted award); $6,000 fee paid for 2-day board meetings.

Average director's annual compensation = $60,000
(assumes all meetings are attended and director sits on the Audit and Compensation committees)

STOCK-BASED COMPENSATION

Grant type(s):	**Restricted Units**
Number of shares:	Formula
Frequency:	Annual
Vesting:	5 years (or longer if elected)
Year-end stock price:	38.8125
Plan type:	Separate
Plan life:	10 years
Plan kitty:	300,000

Comments: Annual award is valued at 20% of prior year's cash compensation ($12,000 used to calculate Average Director's Total Compensation).

COMPENSATION DEFERRAL

Eligible comp: Retainter/meeting

Comments: directors may take restricted stock units in lieu of cash fees (+ 20% premium); must remain restricted at least 5 years.

CASH RETIREMENT BENEFITS

None

INSURANCE BENEFITS

None

OTHER BENEFITS

None

CHANGES

None

U.S. Trust Corporation

Industry: Banks FY97 Revenue (mils): $494

BOARD STRUCTURE/FEES

	No. of Mtgs	Retainer Cash	Retainer Stock	Member Fee	Meeting Fee	Chairman Fee
Board	10	$15,000	400 shr	$ —	$1,000	$ —
Audit	5	—	—	10,000	—	2,500
Compensation & Benefits	3	—	—	7,000	—	3,000
Executive	3	—	—	—	1,000	—
Corporate Responsibility	3	—	—	—	1,000	—

Same day fees: only one meeting attendance fee paid per day

Average director's annual compensation = $67,050
(assumes all meetings are attended and director sits on the Audit and Compensation committees)

STOCK-BASED COMPENSATION

Grant type(s):	**Deferred Units**	**Stock Award**
Number of shares:	$5,000	400
Frequency:	Annual	Annual
Vesting:	After termination	—
Year-end stock price:	62.625	same
Plan type:	Separate	same

Comments: Stock award is reflected in "Stock Retainer" and "Average Director's Annual Compensation" above.

COMPENSATION DEFERRAL

Eligible comp: Cash retainer/meeting
Account types: Cash and/or stock
Interest: 6 investment options
Payment: After termination
Max. installments: 10 years

Comments: at least 50% of deferred amounts must be in stock; payout is lump sum or installments; stock accounts are paid out in stock.

CASH RETIREMENT BENEFITS

Cash plan terminated 12/31/96 and accrued benefits converted to deferred stock units

INSURANCE BENEFITS

None

OTHER BENEFITS

None

CHANGES

None

Vanguard Cellular Systems, Inc.

Industry: Telecommunications FY97 Revenue (mils): $375

BOARD STRUCTURE/FEES

	No. of Mtgs	Retainer Cash	Retainer Stock	Member Fee	Meeting Fee	Chairman Fee
Board	4	$12,000	$—	$—	$1,000	$—
Audit	2	—	—	—	1,000	—
Compensation	3	—	—	—	1,000	—

Comments: The VCOB and the Co-CEO are on the board of a Compensation Committee member's company.

Misc fees: $500 for telephonic meetings

Same day fees: $500 paid for the second meeting on a day

Average director's annual compensation = $18,500
(assumes all meetings are attended and director sits on the Audit and Compensation committees)

STOCK-BASED COMPENSATION

The executive stock plan provides for discretionary grants to outside directors

COMPENSATION DEFERRAL

None

CASH RETIREMENT BENEFITS

None

INSURANCE BENEFITS

None

OTHER BENEFITS

None

CHANGES

None

Venator Group, Inc. (formerly Woolworth Corp.)

Industry: Retailing FY97 Revenue (mils): $6,624

BOARD STRUCTURE/FEES

	No. of Mtgs	Retainer Cash	Retainer Stock	Member Fee	Meeting Fee	Chairman Fee
Board	7	$20,000	$20,000	$—	$—	$—
Audit	7	—	—	—	—	3,000
Compensation	3	—	—	—	—	3,000
Nomin & Organization	3	—	—	—	—	3,000
Executive	0	—	—	—	—	—
Retirement Investment	4	—	—	—	—	3,000
Acquisitions & Finance	0	—	—	—	—	3,000

Comments: directors may elect to have all fees paid in stock; one director serves on board of German subsidiary for DM 15,000 ($8,200) and received $20,000 for consulting; the company leases space to Bank of NY for $554,000 in 1997.

Average director's annual compensation = $40,000
(assumes all meetings are attended and director sits on the Audit and Compensation committees)

STOCK-BASED COMPENSATION

Grant type(s):	**Stock Award**
Number of shares:	50% of retainer ($20,000)
Frequency:	Annual
Year-end stock price:	20.375
Plan type:	Separate
Plan life:	10 years
Plan kitty:	250,000

Comments: The value of the stock award is reflected in "Stock Retainer" and "Avg. Director's Annual Comp" above.

COMPENSATION DEFERRAL

None

CASH RETIREMENT BENEFITS

Mandatory retirement age: 70

Cash plan was previously terminated; current eligible directors will receive retirement benefits of $24,000/yr for the number of years of service, up to 10

INSURANCE BENEFITS

None

OTHER BENEFITS

Financial Planning

CHANGES

None

VF Corporation

Industry: Consumer Products | FY97 Revenue (mils): $5,222

BOARD STRUCTURE/FEES

	No. of Mtgs	Retainer Cash	Retainer Stock	Member Fee	Meeting Fee	Chairman Fee
Board	8	$28,000	$—	$—	$1,200	$25,000
Audit	3	—	—	—	1,000	300
Executive	0	—	—	—	1,000	0
Finance	0	—	—	—	1,000	0
Organiz & Compensation	2	—	—	—	1,000	200
Nominating	3	—	—	—	1,000	300
Pension Advisory	0	—	—	—	1,000	0

Same Day Mtg Fees: $500 for attendance at committee meeting on same day as board meeting

Comments: chairman fees reflect additional payment of $200 per meeting ($100 for "same day" meetings); the COB receives $25,000/yr in lieu of meeting attendance fees.

Average director's annual compensation = $40,100
(assumes all meetings are attended and director sits on the Audit and Compensation committees)

STOCK-BASED COMPENSATION

Grant type(s):	**Stock Option**
Number of shares:	Formula
Frequency:	Annual
Vesting:	6 months
Year-end stock price:	46.50
Plan type:	Combined w/ exec.
COC provision:	Yes

Comments: Directors are also eligible for discretionary awards of restricted stock.

Number of options ranges from 1,200 to 4,800 depending on FMV on grant date (4,800 shares on 2/10/98);

less than $5: 1,200 shares	$15–20: 3,000 shares	> $30: 4,800 shares
$5–10: 1,800 shares	$20–25: 3,600 shares	
$10–15: 2,400 shares	$25–30: 4,200 shares	

COMPENSATION DEFERRAL

Eligible comp: Retainter/meeting
Account types: Stock
Payment: After termination

CASH RETIREMENT BENEFITS

Mandatory retirement age: 70
None

INSURANCE BENEFITS

None

OTHER BENEFITS

Matching Gift Program up to $10,000 per year

CHANGES

- Eliminated deferrals in cash

Viacom Inc.

Industry: Leisure FY97 Revenue (mils): $13,505

BOARD STRUCTURE/FEES

	No. of Mtgs	Retainer Cash	Retainer Stock	Member Fee	Meeting Fee	Chairman Fee
Board	9	$40,000	$ —	$ —	$1,500	$ —
Audit	3	—	—	—	500	7,500
Compensation	9	—	—	—	500	7,500
Governance & Nominations	(new)	—	—	—	500	7,500
Sr. Executive Compensation	9	—	—	—	—	—

Comments: One Compensation Committee member provides legal and governmental consulting services and was paid $120,000 in 1997; compensation for two directors from Bell Atlantic is paid to that company.

Average director's annual compensation = $59,500
(assumes all meetings are attended and director sits on the Audit and Compensation committees)

STOCK-BASED COMPENSATION

Grant type(s):	**Stock Option**	**Stock Option**
Number of shares:	10,000	1,500
Frequency:	One-time	Annual (max. 10)
Vesting:	1 year	1 year
Year-end stock price:	41.4375	Same
Plan type:	Separate	Separate
Plan life:	10 years	10 years
Plan kitty:	100,000	200,000
COC provision:	Yes	Yes

Comments: Plan providing for annual grants also authorizes initial grants of 5,000 shares.

COMPENSATION DEFERRAL

Eligible comp: Retainter/meeting
Account types: Cash and/or stock
Max. installments: 5 years
Payment: After termination
Comments: payout may be in lump sum or three or five annual installments beginning 7 months after retirement.

CASH RETIREMENT BENEFITS

Mandatory service: 3 years
Basic benefits: Retainer
Payment term: Matching service
Death benefit: Yes

INSURANCE BENEFITS

None

OTHER BENEFITS

None

CHANGES

None

Vulcan Materials Company

Industry: Housing — FY97 Revenue (mils): $1,679

BOARD STRUCTURE/FEES

	No. of Mtgs	Retainer Cash	Retainer Stock	Member Fee	Meeting Fee	Chairman Fee
Board	7	$30,000	—	$—	$1,500	$—
Audit Review	2	—	—	—	1,500	5,000
Compensation	2	—	—	—	1,500	5,000
Governance & Succession	3	—	—	—	1,500	5,000
Finance & Pension Funds	2	—	—	—	1,500	5,000
Executive	1	—	—	—	1,500	5,000
Safety, Health & Env Affairs	2	—	—	—	1,500	5,000

Misc. Fees: Telephone Meetings (committees only): $1,500

Comments: meeting fees also are paid for each unanimous consent to action taken in lieu of meeting.

Average director's annual compensation = $46,500
(assumes all meetings are attended and director sits on the Audit and Compensation committees)

STOCK-BASED COMPENSATION

Grant type(s):	**Deferred Units**	**Restricted**
Number of shares:	Value = 40% of Retainer ($12,000)	65
Frequency:	Annual	Annual
Vesting:	At Termination	Retirement at age 70/death/disability
Year-end stock price:	102.125	Same
Plan type:	Separate	Separate
Plan life:	Indefinite	Undisclosed
Plan kitty:	100,000	Undisclosed
COC provision:	Yes	Undisclosed

Comments: Vesting: for restricted stock may be waived by the CEO if retirement before age 70 occurs; dividend equivalents accrue on restricted shares and are paid out at termination regardless of whether shares vest or not.

COMPENSATION DEFERRAL

Eligible comp: Retainter/meeting
Account types: Cash and/or stock
Payment: Date specified by director
COC provision:: Yes
Comments: payout is made in cash; lump sum payouts if COC occurs.

CASH RETIREMENT BENEFITS

Mandatory retirement age: 70
Cash plan terminated in 1996 with the present value of accrued benefits converted to deferred stock units

INSURANCE BENEFITS

None

OTHER BENEFITS

None

CHANGES

- Added restricted stock grants

Wal-Mart Stores, Inc.

Industry: Retailing

FY97 Revenue (mils): $119,299

BOARD STRUCTURE/FEES

	No. of Mtgs	Retainer Cash	Retainer Stock	Member Fee	Meeting Fee	Chairman Fee
Board	8	$25,000	$25,000	$ —	$ —	$ —
Audit	5	—	—	—	—	3,000
Stock Option	2	—	—	—	—	3,000
Compensation & Nominating	6	—	—	—	—	3,000
Executive	0	—	—	—	—	3,000
Strategic Plan & Finance	4	—	—	—	—	3,000

Misc. Fees: number of board meetings includes four telephonic meetings

Comments: One director is paid $150,000/yr in consulting fees plus benefits; $1,500 per day is paid for special services, up to 30 days per year; stock may be deferred; one director received rent, utility service payments and other items totaling $18.8-mil in 1997.

Average director's annual compensation = $50,000
(assumes all meetings are attended and director sits on the Audit and Compensation committees)

STOCK-BASED COMPENSATION

Grant type(s):	**Stock Award**
Value of award:	50% of retainer ($25,000)
Frequency:	Annual
Year-end stock price:	39.4375
Plan type:	Separate
Plan kitty:	1,000,000

Comments: The 1998 Stock Incentive Plan includes discretionary grants to directors of: stock options, reload options, restricted stock, SARs and other stock-based awards; the value of this award is reflected in "Stock Retainer" and "Average Director's Annual Compensation" above.

COMPENSATION DEFERRAL

Eligible comp:	Retainer/meeting/stock retainer
Account types:	Cash and/or stock
Interest rate:	determined by board
Payment:	After termination
Max. installments:	10 years

Comments: interest is compounded annually; deferred units are paid out in shares; account conversions are permitted.

CASH RETIREMENT BENEFITS

None

INSURANCE BENEFITS

None

OTHER BENEFITS

None

CHANGES

- Directors are now eligible for discretionary awards under the newly approved 1998 Stock Incentive Plan

The Walt Disney Company

Industry: Leisure

FY97 Revenue (mils): $22,473

BOARD STRUCTURE/FEES

	No. of Mtgs	Retainer Cash	Retainer Stock	Member Fee	Meeting Fee	Chairman Fee
Board	6	$35,000	—	$ —	$1,000	$ —
Executive	0	—	—	—	1,000	—
Compensation	8	—	—	—	1,000	—
Audit Review	3	—	—	—	1,000	—
Nominating	0	—	—	—	1,000	—
Exec. Performance Plan	8	—	—	—	1,000	—

Comments: one member of the Compensation Committee is a former COB; one director's architectural firm received $546,905 in 1997; one director consulted for $50,000 in 1997; directors may elect to have fees paid in common stock.

Average director's annual compensation = $52,000
(assumes all meetings are attended and director sits on the Audit and Compensation committees)

STOCK-BASED COMPENSATION

Grant type(s):	**Stock Option**
Number of shares:	2,000
Frequency:	Annual
Vesting:	20% per year
Year-end stock price:	99.00
Plan type:	Separate
Plan life:	10 years
Plan kitty:	250,000

COMPENSATION DEFERRAL

Eligible comp:	Retainter/meeting
Account types:	Stock
Payment:	After termination

CASH RETIREMENT BENEFITS

None

INSURANCE BENEFITS

None

OTHER BENEFITS

None

CHANGES

- Increased cash retainer by $5,000
- Added alternative for directors to receive stock in lieu of cash fees

Warner-Lambert Company

Industry: Health Care FY97 Revenue (mils): $8,180

BOARD STRUCTURE/FEES

	No. of Mtgs	Retainer Cash	Retainer Stock	Member Fee	Meeting Fee	Chairman Fee
Board	6	$40,000	$ —	$ —	$1,000	$ —
Executive	0	—	—	4,000	—	3,000
Audit	3	—	—	—	1,000	3,000
Compensation	4	—	—	—	1,000	3,000
Nominating & Organiz	2	—	—	—	1,000	3,000
Retirement & Savings Plan	2	—	—	—	1,000	3,000
Corp Public Policy	2	—	—	—	1,000	3,000

Comments: Executive Committee members receive $4,000 fee in lieu of attendance fees for first four meetings; $1,000 fee paid for special meetings or other board-related activities.

Average director's annual compensation = $53,000
(assumes all meetings are attended and director sits on the Audit and Compensation committees)

STOCK-BASED COMPENSATION

Grant type(s):	**Restricted**	**Deferred**
Number of shares:	4,000	Value = 50% of Retainer ($20,000)
Frequency:	One-time	Annual (up to 10 years)
Vesting:	1/10th for each full service year	At Termination
Year-end stock price:	124.1875	Same
Plan type:	Separate	Combined w/ exec.
COC provision:	Yes	Yes

Comments: Restrictions also lapse upon death/disability/retirement/nonelection; directors would receive the full value of restricted shares in cash after a COC. Deferred stock grants are made for a maximum of 10 years (to replace cash pension benefits).

COMPENSATION DEFERRAL

Eligible comp: Retainter/meeting/consulting
Account types: Cash and/or stock
Max. installments: 10 years
Payment: After termination
COC provision:: Yes
Comments: interest accrues annually.

CASH RETIREMENT BENEFITS

Cash plan terminated 1/1/96; accrued benefits for at least 5 years' service are converted to deferred stock accounts. In the future, 50% of the retainer value is credited each year to deferred stock accounts.

INSURANCE BENEFITS

Accidental Death/Disability
Group Life
Medical/Dental

OTHER BENEFITS

None

CHANGES

None

Waste Management, Inc.

Industry: Service Industries FY97 Revenue (mils): $9,273

BOARD STRUCTURE/FEES

	No. of Mtgs	Retainer Cash	Retainer Stock	Member Fee	Meeting Fee	Chairman Fee
Board	17	$50,000	$ —	$ —	$ —	$ —
Compensation & Stock Option	11	—	—	—	1,000	—
Audit	6	—	—	—	1,000	—
Nominating & Governance	4	—	—	—	1,000	—

Same day fees: The committee fee covers all meetings held on one day

Average director's annual compensation = $67,000
(assumes all meetings are attended and director sits on the Audit and Compensation committees)

STOCK-BASED COMPENSATION

Grant type(s):	**Stock Option**
Number of shares:	3,000
Frequency:	Annual (max. 5 years)
Vesting:	1 year
Year-end stock price:	27.50
Plan type:	Separate
Plan life:	10 years
Plan kitty:	150,000
COC provision:	Yes

Comments: Payment in shares or promissory notes permitted.

Ownership Guidelines: Three times the annual retainer within 5 years

COMPENSATION DEFERRAL

Eligible comp: Retainter/meeting
Account types: Cash
Interest rate: 10-year T-note
Payment: After termination
COC provision:: Yes
Comments: Payout may be lump sum or installments.

CASH RETIREMENT BENEFITS

None

INSURANCE BENEFITS

Medical/Dental

OTHER BENEFITS

Charitable Award Program
Amount: $1,000,000
Comments: donation = $100,000 for each service year up to 10; life insurance funded.

CHANGES

- Added stock ownership guidelines
- Changed deferral plan from stock-based to cash-based

Wells Fargo & Company

Industry: Banks

FY97 Revenue (mils): $9,608

BOARD STRUCTURE/FEES

	No. of Mtgs	Retainer Cash	Retainer Stock	Member Fee	Meeting Fee	Chairman Fee
Board	10	$32,000	$ —	$ —	$1,500	$ —
Executive	4	—	—	—	1,150	—
Examination & Audits	8	—	—	5,000	1,150	5,000
Mgmt Dev & Compensation	6	—	—	2,000	1,150	3,000
Nominating	2	—	—	—	1,150	—

Same Day Mtg Fees: fees cover combined or same-day meetings of company and bank

Comments: 3 directors have consulting agreements for $100,000, $75,000/yr and $2,500/month. Discount options may be taken in lieu of retainer (see STOCK)

Average director's annual compensation = $70,100
(assumes all meetings are attended and director sits on the Audit and Compensation committees)

STOCK-BASED COMPENSATION

Grant type(s):	**Stock Option**	**Discounted Options**
Number of shares:	500	As elected by director
Frequency:	Annual	Annual
Vesting:	1 year	Same
Year-end stock price:	339.4375	Same
Plan type:	Separate	Same
Plan kitty:	200,000	Same

Comments: No more than 20,000 shares may be subject to options in any calendar year; discount options may be taken in lieu of retainer with an exercise price = 50% of FMV.

COMPENSATION DEFERRAL

Eligible comp: Retainter/meeting
Account types: Cash and/or stock
Interest rate: T-bills
Comments: payable in lump sum or over undisclosed period of years.

CASH RETIREMENT BENEFITS

Mandatory retirement age: 70
Cash plan terminated for future elected directors. Current directors continue in plan.

INSURANCE BENEFITS

None

OTHER BENEFITS

Financial Planning: $7,500/year
The retired COB receives an office, secretarial services, and a driver for his personal use

CHANGES

None

Wendy's International, Inc.

Industry: Leisure

FY97 Revenue (mils): $2,037

BOARD STRUCTURE/FEES

	No. of Mtgs	Retainer Cash	Retainer Stock	Member Fee	Meeting Fee	Chairman Fee
Board	6	$28,000	$—	$—	$1,500	$—
Audit	4	—	—	—	1,000	—
Board Membership (Nominating)	2	—	—	—	—	—
Compensation	4	—	—	—	1,000	—

Misc. Fees: Telephone Meetings: $1,000

Average director's annual compensation = $45,000
(assumes all meetings are attended and director sits on the Audit and Compensation committees)

STOCK-BASED COMPENSATION

Grant type(s):	**Stock Option**
Number of shares:	2,500
Frequency:	Annual
Vesting:	25% per year
Year-end stock price:	24.0625
Plan type:	Combined w/ exec.
COC provision:	Yes

Comments: Company may cash out exercisable shares without director's consent.

COMPENSATION DEFERRAL
None

CASH RETIREMENT BENEFITS
None

INSURANCE BENEFITS
None

OTHER BENEFITS
None

CHANGES
None

Weyerhaeuser Company

Industry: Paper/Forest FY97 Revenue (mils): $11,210

BOARD STRUCTURE/FEES

	No. of Mtgs	Retainer Cash	Retainer Stock	Member Fee	Meeting Fee	Chairman Fee
Board	7	$25,000	—	$—	$1,500	$100,000
Executive	2	—	—	—	1,000	5,000
Actg. & Reporting Standards	3	—	—	—	1,000	5,000
Compensation	4	—	—	—	1,000	5,000
Nominating & Mgmt Organization	6	—	—	—	1,000	5,000

Comments: $10,000 of the $35,000 annual retainer is mandatorily deferred in a stock account (see DEFERRAL and STOCK); the COB fee is in addition to other fees; a subsidiary purchased an outside director's interest in a partnership for $1,175,000 in 1997.

Misc. Fees: Subsidiary fees paid; one director received Canadian $16,750

Average director's annual compensation = $42,500
(assumes all meetings are attended and director sits on the Audit and Compensation committees)

STOCK-BASED COMPENSATION

Grant type(s):	**Deferred**
Value of award	$10,000
Frequency:	Annual
Vesting:	After termination
Year-end stock price:	49.0625
Plan type:	(Deferral plan)

Comments: $10,000 of the annual retainer is mandatorily deferred in stock.

COMPENSATION DEFERRAL

Eligible comp: Retainter/meeting
Account types: Cash and/or stock
Payment: After termination
Comments: $10,000 of retainer is mandatorily deferred in stock.

CASH RETIREMENT BENEFITS

None

INSURANCE BENEFITS

None

OTHER BENEFITS

None

CHANGES

None

Xerox Corporation

Industry: Office Equipment & Services

FY97 Revenue (mils): $18,166

BOARD STRUCTURE/FEES

	No. of Mtgs	Retainer Cash	Retainer Stock	Member Fee	Meeting Fee	Chairman Fee
Board	10	$40,000	$—	$—	$—	$—
Executive	0	—	—	—	—	—
Audit	3	—	—	—	—	—
Exec. Comp. & Benefits	4	—	—	—	—	—
Nominating	2	—	—	—	—	—
Finance	4	—	—	—	—	—

Comments: directors may elect to receive stock in lieu of cash fees; stock may be restricted at the director's election; the COB/CEO serves on the Compensation Committee of a Compensation Committee member's company.

Average director's annual compensation = $40,000
(assumes all meetings are attended and director sits on the Audit and Compensation committees)

STOCK-BASED COMPENSATION

Grant type(s):	**Restricted**	**Stock Option**
Value of award	$25,000	2,500
Frequency:	Annual	Annual
Vesting:	After termination	1/3 per year
Year-end stock price:	73.875	Same
Plan type:	Separate	Separate
Plan life:	—	Indefinite
Plan kitty:	—	1,000,000
COC provision:	Yes	Yes

COMPENSATION DEFERRAL

Eligible comp: Retainer
Account types: Cash
Comments: no additional information disclosed.

CASH RETIREMENT BENEFITS

Cash plan terminated 5/96 with vested accrued benefits converted to deferred accounts.

INSURANCE BENEFITS

None

OTHER BENEFITS

None

CHANGES

None

Appendix I. List of Companies by Revenue Ranges

Below is a quick reference to the companies included in this study, listed within the revenue ranges used throughout the analyses.

Greater than $10 billion

Aetna Inc.
Albertson's Inc.
Allied-Signal Inc.
American Express Co.
American International Group, Inc.
AMR Corp.
Anheuser-Busch Companies, Inc.
Ashland Inc.
AT&T Corp.
BankAmerica Corp.
Bell Atlantic Corp.
The Boeing Co.
Bristol-Myers Squibb Co.
Caterpillar, Inc.
Chase Manhattan Corp.
Chrysler Corp.
Cigna Corp.
Citicorp
The Coca-Cola Co.
Dayton Hudson Corp.
Delta Air Lines
The Dow Chemical Co.
E. I. DuPont de Nemours & Co.
Electronic Data Systems Corp.
Emerson Electric Co.
ENRON Corp.
Exxon Corp.
FDX Corp.
Fluor Corp.
Ford Motor Co.
General Electric Co.
General Motors Corp.
The Goodyear Tire & Rubber Co.
GTE Corp.
Hewlett-Packard Co.
International Business Machines
J. C. Penney Company, Inc.
Johnson & Johnson
Kimberly-Clark Corp.
Marriott International Corp.
The May Department Stores Co.
McDonald's Corp.
Merck & Company, Inc.
Merrill Lynch & Company, Inc.
Minnesota Mining & Mfg Co.
Mobil Corp.
Motorola, Inc.
PepsiCo Inc.
Pfizer Inc.
PG&E Corp.
Philip Morris Companies Inc.
The Procter & Gamble Co.
Sara Lee Corp.
SBC Communications
Sears, Roebuck & Co.
Southern Co.
Sprint Corp.
Texaco Inc.
Texas Instruments
Textron Inc.
Time Warner Inc.
Travelers Group
TRW
Union Pacific Corp.
United Healthcare Corp.
United Technologies Corp.
Viacom Inc.
Wal-Mart Stores, Inc.
The Walt Disney Co.
Weyerhaeuser Co.
Xerox Corp.

$5 < $10 billion

AFLAC Inc.
American Electric Power Company, Inc.
American General Corp.
Aon Corp.
Apple Computer Corp.
Bank of New York
Baxter International Inc.
Bestfoods Inc.
Boise Cascade Corp.
Browning-Ferris Industries
Campbell Soup Co.
CBS Corp.
CISCO Systems, Inc.
Colgate-Palmolive Co.

Computer Sciences Corp.
Consolidated Natural Gas Co.
Cooper Industries, Inc.
Cummins Engine Co.
Eaton Corp.
Eli Lilly & Co.
Fleet Financial Group
Fortune Brands, Inc.
FPL Group, Inc.
Gap, Inc.
General Mills, Inc.
Genuine Parts Co.
Honeywell Inc.
Household International
IKON Office Solutions, Inc.
Illinois Tool Works Inc.
Ingersoll-Rand
Kellogg Co.
Marsh & McClennan Companies
Mcad Corp.
Monsanto Co.
Nike, Inc.
Norfolk Southern Corp.
Northrop Grumman
Paine Webber Group, Inc
Pharmacia & Upjohn, Inc
PPG Industries, Inc.
Public Service Enterprise Group Inc.
Quaker Oats
Reynolds Metals Co.
Ryder System, Inc.
Schering-Plough Corp.
St. Paul Companies
Sun Co.
Tenet Healthcare Corp.
TJX Companies
Transamerica
Unicom Corp.
Unisys Corp.
Unocal Corp.
Venator Group, Inc.
VF Corp.
Warner-Lambert Co.
Waste Management Inc.
Wells Fargo & Co.

$3 < $5 billion

Air Products and Chemicals, Inc.
AirTouch Communications
American Financial Corp.
Baltimore Gas & Electric Co.
Beverly Enterprises, Inc.
The Black & Decker Corp.
Brunswick Corp.
Corning Inc.
Cyprus Amax Minerals Co.
General Dynamics Corp.
Hannaford Bros.
Harcourt General, Inc.
Hormel Foods
Interpublic Group of Companies
Kelly Services, Inc.
Knight-Ridder Inc.
McDermott International, Inc.
McGraw-Hill, Inc.
Micro Age, Inc.
Morton International
Nordstrom, Inc.
Omnicom Group
Owens-Corning Fiberglas
Phelps Dodge Corp.
Pittston Co.
Reebok International Ltd.
Sherwin-Williams Co.
Silicon Graphics, Inc.
Temple-Inland, Inc.

$1–$3 billion

Allergan, Inc.
Analog Devices, Inc.
Apache Corp.
Ball Corp.
Beckman Coulter, Inc.
Becton Dickinson & Co.
Bowater Inc.
Burlington Resources Inc.
Ceridian Corp.
Charles Schwab Corp.
Cracker Barrel Old Country Store
Crestar Financial Corp.
Dexter Corp.
Dow Jones & Co.
Dun & Bradstreet
Federal Mogul
First Tennessee National Corp.
Freeport-McMoRan Copper & Gold, Inc.
Fruit of the Loom, Inc.
Louisiana-Pacific Corp.

Manor Care, Inc.
Montana Power Co.
The Neiman Marcus Group, Inc.
Old Kent Financial Corp.
Oryx Energy Co.
Pacific Enterprises
Pioneer Hi-Bred International, Inc.
Premark International
Qualcomm, Inc.
Rubbermaid Inc.
Russell Corp.
Shoney's Inc.
Snap-On Inc.
Sonoco Products Co.
Southern New England Telecom
Springs Industries, Inc.
The Stanley Works
Stone & Webster, Inc.
SunAmerica Inc.
Talbots, Inc.
Vulcan Materials Co.
Wendy's International, Inc.

Less than $1 billion

Anadarko Petroleum
BMC Software, Inc.
Bob Evans Farms, Inc.
Cintas Corp.
Houghton Mifflin
Huffy Corp.
Idacorp, Inc.
Lee Enterprises, Inc.
Media General, Inc.
Mentor Graphics Corp.
MGM Grand, Inc.
Millipore Corp.
Oshkosh B'Gosh Inc.
Policy Management Systems
Questar Corp.
The Rouse Co.
SPX Corp.
St. Joe Co.
St. Jude Medical
Standard Register Co.
Tootsie Roll
U.S. Trust Corp.
Universal Foods Corp.
Vanguard Cellular Systems, Inc.

Appendix II. List of Companies by Industry Groupings

Below is a quick reference to the companies included in this study, listed within the industry groupings used throughout the analyses.

Financial

Aetna Inc.
AFLAC Inc.
American Express Co.
American General Corp.
American International Group, Inc.
Aon Corp.
Bank of New York Company, Inc.
BankAmerica Corp.
Charles Schwab Corp.
Chase Manhattan Corp.
Cigna Corp.
Citicorp
Crestar Financial Corp.
First Tennessee National Corp.
Fleet Financial Group
Marsh & McLennan Companies
Merrill Lynch & Company, Inc.
Old Kent Financial Corp.
Paine Webber Group, Inc.
The St. Paul Companies, Inc.
SunAmerica Inc.
Transamerica Corp.
The Travelers Group
U.S. Trust Corp.
Wells Fargo & Co

Health Care

Allergan, Inc.
Baxter International Inc.
Becton Dickinson & Co.
Beverly Enterprises, Inc.
Bristol-Myers Squibb Co.
Eli Lilly & Co.
Johnson & Johnson
Manor Care, Inc.
Merck & Company, Inc.
Pfizer Inc.
Pharmacia & Upjohn, Inc.
Schering-Plough Corp.
St. Jude Medical
Tenet Healthcare Corp.
United Healthcare Corp.
Warner-Lambert Co.

Hi-Tech

AirTouch Communications
Analog Devices, Inc.
Apple Computer, Inc.
AT&T Corp.
Beckman Coulter, Inc.
Bell Atlantic Corp.
BMC Software, Inc.
The Boeing Co.
CBS Corp.
Ceridian Corp.
CISCO Systems, Inc.
Computer Sciences Corp.
Cooper Industries, Inc.
Electronic Data Systems Corp.
Emerson Electric Co.
General Dynamics Corp.
GTE Corp.
Hewlett-Packard Co.
Honeywell Inc.
International Business Machines
Mentor Graphics Corp.
Millipore Corp.
Motorola, Inc.
Northrop Grumman
Policy Management Systems
Qualcomm, Inc.
SBC Communications
Silicon Graphics, Inc.
Southern New England Telecom.
Sprint Corp.
Standard Register Co.
Texas Instruments
Unisys Corp.
United Technologies Corp.
Vanguard Cellular Systems, Inc.
Xerox Corp.

Manufacturing/Industrials

Anheuser-Busch Companies, Inc.
Ball Corp.
The Black & Decker Corp.
Boise Cascade Corp.
Bowater Inc.
Caterpillar, Inc.
Chrysler Corp.
The Coca-Cola Co.
Colgate-Palmolive Co.
Corning Inc.
Cummins Engine Company, Inc.
Eaton Corp.
Federal Mogul
Ford Motor Co.
Fortune Brands, Inc.
Fruit of the Loom, Inc.
General Motors Corp.
The Goodyear Tire & Rubber Co.
Illinois Tool Works Inc.
Ingersoll-Rand Co.
Kimberly-Clark Corp.
Louisiana-Pacific Corp.
The Mead Corp.
Minnesota Mining & Mfg. Co.
Nike, Inc.
Owens-Corning Fiberglas Corp.
PepsiCo Inc.
Philip Morris Companies Inc.
PPG Industries, Inc.
Premark International, Inc.
The Procter & Gamble Co.
Reebok International Ltd.
The Rouse Co.
Rubbermaid Inc.
Russell Corp.
The Sherwin-Williams Co.
Snap-On Inc.
Sonoco Products Co.
Springs Industries, Inc.
SPX Corp.
St. Joe Co.
The Stanley Works
Temple-Inland, Inc.
VF Corp.
Vulcan Materials Co.
Weyerhaeuser Co.

Other Industrials

Air Products and Chemicals, Inc.
Anadarko Petroleum Corp.
Apache Corp.
Ashland Oil, Inc.
Burlington Resources Inc.
Cyprus Amax Minerals Co.
The Dexter Corp.
The Dow Chemical Co.
E. I. DuPont de Nemours & Co.
Exxon Corp.
Freeport-McMoRan Copper & Gold Inc.
Mobil Corp.
Monsanto Co.
Morton International
Oryx Energy Co.
Phelps Dodge Corp.
The Pittston Co.
Reynolds Metals Co.
Sun Company, Inc.
Texaco Inc.
Unocal Corp.

Service

AMR Corp.
Bob Evans Farms, Inc.
Browning-Ferris Industries, Inc.
Brunswick Corp.
Cintas Corp.
Cracker Barrel Old Country Store, Inc.
Delta Air Lines
Dow Jones & Co.
Dun & Bradstreet Corp.
FDX Corp.
Fluor Corp.
Genuine Parts Co.
Harcourt General, Inc.
Houghton Mifflin
Huffy Corp.
Interpublic Group of Companies Inc.
Kelly Services, Inc.
Knight-Ridder, Inc.
Lee Enterprises, Inc.
Marriott International, Inc.
McDermott International, Inc.
McDonald's Corp.

McGraw-Hill, Inc.
Media General, Inc.
MGM Grand, Inc.
Micro Age, Inc.
Norfolk Southern Corp.
Omnicom Group
Ryder System, Inc.
Shoney's Inc.
Stone & Webster, Inc.
Time Warner Inc.
Union Pacific Corp.
Viacom Inc.
The Walt Disney Co.
Waste Management, Inc.
Wendy's International, Inc.

Utilities

American Electric Power Co.
Baltimore Gas & Electric Co.
Consolidated Natural Gas Co.
Enron Corp.
FPL Group, Inc.
Idacorp, Inc.
Montana Power Co.
Pacific Enterprises
PG&E Co.
Public Service Enterprise Group Inc.
Questar Corp.
Southern Co.
Unicom Corp.

Other

Albertson's Inc.
Allied-Signal Inc.
American Financial Corp.
Bestfoods Inc.
Campbell Soup Co.
Dayton Hudson Corp.
The Gap, Inc.
General Electric Co.
General Mills, Inc.
Hannaford Bros. Co.
Hormel Foods
Household International
IKON Office Solutions, Inc.
C. Penney Company, Inc.
Kellogg Co.
The May Department Stores Co.
The Neiman Marcus Group, Inc.
Nordstrom, Inc.
Oshkosh B'Gosh, Inc.
Pioneer Hi-Bred International, Inc.
Quaker Oats
Sara Lee Corp.
Sears, Roebuck & Co.
Talbots, Inc.
Textron Inc.
The TJX Companies, Inc.
Tootsie Roll
TRW Inc.
Universal Foods Corp.
Venator Group, Inc.
Wal-Mart Stores, Inc.

Appendix III. Compensation Committee Members by Company

Aetna
Betsy Z. Cohen
Gerald Greenwald
Michael H. Jordan
Jack D. Kuehler
Frank R. O'Keefe, Jr.*

AFLAC
M. Delmar Edwards
Joe F. Harris*
Glenn Vaughn, Jr.
Air Products & Chemicals
Tom H. Barrett
Robert Cizik
Terry R. Lautenbach*

AirTouch Communications
Carol A. Bartz
Donald G. Fisher*
Charles R. Schwab
George P. Shultz

Albertson's
A. Gary Ames
John B. Fery*
Clark A. Johnson
Will M. Storey

Allergan
Tamara J. Erickson
Handel E. Evans
William R. Grant*
Leslie G. McCraw

Allied-Signal
Hans W. Becherer
Robert P. Luciano*
Ivan G. Seidenberg
Andrew C. Sigler
John R. Stafford

American Electric Power
John P. DesBarres
Lester A. Hudson, Jr.
Donald G. Smith
Morris Tanenbaum*

American Express
Anne L. Armstrong
Edwin L. Artzt
Beverly S. Greenough
F. Ross Johnson
Frank P. Popoff*

American Financial Group
Theodore H. Emmerich
Thomas H. Hunt
William R. Martin*

American General
Larry D. Horner*
Richard J. Johnson
Robert E. Smittcamp
Anne M. Tatlock

American Internat'l Group
Marshall A. Cohen
Barber B. Conable, Jr.
Frank J. Hoenemeyer

AMR
Edward A. Brennan*
Christopher F. Edley
Charles H. Pistor, Jr.
Joe M. Rodgers
Judith Rodin
Maurice Segall

Anadarko Petroleum
Ronald Brown*
James L. Bryan
John R. Gordon
Analog Devices
Samuel H. Fuller*
Gordon C. McKeague
Lester C. Thurow

Anheuser-Busch Companies
Bernard A. Edison*
Vernon R. Loucks, Jr.
Vilma S. Martinez
William P. Payne

---

* Denotes committee chairperson.

Aon
Edgar D. Jannotta
Andrew J. McKenna
Newton N. Minow
Donald S. Perkins*
George A. Schaefer
Fred L. Turner

Apache
Frederick M. Bohen*
A. D. Frazier, Jr.
John A. Kocur
George D. Lawrence, Jr.
Joseph A. Rice

Apple Computer
Gareth C.C. Chang
Edgar S. Woolard, Jr.*

Ashland
Frank C. Carlucci*
James B. Farley
Mannie L. Jackson
Patrick F. Noonan
W. L. Rouse, Jr.

AT&T
Kenneth T. Derr
George M.C. Fisher
Donald F. McHenry
Michael I. Sovern
Thomas H. Wyman*

Ball
Howard M. Dean*
John T. Hackett
John F. Lehman
William P. Stiritz

Baltimore Gas & Electric
J. Owen Cole
Dan A. Colussy
Jerome W. Geckle*
Michael D. Sullivan

Bank of New York
William R. Chaney
Richard J. Kogan
John C. Malone
Donald L. Miller
H. Barclay Morley*
Harold E. Sells

BankAmerica
Joseph F. Alibrandi
Timm F. Crull*
Kathleen Feldstein
Frank Hope, Jr.
A. Michael Spence

Baxter International
Mary J. Evans
Frank R. Frame
Martha R. Ingram
Georges C. St. Laurent, Jr.*

Beckman Coulter
Hugh K. Coble
Dennis C. Fill*
William N. Kelley
Betty Woods

Becton Dickinson & Co.
Henry P. Becton, Jr.*
Albert J. Costello
Richard W. Hanselman
Frank A. Olson
James E. Perrella
Raymond S. Troubh

Bell Atlantic
Richard L. Carrion
James H. Gilliam, Jr.
Elizabeth T. Kennan
Thomas H. O'Brien*

Beverly Enterprises
Beryl F. Anthony, Jr.*
James R. Greene
Risa J. Lavizzo-Mourey
Louis W. Menk

Black & Decker
Anthony Luiso
Mark H. Willes*
M. Cabell Woodward, Jr.

BMC Software
John W. Barter*
B. Garland Cupp
Meldon K. Gafner
Bob Evans Farms
Daniel A. Fronk
Cheryl L. Krueger
G. Robert Lucas II*

Boeing
John H. Biggs
William J. Perry
Donald E. Petersen*
Charles M. Pigott
George H. Weyerhaeuser

Boise Cascade
Anne L. Armstrong
Philip J. Carroll
Paul J. Phoenix
A. William Reynolds
Ward W. Woods, Jr.*

Bowater
Francis J. Aguilar
H. David Aycock*
Donald R. Melville

Bristol-Myers Squibb
Robert E. Allen
John D. Macomber
Andrew C. Sigler*
Louis W. Sullivan

Browning-Ferris Industries
William T. Butler
Gerald Grinstein*
Marina v.N. Whitman

Brunswick
Nolan D. Archibald
Manuel A. Fernandez
George D. Kennedy
Roger W. Schipke*

Burlington Resources
S. Parker Gilbert
John T. LaMacchia
John F. Schwarz
Walter Scott, Jr.*
William E. Wall

Campbell Soup
Edmund M. Carpenter
Thomas W. Field, Jr.
Harvey Golub
Philip E. Lippincott*
Mary Alice Malone
George Strawbridge, Jr.
Charlotte C. Weber

Caterpillar
Lilyan H. Affinito
John T. Dillon
David R. Goode
James P. Gorter*
Peter A. Magowan
Clayton K. Yeutter

CBS
George H. Conrades*
David K. Li
David T. McLaughlin
Richard R. Pivirotto
Raymond W. Smith
Robert D. Walter

Ceridian
Ronald T. LeMay
Charles Marshall
Carole J. Uhrich
Paul S. Walsh*
Charles Schwab
Nancy H. Bechtle
C. Preston Butcher
Stephen T. McLin
George P. Shultz
Roger O. Walther*

Chase Manhattan
H. Laurance Fuller
Melvin R. Goodes
William H. Gray III
John R. Stafford*

Chrysler
Robert E. Allen
Robert J. Lanigan*
Peter A. Magowan
Lynton R. Wilson

Cigna
Robert P. Bauman
Alfred C. DeCrane, Jr.*
Paul F. Oreffice
Charles R. Shoemate
Louis W. Sullivan, M.D.

Cintas
Gerald V. Dirvin
Roger L. Howe
John S. Lillard*

CISCO Systems
James F. Gibbons
Robert L. Puette*

Citicorp
D. Wayne Calloway
Kenneth T. Derr
Frank A. Shrontz*
Franklin A. Thomas
Edgar S. Woolard, Jr.

Coca-Cola
Herbert A. Allen*
Susan B. King
Paul F. Oreffice
Peter V. Ueberroth

Colgate-Palmolive
Jill K. Conway*
Ronald E. Ferguson
David W. Johnson
John P. Kendall
Delano E. Lewis

Computer Sciences
Howard P. Allen*
Irving W. Bailey II
James R. Mellor

Consolidated Natural Gas
J. W. Connolly
Paul E. Lego
Margaret A. McKenna
Steven A. Minter*

Cooper Industries
Warren L. Batts
Clifford J. Grum
Harold S. Hook
Constantine S. Nicandros*
Frank A. Olson
Ralph H. Robins

Corning
James W. Kinnear*
James J. O'Connor
Catherine A. Rein
William D. Smithburg

CPC International
Alfred C. DeCrane, Jr.
Ellen R. Gordon
George V. Grune
Eileen W. Kraus
William S. Norman*

Cracker Barrel Old Country
Robert V. Dale*
Edgar W. Evins
William D. Heydel
Robert C. Hilton

Crestar Financial Corp
Charles R. Longsworth*
Frank E. McCarthy
Paul D. Miller
Gilmer Minor, III

Cummins Engine Co
Harold Brown
Walter Y. Elisha
Hanna H. Gray*
William D. Ruckelshaus
Franklin A. Thomas

Cyprus Amax Minerals
George S. Ansell
Thomas V. Falkie
Ann M. Gray
Theodore M. Solso
James A. Todd, Jr.
Billie B. Turner*

Dayton Hudson
Roger A. Enrico*
Stephen W. Sanger
Solomon D. Trujillo

Delta Air Lines
James L. Broadhead
Raymond E. Cartledge
Mary J. Evans
Gerald Grinstein*

Dexter
Henrietta H. Fore
Bernard M. Fox
Robert M. Furek*
Martha C. Goss
Edgar G. Hotard

Dow Chemical
Willie D. Davis
Barbara H. Franklin
Allan D. Gilmour
Harold T. Shapiro*
Paul G. Stern

Dow Jones & Co.
Bettina Bancroft
Irvine O. Hockaday, Jr.*
Jane C. MacElree
James Q. Riordan
William C. Steere, Jr.

Dun & Bradstreet
Ronald L. Kuehn, Jr.*
Robert J. Lanigan
Vernon R. Loucks, Jr.
Henry A. McKinnell
James R. Peterson
Michael R. Quinlan

E.I. DuPont de Nemours
Charles M. Harper*
Lois D. Juliber
H. Rodney Sharp III
Charles M. Vest

Eaton
Phyllis B. Davis
Ned C. Lautenbach
John R. Miller*
Victor A. Pelson
Gary L. Tooker

Electronic Data Systems
William H. Gray III
Ray J. Groves
C. Robert Kidder*

Eli Lily & Co.
Steven C. Beering*
Karen N. Horn
Kenneth L. Lay
Alva O. Way

Emerson Electric
D. C. Farrell
J. A. Frates
Vernon R. Loucks, Jr.*
E. F. Williams

Enron
Norman P. Blake, Jr.
John H. Duncan
Robert K. Jaedicke
Charles A. LeMaistre*

Exxon
Michael J. Boskin
D. Wayne Calloway
Jess T. Hay
William R. Howell*
Philip E. Lippincott

FDX
Robert H. Allen
Ralph D. DeNunzio
J. R. Hyde III
Charles T. Manatt
Jackson W. Smart*
Paul S. Walsh
Federal Mogul
John J. Fannon*
Antonio Madero
John C. Pope

First Tennessee National
Carlos H. Cantu
R. Brad Martin*
Michael D. Rose
William B. Sansom

Fleet Financial Group
Bradford R. Boss
John T. Collins
James F. Hardymon*
Thomas D. O'Conner
Paul R. Tregurtha

Fluor Corp
Peter J. Fluor
David P. Gardner
Thomas L. Gossage
Bobby R. Inman*
Dean O'Hare

Ford Motor
Michael D. Dingman*
Carl E. Reichardt

Fortune Brands
Eugene R. Anderson
Patricia O. Ewers
John W. Johnstone, Jr.
Sidney Kirschner
Gordon R. Lohman*
Charles H. Pistor, Jr.

FPL Group
H. Jesse Arnelle
Robert M. Beall II
Hyatt Brown*
Armando M. Codina
B. F. Dolan
Drew Lewis
Paul R. Tregurtha

Freeport-McMoRan
Robert W. Bruce III*
William B. Harrison, Jr.
Gabrielle K. McDonald
George Putnam
J. Taylor Wharton

Fruit of the Loom
Dennis S. Bookshester*
A. Lorne Weil
Brian G. Wolfson

Gap
Adrian D. Bellamy
John G. Bowes
Lucie J. Fjeldstad
John M. Lillie*

General Dynamics
James S. Crown
Charles H. Goodman
Frank C. Sullivan
Carlisle A. Trost*

General Electric
Silas S. Cathcart*
Claudio X. Gonzalez
Gertrude G. Michelson
Frank H. Rhodes
Andrew C. Sigler

General Mills
Richard M. Bressler*
Livio D. DeSimone
Kenneth A. Macke
Michael D. Rose

General Motors
John H. Bryan*
George M.C. Fisher
J. Willard Marriott, Jr.
John G. Smale
Dennis Weatherstone
Thomas H. Wyman

Genuine Parts
Bradley Currey, Jr.
J. Hicks Lanier
William A. Parker, Jr.*
James B. Williams

Goodyear Tire & Rubber
John G. Breen*
William E. Butler
Thomas H. Cruikshank
William J. Hudson, Jr.
Gertrude G. Michelson
Steven A. Minter
Agnar Pytte
George H. Schofield
William C. Turner
Martin D. Walker

GTE
James R. Barker
Edward H. Budd
James L. Ketelsen
Russell E. Palmer*

Hannaford Bros.
Bruce G. Allbright
William T. End*
Richard K. Lochridge
Robert L. Strickland

Harcourt General
William F. Connell
Jack M. Greenberg
Lynn M. Martin
Maurice Segall*
Hugo Uyterhoeven

Hewlett-Packard
Thomas E. Everhart
John B. Fery
Samuel L. Ginn
David M. Lawrence
Susan P. Orr*

Honeywell
Albert J. Baciocco, Jr.
James J. Howard
Bruce Karatz
A. Barry Rand*
Michael W. Wright

Hormel Foods
William S. Davila*
E. Peter Gillette, Jr.
Joseph T. Mallof

Houghton Mifflin
Mary H. Lindsay
Charles R. Longsworth
George Putnam
Ralph Z. Sorenson
Deroy C. Thomas*

Household International
Robert J. Darnall
John A. Edwardson
George A. Lorch*
S. Jay Stewart
Louis W. Sullivan

Huffy
Patrick W. Rooney
Thomas C. Sullivan*
Joseph P. Viviano

Idacorp
John B. Carley*
Peter T. Johnson
Evelyn Loveless
Peter S. O'Neill

IKON Office Solutions
James R. Birle
Frederick S. Hammer
Barbara B. Hauptfuhrer*
Richard A. Jalkut

Illinois Tool Works
Michael J. Birck
L. Richard Flury
Robert C. McCormack
Phillip B. Rooney*
Ormand J. Wade

Ingersoll-Rand
Joseph P. Flannery*
H. William Lichtenberger
Orin R. Smith
Richard J. Swift

Internat'l Business Machines
Charles F. Knight*
Alex Trotman
Charles M. Vest

Interpublic Group of Cos
Frank J. Borelli
Reginald K. Brack
Jill M. Considine
Leif H. Olsen*
Allen Questrom
J. Phillip Samper
J. C. Penney
George Nigh
Jane C. Pfeiffer*
R. Gerald Turner
Joseph D. Williams

Johnson & Johnson
Joan G. Cooney
James G. Cullen
Philip M. Hawley
Arnold G. Langbo
Thomas S. Murphy*

Kellogg
Claudio X. Gonzalez*
Gordon Gund
Russell G. Mawby
J. Richard Munro
Donald H. Rumsfeld
John L. Zabriskie

Kelly Services
Maureen A. Fay
Cedric V. Fricke
B. Joseph White*

Kimberly-Clark
Pastora S. Cafferty
Louis E. Levy*
Frank A. McPherson
Randall L. Tobias

Knight-Ridder
Barbara B. Hauptfuhrer
C. Peter McColough
Thomas L. Phillips
Randall L. Tobias
John L. Weinberg*

Lee Enterprises
Rance E. Crain
Andrew E. Newman
Phyllis Sewell*
Mark Vittert

Louisiana-Pacific
William S. Brooks
Archie W. Dunham
William E. Flaherty*
Bonnie G. Hill
Charles E. Yeager
Manor Care
Stewart Bainum
William H. Longfield
Frederic V. Malek
Jerry E. Robertson*

Marriott International
Floretta D. McKenzie*
W. Mitt Romney
Roger W. Sant
Lawrence M. Small
Marsh & McClennan
Lewis W. Bernard
Robert F. Erburu
Ray J. Groves

May Department Stores
Edward H. Meyer*
Russell E. Palmer
Edward E. Whitacre, Jr.

McDermott International
Theodore H. Black*
John W. Johnstone, Jr.
William McCollam, Jr.

McDonald's
Donald R. Keough
Terry L. Savage
Robert N. Thurston*

McGraw-Hill
Vartan Gregorian
John T. Hartley
Lisa K. Lorimer
Lois D. Rice
Paul J. Rizzo*
Sidney Taurel

Mead
John G. Breen*
Susan J. Kropf
Charles S. Mechem, Jr.
Lee J. Styslinger, Jr.
J. Lawrence Wilson

Media General
Robert P. Black
Robert V. Hatcher, Jr.*
John G. Medlin, Jr.

Mentor Graphics
Marsha B. Congdon
Fontaine K. Richardson
Jon A. Shirley

Merck & Co.
H. Brewster Atwater, Jr.*
Lawrence A. Bossidy
William G. Bowen
Johnetta B. Cole
Lloyd C. Elam

Merrill Lynch & Co.
Jill K. Conway*
Earle H. Harbison, Jr.
Robert P. Luciano
John J. Phelan, Jr.
William L. Weiss

MGM Grand
James D. Aljian*
Walter M. Sharp
Jerome B. York

MicroAge
Lynda M. Applegate
Fred Israel
William H. Mallender
Steven G. Mihaylo

Millipore
Robert E. Caldwell
Mark Hoffman
John F. Reno*

Minnesota Mining & Mfg
Edward A. Brennan*
Allen E. Murray
Rozanne L. Ridgway
Frank A. Shrontz

Mobil
Donald V. Fites
Allen F. Jacobson
Samuel C. Johnson
J. Richard Munro
Charles S. Sanford, Jr.
Robert G. Schwartz*

Monsanto
Robert M. Heyssel
Gwendolyn S. King
Philip Leder
William D. Ruckelshaus*

Montana Power
R.D. Corette
Kay Foster
Chase T. Hibbard
John R. Jester
Carl Lehrkind III*
Noble E. Vosburg

Morton International
Ralph M. Barford
Dennis C. Fill
Richard L. Keyser
Edward J. Mooney
Roger W. Stone*

Motorola
Thomas J. Murrin
John E. Pepper, Jr.
Samuel C. Scott III*

Neiman Marcus Group
Matina S. Horner
Vincent M. O'Reilly
Walter J. Salmon*
Jean H. Sisco

Nike
Jill K. Conway
Ralph D. DeNunzio*
John E. Jaqua
John R. Thompson

Nordstrom
D. Wayne Gittinger
Ann D. McLaughlin
John A. McMillan
Alfred E. Osborne, Jr.
William D. Ruckelshaus*
Elizabeth C. Vaughan

Norfolk Southern Corp
L. E. Coleman
T. Marshall Hahn, Jr.
E. B. Leisenring, Jr.*

Northrop Grumman
Jack R. Borsting
John T. Chain
Jack Edwards
John E. Robson
Brent Scowcroft
Richard J. Stegemeier*

Old Kent Financial
John M. Bissell*
Earl D. Holton
Michael J. Jandernoa
John P. Keller

Omnicom Group
Robert J. Callander
Quentin I. Smith, Jr.*
Egon P. Zehnder

Oryx Energy
David C. Genever-Watling
Robert B. Gill*
David S. Hollingsworth
Charles H. Pistor, Jr.
Ian L. White-Thomson

Oshkosh B'Gosh
Orren J. Bradley
Jerry M. Hiegel*
Stig A. Kry

Owens-Corning Fiberglas
Norman P. Blake, Jr.
John H. Dasburg
Landon Hilliard*
Furman C. Moseley, Jr.
W. Ann Reynolds

Pacific Enterprises
Wilford D. Godbold, Jr.
Ignacio E. Lozano, Jr.
Richard J. Stegemeier*

Paine Webber Group
E. Garrett Bewkes, Jr.
Frank P. Doyle*
Robert M. Loeffler

PepsiCo
John F. Akers
Robert E. Allen
Peter Foy
Ray L. Hunt
John J. Murphy*
Sharon P. Rockefeller
Franklin A. Thomas
P. Roy Vagelos
Arnold R. Weber

Pfizer
M. Anthony Burns*
George B. Harvey
Thomas G. Labrecque
Dana G. Mead

PG&E
David A. Coulter
David M. Lawrence
Carl E. Reichardt*
John C. Sawhill
Alan Seelenfreund

Pharmacia & Upjohn
Richard H. Brown
Jan Ekberg
Daryl F. Grisham
Berthold Lindqvist

Phelps Dodge
Robert N. Burt
Paul W. Douglas
Paul Hazen
Southwood J. Morcott*

Philip Morris Companies
Harold Brown
Robert E. Huntley
Richard D. Parsons
John S. Reed*
Stephen M. Wolf

Pioneer Hi-Bred Internat'l
Pedro Cuatrecasas
Fred S. Hubbell*
Luiz Kaufmann

Pittston
Roger G. Ackerman*
James R. Barker
Adam H. Zimmerman

Policy Management Systems
Alfred R. Berkeley III
John M. Palms
Joseph D. Sargent*

PPG Industries
Erroll B. Davis, Jr.
Steven C. Mason
Harold A. McInnes
Thomas J. Usher
David G. Vice
David R. Whitwam

Premark International
Harry W. Bowman
Lloyd C. Elam
Richard S. Friedland
Janice D. Stoney*

Procter & Gamble
Norman R. Augustine*
Donald R. Beall
Richard B. Cheney
Joseph T. Gorman
Marina v.N. Whitman

Public Svc Enterprise Group
T. J. Dunphy
Raymond V. Gilmartin
Irwin Lerner*
Marilyn M. Pfaltz
Josh S. Weston

Quaker Oats
Silas S. Cathcart*
Kenneth I. Chenault
Vernon R. Loucks, Jr.
William L. Weiss

Qualcomm
Jerome S. Katzin*
Duane A. Nelles
Marc I. Stern

Questar
Patrick J. Early
U. Edwin Garrison
W. Whitley Hawkins*
William N. Jones
Robert E. Kadlec
Gary G. Michael
Scott S. Parker

Reebok International Ltd
William F. Glavin
Geoffrey Nunes*
Reynolds Metals
John R. Hall*
William H. Joyce
Mylle B. Mangum
D. Larry Moore
James M. Ringler
Samuel C. Scott
Joe B. Wyatt

Rouse
Jeremiah E. Casey*
Juanita T. James
Thomas J. McHugh
Alexander B. Trowbridge

Rubbermaid
Scott S. Cowen
Robert M. Gerrity
Karen N. Horn
William D. Marohn*
Gordon R. Sullivan

Russell
Herschel M. Bloom
Ronald G. Bruno
C. V. Nalley III

Ryder System
Edward T. Foote II
Lynn M. Martin
Paul J. Rizzo
Alva O. Way*

Sara Lee
Charles W. Coker
Allen F. Jacobson*
James L. Ketelsen
Joan D. Manley
Rozanne L. Ridgway

SBC Communications
August A. Busch III
Jess T. Hay*
Bobby R. Inman
S. Donley Ritchey

Schering-Plough
Hans W. Becherer
H. Barclay Morley
Richard de J. Osborne
William A. Schreyer
James Wood*

Sears, Roebuck & Co.
Alston D. Correll, Jr.
Michael A. Miles
Clarence B. Rogers, Jr.*
Donald H. Rumsfeld
Patrick G. Ryan
Dorothy A. Terrell

Sherwin-Williams
James M. Biggar
Duane E. Collins
Robert W. Mahoney
Willaim G. Mitchell*
A. Malachi Mixon III

Shoney's
Carole F. Hoover*
Carroll D. Shanks
Felker W. Ward, Jr.
James D. Yancey

Silicon Graphics
C. Richard Kramlich*
Robert B. Shapiro
James G. Treybig

Snap-On
Donald W. Brinckman
Bruce S. Chelberg*
Raymond F. Farley*
Leonard A. Hadley
Edward H. Rensi

Sonoco Products
C. J. Bradshaw
A. T. Dickson*
R. E. Elberson
Paul Fulton
B. L. Kasriel
E. H. Lawton, Jr.
Dona D. Young

Southern
Alston D. Correll, Jr.*
L. G. Hardman III
Herbert Stockham
Gerald J. St. Pe

Southern N. England Telcom
Robert L. Bennett
Frank J. Connor*
William R. Fenoglio
Claire L. Gaudiani
Ira D. Hall

Springs Industries
John F. Akers
John L. Clendenin
Charles W. Coker*
Sherwood H. Smith
Robin B. Smith

Sprint
Harold S. Hook
Linda K. Lorimer
Charles E. Rice
Ron Sommer
Stewart Turley*

SPX
J. Kermit Campbell
Sarah R. Coffin
Frank A. Ehmann*
David P. Williams
St. Joe
John J. Quindlen
Frank S. Shaw, Jr.
John D. Uible*

St. Jude Medical
Kenneth G. Langone
William R. Miller
Walter L. Sembrowich

St. Paul Companies
Michael R. Bonsignore*
John H. Dasburg
Pierson M. Grieve
David G. John
Glen D. Nelson, M.D.
Gordon M. Sprenger

Standard Register
F. David Clarke III*
Dennis L. Rediker
Ann Scavullo
John Q. Sherman II

Stanley Works
Stillman B. Brown*
Mannie L. Jackson
James G. Kaiser
Walter W. Williams

Stone & Webster
Frank J. Cilluffo
Elvin R. Heiberg III
David N. McCammon
John P. Merrill, Jr.
Bernard W. Reznicek*

Sun Company
Raymond E. Cartledge*
Robert E. Cawthorn
Mary J. Evans
James G. Kaiser
Robert D. Kennedy

SunAmerica
William F. Aldinger, III
Karen Hastie-Williams
David O. Maxwell*
Carl E. Reichardt
Harold M. Williams

Talbots
Elizabeth T. Kennan
Mark H. Willes*

Temple-Inland
Robert Cizik
Anthony M. Frank*
Bobby R. Inman
Herbert A. Sklenar
Arthur Temple III

Tenet Healthcare
Bernice B. Bratter*
Maurice J. DeWald
Lester B. Korn

Texaco
Willard C. Butcher*
Edmund M. Carpenter
Charles H. Price II
William C. Steere
Thomas A. Vanderslice

Texas Instruments
David L. Boren
Gerald W. Fronterhouse*
David R. Goode
Wayne R. Sanders

Textron
H. Jesse Arnelle
John D. Macomber
Dana G. Mead
Barbara S. Preiskel
Sam F. Segnar
Martin D. Walker*

Time Warner
Stephen F. Bollenbach
Carla A. Hills
Reuben Mark*
Raymond S. Troubh
Francis T. Vincent, Jr.

TJX Companies
Dennis F. Hightower
John M. Nelson
John F. O'Brien
Robert F. Shapiro*
Willow B. Shire

Tootsie Roll Industries
Lana J. Lewis-Brent
Charles W. Seibert
William Touretz

Transamerica
Samuel L. Ginn
Robert W. Matschullat
Forrest N. Shumway
Peter V. Ueberroth*

Travelers Group
Gerald R. Ford
Ann D. Jordan
Michael T. Masin
Andrall E. Pearson
Linda J. Wachner
Arthur Zankel*

TRW
Martin Feldstein
Carl H. Hahn
Karen N. Horn
William S. Kiser*
David B. Lewis
John D. Ong

Unicom
Edward A. Brennan*
James W. Compton
Bruce DeMars
Sue L. Gin
Donald P. Jacobs
Edgar D. Jannotta
George E. Johnson

Union Pacific
Robert P. Bauman
Richard B. Cheney
E. Virgil Conway*
William H. Gray III
Thomas A. Reynolds, Jr.
James D. Robinson III
Richard D. Simmons

Unisys
Melvin R. Goodes
Edwin A. Huston
Kenneth A. Macke

United Healthcare
William C. Ballard, Jr.
Thomas H. Kean
Mary O. Mundinger
Robert L. Ryan
William G. Spears*

United Technologies
Charles W. Duncan, Jr.
Jean-Pierre Garnier
Frank P. Popoff
Harold A. Wagner*
Jacqueline G. Wexler

Universal Foods
John F. Bergstrom
James H. Keyes*
Essie Whitelaw

Unocal
John W. Amerman
Malcolm R. Currie
Frank C. Herringer
Donald P. Jacobs*

U.S. Trust
Peter O. Crisp
Frederic C. Hamilton
Philip L. Smith*
Robert N. Wilson
Ruth A. Wooden

Vanguard Cellular Systems
Robert M. DeMichele
Robert A. Silverberg

Venator Group
Philip H. Geier, Jr.
Margaret P. MacKimm
James E. Preston*

VF
Robert D. Buzzell
Edward E. Crutchfield
Ursula F. Fairbairn
Barbara S. Feigin
William E. Pike*

Viacom
George S. Abrams
Ken Miller
Brent D. Redstone
Shari Redstone
Frederic V. Salerno
William Schwartz*
Ivan G. Seidenberg

Vulcan Materials
Marion H. Antonini
Livio D. DeSimone
Douglas J. McGregor
James V. Napier
Orin R. Smith*

Wal-Mart Stores
John A. Cooper, Jr.
Frederick S. Humphries
John T. Walton

Walt Disney
Reveta F. Bowers
Stanley P. Gold
Ignacio E. Lozano, Jr.*
Thomas S. Murphy
Sidney Poitier
Irwin E. Russell
Raymond L. Watson

Warner-Lambert
Donald C. Clark*
John A. Georges
William R. Howell
Alex J. Mandl
Lawrence G. Rawl

Waste Management
H. Jesse Arnelle
Pastora S. Cafferty
James B. Edwards
Paul M. Montrone
Peer Pedersen*
James R. Peterson

Wells Fargo & Co.
Michael R. Bowlin
William S. Davila
Myron DuBain
Philip J. Quigley
Donald B. Rice
Richard J. Stegemeier
Susan G. Swenson
David M. Tellep
John A. Young*

Wendy's International
Janet Hill
True H. Knowles
Fielden B. Nutter, Sr.*
Thekla R. Shackelford

Weyerhaeuser
W. John Driscoll
Philip M. Hawley*
John I. Kieckhefer

Xerox
Bobby R. Inman
Antonio A. Johnson
Ralph S. Larsen*
John D. Macomber
John E. Pepper, Jr.
Patricia F. Russo

Appendix IV. Compensation Committee Members by Name

George S. Abrams
Viacom
Roger G. Ackerman*
Pittston
Lilyan H. Affinito
Caterpillar
Francis J. Aguilar
Bowater
John F. Akers
PepsiCo
Springs Industries
William F. Aldinger, III
SunAmerica
Joseph F. Alibrandi
BankAmerica
James D. Aljian*
MGM Grand
Bruce G. Allbright
Hannaford Bros.
Herbert A. Allen*
Coca-Cola
Howard P. Allen*
Computer Sciences
Robert E. Allen
Bristol-Myers Squibb
Chrysler
PepsiCo
Robert H. Allen
FDX
John W. Amerman
Unocal
A. Gary Ames
Albertson's
Eugene R. Anderson
Fortune Brands
George S. Ansell
Cyprus Amax Minerals
Beryl F. Anthony, Jr.*
Beverly Enterprises
Marion H. Antonini
Vulcan Materials
Lynda M. Applegate
MicroAge
Nolan D. Archibald
Brunswick

* Denotes that director chairs the Compensation Committee at one or more companies.

Anne L. Armstrong
American Express
Boise Cascade
H. Jesse Arnelle
FPL Group
Textron
Waste Management
Edwin L. Artzt
American Express
H. Brewster Atwater, Jr.*
Merck & Company
Norman R. Augustine*
Procter & Gamble
H. David Aycock*
Bowater
Albert J. Baciocco, Jr.
Honeywell
Irving W. Bailey II
Computer Sciences
Stewart Bainum
Manor Care
William C. Ballard, Jr.
United Healthcare
Bettina Bancroft
Dow Jones & Company
Ralph M. Barford
Morton International
James R. Barker
GTE
Pittston
Tom H. Barrett
Air Products & Chemicals
John W. Barter*
BMC Software
Carol A. Bartz
AirTouch Communications
Warren L. Batts
Cooper Industries
Robert P. Bauman
Cigna
Union Pacific
Donald R. Beall
Procter & Gamble
Robert M. Beall II
FPL Group
Hans W. Becherer
Allied-Signal
Schering-Plough
Nancy H. Bechtle
Charles Schwab

Henry P. Becton, Jr.*
Becton Dickinson & Company
Steven C. Beering*
Eli Lily & Company
Adrian D. Bellamy
Gap
Robert L. Bennett
Southern New England
John F. Bergstrom
Universal Foods
Alfred R. Berkeley III
Policy Management Systems
Lewis W. Bernard
Marsh & McClennan Companies
E. Garrett Bewkes, Jr.
Paine Webber Group
James M. Biggar
Sherwin-Williams
John H. Biggs
Boeing
Michael J. Birck
Illinois Tool Works
Jame R. Birle
IKON Office Solutions
John M. Bissell*
Old Kent Financial
Robert P. Black
Media General
Theodore H. Black*
McDermott International
Norman P. Blake, Jr.
Enron
Owens-Corning Fiberglas
Herschel M. Bloom
Russell
Frederick M. Bohen*
Apache
Stephen F. Bollenbach
Time Warner
Michael R. Bonsignore*
St. Paul Companies
Dennis S. Bookshester*
Fruit of the Loom
Frank J. Borelli
Interpublic Group of Companies
David L. Boren
Texas Instruments
Jack R. Borsting
Northrop Grumman
Michael J. Boskin
Exxon
Bradford R. Boss
Fleet Financial Group
Lawrence A. Bossidy
Merck & Company
William G. Bowen
Merck & Company
Reveta F. Bowers
Walt Disney
John G. Bowes
Gap
Michael R. Bowlin
Wells Fargo & Company
Harry W. Bowman
Premark International
Reginald K. Brack
Interpublic Group of Companies
Orren J. Bradley
Oshkosh B'Gosh
C. J. Bradshaw
Sonoco Products
Bernice B. Bratter*
Tenet Healthcare
John G. Breen*
Goodyear Tire & Rubber
Mead
Edward A. Brennan*
AMR
Minnesota Mining & Mfg
Unicom
Richard M. Bressler*
General Mills
Donald W. Brinckman
Snap-On
James L. Broadhead
Delta Air Lines
William S. Brooks
Louisiana-Pacific
Harold Brown
Cummins Engine
Philip Morris Companies
J. Hyatt Brown*
FPL Group
Richard H. Brown
Pharmacia & Upjohn
Ronald Brown*
Anadarko Petroleum
Stillman B. Brown*
Stanley Works
Robert W. Bruce III*
Freeport-McMoRan C&G
Ronald G. Bruno
Russell
James L. Bryan
Anadarko Petroleum
John H. Bryan*
General Motors

Edward H. Budd
GTE
M. Anthony Burns*
Pfizer
Robert N. Burt
Phelps Dodge
August A. Busch III
SBC Communications
C. Preston Butcher
Charles Schwab
Willard C. Butcher*
Texaco
William E. Butler
Goodyear Tire & Rubber
William T. Butler
Browning-Ferris Industries
Robert D. Buzzell
VF
Pastora S. Cafferty
Kimberly-Clark
Waste Management
Robert E. Caldwell
Millipore
Robert J. Callander
Omnicom Group
D. Wayne Calloway
Citicorp
Exxon
J. Kermit Campbell
SPX
Carlos H. Cantu
First Tennessee National
John B. Carley*
Idacorp
Frank C. Carlucci*
Ashland
Edmund M. Carpenter
Campbell Soup
Texaco
Richard L. Carrion
Bell Atlantic
Philip J. Carroll
Boise Cascade
Raymond E. Cartledge*
Sun Company
Delta Air Lines
Jeremiah E. Casey*
Rouse
Silas S. Cathcart*
General Electric
Quaker Oats
Robert E. Cawthorn
Sun Company
John T. Chain
Northrop Grumman
William R. Chaney
Bank of New York Company
Gareth C.C. Chang
Apple Computer
Bruce S. Chelberg*
Snap-On
Kenneth I. Chenault
Quaker Oats
Richard B. Cheney
Procter & Gamble
Union Pacific
Frank J. Cilluffo
Stone & Webster
Robert Cizik
Air Products & Chemicals
Temple-Inland
Donald C. Clark*
Warner-Lambert
F. David Clarke III*
Standard Register
John L. Clendenin
Springs Industries
Hugh K. Coble
Bechman Coulter
Armando M. Codina
FPL
Sarah R. Coffin
SPX
Betsy Z. Cohen
Aetna
Marshall A. Cohen
American International Group
Charles W. Coker*
Springs Industries
Sara Lee
J. Owen Cole
Baltimore Gas & Electric
Johnetta B. Cole
Merck & Company
L. E. Coleman
Norfolk Southern
Duane E. Collins
Sherwin-Williams
John T. Collins
Fleet Financial Group
Dan A. Colussy
Baltimore Gas & Electric
James W. Compton
Unicom
Barber B. Conable, Jr.
American International Group

Marsha B. Congdon
Mentor Graphics
William F. Connell
Harcourt General
J. W. Connolly
Consolidated Natural Gas
Frank J. Connor*
Southern New England
George H. Conrades*
CBS
Jill M. Considine
Interpublic Group of Cos.
E. Virgil Conway*
Union Pacific
Jill K. Conway*
Colgate-Palmolive
Merrill Lynch & Company
Nike
Joan G. Cooney
Johnson & Johnson
John A. Cooper, Jr.
Wal-Mart Stores
R. D. Corette
Montana Power
Alston D. Correll, Jr.*
Southern
Sears, Roebuck & Company
Albert J. Costello
Becton Dickinson & Company
David A. Coulter
PG&E
Scott S. Cowen
Rubbermaid
Rance E. Crain
Lee Enterprises
Peter O. Crisp
U.S. Trust
James S. Crown
General Dynamics
Thomas H. Cruikshank
Goodyear Tire & Rubber
Timm F. Crull*
BankAmerica
Edward E. Crutchfield
VF
Pedro Cuatrecasas
Pioneer Hi-Bred International
James G. Cullen
Johnson & Johnson
B. Garland Cupp
BMC Software
Bradley Currey, Jr.
Genuine Parts

Malcolm R. Currie
Unocal
Robert V. Dale*
Cracker Barrel Old Country
Robert J. Darnall
Household International
John H. Dasburg
Owens-Corning Fiberglas
St. Paul Companies
William S. Davila*
Hormel Foods
Wells Fargo & Company
Phyllis B. Davis
Eaton
Willie D. Davis
Dow Chemical
Erroll B. Davis, Jr.
PPG Industries
Howard M. Dean*
Ball
Alfred C. DeCrane, Jr.*
Cigna
CPC International
Bruce DeMars
Unicom
Robert M. DeMichele
Vanguard Cellular Systems
Ralph D. DeNunzio*
FDX
Nike
Kenneth T. Derr
AT&T
Citicorp
John P. DesBarres
American Electric Power
Livio D. DeSimone
General Mills
Vulcan Materials
Maurice J. DeWald
Tenet Healthcare
A. T. Dickson*
Sonoco Products
John T. Dillon
Caterpillar
Michael D. Dingman*
Ford Motor
Gerald V. Dirvin
Cintas
B. F. Dolan
FPL Group
Paul W. Douglas
Phelps Dodge
Frank P. Doyle*
Paine Webber Group

W. John Driscoll
Weyerhaeuser
Myron DuBain
Wells Fargo & Company
John H. Duncan
Enron
Charles W. Duncan, Jr.
United Technologies
Archie W. Dunham
Louisiana-Pacific
T. J. Dunphy
Public Service Enterprise Group
Patrick J. Early
Questar
Bernard A. Edison*
Anheuser-Busch Companies
Christopher F. Edley
AMR
Jack Edwards
Northrop Grumman
James B. Edwards
Waste Management
M. Delmar Edwards
AFLAC
John A. Edwardson
Household International
Frank A. Ehmann*
SPX
Jan Ekberg
Pharmacia & Upjohn
Lloyd C. Elam
Merck &
Premark International
R. E. Elberson
Sonoco Products
Walter Y. Elisha
Cummins Engine Company
Theodore H. Emmerich
American Financial Group
William T. End*
Hannaford Bros.
Roger A. Enrico*
Dayton Hudson
Robert F. Erburu
Marsh & McLennan
Tamara J. Erickson
Allergan
Handel E. Evans
Allergan
Mary J. Evans
Baxter International
Delta Air Lines
Sun Company
Thomas E. Everhart
Hewlett-Packard
Edgar W. Evins
Cracker Barrel Old Country
Patricia O. Ewers
Fortune Brands
Ursula F. Fairbairn
VF
Thomas V. Falkie
Cyprus Amax Minerals
John J. Fannon*
Federal Mogul
James B. Farley
Ashland
Raymond F. Farley*
Snap-On
D. C. Farrell
Emerson Electric
Maureen A. Fay
Kelly Services
Barbara S. Feigin
VF
Kathleen Feldstein
BankAmerica
Martin Feldstein
TRW
William R. Fenoglio
Southern New England
Ronald E. Ferguson
Colgate-Palmolive
Manuel A. Fernandez
Brunswick
John B. Fery*
Albertson's
Hewlett-Packard
Thomas W. Field, Jr.
Campbell Soup
Dennis C. Fill*
Beckman Coulter
Morton International
Donald G. Fisher*
AirTouch Communications
George M.C. Fisher
AT&T
General Motors
Donald V. Fites
Mobil
Lucie J. Fjeldstad
Gap
William E. Flaherty*
Louisiana-Pacific
Joseph P. Flannery*
Ingersoll-Rand

Peter J. Fluor
Fluor
L. Richard Flury
Illinois Tool Works
Edward T. Foote II
Ryder System
Gerald R. Ford
Travelers Group
Henrietta H. Fore
Dexter
Kay Foster
Montana Power
Bernard M. Fox
Dexter
Peter Foy
PepsiCo
Frank R. Frame
Baxter International
Anthony M. Frank*
Temple-Inland
Barbara H. Franklin
Dow Chemical
J. A. Frates
Emerson Electric
A.D. Frazier, Jr.
Apache
Cedric V. Fricke
Kelly Services
Richard S. Friedland
Premark
Daniel A. Fronk
Bob Evans Farms
Gerald W. Fronterhouse*
Texas Instruments
H. Laurance Fuller
Chase Manhattan
Samuel H. Fuller*
Analog Devices
Paul Fulton
Sonoco Products
Robert M. Furek*
Dexter
Meldon K. Gafner
BMC Software
David P. Gardner
Fluor
Jean-Pierre Garnier
United Technologies
U. Edwin Garrison
Questar
Claire L. Gaudiani
Southern New England
Jerome W. Geckle*
Baltimore Gas & Electric
Philip H. Geier, Jr.
Venator Group
David C. Genever-Watling
Oryx Energy
John A. Georges
Warner-Lambert
Robert M. Gerrity
Rubbermaid
James F. Gibbons
CISCO Systems
S. Parker Gilbert
Burlington Resources
Robert B. Gill*
Oryx Energy
E. Peter Gillette, Jr.
Hormel Foods
James H. Gilliam, Jr.
Bell Atlantic
Raymond V. Gilmartin
Public Service Enterprise Group
Allan D. Gilmour
Dow Chemical
Sue L. Gin
Unicom
Samuel L. Ginn
Hewlett-Packard
Transamerica
D. Wayne Gittinger
Nordstrom
William F. Glavin
Reebok International Ltd
Wilford D. Godbold, Jr.
Pacific Enterprises
Stanley P. Gold
Walt Disney
Harvey Golub
Campbell Soup
Claudio X. Gonzalez*
General Electric
Kellogg
David R. Goode
Caterpillar
Texas Instruments
Melvin R. Goodes
Chase Manhattan
Unisys
Charles H. Goodman
General Dynamics
Ellen R. Gordon
CPC International
John R. Gordon
Anadarko Petroleum
Joseph T. Gorman
Procter & Gamble

James P. Gorter*
Caterpillar
Martha C. Goss
Dexter
Thomas L. Gossage
Fluor
William R. Grant*
Allergan
Ann M. Gray
Cyprus Amax Minerals
Hanna H. Gray*
Cummins Engine
William H. Gray III
Chase Manhattan
Electronic Data Systems
Union Pacific
Jack M. Greenberg
Harcourt General
James R. Greene
Beverly Enterprises
Beverly S. Greenough
American Express
Gerald Greenwald
Aetna
Vartan Gregorian
McGraw-Hill
Pierson M. Grieve
St. Paul Companies
Gerald Grinstein*
Browning-Ferris Industries
Delta Air Lines
Daryl F. Grisham
Pharmacia & Upjohn
Ray J. Groves
Electronic Data Systems
Marsh & McClennan Companies
Clifford J. Grum
Cooper Industries
George V. Grune
CPC International
Gordon Gund
Kellogg
John T. Hackett
Ball
Leonard A. Hadley
Snap-On
Carl H. Hahn
TRW
T. Marshall Hahn, Jr.
Norfolk Southern
Ira D. Hall
Southern New England
John R. Hall*
Reynolds Metals
Frederic C. Hamilton
U.S. Trust
Frederick S. Hammer
IKON Office Solutions
Richard W. Hanselman
Becton Dickinson & Company
Earle H. Harbison, Jr.
Merrill Lynch & Company
L. G. Hardman III
Southern
James F. Hardymon*
Fleet Financial Group
Charles M. Harper*
E.I. DuPont de Nemours
Joe F. Harris*
AFLAC
William B. Harrison, Jr.
Freeport-McMoRan C&G
John T. Hartley
McGraw-Hill
George B. Harvey
Pfizer
Karen Hastie-Williams
SunAmerica
Robert V. Hatcher, Jr.*
Media General
Barbara B. Hauptfuhrer*
IKON Office Solutions
Knight-Ridder
W. Whitley Hawkins*
Questar
Philip M. Hawley*
Johnson & Johnson
Weyerhaeuser
Jess T. Hay*
Exxon
SBC Communications
Paul Hazen
Phelps Dodge
Elvin R. Heiberg III
Stone & Webster
Frank C. Herringer
Unocal
William D. Heydel
Cracker Barrel Old Country
Robert M. Heyssel
Monsanto
Chase T. Hibbard
Montana Power
Jerry M. Hiegel*
Oshkosh B'Gosh
Dennis F. Hightower
TJX Companies

Bonnie G. Hill
Louisiana-Pacific
Janet Hill
Wendy's International
Landon Hilliard*
Owens-Corning Fiberglas
Carla A. Hills
Time Warner
Robert C. Hilton
Cracker Barrel Old Country
Irvine O. Hockaday, Jr.*
Dow Jones & Company
Frank J. Hoenemeyer
American International Group
Mark Hoffman
Millipore
David S. Hollingsworth
Oryx Energy
Earl D. Holton
Old Kent Financial
Harold S. Hook
Cooper Industries
Sprint
Carole F. Hoover*
Shoney's
Frank Hope, Jr.
BankAmerica
Karen N. Horn
Eli Lily & Company
Rubbermaid
TRW
Larry D. Horner*
American General
Matina S. Horner
Neiman Marcus Group
Edgar G. Hotard
Dexter
James J. Howard
Honeywell
Roger L. Howe
Cintas
William R. Howell*
Exxon
Warner-Lambert
Fred S. Hubbell*
Pioneer Hi-Bred International
Lester A. Hudson, Jr.
American Electric Power
William J. Hudson, Jr.
Goodyear Tire & Rubber
Frederick S. Humphries
Wal-Mart Stores
Ray L. Hunt
PepsiCo
Thomas H. Hunt
American Financial Group
Robert E. Huntley
Philip Morris Companies
Edwin A. Huston
Unisys
J. R. Hyde III
FDX
Martha R. Ingram
Baxter International
Bobby R. Inman*
Fluor
SBC Communications
Temple-Inland
Xerox
Fred Israel
MicroAge
Mannie L. Jackson
Ashland
Stanley Works
Donald P. Jacobs*
Unocal
Unicom
Allen F. Jacobson*
Mobil
Sara Lee
Robert K. Jaedicke
Enron
Richard A. Jalkut
IKON Office Solutions
Juanita T. James
Rouse
Michael J. Jandernoa
Old Kent Financial
Edgar D. Jannotta
Aon
Unicom
John E. Jaqua
Nike
John R. Jester
Montana Power
David G. John
St. Paul Companies
Antonio A. Johnson
Xerox
Clark A. Johnson
Albertson's
David W. Johnson
Colgate-Palmolive
F. Ross Johnson
American Express
George E. Johnson
Unicom

Peter T. Johnson
Idacorp
Richard J. Johnson
American General
Samuel C. Johnson
Mobil
John W. Johnstone, Jr.
Fortune Brands
McDermott International
William N. Jones
Questar
Ann D. Jordan
Travelers Group
Michael H. Jordan
Aetna
William H. Joyce
Reynolds Metals
Lois D. Juliber
E.I. DuPont de Nemours
Robert E. Kadlec
Questar
James G. Kaiser
Stanley Works
Sun Company
Bruce Karatz
Honeywell
B. L. Kasriel
Sonoco Products
Jerome S. Katzin*
Qualcomm
Luiz Kaufmann
Pioneer Hi-Bred International
Thomas H. Kean
United Healthcare
John P. Keller
Old Kent Financial
William N. Kelley
Beckman Coulter
John P. Kendall
Colgate-Palmolive
Elizabeth T. Kennan
Bell Atlantic
Talbots
George D. Kennedy
Brunswick
Robert D. Kennedy
Sun
Donald R. Keough
McDonald's
James L. Ketelsen
GTE
Sara Lee
James H. Keyes*
Universal Foods
Richard L. Keyser
Morton International
C. Robert Kidder*
Electronic Data Systems
John I. Kieckhefer
Weyerhaeuser
Gwendolyn S. King
Monsanto
Susan B. King
Coca-Cola
James W. Kinnear*
Corning
Sidney Kirschner
Fortune Brands
William S. Kiser*
TRW
Charles F. Knight*
International Business Machines
True H. Knowles
Wendy's International
John A. Kocur
Apache
Richard J. Kogan
Bank of New York Company
Lester B. Korn
Tenet Healthcare
C. Richard Kramlich*
Silicon Graphics
Eileen S. Kraus
CPC International
Susan J. Kropf
Mead
Cheryl L. Krueger
Bob Evans Farms
Stig A. Kry
Oshkosh B'Gosh
Jack D. Kuehler
Aetna
Ronald L. Kuehn, Jr.*
Dun & Bradstreet
Thomas G. Labrecque
Pfizer
John T. LaMacchia
Burlington Resources
Arnold G. Langbo
Johnson & Johnson
Kenneth G. Langone
St. Jude Medical
J. Hicks Lanier
Genuine Parts
Robert J. Lanigan*
Chrysler
Dun & Bradstreet

Ralph S. Larsen*
Xerox
Ned C. Lautenbach
Eaton
Terry R. Lautenbach*
Air Products & Chemicals
Risa J. Lavizzo-Mourey
Beverly Enterprises
David M. Lawrence
Hewlett-Packard
PG&E
George D. Lawrence, Jr.
Apache
E. H. Lawton, Jr.
Sonoco Products
Kenneth L. Lay
Eli Lily & Company
Philip Leder
Monsanto
Paul E. Lego
Consolidated Natural Gas
John F. Lehman
Ball
Carl Lehrkind III*
Montana Power
E. B. Leisenring, Jr.*
Norfolk Southern
Charles A. LeMaistre*
Enron
Ronald T. LeMay
Ceridian
Irwin Lerner*
Public Service Enterprise Group
Louis E. Levy*
Kimberly-Clark
David B. Lewis
TRW
Delano E. Lewis
Colgate-Palmolive
Drew Lewis
FPL Group
Lana J. Lewis-Brent
Tootsie Roll Industries
David K. Li
CBS
H. William Lichtenberger
Ingersoll-Rand
John S. Lillard*
Cintas
John M. Lillie*
Gap
Berthold Lindqvist
Pharmacia & Upjohn
Mary H. Lindsay
Houghton Mifflin
Philip E. Lippincott*
Campbell Soup
Exxon
Richard K. Lochridge
Hannaford Bros.
Robert M. Loeffler
Paine Webber Group
Gordon R. Lohman*
Fortune Brands
William H. Longfield
Manor Care
Charles R. Longsworth*
Crestar Financial
Houghton Mifflin
George A. Lorch*
Household International
Linda K. Lorimer
Sprint
Lisa K. Lorimer
McGraw-Hill
Vernon R. Loucks, Jr.*
Emerson Electric
Anheuser-Busch Companies,
Dun & Bradstreet
Quaker Oats
Evelyn Loveless
Idacorp
Ignacio E. Lozano, Jr.*
Pacific Enterprises
Walt Disney
G. Robert Lucas II*
Bob Evans Farms
Robert P. Luciano*
Allied-Signal
Merrill Lynch & Company
Anthony Luiso
Black & Decker
Jane C. MacElree
Dow Jones & Company
Kenneth A. Macke
General Mills
Unisys
Margaret P. MacKimm
Venator Group
John D. Macomber
Bristol-Myers Squibb
Textron
Xerox
Antonio Madero
Federal Mogul

Peter A. Magowan
Caterpillar
Chrysler
Robert W. Mahoney
Sherwin-Williams
Frederic V. Malek
Manor Care
William H. Mallender
MicroAge
Joseph T. Mallof
Hormel Foods
John C. Malone
Bank of New York Company
Mary Alice Malone
Campbell Soup
Charles T. Manatt
FDX
Alex J. Mandl
Warner-Lambert
Mylle B. Mangum
Reynolds Metals
Joan D. Manley
Sara Lee
Reuben Mark*
Time Warner
William D. Marohn*
Rubbermaid
J. Willard Marriott, Jr.
General Motors
Charles Marshall
Ceridian
Lynn M. Martin
Harcourt General
Ryder System
R. Brad Martin*
First Tennessee National
William R. Martin*
American Financial Group
Vilma S. Martinez
Anheuser-Busch Companies
Michael T. Masin
Travelers Group
Steven C. Mason
PPG Industries
Robert W. Matschullat
Transamerica
Russell G. Mawby
Kellogg
David O. Maxwell*
SunAmerica
David N. McCammon
Stone & Webster
Frank E. McCarthy
Crestar Financial
William McCollam, Jr.
McDermott International
C. Peter McColough
Knight-Ridder
Robert C. McCormack
Illinois Tool Works
Leslie G. McCraw
Allergan
Gabrielle K. McDonald
Freeport-McMoRan C&G
Douglas J. McGregor
Vulcan Materials
Donald F. McHenry
AT&T
Thomas J. McHugh
Rouse
Harold A. McInnes
PPG Industries
Gordon C. McKeague
Analog Devices
Andrew J. McKenna
Aon
Margaret McKenna
Consolidated Natural Gas
Floretta D. McKenzie*
Marriott International
Henry A. McKinnell
Dun & Bradstreet
Ann D. McLaughlin
Nordstrom
David T. McLaughlin
CBS
Stephen T. McLin
Charles Schwab
John A. McMillan
Nordstrom
Frank A. McPherson
Kimberly-Clark
Dana G. Mead
Pfizer
Textron
Charles S. Mechem, Jr.
Mead
John G. Medlin, Jr.
Media General
James R. Mellor
Computer Sciences
Donald R. Melville
Bowater
Louis W. Menk
Beverly Enterprises
John P. Merrill, Jr.
Stone & Webster

Edward H. Meyer*
May Department Stores
Gary G. Michael
Questar
Gertrude G. Michelson
General Electric
Goodyear Tire & Rubber
Steven G. Mihaylo*
MicroAge
Michael A. Miles
Sears, Roebuck & Company
Donald L. Miller
Bank of New York Company
John R. Miller*
Eaton
Ken Miller
Viacom
Paul D. Miller
Crestar Financial
William R. Miller
St. Jude Medical
Gilmer Minor, III
Crestar Financial
Newton N. Minow
Aon
Steven A. Minter*
Consolidated Natural Gas
Goodyear Tire & Rubber
William G. Mitchell*
Sherwin-Williams
A. Malachi Mixon III
Sherwin-Williams
Paul M. Montrone
Waste Management
Edward J. Mooney
Morton International
D. Larry Moore
Reynolds Metals
Southwood J. Morcott*
Phelps Dodge
H. Barclay Morley*
Bank of New York Company
Schering-Plough
Furman C. Moseley, Jr.
Owens-Corning Fiberglas
Mary O. Mundinger
United Healthcare
J. Richard Munro
Kellogg
Mobil
John J. Murphy*
PepsiCo
Thomas S. Murphy*
Johnson & Johnson
Walt Disney
Allen E. Murray
Minnesota Mining & Mfg
Thomas J. Murrin
Motorola
C. V. Nalley III
Russell
James V. Napier
Vulcan Materials
Duane A. Nelles
Qualcomm
John M. Nelson
TJX Companies
Glen D. Nelson, M.D.
St. Paul Companies
Andrew E. Newman
Lee Enterprises
Constantine S. Nicandros*
Cooper Industries
George Nigh
J. C. Penney
Patrick F. Noonan
Ashland
William S. Norman*
CPC International
Geoffrey Nunes*
Reebok International Ltd
Fielden B. Nutter, Sr.*
Wendy's International
John F. O'Brien
TJX Companies
Thomas H. O'Brien*
Bell Atlantic
Thomas D. O'Conner
Fleet Financial Group
James J. O'Connor
Corning
Dean O'Hare
Fluor
Frank R. O'Keefe, Jr.*
Aetna
Leif H. Olsen*
Interpublic Group of Companies
Frank A. Olson
Becton Dickinson & Company
Cooper Industries
Peter S. O'Neill
Idacorp
John D. Ong
TRW

Paul F. Oreffice
Cigna
Coca-Cola
Vincent M. O'Reilly
Neiman Marcus Group
Susan P. Orr*
Hewlett-Packard
Richard de J. Osborne
Schering-Plough
Alfred E. Osborne, Jr.
Nordstrom
Russell E. Palmer*
GTE
May Department Stores
John M. Palms
Policy Management Systems
Scott S. Parker
Questar
William A. Parker, Jr.*
Genuine Parts
Richard D. Parsons
Philip Morris Companies
William P. Payne
Anheuser-Busch Companies
Andrall E. Pearson
Travelers Group
Peer Pedersen*
Waste Management
Victor A. Pelson
Eaton
John E. Pepper, Jr.
Motorola
Xerox
Donald S. Perkins*
Aon
James E. Perrella
Becton Dickinson & Company
William J. Perry
Boeing
Donald E. Petersen*
Boeing
James R. Peterson
Dun & Bradstreet
Waste Management
Marilyn M. Pfaltz
Public Service Enterprise Group
Jane C. Pfeiffer*
J. C. Penney
John J. Phelan, Jr.
Merrill Lynch & Company
Thomas L. Phillips
Knight-Ridder
Paul J. Phoenix
Boise Cascade
Charles M. Pigott
Boeing
William E. Pike*
VF
Charles H. Pistor, Jr.
AMR
Fortune Brands
Oryx Energy
Richard R. Pivirotto
CBS
Sidney Poitier
Walt Disney
John C. Pope
Federal Mogul
Frank P. Popoff*
American Express
United Technologies
Barbara S. Preiskel
Textron
James E. Preston*
Venator Group
Charles H. Price II
Texaco
Robert L. Puette*
CISCO Systems
George Putnam
Freeport-McMoRan C&G
Houghton Mifflin
Agnar Pytte
Goodyear Tire & Rubber
Allen Questrom
Interpublic Group of Companies
Philip J. Quigley
Wells Fargo & Company
John J. Quindlen
St. Joe
Michael R. Quinlan
Dun & Bradstreet
A. Barry Rand*
Honeywell
Lawrence G. Rawl
Warner-Lambert
Dennis L. Rediker
Standard Register
Brent D. Redstone
Viacom
Shari Redstone
Viacom
John S. Reed*
Philip Morris Companies
Carl E. Reichardt*
Ford Motor
PG&E
SunAmerica

Catherine A. Rein
Corning
John F. Reno*
Millipore
Edward H. Rensi
Snap-On
A. William Reynolds
Boise Cascade
W. Ann Reynolds
Owens-Corning Fiberglas
Thomas A. Reynolds, Jr.
Union Pacific
Bernard W. Reznicek*
Stone & Webster
Frank H. Rhodes
General Electric
Charles E. Rice
Sprint
Donald B. Rice
Wells Fargo & Company
Joseph A. Rice
Apache
Lois D. Rice
McGraw-Hill
Fontaine K. Richardson
Mentor Graphics
Rozanne L. Ridgway
Minnesota Mining & Mfg
Sara Lee
James M. Ringler
Reynolds Metals
James Q. Riordan
Dow Jones & Company
S. Donley Ritchey
SBC Communications
Paul J. Rizzo*
McGraw-Hill
Ryder System
Jerry E. Robertson*
Manor Care
Ralph H. Robins
Cooper Industries
James D. Robinson III
Union Pacific
John E. Robson
Northrop Grumman
Sharon P. Rockefeller
PepsiCo
Joe M. Rodgers
AMR
Judith Rodin
AMR
Clarence B. Rogers, Jr.*
Sears, Roebuck & Company
W. Mitt Romney
Marriott International
Patrick W. Rooney
Huffy
Philip B. Rooney*
Illinois Tool Works
Michael D. Rose
First Tennessee National
General Mills
W. L. Rouse, Jr.
Ashland
William D. Ruckelshaus*
Cummins Engine
Monsanto
Nordstrom
Donald H. Rumsfeld
Kellogg
Sears, Roebuck & Company
Irwin E. Russell
Walt Disney
Patricia F. Russo
Xerox
Patrick G. Ryan
Sears, Roebuck & Company
Robert L. Ryan
United Healthcare
Frederic V. Salerno
Viacom
Walter J. Salmon*
Neiman Marcus Group
J. Phillip Samper
Interpublic Group of Companies
Wayne R. Sanders
Texas Instruments
Charles S. Sanford, Jr.
Mobil
Stephen W. Sanger
Dayton Hudson
William B. Sansom
First Tennessee National
Roger W. Sant
Marriott International
Joseph D. Sargent*
Policy Management Systems
Terry L. Savage
McDonald's
John C. Sawhill
PG&E
Ann Scavullo
Standard Register
George A. Schaefer
Aon
Roger W. Schipke*
Brunswick

George H. Schofield
Goodyear Tire & Rubber
William A. Schreyer
Schering-Plough
Charles R. Schwab
AirTouch Communications
Robert G. Schwartz*
Mobil
William Schwartz*
Viacom
John F. Schwarz
Burlington Resources
Samuel C. Scott III*
Motorola
Reynolds Metals
Walter Scott, Jr.*
Burlington Resources
Brent Scowcroft
Northrop Grumman
Alan Seelenfreund
PG&E
Maurice Segall*
Harcourt General
AMR
Sam F. Segnar
Textron
Charles W. Seibert
Tootsie Roll Industries
Ivan G. Seidenberg
Allied-Signal
Viacom
Harold E. Sells
Bank of New York Company
Walter L. Sembrowich
St. Jude Medical
Phyllis Sewell*
Lee Enterprises
Thekla R. Shackelford
Wendy's International
Carroll D. Shanks
Shoney's
Harold T. Shapiro*
Dow Chemical
Robert B. Shapiro
Silicon Graphics
Robert F. Shapiro*
TJX Companies
Walter M. Sharp
MGM Grand
H. Rodney Sharp III
E.I. DuPont de Nemours
Frank S. Shaw, Jr.
St. Joe
John Q. Sherman II
Standard Register
Willow B. Shire
TJX Companies
Jon A. Shirley
Mentor Graphics
Charles R. Shoemate
Cigna
Frank A. Shrontz*
Citicorp
Minnesota Mining & Mfg
George P. Shultz
AirTouch Communications
Charles Schwab
Forrest N. Shumway
Transamerica
Andrew C. Sigler*
Allied-Signal
Bristol-Myers Squibb
General Electric
Robert A. Silverberg
Vanguard Cellular Systems
Richard D. Simmons
Union Pacific
Jean H. Sisco
Neiman Marcus Group
Herbert A. Sklenar
Temple-Inland
John G. Smale
General Motors
Lawrence M. Small
Marriott International
Jackson W. Smart*
FDX
Donald G. Smith
American Electric Power
Orin R. Smith*
Vulcan Materials
Ingersoll-Rand
Philip L. Smith*
U.S. Trust
Quentin I. Smith, Jr.*
Omnicom Group
Raymond W. Smith
CBS
Robin B. Smith
Springs Industries
Sherwood H. Smith
Springs Industries
William D. Smithburg
Corning
Robert E. Smittcamp
American General

Theodore M. Solso
Cyprus Amax Minerals
Ron Sommer
Sprint
Ralph Z. Sorenson
Houghton Mifflin
Michael I. Sovern
AT&T
William G. Spears*
United Healthcare
A. Michael Spence
BankAmerica
Gordon M. Sprenger
St. Paul Companies
Georges C. St. Laurent, Jr.*
Baxter International
Gerald J. St. Pe
Southern
John R. Stafford*
Chase Manhattan
Allied-Signal
William C. Steere, Jr.
Dow Jones & Company
Texaco
Richard J. Stegemeier*
Northrop Grumman
Pacific Enterprises
Wells Fargo & Company
Marc I. Stern
Qualcomm
Paul G. Stern
Dow Chemical
S. Jay Stewart
Household International
William P. Stiritz
Ball
Herbert Stockham
Southern
Roger W. Stone*
Morton International
Janice D. Stoney*
Premark International
Will M. Storey
Albertson's
George Strawbridge, Jr.
Campbell Soup
Robert L. Strickland
Hannaford
Lee J. Styslinger, Jr.
Mead
Frank C. Sullivan
General Dynamics
Gordon R. Sullivan
Rubbermaid
Louis W. Sullivan
Bristol-Myers Squibb
Household International
Michael D. Sullivan
Baltimore Gas & Electric
Thomas C. Sullivan*
Huffy
Louis W. Sullivan, M.D.
Cigna
Susan G. Swenson
Wells Fargo & Company
Richard J. Swift
Ingersoll-Rand
Morris Tanenbaum*
American Electric Power
Anne M. Tatlock
American General
Sidney Taurel
McGraw-Hill
David M. Tellep
Wells Fargo & Company
Arthur Temple III
Temple-Inland
Dorothy A. Terrell
Sears, Roebuck & Company
Deroy C. Thomas*
Houghton Mifflin
Franklin A. Thomas
Citicorp
Cummins Engine
PepsiCo
John R. Thompson
Nike
Lester C. Thurow
Analog Devices
Robert N. Thurston*
McDonald's
Randall L. Tobias
Kimberly-Clark
Knight-Ridder
James A. Todd, Jr.
Cyprus Amax Minerals
Gary L. Tooker
Eaton
William Touretz
Tootsie Roll Industries
Paul R. Tregurtha
Fleet Financial Group
FPL Group
James G. Treybig
Silicon Graphics
Carlisle A. Trost*
General Dynamics

Alex Trotman
International Business Machines
Raymond S. Troubh
Becton Dickinson & Company
Time Warner
Alexander B. Trowbridge
Rouse
Solomon D. Trujillo
Dayton Hudson
Stewart Turley*
Sprint
Billie B. Turner*
Cyprus Amax Minerals
Fred L. Turner
Aon
Gerald Turner
J.C. Penney
William C. Turner
Goodyear Tire & Rubber
Peter V. Ueberroth*
Transamerica
Coca-Cola
Carole J. Uhrich
Ceridian
John D. Uible*
St. Joe
Thomas J. Usher
PPG Industries
Hugo Uyterhoeven
Harcourt General
P. Roy Vagelos
PepsiCo
Thomas A. Vanderslice
Texaco
Elizabeth C. Vaughan
Nordstrom
Glenn Vaughn, Jr.
AFLAC
Charles M. Vest
E.I. DuPont de Nemours
International Business Machines
David G. Vice
PPG Industries
Francis T. Vincent, Jr.
Time Warner
Mark Vittert
Lee Enterprises
Joseph P. Viviano
Huffy
Noble E. Vosburg
Montana Power
Linda J. Wachner
Travelers Group
Ormand J. Wade
Illinois Tool Works
Harold A. Wagner*
United Technologies
Martin D. Walker*
Goodyear Tire & Rubber
Textron
William E. Wall
Burlington Resources
Paul S. Walsh*
Ceridian
FDX
Robert D. Walter
CBS
Roger O. Walther*
Charles Schwab
John T. Walton
Wal-Mart Stores
Felker W. Ward, Jr
Shoney's
Raymond L. Watson
Walt Disney
Alva O. Way*
Eli Lily & Company
Ryder System
Dennis Weatherstone
General Motors
Arnold R. Weber
PepsiCo
Charlotte C. Weber
Campbell Soup
A. Lorne Weil
Fruit of the Loom
John L. Weinberg*
Knight-Ridder
William L. Weiss
Merrill Lynch & Company
Quaker Oats
Josh S. Weston
Public Service Enterprise Group
Jacqueline G. Wexler
United Technologies
George H. Weyerhaeuser
Boeing
J. Taylor Wharton
Freeport-McMoRan C&G
Edward E. Whitacre, Jr.
May Department Stores
B. Joseph White*
Kelly Services
Essie Whitelaw
Universal Foods
Ian L. White-Thomson
Oryx Energy

Marina v.N. Whitman
Browning-Ferris Industries
Procter & Gamble
David R. Whitwam
PPG Industries
Mark H. Willes*
Talbots
Black & Decker
David P. Williams
SPX
E. F. Williams
Emerson Electric
Harold M. Williams
SunAmerica
James B. Williams
Genuine Parts
Joseph D. Williams
J. C. Penney
Walter W. Williams
Stanley Works
J. Lawrence Wilson
Mead
Lynton R. Wilson
Chrysler
Robert N. Wilson
U.S. Trust
Stephen M. Wolf
Philip Morris Companies
Brian G. Wolfson
Fruit of the Loom
James Wood*
Schering-Plough
Ruth A. Wooden
U.S. Trust
Betty Woods
Beckman Coulter
Ward W. Woods, Jr.*
Boise Cascade
Cabell Woodward, Jr.
Black & Decker
Edgar S. Woolard, Jr.*
Apple Computer
Citicorp
Michael W. Wright
Honeywell
Joe B. Wyatt
Reynolds Metals
Thomas H. Wyman*
AT&T
General Motors
James D. Yancey
Shoney's
Charles E. Yeager
Louisiana-Pacific
Clayton K. Yeutter
Caterpillar
Jerome B. York
MGM Grand
Dona D. Young
Sonoco Products
John A. Young*
Wells Fargo & Company
John L. Zabriskie
Kellogg
Arthur Zankel*
Travelers Group
Egon P. Zehnder
Omnicom Group
Adam H. Zimmerman
Pittston

Appendix V. Average Directors' Total Compensation—Alphabetical List

What the Headings Mean

TOTAL COMP RANK
Shows the company's Total Compensation ranking, out of the 225 study companies

AVG. DIRECT RANK
Shows the company's Direct Compensation ranking, for comparison purposes

REV
Shows the company's fiscal 1997 revenues, in millions of dollars

IND
Shows the company's industry group, using the following codes:

F - Financial	S - Service
H - Health CareT -	Hi Tech
I - Other Industrials	O - Other
	M - Manufacturing/Industrials

AVG. DIRECT COMP
Shows the dollar figure calculated for an "average director" at the company (see page 26 in Chapter 3 for a detailed explanation of this technique). *Note: The value of any annual stock awards that are not restricted for more than one year is included in Avg Direct Comp, as noted in the Comments column.*

+ GRANT VALUE
Reflects the annualized value of any annual or periodic stock grants received by directors.

= TOTAL COMP
Shows the sum of the company's Average Direct Compensation plus Stock Grant Value

COMMENTS
Noted here are: (1) stock awards that are included in the retainer value, (2) one-time stock grants or "initial" awards that differ from regular periodic grants, and (3) the total number of shares/value in periodic grants that do not occur annually

Table 43 Average Director's Total Compensation—Alphabetical

Total Comp Rank	Avg. Direct Rank	Company	Rev ($mils)	Ind	Avg. Direct Comp	+Grant Value	=Total Comp	Comments
96	70	Aetna	18,540	F	55,000	24,697	79,697	initial grant = 1,500 def'd shrs
130	175	AFLAC	7,251	F	35,200	34,083	69,283	initial grant = 10,000 options; 10,000 options every 5 yrs
68	171	Air Products & Chem	4,662	I	36,000	55,867	91,867	
131	70	AirTouch Comm	3,594	T	55,000	13,854	68,854	initial grant = 10,000 options
111	129	Albertson's	14,690	O	43,000	31,500	74,500	
125	146	Allergan	1,138	H	40,500	30,206	70,706	2,700 res't shrs every 3 yrs
53	61	Allied-Signal	14,472	O	57,800	40,875	98,675	1-time 3,000 res't shrs
164	142	Amer Electric Power	6,161	U	41,000	15,488	56,488	
39	13	American Express	17,760	F	81,850	29,750	111,600	200 shrs in retainer value
70	15	Amer Financial Grp	4,021	O	78,000	13,438	91,438	$20,000 shrs in retainer value; also initial grant = 5,000 options
152	45	American General	8,927	F	60,500	0	60,500	1-time 500 res't shrs; also 1-time 1,500 options
1	5	Amer Int'l Group	30,520	F	120,906	181,250	302,156	675 shrs in retainer value
56	159	AMR	18,570	S	38,000	57,825	95,825	
11	63	Anadarko Petroleum	673	I	57,250	101,146	158,396	initial grant = 10,000 options; also 1-time $13,000 def'd shrs
19	115	Analog Devices	1,243	T	45,500	96,906	142,406	
148	38	Anheuser-Busch	11,066	M	62,600	0	62,600	
63	20	Aon	5,751	F	72,322	20,000	92,322	675 shrs in retainer value
175	112	Apache	1,176	I	46,000	7,013	53,013	$5,000 shrs in retainer value; also 1,000 res't shrs every 5 yrs
199	224	Apple Computer	7,081	T	0	43,750	43,750	initial grant = 30,000 options
101	97	Ashland	13,567	I	49,000	28,634	77,634	1,000 res't shrs every 5 yrs
73	117	AT&T	53,261	T	45,000	45,000	90,000	
173	209	Ball	2,389	M	25,900	27,180	53,080	1,000 res't shrs every 3 yrs
183	159	Baltimore Gas & Elec	3,308	U	38,000	13,000	51,000	
20	2	Bank of New York	5,697	F	140,775	0	140,775	1,200 shrs in retainer value
89	41	BankAmerica	23,585	F	62,000	20,000	82,000	
21	217	Baxter International	6,138	H	22,000	117,688	139,688	4,000 res't shrs every 3 yrs
126	148	Beckman Instrum	1,198	T	40,000	30,667	70,667	
116	79	Becton Dickinson	2,811	H	53,000	20,000	73,000	
17	30	Bell Atlantic	30,194	T	67,500	75,833	143,333	
67	90	Bestfoods	9,818	O	51,250	40,800	92,050	
143	148	Beverly Enterprises	3,230	H	40,000	23,400	63,400	

123	152	Black & Decker	4,941	M	39,062	32,552	71,614	500 shrs in retainer value
2	213	BMC Software	731	T	23,000	218,750	241,750	initial grant = 20,000 options
208	201	Bob Evans Farms	822	S	29,900	7,571	37,471	5,133 options every 5 yrs
105	112	Boeing	45,800	T	46,000	29,575	75,575	initial grant = 1,500 options
159	126	Boise Cascade	5,493	M	43,800	15,125	58,925	
178	164	Bowater	1,485	M	37,600	14,813	52,413	
7	40	Bristol-Myers Sqb	16,701	H	62,250	119,146	181,396	
84	128	Browning-Ferris Ind	5,783	S	43,500	40,833	84,333	initial grant = 5,000 options
93	93	Brunswick	3,657	S	50,000	30,313	80,313	$25,000 shrs in retainer value; also 1-time $25,000 stock award
62	70	Burlington Resources	2,000	I	55,000	37,344	92,344	initial grant = 3,000 options
5	1	Campbell Soup	7,964	O	167,000	38,750	205,750	2,400 shrs in retainer value
18	135	Caterpillar	18,925	M	42,000	101,042	143,042	
144	70	CBS	9,632	T	55,000	8,333	63,333	$25,000 shrs in retainer value
87	207	Ceridian	1,664	T	26,000	56,542	82,542	1-time $65,000 res't shrs
118	145	Charles Schwab	2,299	F	40,600	31,453	72,053	
26	4	Chase Manhattan	30,381	F	123,432	0	123,432	500 shrs in retainer value
57	47	Chrysler	61,147	M	60,000	35,188	95,188	$25,000 shrs in retainer value; also 1-time 6,000 def'd shrs
107	36	Cigna	20,038	F	64,250	11,000	75,250	$20,000 shrs in retainer value; also 1-time 1,500 res't shrs
220	221	Cintas	840	S	18,400	13,000	31,400	
4	195	CISCO Systems	6,440	T	32,000	185,833	217,833	initial grant = 20,000 options
158	97	Citicorp	34,697	F	49,000	10,000	59,000	
112	19	Coca-Cola	18,868	M	74,000	0	74,000	
9	7	Colgate-Palmolive	9,057	M	114,738	48,583	163,321	1,300 shrs in retainer value
113	87	Computer Sciences	5,616	T	52,000	21,800	73,800	$109,000 res't shrs every 5 yrs
185	159	Consol Natural Gas	5,710	U	38,000	12,100	50,100	initial grant = 400 res't shrs
79	24	Cooper Industries	5,289	T	70,600	16,333	86,933	400 shrs in retainer value
188	184	Corning	4,129	M	34,500	14,850	49,350	1,200 res't shrs every 3 yrs; also initial grant = 4,000 rest'd shrs
223	203	Cracker Barrel	1,124	S	29,000	0	29,000	regular grant of 25,312 opts not made becuase kitty was depleted
198	166	Crestar Financial	1,997	F	37,000	8,000	45,000	$6,000 shrs in retainer value; also $40,000 res't shrs every 5 yrs
163	65	Cummins Engine	5,625	M	57,000	0	57,000	$18,000 shrs in retainer value
169	122	Cyprus Amax Min	3,346	I	44,688	10,250	54,938	500 shrs in retainer value
81	166	Dayton Hudson	27,757	O	37,000	48,333	85,333	
189	129	Delta Air Lines	13,590	S	43,000	6,300	49,300	$5,000 shrs in retainer value
201	132	Dexter	1,159	I	42,638	0	42,638	$10,000 +200 shrs in retainer value

36	43	Dow Chemical	20,018	I	61,600	51,088	112,688	1,550 options every 5 yrs; also 1-time 1,500 res't shrs
160	155	Dow Jones & Co	2,573	S	38,600	20,000	58,600	
104	117	Dun & Bradstreet	2,154	S	45,000	30,938	75,938	1-time $25,000 res't shrs
83	70	Eaton	7,563	M	55,000	29,750	84,750	initial grant = 5,000 options
27	16	Electronic Data Syst	15,236	T	77,500	43,938	121,438	
64	111	Eli Lily & Co	8,518	H	46,200	46,092	92,292	
78	84	Emerson Electric	12,299	T	52,500	35,000	87,500	
37	37	Enron	20,273	U	63,000	49,459	112,459	
32	16	Exxon	122,379	I	77,500	36,713	114,213	initial grant = 4,000 res't shrs
120	21	E.I. DuPont	41,304	I	72,025	0	72,025	400 shrs in retainer value
35	22	FDX	11,520	S	72,000	40,708	112,708	
99	187	Federal Mogul	1,807	M	33,000	45,708	78,708	$25,000 def'd every 5 yrs; also 1-time 1,000 res't shrs
211	171	First Tennessee Nat'l	1,609	F	36,000	0	36,000	1-time 6,000 res't shrs
89	87	Fleet Financial Grp	8,095	F	52,000	30,000	82,000	
151	135	Fluor	14,299	S	42,000	18,688	60,688	1-time 1,570 res't shrs
77	54	Ford Motor	153,627	M	59,000	29,425	88,425	2,000 res't shrs every 5 yrs
60	28	Fortune Brands	7,001	M	68,105	25,042	93,147	482 shrs in retainer value
176	79	FPL Group	6,369	U	53,000	0	53,000	1-time 200 shrs stock award
75	166	Freeport-McMoRan	2,001	I	37,000	52,083	89,083	
48	70	Fruit of the Loom	2,140	M	55,000	47,406	102,406	initial grant = 2,500 res't shrs
94	171	Gap	6,508	O	36,000	44,297	80,297	initial grant = 15,000 options
161	58	General Dynamics	4,062	T	58,000	0	58,000	
3	12	General Electric	90,840	O	83,600	146,750	230,350	
15	11	General Mills	5,609	O	84,813	59,688	144,501	500 shrs in retainer value
88	57	General Motors	178,174	M	58,250	24,000	82,250	
218	194	Genuine Parts	6,005	S	32,400	0	32,400	
146	79	Goodyear	13,155	M	53,000	10,000	63,000	
38	47	GTE	23,260	T	60,000	52,250	112,250	
49	142	Hannaford Bros.	3,226	O	41,000	60,813	101,813	
210	170	Harcourt General	3,692	S	36,750	0	36,750	
141	34	Hewlett-Packard	42,895	T	65,100	0	65,100	$22,500 shrs in retainer value
72	46	Honeywell	8,028	T	60,400	30,200	90,600	
170	156	Hormel Foods	3,257	O	38,400	15,917	54,317	
85	56	Houghton Mifflin	797	S	58,675	25,583	84,258	1,000 shrs in retainer value
16	159	Household Inter'l	5,503	O	38,000	106,354	144,354	1-time 1,000 shrs stock award
166	158	Huffy	695	S	38,250	17,438	55,688	5,625 options every 3 yrs

219	196	Idacorp	749	U	31,800	0	31,800	
153	197	IKON Office Solut	5,128	O	30,000	30,000	60,000	1-time 25,000 stock options
174	176	Illinois Tool Works	5,220	M	35,000	18,038	53,038	900 res't shrs every 3 yrs; also 1-time 1,000 def'd
47	101	Ingersoll-Rand	7,103	M	48,000	54,675	102,675	
22	210	Int'l Bus Machines	78,508	T	24,000	104,750	128,750	
86	123	Interpublic	3,126	S	44,000	39,888	83,888	3,000 res't shrs every 5 yrs
58	70	Johnson & Johnson	22,629	H	55,000	39,763	94,763	1-time $10,000 stock award
97	96	J. C. Penney	30,546	O	49,200	30,156	79,356	
76	153	Kellogg	6,830	O	39,000	49,625	88,625	
200	131	Kelly Services	3,853	S	42,700	0	42,700	$10,500 shrs in retainer value
102	107	Kimberly-Clark	12,547	M	46,800	29,588	76,388	
34	104	Knight-Ridder	3,139	S	47,500	65,867	113,367	$15,000 shrs in retainer value
192	106	Lee Enterprises	439	S	47,381	0	47,381	500 shrs in retainer value
74	191	Louisiana-Pacific	2,403	M	32,750	57,000	89,750	45,000 options every 5 yrs
204	224	Manor Care	1,617	H	0	41,667	41,667	initial grant = 5,000 options
114	66	Marriott Int'l	12,034	S	56,250	17,313	73,563	$12,500 shrs in retainer value
33	8	Marsh & McClennan	6,009	F	113,738	0	113,738	$10,000 + 600 shrs in retainer value
46	58	May Dept Stores	12,685	O	58,000	45,000	103,000	initial grant = 2,000 res't shrs
108	50	McDermott Int'l	3,308	S	59,950	15,260	75,210	
61	54	McDonald's	11,409	S	59,000	33,417	92,417	
181	183	McGraw-Hill	3,534	S	34,600	17,000	51,600	
172	181	Mead	5,077	M	34,900	18,372	53,272	
167	205	Media General	910	S	27,500	27,500	55,000	
179	219	Mentor Graphics	455	T	20,000	32,292	52,292	
43	64	Merck & Co	23,637	H	57,200	50,333	107,533	
82	35	Merrill Lynch	31,731	F	65,000	20,000	85,000	$100,000 def'd every 5 yrs
197	185	MGM Grand	828	S	33,500	12,042	45,542	initial grant = 5,000 options
147	176	MicroAge	4,446	S	35,000	27,615	62,615	initial grant = 2,500 options and 1,000 res't shrs
194	210	Millipore	619	T	24,000	22,625	46,625	initial grant = 4,000 options
92	14	MMM	15,070	M	80,400	0	80,400	$35,000 shrs in retainer value
45	51	Mobil	59,978	I	59,750	43,313	103,063	
153	117	Monsanto	9,457	I	45,000	15,000	60,000	$50,000 res't shrs every 5 yrs
214	182	Montana Power	1,024	U	34,840	0	34,840	480 shrs in retainer value
150	44	Morton Int'l	3,637	I	60,938	0	60,938	500 shrs in retainer value
44	58	Motorola	29,794	T	58,000	47,656	105,656	
215	187	Neiman Marcus	2,210	O	33,000.	0	33,000	
215	187	Nike	9,187	M	33,000	0	33,000	1-time 30,000 options
202	135	Nordstrom	4,852	O	42,000	0	42,000	$10,000 shrs in retainer value
54	33	Norfolk Southern	5,165	S	66,200	30,500	96,700	1-time 3,000 res't shrs

25	78	Northrop Grumman	9,153	T	54,000	71,500	125,500	$8,400 shrs in retainer value
221	216	Old Kent Financial	1,306	F	22,500	8,500	31,000	
207	153	Omnicom Group	3,125	S	39,000	0	39,000	
91	69	Oryx Energy	1,197	I	55,750	25,500	81,250	$12,000+500 shrs in retainer value; also 9,000 options every 3 yrs; initial stock award = 5,000 shrs
165	213	Oshkosh B'Gosh	395	O	23,000	33,000	56,000	
182	91	Owens-Corning	4,373	M	51,063	0	51,063	500 shrs in retainer value; also 1-time 10,000 options
195	108	Pacific Enterprises	2,777	U	46,600	0	46,600	
Total Comp Rank	Avg Direct Rank	Company	Rev($mils)	Ind	AvgDirect Comp	+GrantValue	=TotalComp	Comments
13	9	Paine Webber Group	6,657	F	101,762	51,844	153,606	1,162 shrs in retainer value; also 22,500 options every 5 yrs
41	26	PepsiCo	29,292	M	70,000	40,000	110,000	
6	22	Pfizer	12,504	H	72,000	115,475	187,475	
98	67	PG&E	15,400	U	56,000	23,333	79,333	
134	27	Pharmacia & Upjohn	6,710	H	68,313	0	68,313	500 shrs in retainer value
128	135	Phelps Dodge	3,914	I	42,000	28,013	70,013	
29	6	Philip Morris	56,114	M	116,673	0	116,673	932 shrs in retainer value
202	135	Pioneer Hi-Bred	1,784	O	42,000	0	42,000	
149	156	Pittston	3,394	I	38,400	22,978	61,378	initial grant = 17,000 options
211	171	Policy Mgmt	583	T	36,000	0	36,000	
136	135	PPG Industries	7,379	M	42,000	25,000	67,000	
183	92	Premark International	2,407	M	51,000	0	51,000	1-time 1,000 shrs stock award
50	70	Procter & Gamble	35,764	M	55,000	46,604	101,604	
162	100	Public Service Enterp	6,370	U	48,400	9,544	57,944	$11,000 shrs in retainer value
40	29	Quaker Oats	5,016	O	68,000	42,200	110,200	
8	223	Qualcomm	2,036	T	10,000	168,333	178,333	initial grant = 20,000 options
133	218	Questar	933	U	20,800	47,600	68,400	
122	142	Reebok International	3,637	M	41,000	30,628	71,628	$10,000 shrs in retainer value; initial grant = 6X avg comp in prior year
124	112	Reynolds Metals	6,900	I	46,000	25,500	71,500	1,000 res't shrs every 5 yrs
157	115	Rouse	930	M	45,500	13,667	59,167	initial grant = 5,000 options
206	206	Rubbermaid	2,400	M	26,150	13,500	39,650	
222	202	Russell	1,228	M	29,200	1,667	30,867	$5,000 shrs in retainer value
127	53	Ryder System	5,351	S	59,300	10,917	70,217	
Total Comp Rank	Avg Direct Rank	Company	Rev($mils)	Ind	AvgDirect Comp	+GrantValue	=TotalComp	Comments

12	39	Sara Lee	19,734	O	62,500	93,854	156,354	
66	42	SBC Comm	24,856	T	61,700	30,500	92,200	
14	3	Schering-Plough	6,778	H	125,338	25,000	150,338	1,100 shrs in retainer value
129	197	Sears, Roebuck & Co	41,296	O	30,000	40,000	70,000	
138	104	Sherwin-Williams	4,881	M	47,500	18,500	66,000	
196	117	Shoney's	1,203	S	45,000	1,083	46,083	5,000 options every 5 yrs
103	176	Silicon Graphics	3,663	T	35,000	41,042	76,042	initial grant = 30,000 options
80	134	Snap-On	1,672	M	42,250	43,625	85,875	$6,500 shrs in retainer value
135	123	Sonoco Products	2,848	M	44,000	23,125	67,125	
136	101	Southern	12,611	U	48,000	19,000	67,000	
191	192	So New England Tele	2,022	T	32,500	15,094	47,594	
211	222	Springs Industries	2,226	M	18,000	18,000	36,000	
69	83	Sprint	14,874	T	52,750	39,083	91,833	1-time 2,500 def'd
100	127	SPX	922	M	43,597	34,500	78,097	
209	166	Standard Register	966	T	37,000	0	37,000	
106	123	Stanley Works	2,670	M	44,000	31,458	75,458	
115	62	Stone & Webster	1,323	S	57,750	15,625	73,375	400 shrs in retainer value; also initial grant = 2,000 options
186	93	St. Joe	346	M	50,000	0	50,000	
132	159	St. Jude Medical	809	H	38,000	30,500	68,500	
110	185	St. Paul Companies	6,219	F	33,500	41,031	74,531	
139	68	Sun Company	8,968	I	55,900	10,000	65,900	$19,880 shrs in retainer value
171	192	SunAmerica	2,084	F	32,500	21,375	53,875	
193	213	Talbots	1,054	O	23,000	24,167	47,167	
190	97	Temple-Inland	3,625	M	49,000	0	49,000	1-time 10,000 options
10	18	Tenet Healthcare	8,691	H	77,200	82,813	160,013	
51	84	Texaco	45,187	I	52,500	48,938	101,438	$15,000 shrs in retainer value
167	176	Texas Instruments	10,562	T	35,000	20,000	55,000	1-time 1,000 def'd
109	108	Textron	10,544	O	46,600	28,200	74,800	1-time 1,000 res't shrs
71	197	Time Warner	13,294	S	30,000	61,000	91,000	
145	141	TJX Companies	7,389	O	41,750	21,459	63,209	initial grant = 1,000 options
223	203	Tootsie Roll	376	O	29,000	0	29,000	
30	101	Transamerica	6,486	F	48,000	68,250	116,250	
52	10	Travelers Group	37,609	F	100,000	0	100,000	$100,000 shrs in retainer value
55	176	TRW	10,831	O	35,000	61,688	96,688	
180	86	Unicom	7,083	U	52,200	0	52,200	$36,200 shrs in retainer value
153	197	Union Pacific	11,014	S	30,000	30,000	60,000	1-time 1,785 res't shrs
153	165	Unisys	6,636	T	37,500	22,500	60,000	
65	207	United Healthcare	11,794	H	26,000	66,250	92,250	initial grant = 9,000 options
42	210	United Technologies	24,713	T	24,000	84,542	108,542	1-time 2,000 res't shrs

215	187	Universal Foods	826	O	33,000	0	33,000	$5,500 shrs in retainer value
121	47	Unocal	6,064	I	60,000	12,000	72,000	
119	31	U.S. Trust	494	F	67,050	5,000	72,050	400 shrs in retainer value
225	220	Vanguard Cellular Systems	375	T	18,500	0	18,500	
205	148	Venator Group	6,624	O	40,000	0	40,000	$20,000 shrs in retainer value
31	147	VF	5,222	M	40,100	74,400	114,500	
795	52	Viacom	13,505	S	59,500	20,719	80,219	1-time 10,000 options; also initial grant = 5,000 options
140	110	Vulcan Materials	1,679	M	46,500	18,638	65,138	
186	93	Wal-Mart Stores	119,29 9	O	50,000	0	50,000	$25,000 shrs in retainer value
28	87	Walt Disney	22,473	S	52,000	66,000	118,000	
116	79	Warner-Lambert	8,180	H	53,000	20,000	73,000	1-time 4,000 res't shrs
59	32	Waste Management	9,273	S	67,000	27,500	94,500	
23	25	Wells Fargo & Co	9,608	F	70,100	56,573	126,673	
142	117	Wendy's Int'l	2,037	S	45,000	20,052	65,052	
177	133	Weyerhaeuser	11,210	M	42,500	10,000	52,500	
24	148	Xerox	18,166	T	40,000	86,563	126,563	

Subject Index

Index to Graphs

ISBN 0-15-606305-0

9 780156 063050